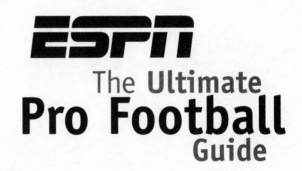

ESPN

The Ultimate
Pro Football
Guide

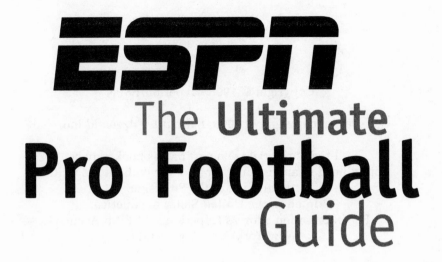

ESPN
The **Ultimate**
Pro Football
Guide

Editors,
Russell S. Baxter and John Hassan
with contributions from the commentators of ESPN

Introduction by
Chris Berman

HYPERION
ESPN®
BOOKS

Designed by Susan Canavan

Balliett & Fitzgerald, Inc.
Project Editor: Thomas Dyja
Editors: Howard Slatkin, Phil Berger
Production Editor: Maria Fernandez
Copyeditor: Phil Presby
Proofreader: Jim Gerard
Associate Editor: Vijay Balakrishnan

Hyperion
Editor: Gretchen Young
Editorial Assistant: Jennifer Morgan
Production Editor: David Lott
Production Manager: Vincent Stanley

Library of Congress Cataloging-in-Publication Data available

ISBN 0-7868-8328-6

First Edition

10 9 8 7 6 5 4 3 2 1

contents

Introduction

It was 1964, and the waiting list for New York football Giants season tickets was just way too long for a father with two young sons. After all, the Giants were perennial champs of the NFL's Eastern Division, and within the last decade, they had become pro football's most marketable team.

In part, it was because they were in New York, a cab ride from Madison Avenue. But they also played outstanding football, and had been participants in "the greatest game ever played," the 1958 overtime loss in the NFL championship game against the Baltimore Colts. That game put pro football on the national TV map, and through the Giants, everyone could see the brilliance of an emerging NFL: Colts quarterback Johnny Unitas, the magnificence of running back Jim Brown, who played for the Giants' main rival of that time, the Cleveland Browns, and the developing legend in Green Bay of Vince Lombardi's Packers.

It was an exciting time, so the father, Jim Berman, decided a waiting list with a 9 and a 7-year old boy was not the way to go.

Instead, he opted for season tickets for the New York Jets of the fledgling AFL as they moved into their spanking new home, Shea Stadium. Mind you, there was certainly no waiting list for Jets seats, and nobody was sure if the AFL would ever be big time.

But this was pro football—with action, excitement, and fervor—and certainly neither Little Chris nor Andy Berman could tell the difference between Jets quarterback Dick Wood and Giants quarterback Y.A. Tittle. They couldn't tell the difference between Jets linebacker Wahoo McDaniel or Giants defensive end Andy Robustelli, either, but what they could learn was that a touchdown was six points, passing the ball was fun, hard hits were eye-opening, and that the game of pro football, played just once a week, was something to look forward to. Who could have guessed that a year later, in 1965, the Jets quarterback would be Joe Namath, and the AFL was here to stay forever. Who would have guessed that within the next three seasons, with apologies to the Colts-Giants game in 1958, the two most important games in pro football history would be played: Namath's "guarantee" and delivery of the Jets' huge upset of the Colts in Super Bowl III, and the Packers-Cowboys epic struggle in the Ice Bowl at Lambeau Field.

What it did was hook America on pro football. It sure hooked me, enough to lead me to a career of talking football on ESPN. And, if you were my age or older, it must have hooked you, too.

You don't have to be "40-something," as I am, to enjoy the splendor of the NFL. There are dads with their young sons and daughters who are experiencing the same thing today that we did back then, and it doesn't have to involve buying tickets. Some of the best NFL fans I know have never been to a game in person because they live too far away from the stadiums. Perhaps that's where this book, *ESPN: The Ultimate Guide to Pro Football*, comes in.

Inside you'll find not only a bit of history about all the NFL teams, but you'll discover anecdotes, facts, quotes and thumbnail looks at their best players and coaches. What's unique about this book, though, is that we'll take you to every league city, let you know about its stadium, where to "dial into" the team on TV and radio, what to read to make you a local football aficionado, and most important: where to eat, visit, and stay when you're in town.

Try watching a game this fall with this book at your side, and then browse through the stuff on each city. You'll think you're right there.

What I've learned through the years of covering the NFL on ESPN's NFL Primetime and NFL Countdown (once upon a time, NFL Gameday) and Sportscenter as "the Swami" is that while everyone roots for his or her favorite teams, football fans are truly national fans, in that they are intrigued by all the teams. The proof is our televising of the NFL draft, where viewers don't just tune in for their teams—they tune in for all the teams.

There's no way somebody growing up near Chicago or rooting for the Bears can possibly know as much about the Miami Dolphins, or somebody growing up near Tampa or rooting for the Bucs can know as much about the Denver Broncos, but they'd like to.

In the following pages, we hope to at least feed your appetite for all of this, and help you enjoy the season that much more.

Hopefully, *ESPN: The Ultimate Guide to Pro Football* will help you imagine you're with Tom Jackson and me as we watch all the Sunday afternoon games at once, getting ready to show you the best highlights on NFL Primetime.

Perhaps it will give you a little more insight into our Sunday night or Monday night game between two teams who you'd like to know a little more about. Better yet, perhaps you've got a ticket to a game in another city, and we're getting you primed for the game and your trip.

This is a collection for the true NFL fan, so I know you qualify. How????

Because it takes one to know one.

Enjoy....

—Chris Berman

The Teams

Arizona
Cardinals

As the oldest continuously run professional football franchise in the country, the Cardinals are woven into the very fiber of American football — even if that tradition doesn't include much in the way of winning. The 1997 season marked the 50th anniversary of the Cardinals' only NFL championship, and fans keep hoping that it won't be another fifty years before they see another title.

Born in the neighborhood streets on the south side of Chicago, Cardinal football began its existence as the Morgan Athletic Club in 1898. By 1901 the club had become the Normals and shortly after that the Racine Cardinals. Lack of competition, the influenza epidemic and World War I forced the club to suspend play off and on during the early part of the 20th century. The Racine Cardinals eventually became one of the twelve charter members of the American Professional Football Association, forerunner of the NFL, then joined the league in 1922, with one of the game's first superstars, Paddy Driscoll, in the backfield. Three years later the Cards won their first championship, one that would have to last a long time. Playing in the shadow of the Bears, the Cardinals slogged through the '30s and '40s, losing crucial players such as Johnny Clement and Bill Dewell to the military during the war, and even joining forces with the Steelers for a time to pool resources. The Cardinals' one burst of greatness in Chicago came after the war, when coach Jimmy Conzelman took the

Franchise History

Chicago Cardinals (NFL)
(1920–1943)
Card-Pitt
(1944)
Chicago Cardinals
(1954–59)
St. Louis Cardinals
(1960–1987)
Phoenix Cardinals
(1988–93)
Arizona Cardinals
(1994-present)

By the Numbers

(Since 1970)
Regular Season: 174-244-6
Postseason: 0-3
Division Titles: 2
Vs. Division: 81-137-3
Playoff Appearances: 3
Home: 100-108-3
Away: 74-136-3

(Overall)
Regular Season: 406-555-39
Postseason: 1-4
Playoff Appearances: 5
Home: 233-243-22
Away: 173-312-17

Most Revered Football Figures

Larry Wilson. Now a vice president with the team, Wilson revolutionized the safety position and was one of the Cardinals' greatest players.
Ollie Matson. The do-everything, Hall of Fame back was so good that his 1959 trade brought eight players and a draft pick to the Cardinals.
Terry Metcalf. A rushing, receiving and returning star; his son Eric came to wear his number 21 for the Cards in 1998.

Rivalries

The **Cowboys** are a great rival, although the series has been one-sided, with the Cowboys enjoying a 47-23-1 edge. Before pro football arrived in Phoenix, Dallas games usually were televised in Arizona and they quickly became Arizona's team. Typically, Dallas fans outnumber Cardinals fans when the teams play in Arizona, which annoys Cardinals players greatly. The **Bears** are villains for two reasons. First, the Bears used to be a crosstown rival. It's still an important game to Cardinals owner Bill Bidwill. Second, the Bears are immensely popular in Arizona, where there are many transplanted Chicagoans. The Bears lead the series, 54-26-6. In one of the league's oldest rivalries dating back to 1926, the **Giants** have dominated, 72-37-2. Bidwill loves the NFC East and has refused to move into another division, mainly because he didn't want to give up rivalries such as this one.

team all the way to the 1947 NFL title with the Million Dollar Backfield — Pat Harder, Elmer Angsman and Charley Trippi and tackle Stan Mauldin leading the way.

In 1960 the team moved to St. Louis. In Chicago, at least the Cardinals were underdogs; here they were just mediocre. Safety Larry Wilson was the heart of the St. Louis team for 12 years, but he never played in a playoff game. Under Don Coryell the Cards stitched together a couple good years in

> "It was a good shot, all right. I earholed him."
> — Larry Wilson in 1961, after hitting Giants QB Charlie Conerly on the first acknowledged safety blitz.

the '70s with Jim Hart at quarterback, J.V. Cain and Mel Gray at wide receiver, Terry Metcalf at running back and a fierce offensive line featuring Dan Dierdorf and Conrad Dobler. St. Louis made the playoffs in 1974 and 1975.

did you know?
The Cardinals have gone into overtime in 14 of their last 67 contests dating back to December 19, 1993. They had not played an OT game in an NFL-record 110 outings prior to that.

They haven't been back since. After 28 years in St. Louis, the Cardinals relocated to Arizona in the spring of 1988. Their lone .500 year in Arizona came in 1994 under Buddy Ryan in his first of only two years as head coach.

While the team's nucleus has been strong, their inability to find a franchise quarterback has plagued them. The Cardinals have had a string of 15 different starting quarterbacks since 1988. Now, under head coach Vince Tobin, the current squad is led by four-time Pro Bowler

Aeneas Williams and 1996 Defensive Rookie of the Year Simeon Rice. But the hopes of the franchise could rest on the shoulders of former Arizona State standout quarterback Jake Plummer. Plummer's exciting style and big-play ability may not only put fans back in the stands but also bring a winning record to Arizona.

—Mike Golic

Sun Devil Stadium

Sun Devil Stadium is not a dump on the order of Philadelphia's Veterans Stadium. It's no palace, though, and the Cardinals are the only NFL team that plays in a facility on a college campus.

Many of the seats have no backs. The restroom facilities are inadequate, and the concourses where vendors are located are small and become crowded easily. There's one benefit of losing, though: It's so easy to get to the stadium that fans can play 18 holes of golf and still arrive for a 1 p.m. game 45 minutes early. Fans at Cardinals games are unique because they often make the visiting team feel welcome. It's not uncommon for teams such as Dallas, Pittsburgh, San Francisco, Denver and Chicago to see more of their colors in the crowd.

Another advantage to the Cardinals status as a perennial loser is that tickets are rarely tough to find. Games against Dallas are the only ones that consistently sell out, and tickets for other games can be purchased at the box office on the day of the game. We are not talking about a rabid fan base here.

If you are getting tickets for an early-season game, remember to sit on the west side of the stadium. The sun beats down on the east side, and you could end up roasted.

The "I Was There" Game

September 7, 1997: With the Sun Devil Stadium crowd full of Cowboys fans, the Cardinals pulled out the overtime upset, breaking a 13-game losing streak to Dallas. Cardinals 25, Cowboys 22.

The Paper Bag Game

September 24, 1950: In the regular-season debut of head coach Earle "Curly" Lambeau, the Cards had a whopping eight passes intercepted, tied for the second most in an NFL game. They also fumbled the ball away four times, giving them a record-tying dozen turnovers for the game. Eagles 45, Cardinals 7.

did you know?
The Cardinals drafted Joe Namath in 1965 but lost him to the Jets in a bidding war.

Great Names

John Booty (DB, 1993)
Stoney Case (QB, 1995-present)
Marshall "Biggie" Goldberg (DB/RB, 1939-40, 1946-48)
Mac Arthur Lane (RB, 1968-71)
Tom Wham (E, 1949-51)

Hall of Fame

Ernie Nevers	(FB 1963)
Jim Thorpe	(HB 1963)
Jimmy Conzelman	(Coach 1964)
Guy Chamberlin	(E/Coach 1965)
Paddy Driscoll	(HB 1965)
Walt Kiesling	(G 1966)
Charles W. Bidwill Sr.	(Owner 1967)
Charley Trippi	(HB 1968)
Ollie Matson	(HB 1972)
Dick Lane	(DB 1974)
Larry Wilson	(DB 1978)
Jackie Smith	(TE 1994)
Dan Dierdorf	(T 1996)

Our Top Story

`"One Shining Moment"`
`December 28, 1947`
The Cardinals defeated Philadelphia, 28-21, to win their only NFL championship. Violet Bidwill, who owned the team, broke into tears afterward in remembrance of her husband, Charley, who had died the previous spring.

`"Football Hits Monday Night TV"`
`October 31, 1966`
The Cardinals defeat the visiting Bears, 24-17, in the first televised Monday night game. Frank Gifford was in the booth for CBS; Dan Dierdorf was still in high school.

`"Welcome to Arizona"`
`September 12, 1988`
After years of sagging attendance in St. Louis, the Cardinals played their first home game in Arizona's Sun Devil Stadium. A crowd of 67,139 showed up to see the Cards fall to the Cowboys, 17-14.

Worst Team

1939 (1-10):The then-Chicago Cardinals played eight of their 11 games away from home, but no matter where this undermanned team lined up, points were at a premium. Head coach Ernie Nevers saw his club outscored by a combined 254-84 for the season, with nearly one-fourth of their points coming in a 27-20 loss at Green Bay in early October.

did you know?

Never had Cardinals quarterbacks been under such duress as they were in 1997. Arizona surrendered an incredible 78 sacks, the second-worst mark in NFL annals.

Tailgating parties don't kick in until mid-October, when the weather finally cools. Fans do the typical stuff. The best parties are in the parking lots north and east of the stadium. If you want any special food, you better bring it and tailgate. The stadium food is fairly basic, mostly hamburgers and hot dogs, and they don't serve much food that's indigenous to the area.

The Bottom Line on Sun Devil Stadium

Address: Fifth Street, Tempe, AZ 85287.
Tickets: It's a big stadium, and tickets are readily available. (602) 379-0102 (800) 999-1402.
1998: $200/$125/$75/$50/$40/$30/$20
1994: $200/$100/$60/$50/$35/$20/$15
Parking: Parking is adequate, with large lots north and east of the stadium; prices run around $5. One of the most attractive things about Cardinals games is the lack of traffic on the way there.
Public Transportation: Valley Metro buses run in the area, but not on Sundays, so unless it's a Saturday game, you're pretty much out of luck. (602) 253-5000.
Capacity: 73,273.
Restrooms: 30.

Where to Go . . . in Phoenix/Tempe

Best Bars

Best pre-game warm-up. It may be across town from the stadium, but **Max's Sports Lounge** is worth the trip. The bar has an amazing collection of helmets from college teams, and there is no bet-

Best of the Cardinals

Best Team

1975 (11-4): One year after surprising many and capturing their first-ever NFC East title, Don Coryell's club proved 1974 was no fluke and repeated as division champions. Quarterback Jim Hart led an attack that featured explosive wide receiver Mel Gray, NFC rushing champion Jim Otis and versatile Terry Metcalf. But a suspect defense proved to be their undoing as the Rams ended the Cards' season in the playoffs.

> "He's got two speeds — here-he-comes and there-he-goes."
> — Redskins DB Barry Wilburn, on Cardinals WR Roy Green.

Greatest Players by Position

Pos:	Player
QB:	Jim Hart
RB:	Ottis Anderson
WR:	Roy Green
TE:	Jackie Smith
OL:	Dan Dierdorf
DL:	Eric Swann
LB:	E.J. Junior
DB:	Larry Wilson
P/K:	Jim Bakken
ST:	Ron Wolfley

And Don't Forget...

QB: Neil Lomax. Injuries cut short a potentially great career. He threw for better than 22,000 yards and 136 scores in just nine seasons.
CB: Roger Wehrli. Seven-time Pro Bowler and one of the Cardinals' best players in the 1970s.
WR: Pat Tilley. Sure-handed possession receiver who totaled 469 catches in 11 seasons.

CB: Aeneas Williams. Four-time Pro Bowler who has emerged as a big-play defender and one of the top cover artists in the league.
RB: Terry Metcalf. A do-it-all home run threat from anywhere on the field, excelling on offense as well as kick returns.

Best Argument

Wide Receiver: Roy Green or Mel Gray? The Cardinals have had their share of big-play wide receivers, and Green and Gray were two of the most feared. The latter was the focal point of Don Coryell's passing attack in the mid-70s. Meanwhile, Green actually began his NFL career as a defensive back, playing two ways for a short time, then made the full-time conversion to wideout.

> "We've got the same letter-head as always. The Chicago Cardinals will remain the Chicago Cardinals."
> — Managing director Walter Wolfner in 1960, four days before announcing that the team would move to St. Louis.

Best Coach

Don Coryell (1973-77): The Cardinals have had more head coaches than any team in the NFL, and not just because they've been around since 1920. The excitable Coryell led the Big Red to their only pair of NFC East titles (1974-75), not an easy feat considering both Tom Landry and George Allen were leading the charge those years in Dallas and Washington, respectively.

Pressbox

Who to Read...

It's agreed that the preeminent football writer in the area is *The Arizona Republic*'s Steve Schoenfeld, who has covered the team since it moved west in 1988. Don't miss his "NFL Notes" column on Sundays. On weekends, the *Republic* offers a "GameDay Extra" section, which includes a complete breakdown of the upcoming Cardinals game. Lynn DeBruin's column stands out from the *Mesa Tribune*'s otherwise limited coverage. With Arizona State's recent gridiron success, the struggling Cards have had a hard time getting attention in the press, particularly as they fade late in the season.

Who to Watch...

Sports anchor Jude LaCava on KSAZ–CBS does a great job of breaking down a game on Sunday evenings. Reporters Kevin McCabe and Kirby Maus back up LaCava's coverage. KPHO–CBS shows the Cardinals' preseason games. "Sports Tonight" hosted by Mark Curtis on KPNX–NBC draws a loyal viewership.

Who to Listen To...

Cardinals games are carried on KSLX (100.7 FM) and KDUS (1060 AM). Even though Phoenix isn't a pro football–crazy town, it fields a trio of all-sports radio stations, KGME (1360 AM), KMVP (860 AM) and KDUS, the most recent entry into the field. KMVP's Tony Femino, who describes himself as "The Ultimate Giver," is the area's leading outrageous radio personality. Afternoon host John Cannon on KDUS is more cerebral and sophisticated, and doesn't cater to the lowest common denominator.

ter place to warm up for Sunday's game. *6727 N. 47th Ave., Glendale, (602) 937-1671. Seven days 11am-1am.*

Best neighborhood pre-game lube job. Just a short walk from Sun Devil Stadium, **McDuffy's** features a raucous crowd, and you can catch the early games on one of the many televisions. *230 W. 5th St., Tempe, (602) 966-5600. M-F 11am-1am, Sa-Su 10am-1am, game days 9am-1am.*

Back to college. Want a bar that reminds you of your college days? Try **The Bandersnatch**, a quick walk across the street from Sun Devil Stadium. The beer is cold, and the nachos are as good as you'll find. *125 E. 5th St., Tempe, (602) 966-4438. Seven days 11am-1am, opens early on game days.*

Best Restaurants

Best cheap pre-game breakfast. For a great meal that will stick with you through an early afternoon game, don't miss the Eggs Maximillian with chorizo at **May West Restaurant**. It never closes, and the price is right. *1825 E. University Dr.,Tempe, (602) 966-2761. 24 hours. All major credit cards. $*

Best funky cafe. Cafe Boa is a quiet, out-of-the-way cafe where the staff is into grunge but the food is unbelievable. They specialize in pasta — don't miss the *agnolotti*, triangle-shaped ravioli stuffed with mushrooms, in a tomato cream sauce. *709 S. Mill Ave., Tempe, (602) 968-9112. M-Th 10am-10pm, F 10am-11pm, Sa 12pm-11pm, Su 12pm-10pm. All major credit cards. $$*

Best kiss-up dinner. OK, you've convinced your spouse to go to the game with you — be good and go to the **Top of the Rock** the night before. The panoramic view of Phoenix will score you major points. *2000 Westcourt Way, Phoenix, (602) 431-2370. Su-Th 5pm-10pm, F-Sa 5pm-11pm, Su (brunch) 10am-2pm. All major credit cards. $$$$.*

Swami Sez:

With a defense that could be downright nasty, and a local folk hero at quarterback, there's excitement about the local football team in Arizona for the first time since the desert was painted.

Best Accommodations

Tempe Mission Palms. You can't get any closer to the stadium than this: it's literally next door. A beautiful place, it's close to the nightlife of Mill Avenue but peaceful enough that a good night's sleep is possible. More expensive than a motel, and it's worth it. *60 E. 5th St. (602) 894-1400. $$*

"That's not maroon! It's Cardinal red!" — Original owner Chris O'Brien about the jerseys he bought from the University of Chicago, thus christening his team.

The Buttes. A gorgeous hotel with a beautiful pool and a great restaurant. It's a splurge, though. *2000 W. Westcourt Way, Phoenix, (602) 225-9000. $$$$*

Super 8 Motel. Cheap, simple lodgings — you know the drill here. *1020 E. Apache Blvd.,Tempe, (602) 967-8891. $*

Ready For Primetime (Monday Night)

December 25, 1995: The Cardinals have played just twice on Monday night since moving to Arizona. This game was one of the most embarrassing in team history, and not only because of the score. Two players got into a fight before the game, and at the end, Buddy Ryan jogged off the field, but a penalty had delayed the final play. Ryan watched from the tunnel. He was fired the next day. Cowboys 37, Cardinals 13.

Overall Monday Night: 5-9-1

Thursday night record: 0-1

Overall Sunday night: 2-7

Think About the Weather

December 4, 1983: Arizona is usually associated with heat, but this cold and rainy day in East Rutherford, NJ, saw the teams combine for only 16 points and just over 300 yards of total offense. The 51,589 no-shows tell the story. Cardinals 10, Giants 6.

Team Leaders

Rushing Yards
7,999   Ottis Anderson, 1979-86
Passing Yards
34,639   Jim Hart, 1966-83
Passing Touchdowns
209   Jim Hart, 1966-83
Receptions
522   Roy Green, 1979-90
Interceptions
52   Larry Wilson, 1960-72
Touchdowns
69   Roy Green, 1979-90
Points
1,380   Jim Bakken, 1962-78

Fans' notes

On Screen

Cuba Gooding Jr. won an Academy Award for best supporting actor playing Rod Tidwell, a wide receiver for the Arizona Cardinals in **Jerry Maguire.** Few people recall the Cardinals' near-triumph in the 1968 movie **Paper Lion,** based on author George Plimpton's stint with the Detroit Lions. The Cards are the team Plimpton faces when he appears at quarterback in a preseason game, and they surely would have won had the Lions left Plimpton in.

Fight Song, Etc.

One of the first things head coach Jimmy Conzelman did after his initial hiring in 1940 was pen a fight song for the team. It was entitled "It's in the Cards to Win." Eventually, the Cards did win — in 1947, during his second stint at head coach, Conzelman gave the Cardinals their only undisputed NFL championship. Coincidence? Don't be surprised if the team's next head coach is Elton John.

Bookshelf

Third and Long. Neil Lomax (Fleming H. Revell 1986).
They Call Me Dirty. Conrad Dobler and Vic Carucci (Jove 1989).
John David Crow: Heart of a Champion. Steve Pate and Dan Jenkins (Masters Press 1998).

You Gotta See...

▶Try coming to the stadium a day early and catching an **Arizona State game** — Sun Devil Stadium and the whole campus come to life in a different way than on Sundays.
▶If you are looking for some culture, visit **Taliesin West,** the winter home of America's greatest architect, Frank Lloyd Wright.
▶Not far away from the Phoenix-Tempe area are the **Tonto** and **Prescott National Forests,** which encompass over 4 million acres of parkland.

While You Were Eating Turkey....

November 24, 1977: Thanksgiving Day football hasn't been a hit with the Cardinals in recent years, probably because they have tended to play the part of the turkey. In 1977, they treated the visiting Miami Dolphins to a feast of 55 points, tied for the second-most points the team had ever allowed. Bob Griese threw six touchdown passes in handing the Cardinals their third consecutive Thanksgiving Day loss, 55-14.
Overall: 4-15-1

Against the Odds

It wasn't the road most traveled, but the destination was reached just the same. **Eric Swann** (1991-present) is one of the rare individuals who gained entrance into the NFL fraternity despite never playing a down of college football, after being ruled academically ineligible. The two-time Pro Bowler and defensive menace instead honed his skills as a member of the minor-league Bay State Titans, where his combination of power and quickness caught the NFL's attention. Swann, the sixth overall pick in 1991, is the only player without a college background to be a first-round choice, and the first to be drafted at all since 1946.

Atlanta
Falcons

To some pioneers of the game, it seemed sacreligious — in the South, a part of the nation where football was supposed to be a religion, there was no pro game. It took the American Football League to provide the push. In 1965, the AFL initiated plans to bring pro football southward by awarding Atlanta a franchise. Enter Pete Rozelle, the proactive NFL commissioner, and presto, the Atlanta Falcons were born. Owner Rankin M. Smith paid a then-record $8.5 million to adopt the team, and the AFL abandoned its move south.

Franchise History

Atlanta Falcons
(1966–present)

Although the franchise established itself in the wrong direction, the formative years provided some memories. In 1966, the Falcons' inaugural season, first-round draft choice Tommy Nobis, an All-America line-backer out of Texas, became a source of pride for the eager Atlanta fans who filled Atlanta-Fulton County Stadium after church on Sundays. Nobis became a five-time Pro Bowl player and dominated the team's highlight films as he ravaged opposing quarterbacks and running backs. The franchise finally spiked itself with color when Smith hired fiery Norm Van Brocklin as his second coach, replacing Norb Hecker three games into the 1968 season. Van Brocklin captured the fancy of fans and players with his no-holds-barred approach and delivered the team's first winning season (7-6-1) in 1971.

But the Atlanta franchise has been known to make a wrong turn here, a slip there, and the team stumbled until 1977, when Smith conducted a search for a true front office football boss and new coach. While he considered a Miami Dolphins scout named Bobby Beathard for general manager and a promising

By the Numbers

(Since 1970)
Regular Season: 170-250-4
Postseason: 2-5
Division Titles: 1
Vs. Division: 75-94-3 (Playoffs: 1-0)
Playoff Appearances: 5
Home: 104-108-1
Away: 66-142-3

(Overall)
Regular Season: 182-293-5
Postseason: 2-5
Playoff Appearances: 5
Home: 111-128-2
Away: 71-165-3

Most Revered Football Figures

Steve Bartkowski. Despite bad knees brought on by constant abuse behind a weak offensive line, Bartkowski was one of the game's most dangerous deep-threat quarterbacks. He still holds a majority of club passing records.

Claude Humphrey. A six-time Pro Bowl selection, Humphrey was the force behind the Falcons "Grits Blitz" defense which set an NFL record in 1977 for fewest points allowed in a 14-game season (129).

Tommy Nobis. Mister Falcon. Nobis was Atlanta's first draft pick, Rookie of the Year and first Pro Bowl player. Currently the team's director of player development, he has spent three decades working for the Falcons.

Jeff Van Note. A six-time Pro Bowl selection, "Noter's" career spanned the worst and best of times in Falcons history. In addition to playing a league-record 246 games at center, he played in 155 consecutive games, a club record, including 112 consecutive starts, also a club record.

William Andrews. This four-time Pro Bowler ran for more than 1,000 yards four of his first five seasons, until he tore up his knee in 1984, leaving Atlanta to always wonder what more could have been.

did you know?

The Falcons nickname was chosen from thousands of nominations in 1965. The winning entry came from school teacher Julia Elliott, who stated: "The Falcon is proud and dignified with great courage and fight. It never drops its prey. It is deadly and has a great sporting tradition." Of course, this was before the team began actually playing any games.

young coach named Dan Reeves for head coach, Smith instead tabbed Eddie LeBaron and Leeman Bennett for the jobs. Regardless of the promise Beathard and Reeves would have brought, LeBaron and Bennett provided the franchise with its greatest spark. Building around quarterback Steve Bartkowski, a golden-armed passer who was the club's No. 1 pick in 1975, a little-known back named William Andrews and a crazed "Grits-Blitz" defense headed by end Claude Humphrey, the Falcons finally made their first playoff appearance in 1978. The crescendo came when the Falcons won their first NFC Western Division title in 1980 with a 12-4 record. Visions of a Super Bowl were blurred when Danny White led the Dallas Cowboys from behind to defeat the Falcons, 30-27, in the playoffs. People in Atlanta will tell you the franchise was never the same, as Smith turned repeatedly to a variety of coaches who fell short of the glory which had once been captured.

Though Smith's football team failed on the field, the owner succeeded in building the Georgia Dome in 1989, which enabled Atlanta to host its first Super Bowl in 1994, with an encore set for 2000. Smith passed away on Oct. 26, 1997. Appropriately, in one of his final acts as franchise owner, Smith hired the coach he had passed over 21 years earlier — Dan Reeves — to take over the club in 1997. The Falcons lost that night to the Carolina Panthers, but Reeves proceeded to guide the team to six wins in their next seven games before closing the season with a last-minute loss at Arizona. Hope, at least, was restored for pro football in Atlanta.

—Chris Mortensen

Georgia Dome

Ironically, in a city known for its crisp, clear fall climate, the Falcons host their games indoors. The now-demolished Atlanta Fulton County Stadium provided, if not great sight lines, at least a more traditional football "feel" than does the current anti-septic atmosphere of the Georgia Dome. When the Dome opened on August 23, 1992, the oddity of both the facility and the Jerry Glanville-coached team made for some excitement, with MC Hammer, Travis Tritt, Trisha Yearwood and John Denver on the performers' list at the first game played there. But in recent years the team's on-field fortunes have led to dwindling crowds, and the location of the Dome, with its limited parking, has done little to encourage tailgating or life around the stadium. Most fans drive or take MARTA into downtown, and return to the suburbs after the game. As for indoor comfort, the $210 million facility remains state-of-the-art as football domes go. It's perhaps too cozy for Southern football fans, who pride themselves on their rowdy behavior and football knowledge.

The Dome has yet to maintain enthusiastic crowds. The most memorable moment

> **did you know?**
> The Falcons are 0-4 on Monday Night Football at the Georgia Dome, and have been outscored a combined 161-47 in those games.

> **"This is my house. I built this house."**
> — Deion Sanders upon his return to the Georgia Dome as a member of the San Francisco 49ers. (1994)

Rivalries

Starting in 1967, the rivalry with the New Orleans **Saints** (34-24) is based on three factors: Both teams are in the Deep South, both teams are usually no good and the games between them have usually been good. One year, though, the rivalry even made the playoffs. On December 28, 1991, at the Superdome in New Orleans, Jerry Glanville's Falcons rallied from ten points down to post the franchise's first playoff victory on the road. New Orleans native Michael Haynes scored two touchdowns for the Falcons, including the game-winning 61-yarder in the fourth quarter. The **49ers** (22-39-1) have been killing Atlanta the last few decades, winning 22 out of 29 games since 1984. Before it all fell apart, though, the Falcons and Niners had some classic games, including "Big Ben II" on November 20, 1983. This game was named after the play Bartkowski called in which his last-minute desperation toss landed in the hands of Billy "White Shoes" Johnson for the game-winning score.

Great Names

Bubba Bean (RB, 1976-80)
Charlie Brown (WR, 1985-87)
Rudy Holmes (DE, 1974)
Billy Martin (TE, 1966-67)
Tom Moriarty (S, 1977-79, 1981)
Marion Rushing (LB, 1966-68)
Jessie Tuggle (LB, 1987-present)

The "I Was There" Game

December 14, 1980: Perhaps the greatest regular-season game in Falcons history came at the close of a club record nine-game winning streak. Steve Bartkowski threw three touchdown passes to give him 30 on the season, and William Andrews rushed 105 yards as the Falcons crushed the 49ers (led by young QB Joe Montana) to secure the NFC West title (Falcons 35, 49ers 10).

Swami Sez:

Year one of Dan Reeves' rebuilding efforts almost spelled .500. Will Atlanta's wheel of fortune continue to spin upwards???

The Paper Bag Game

December 4, 1976: This 59-0 defeat by the Rams in 1976 stands out as a real keeper. It was the third time that season the Falcons were shut out and the largest margin of defeat in franchise history. That year, then-unknown and since-unheard-of Pat Peppler replaced head coach Marion Campbell in mid-season, and the Falcons were enroute to a 4-10 finish. (Rams 59, Falcons 0).

of recent years, in fact, came as the result of baggy pants. A local radio station, Z93, hired a very hefty man billed as "Whalon Elephant" to dance every week some time in the third quarter wearing one of their T-shirts. His jiggling body would be captured by cameras and thus provide a human billboard for the radio station. In the 1997 season, Whalon's back-side was flashed on the stadium's big screen after his pants fell down. He lost his job, and the Falcons lost a big third-quarter diversion.

The Bottom Line on Georgia Dome

Address: 1 Georgia Dome Dr. NW, Atlanta, GA 30313. (404) 223-9200

Tickets: A big stadium and a struggling team add up to lots of season and single-game tickets to be had. Call (404) 223-9200, and they will be very willing to sell you some.

1998: $33/$30/$20

1994: $27 (all seats)

Parking: Suite and club seat ticketholders enjoy special parking, which means the only parking actually at the Dome. For everyone else, private lots in the area offer spaces for between $6 and $10. There are an estimated 20,000 spaces within a 10-block radius of the Dome, so if you don't mind a short walk, you should have no problems.

Public Transportation: Cobb County Transit (770/528-7950) runs buses to and from the Georgia Dome, and there are MARTA (404/848-4711) train stations on both sides.

Extras: For those who want to really get

Best of the Falcons

Best Team

1980 (12-5): Two years earlier, Leeman Bennett led the club to their first-ever playoff berth, but in 1979 the team slumped to 6-10. Atlanta started slow in '80 (3-3), but a nine-game winning streak followed, resulting in the franchise's first and only division title. The Falcons owned home field advantage in the NFC, but were stunned in the divisional playoffs as Danny White rallied Dallas to a 30-27 win.

Greatest Players by Position

Pos:	Player
QB:	Steve Bartkowski
RB:	William Andrews
WR:	Andre Rison
TE:	Jim Mitchell
OL:	Mike Kenn
DL:	Claude Humphrey
LB:	Tommy Nobis
DB:	Deion Sanders
P/K:	Mick Luckhurst
ST:	Elbert Shelley

"Our mascot had abandoned us before the first snap. It was a preview of things to come."
— Falcons wide receiver Alex Hawkins before the team's first NFL game. A live falcon was supposed to circle the field three times and return to its perch, but it made just one lap before flying away for good. (1966)

And Don't Forget...

C: Jeff Van Note. Reliable professional and six-time Pro Bowler whose career spanned three decades (1969-86).
TE: Junior Miller. Tight ends were virtually invisible during Atlanta's "Run and Shoot" era, but don't forget this two-time Pro Bowler from the '80s.
LB: Jessie Tuggle. A tackling machine who is always around the ball, and one of the Falcons' most consistent defenders ever.
T: Bill Fralic. The second overall pick in 1985, he was considered one of the best run-blocking linemen in the NFL until injuries wore him down.
WR: Alfred Jenkins. A very consistent, big-play wideout who came up with his share of clutch catches.

Best Argument

Running Back: William Andrews or Gerald Riggs? If not for a severe injury suffered during the summer of '84, who knows how good the former Auburn standout would have been. Named to four Pro Bowls in his first five years in the league, Andrews could do it all. Riggs was an unsung and productive runner, continuing the legacy of big backs in the Falcon backfield.

Best Coach

Leeman Bennett (1977-82): The Falcons' playoff appearances have been few and far between, but Bennett got there in varying ways. In '77, Atlanta gave up just 129 points, a record-low for a 14-game season, while the early 1980s saw QB Steve Bartkowski and company light up the scoreboard. All told, Bennett produced three playoff teams in six seasons.

Pressbox

Who to Read...

Print legends Furman Bisher and Jesse Outlar defined the game for generations, and Bisher's voice is still heard loud — and often critically — clear. Though Outlar has retired, you can still read Bisher in the *Atlanta Journal Constitution*. Len Pasquarelli has for many years served as the beat writer for the *Atlanta Journal Constitution*. The *Marietta Daily Journal* also offers Falcons coverage.

Who to Watch...

Football is king in the South, at least on Saturday. Sunday is pretty important, too. Carolina and Jacksonville have taken some of the regional interest from the Falcons, and fans expect a competitive level of play, since their college teams are a good alternative for their loyalty. Jeff Hullinger is the voice of the Falcons. He does preseason games on WAGA–FOX with former Falcons tackle Tim Green doing color. "The Dan Reeves Show" is telecast on Saturdays at 6:30 pm on WAGA.

Who to Listen To...

Falcons games are broadcast on WGST (920 AM), with Hullinger and Falcons great Jeff Van Note. On Mondays, WGST offers Dan Reeves at 7pm, followed at 7:30 by a show featuring different players every week. The only station in town for sports talk is WQXI (790 AM).

intimate with the Dome, tours are available Wednesdays, Thursdays and Fridays from 10-4 at the top of the hour. Four dollars for adults, $3 for seniors and kids under 5. Call (404) 223-8687 for information.

Capacity: 71,500.

Restrooms: 34 men's, 34 women's.

Where To Go . . . in Atlanta

Best Bars

Best straightforward sports bar experience. In downtown Atlanta, **Champion's** has everything a sports bar needs — a couple dozen TVs, plenty of memorabilia on the walls and even periodic visits from sports celebrities. Oh yeah, and beer. *265 Peachtree Center Ave. (404) 586-6017. Seven days 11:30am-2am.*

Best blues bar. When a prominent blues outfit comes through town, they're most likely to jot this joint down on their itinerary. **Blind Willie's.** *828 N. Highland Ave. NE. (404) 873-2583. Open daily at 8pm, music starts around 10pm.*

Best misnomer. Your first clue should be that Atlanta is not a maritime city — there are no boats to be found at the **Euclid Avenue Yacht Club**. There are no sailors, either, but a varied cast of characters can be found at this neighborhood dive with a good selection of beers. *1136 Euclid Ave. NE. (404) 688-2582. Seven days 11am-2:30am.*

Best Restaurants

Best sports bar chain. In the CNN Center across from the Georgia Dome, formerly known as the Omni International, **Jocks & Jills** is a good pre-game choice. Owned by a group of former Atlanta athletes and sportscaster Craig Sager, Jocks & Jills is an Atlanta-based chain of sports bars sporting good screen-viewing and full-menu fare. *1 CNN Center, Ste. 230; other locations. (404) 688-4225. M-Su 11am-11pm. AE, DC, MC, V. $$*

Best local color. There is one legend for game-day eating in Atlanta: **The Varsity.** Founded in 1928, the Varsity bills itself as the "World's Largest Drive-In Restaurant, selling more Coca-Cola than any other single outlet in the world." Known for its fried fast food menu, with chili dogs and onion rings among the highlights, orders are served from behind a 150-foot long stainless steel counter where the Varsity's attendants

> **"We are the best defensive team in the whole world, in the whole wide world."**
> **—Defensive end Claude Humphrey** about the Falcons 1977 season, during which they allowed just 129 points.

will greet you with their legendary lingo, from "Whaddya have?" to "Walk a dog sideways, bag of rags and a n.i.p.c.," which in Varsity-speak translates to, "a hot dog to go with onions on the side, potato chips, and a chocolate milk without ice . . . Next!" *61 North Ave., adjacent to I-75 and the Georgia Tech campus. (404) 881-1706. Su-Th 9am-11:30pm, F-Sa 9am-1:30am. AE, MC, V. $*

Our Top Story

`"Deion's Doubleheader"`
`October 11, 1992`
Deion Sanders figured prominently in several of the franchise's top days in the news. On this day, Sanders played two pro sports on the same day. After appearing in a Braves playoff game in Pittsburgh on Saturday night, he flew to Miami, where the Falcons played the Dolphins on Sunday afternoon. The Falcons lost, 21-17, to the Dolphins before Sanders flew back to Pittsburgh for Sunday night's baseball game.

`"George vs. Jones"`
`September 22, 1996`
During a Sunday night matchup against the Eagles, quarterback Jeff George and head coach June Jones clashed over the offensive-play calling. Jones pulled George in favor of backup Bobby Hebert, and George made his displeasure known by yelling at Jones on the sideline. Jones responded by benching the highly paid George indefinitely. By season's end, neither George nor Jones was a Falcon any longer.

`"Farewell to Rankin Smith"`
`October 26, 1997`
One of the more somber days in franchise history came when Falcons owner Rankin Smith, Sr., died of heart failure in 1997. He was one of the more respected owners around the league during his tenure, and played a prominent role in building the Georgia Dome and Atlanta's hosting of the Super Bowl.

Ready For Primetime (Monday Night)

November 19, 1973: Bud Grant's Super Bowl VIII-bound Vikings were a perfect 9-0 when they visited Atlanta. The Falcons were riding their own five-game winning streak following a puzzling 1-3 start. Minnesota's vaunted defense had its hands full with QB Bob Lee and especially RB Dave Hampton, who ran for 108 yards and scored on a 19-yard reception. Lee's scramble on a 39-yard TD pass made for what would be voted 16 years later as "the best QB scramble in ABC-TV's first 20 years." Falcons great Tommy Nobis said the atmosphere that night was second-to-none in his playing career (Falcons 20, Vikings 14).
Overall Monday night: 5-15
Overall Thursday night: 1-2
Overall Sunday night: 3-4

Think About the Weather

January 4, 1992: With winds of 30 miles per hour mixed with a steady downpour, the conditions for this NFC divisional playoff were not ideal for Jerry Glanville's high-flying "Run and Shoot" attack. Atlanta managed just 193 total yards and committed six turnovers. Considering this was a Washington team en route to a Super Bowl title, perhaps the weather was the least of the Falcons' concerns. (Redskins 24, Falcons 7).

did you know?

With starter Steve Bartkowski injured, a backup quarterback named June Jones helped set up five Tim Mazzetti field goals, leading the Falcons to a 15-7 win over the 1977 NFC West champion Rams on Monday Night Football.

Best sports memorabilia. Although original owner Frank Diesa has since sold the business to the Jocks & Jills folks, **Frankie's on the Prado** retains its ambiance and thus its status as Atlanta's premier spot for sports memorabilia. Once selected by *USA Today* as the number one sports restaurant in the U.S., Frankie's offers a more extensive menu than some sports bars. *5600 Roswell Rd. (404) 843-9444. Seven days 11am-1am. All major credit cards. $$*

Best Accommodations

Sheraton Colony Square. A 27-story hotel on the corner of Peachtree Street, one of the main drags in town. There's an outdoor pool, a 24-hour exercise room, a bar and grill downstairs, a great view on the upper floors and the Colony Square Mall is next door. *188 14th St. NE. (404) 892-6000. $$$*

Omni Hotel at CNN Center. Smack-dab in the middle of Atlanta's business district. A variety of rooms, a pair of restaurants and location, location, location. Yes, that was Bobbie Batista. *100 CNN Center. (404) 659-0000. $$$-$$$$, weekend packages available.*

Westin Peachtree Plaza. This edifice towers over downtown Atlanta, just a few blocks from Centennial Olympic Park. Over 1,000 guest rooms, an indoor pool and a fitness center are sandwiched between a ground-floor and a rooftop restaurant. The steakhouse up top has views in every direction and rotates 360 degrees. *210 Peachtree St. (404) 659-1400. $$$$.*

Fans' notes

On Screen

Jerry Glanville and the Falcons may not have parted company on the best of terms, but at least Glanville isn't buried in the end zone of the Georgia Dome. He did, however, play a minor role in the 1992 movie **Hoffa**, about the labor leader whom urban legend speculates is buried in the end zone at Giants Stadium. Before he became the Falcons' second head coach, Norm Van Brocklin appeared in the 1955 John Ford film **The Long Gray Line**, a biographical movie based on the life of West Point's Marty Maher.

> "Well men, see ya next year."
> — Leeman Bennett, after his team closed out the 1982 season with a playoff loss at Minnesota. After saying this, Bennett turned and found the door behind him locked, much to his chagrin. He was fired two days later.

Fight Songs, etc.

He may never be enshrined in Canton, Ohio, but Jerry Glanville has already been inducted into the Atlanta Country Music Hall of Fame. He appeared not only in two music videos for the group Confederate Railroad, but also crossed over to appear in the video for Hammer's "Too Legit To Quit." The tumultuous relationship between sometime Falcon Andre Rison and the fashionably eyepatched Lisa "Left Eye" Lopes of the R&B group TLC made headlines when she burned down his house. (He forgave her.)

Bookshelf

The Dark Side of the Game. Tim Green (Warner 1996). Linebacker-turned-novelist Green also wrote this well-received, updated expose on the drugs and violence that fuels the latter-day NFL. Turner Publishing also released the following novels by Green: *Ruffians* (1993) *Titans* (1994), *Outlaws* (1996), *Marauders*, (1997). *The Atlanta Falcons: Violence and Victory* Furman Bisher (Prentice Hall 1976).

You Gotta See...

▶The 1996 Olympics may not have gone off without a hitch, but they at least temporarily transformed Atlanta into the center of the athletic world. They also left behind a number of new sports facilities, including **Turner Field**, the new home of the Braves.
▶The Falcons' first two playoff appearances came in 1978 and 1980, both during the administration of President Carter, native of Georgia. Coincidence? Research yourself at the **Jimmy Carter Library and Museum** in Atlanta, full of historical items dating from the Carter administration.
▶Atlanta also holds the **birthplace and grave of Dr. Martin Luther King, Jr.**, sites well worth anyone's time.
▶It's hard to avoid seeing all things Coke in Atlanta, but you can dive in headfirst at the **World of Coca-Cola**, which bubbles over with Coke-related gifts and paraphernalia, as well as the actual beverage itself.

Worst Team

1974 (3-11): Ugly. The season began with a 24-0 loss to the Cowboys, one of three shutouts that year for a team that was the lowest scoring (111) in franchise history and limited to seven or fewer points in half of their games. A 42-7 loss at Miami in early November ended Norm Van Brocklin's reign as head coach, and replacement Marion Campbell managed just one victory in the final six weeks.

Hall of Fame

Norm Van Brocklin   (QB 1971)
Tommy McDonald   (WR 1998)

Team Leaders

Rushing Yards
6,631   Gerald Riggs, 1982-88
Passing Yards
23,468   Steve Bartkowski, 1975-85
Passing Touchdowns
154   Steve Bartkowski, 1975-85
Receptions
423   Andre Rison, 1990-94
Interceptions
39   Rolland Lawrence, 1973-80
Touchdowns
56   Andre Rison, 1990-94
Points
558   Mick Luckhurst, 1981-97

Against the Odds

Former Appalachian State star **John Settle** (1987-90) didn't have a pedigree or a long, productive career, but he owns a place in NFL history just the same. Settle is the only undrafted free agent since the league merger in 1970 to crack the 1,000-yard rushing barrier — he totaled 1,024 yards in 1988 to earn his only trip to the Pro Bowl. The Chargers' Paul Lowe and the Raiders' Clem Daniels were the only other players to turn the trick, doing so as members of the AFL in 1963 and '65, respectively.

Baltimore Ravens

If you're looking for information about the Colts in the ESPN guide you're holding, look under "Indianapolis;" if it's the Browns you're after, go directly to "Cleveland." The Ravens don't seem quite as certain, though. The media and fan guide published by the Baltimore Ravens has a two-page section outlining the history of pro football in Maryland's harbor city. A Kremlinologist would appreciate it: Nearly the entire history of the Ravens is about the Colts, an NFL franchise which abandoned Baltimore in 1984 and now plays in Indianapolis. The old Colts stars — Johnny Unitas, Raymond Berry and Lenny Moore — are highlighted. It's as if the Ravens were trying to confiscate another team's past and adopt it as their own.

Franchise History

Baltimore Ravens
(1996–present)

The guide next talks about the Cleveland Browns, the team that moved to Baltimore in 1996 and renamed itself the Ravens. It neglects altogether to mention that the Browns name, colors and history remain in Cleveland, where a new franchise named the Browns will begin play in 1999.

Art Modell, who bought the Browns in 1961, abandoned Cleveland in 1996 and created the Ravens franchise, knows a little bit about creating new images. Modell started as a television producer and became an advertising executive before getting involved in the NFL. In the 1960s, he negotiated the NFL's first collective bargaining agreement with the players union. He chaired the NFL's television committee for 31 years, making his fellow owners richer beyond their wildest dreams. In short, at this stage of his career, Modell shouldn't need to come up with a new history. But like another Brooklynite — Walter O'Malley, who moved the Dodgers to Los Angeles — Modell and his team are searching for a new identity and having a hard time breaking from the past.

Slow progress on the football field hasn't helped. In their inaugural season,

By the Numbers

(Overall)

Regular Season: 10-21-1
Postseason: 0-0
Division Titles: 0
Vs. Division: 4-12
Playoff Appearances: 0
Home: 7-8-1
Away: 3-13

Most Revered Football Figures

Ted Marchibroda. He's the link to both the good news and the bad: Football is back in Baltimore, but it's not the Colts.

Ray Lewis. For the younger generation who has adopted the Ravens, Lewis has become the most popular player with his gung-ho style as he goes sideline to sideline to make hits. He led the league with 210 tackles in 1997.

Rivalries

For Baltimore fans, the Indianapolis **Colts** and Washington **Redskins** are the top rivals. They even cheered when it was announced that Pittsburgh had beaten Washington in the second game of the 1997 season. Baltimore's fans still root against Indianapolis because they lost their heritage when the Colts moved there in 1984. In 1996, the Ravens lost to the Colts, 26-21, in the teams' only meeting. But in what will surely be 1998's top attraction, the Colts will make their first visit to Baltimore since they skipped town in the middle of the night. Washington is a rival because Baltimore fans have an inferiority complex from living in the shadow of the nation's capital and love to root against Washington teams. The rivalry was enhanced when Washington owner Jack Kent Cooke was perceived to have blocked Baltimore's bid for an expansion team. The Baltimore fans loved it when the Ravens beat the Redskins, 20-17, in 1997.

the Ravens finished 4-12 with essentially the same team that had been a perennial playoff contender in Cleveland. Some players just couldn't handle the upheaval of the move.

"Leaving our friends and all we had in Cleveland, with the way it was done, was something a lot of us couldn't forget," said center Steve Everitt, who left the Ravens after their first season in Baltimore.

But with the brilliant talent evaluation of team vice president Ozzie Newsome, the Ravens replenished the team through the draft and free agency. The Ravens passed over troubled Nebraska running back Lawrence Phillips and instead chose UCLA offensive lineman Jonathan Ogden, who quickly got involved in Baltimore charities and made the Pro Bowl in his second year. In year two, the Ravens

> ### did you know?
> The name "Ravens" was selected through a telephone phone-in poll conducted through *The Baltimore Sun*. Other names suggested in a focus group: "Americans," "Marauders," "Mustangs," "Bulldogs," "Railers" and — not surprisingly — "Colts."

improved to 6-9-1, but by year's end decided to go in a different direction than they had with 35-year-old Vinny Testaverde just one year after he was named to his first Pro Bowl. Instead, they will start Jim Harbaugh, another 35-year-old quarterback, obtained in a trade with — ironically enough — the Indianapolis Colts. Harbaugh will be reunited with head coach Ted Marchibroda, who was head coach of the Colts in both Baltimore and Indianapolis. Got that?

Perhaps this will all begin to sort itself out in the 1998 season, when the Ravens — who played their first two seasons in

Memorial Stadium, where the old Colts played — move into a new stadium downtown.

Sal Paolantonio

"Your Name Here" Park

After playing two years at Memorial Stadium, the Ravens will move into a new $220-million football-only stadium at Camden Yards near Oriole Park. It — the corporate name hasn't been determined yet — will be a showplace with brick on the outside to give the new stadium an old look reminiscent of Oriole Park. The brick will be a deeper red than Oriole Park to highlight the industrial nature of that end of the complex. It will have wings (or openings) in the upper deck in each of the four corners of the end zone, and two of them will provide a view of downtown. It will seat over 68,000 fans, with 7,900 club seats and 108 luxury boxes.

The two scoreboards will be 90 feet wide and 25 feet high — three times the size of the Oriole Park scoreboard. They will be the first to feature LED lighting used in computers. A first generation model was used by the rock group U-2 on tour and will provide much sharper colors than the scoreboards in most stadiums. They're also thinking about putting a huge Raven on top of the stadium. The Ravens believe

> "The way I play this game is like a dog. You take food away from a dog and run from him, he's going to come and get you." — Ray Lewis, who led the NFL in tackles. (1997)

did you know?

Before moving to Indianapolis, the Colts beat the Oilers, 20-10, in their final contest in Baltimore. In '97, the Ravens played the last game at the same Memorial Stadium, a 21-19 win over the freshly relocated Oilers.

The "I Was There" Game

December 14, 1997: In the final game at Memorial Stadium, the home for so many memorable Colts moments, the Ravens not only beat the Tennessee Oilers, 21-19, they brought back many of the former Colts players to run a final play at the end of the game. Unitas handed off one more time to Lenny Moore. It was a day that recaptured the electricity of the heyday of the Colts and of football in Baltimore.

The Paper Bag Game

November 9, 1997: In their only Sunday night prime time appearance of the year, the Ravens were routed by the Steelers, 37-0, for the worst defeat in their brief history. Vinny Testaverde, ailing with the flu, threw interceptions on the first three series.

Great Names

Dan Footman (DE, 1996-present)
Anthony Pleasant (DE, 1996-present)
Michael Jackson (WR, 1996-present)

Worst Team

1996 (4-12): Strapped by the salary cap, the Ravens had problems keeping 53 players on the roster. On the field, injuries to the defense forced a mid-season shift from a four-man front to a 3-4 scheme, and the results were disastrous. Vinny Testaverde had a breakout season, but the Ravens couldn't stop a runaway baby carriage.

Our Top Story

"Colts Bolt"
March 28, 1984
In the rain and the sleet, a caravan of Mayflower Moving Vans arrived at the Colts complex in Owings Mills, MD., to move the Colt franchise to Indianapolis. By dawn on March 29, the trucks were packed and had departed. The franchise was gone. The hole in the city's psyche remained until the Ravens flew into town, after delivering a similar blow to the citizens of Cleveland.

"From Brown to Purple"
February 9, 1996
The NFL approves owner Art Modell's proposal to move his Cleveland Browns team to Baltimore. The catch: The Browns name, uniform, and franchise records remain in Cleveland.

"Road Win!"
September 14, 1997
Matt Stover kicks a 37-yard field goal with under a minute remaining to give the Ravens a 24-23 win over the Giants in East Rutherford, NJ. It was the team's first win on the road after eight straight losses.

this new stadium will be the one by which all future football stadiums will be measured, just as Oriole Park at Camden Yards became a trend setter for baseball.

The Ravens hope to turn each home game into a day-long experience with an entertainment zone with picnic tables and concession stands and an NFL Experience entertainment zone, where families can take their kids before the game. They'll also have a tailgating zone. They're so determined to foster a family atmosphere that they promise to eject drunk and rowdy fans and buy back their PSLs.

The Bottom Line on "Your Name Here" Park

Address: 1101 Russell St., Baltimore, MD 21230

Tickets: The team still has almost 10,000 personal seat licenses available at $500 (plus $30 per ticket) and $750 (plus $35 per ticket). They've promised to freeze prices for the first three years at the new stadium and may extend the freeze because of the new TV contract. To get information about PSLs, call (410) 261-RAVE or (888) 919-9737. The team's ticket offices are at 200 St. Paul St., Ste 2400, Baltimore, MD. 21202. They also sell 6,000 tickets per game throughout the stadium at prices ranging from $20 to $60. These tickets go on sale at the start of the season.

Public Transportation: Fans will be encouraged to take public transportation to the downtown stadium. There is a light rail stop at the stadium, as well as an MTA (410/682-4636) shuttle bus service from

did you know?

The Ravens are seemingly never out of a game. In their first two years of existence, 20 of Baltimore's 32 contests were decided by seven or fewer points, 13 by a field goal or less (1 tie).

Best of the Ravens

Best Team

1997 (6-9-1): In 1996, the Ravens were an offensive juggernaut that received little or no help from their defense. By the end of 1997, there had been a complete reversal of fortune, as youngsters such as rookie LBs Peter Boulware and Jamie Sharper and ex-Seahawk DE Michael McCrary meshed down the stretch. Too bad the Baltimore offense never regained its form from the previous season.

Greatest Players by Position

Pos:	Player
QB:	Vinny Testaverde
RB:	Earnest Byner
WR:	Michael Jackson
TE:	Eric Green
OL:	Jonathan Ogden
DL:	Rob Burnett
LB:	Ray Lewis
DB:	Stevon Moore
P/K:	Matt Stover
ST:	Jermaine Lewis

And Don't Forget...

QB: Eric Zeier. When he's been in the lineup, he's made things happen. The former Bulldog has made the most of his abilities.

T: Tony Jones. One of the most consistent and underrated tackles in the league, Jones made the most out of never being drafted.

LB: Peter Boulware. His debut season in '97 produced 11.5 sacks and earned him Defensive Rookie of the Year honors.

TE: Brian Kinchen. A former 12th-round draft choice of the Dolphins in '88, he can block, catch and is a key performer on special teams.

DB/ST: Bennie Thompson. A standout defender and one of the league's big hitters, Thompson sets the tone on the coverage units.

> "I was tired. I was beat. I was whipped. I could not believe what those guys go through every week." — Former Raven Leroy Hoard describing his experience with the pro bowling tour.

Best Argument

Wide Receiver: Michael Jackson or Derrick Alexander? Throughout his pro career, Jackson has been one of the most overlooked wideouts in the league. Injuries have plagued the speedster, but he's played his best football over the last few years. Alexander is a former first-round draft choice who has all the tools to be a star, but he was inconsistent before leaving the Ravens for the Chiefs in 1998.

Best Coach

Ted Marchibroda (1996-current): The city of Baltimore has certainly been good to Marchibroda, who led the since-departed Colts to three straight AFC East titles from 1975-77 and has made the Ravens one of the more entertaining teams in the league. He remains one of the better offensive minds in the league, and over time has had a hand in the development of many of the game's top quarterbacks.

Swami Sez:

Quoth the Ravens..."Can we please win a close game ???"

Pressbox

Who to Read...

Despite the Ravens' tribulations, many writers are quite forgiving of the team simply because they're still thrilled about football's return to Baltimore. *Baltimore Sun* columnist Ken Rosenthal isn't one of them — you can count on him to provide counterpoint to Art Modell's rosy team forecasts. Mike Preston and Gary Lambrecht are among those providing daily Ravens coverage for the *Sun,* along with John Eisenberg, John Steadman and Vito Stellino.

> "When you lose a step, you gain knowledge." — Rod Woodson on experience. (1998)

Who to Watch...

The Ravens' three primary TV shows have all migrated to WJZ–CBS for the 1998 season. Ted Marchibroda has a weekly hour at 7pm Saturdays. "Ravens Kickoff," a game-day preview show, airs at 11:30am on Sundays. And WJZ airs a Ravens postgame show as well.

Who to Listen To...

WJFK (1300 AM) broadcasts Ravens games, with Scott Garceau doing play by play and former Colts great Tom Matte doing color. The most boisterous sports radio personality in town has to be "Nasty" Nestor Aparicio of WWLG (1360 AM). He is known for his off-the-wall show "Sports Forum," as well as for his habit of attending games wearing a helmet with a light on top. In contrast, "Sportsline" with Jerry Sandusky (son of John Sandusky) on WBAL (1090 AM) presents a more composed brand of sports radio featuring a Ravens pre-game show and NFL preview with Stan White and Mel Kiper, Jr. At 7pm weekday evenings, Stan "the Fan" Charles of WJFK lives up to his nickname with a hearty enthusiasm. "Sports Final" at 10pm weeknights on WCBM is hosted by Phil Wood, an insider-y guy with a storehouse of trivia knowledge.

---

various points in Baltimore. Maryland MARC (800/325-RAIL) commuter trains run to the complex as well.

Parking: There are only 10,000 parking spaces within a half mile walk of the stadium, although many more are available in downtown garages.

Capacity: 68,400.

Restrooms: 74.

Where to Go . . . in Baltimore

Best Bars

Best sports bar: A traditional sports bar, **Rootie Kazootie's** has nine TVs showing all the games and a football field painted on the floor. *2701 N. Charles St. (410) 889-9977. Seven days 11:30am-2am*

Best location: Wharf Rat-Camden Yards is a brew pub with a patio that is popular with sports fans because it's across the street from Oriole Park. It's a hangout on game days. *206. Pratt St, (410) 244-8900. Seven days 11:30am-2am.*

Second best location. Although it has only three TV sets, **Downtown Sports Exchange Tavern** is a football fan hangout on game days because of its proximity to the sports complex. *102 N. Liberty St. (410) 539-7587. Seven days 12pm-12am.*

did you know?

Pat Modell, the wife of owner Art Modell, actually owns 70 per cent of the team. Art, who owns 30 per cent, remains the general partner who runs the team. Modells switched 70 per cent of the team to his wife for accounting reasons.

Best Restaurants

Best crabs. In the Fells Point section of Baltimore, **Obrycki's** is the classic Baltimore crab house, with heaping platters of steamed crabs the most popular attraction. *1727 E. Pratt St, (410) 732-6399. Su 12pm-9:30pm, M-Sa 12pm-11pm. All major credit cards. $$$*

Best Italian. In the heart of Little Italy, **Sabatino's** is popular with locals as well as the tourists and business travelers. It features both northern and southern Italian cuisine. *901 Fawn St. (410) 727-9414. Seven days 12pm-3am. All major credit cards. $$-$$$*

Ultimate destination for sports fans. Be like the Swami! The best place in Baltimore to eat, drink, watch and play is **ESPNZone**, with a sports theme restaurant, a screening room and a game area. *601 E. Pratt St. $$*

Best Accommodations

Harbor Court Hotel. This is the hotel where Art Modell stayed when he first came to Baltimore. It's a 203-room modern rendition of a classic hotel with oil paintings, oriental carpets and marble

Ready For Primetime (Sunday Night)

October 13, 1996: Some of the previews for this tilt read "Colts host Baltimore" — which certainly had a peculiar ring to it. More important, it was an emotional evening at the RCA Dome as Ravens coach Ted Marchibroda faced the club he had brought within a game of Super Bowl XXX. Colts 26, Ravens 21.

Overall Sunday night: 0-2

Think About the Weather

December 1, 1996: A rainy December day at Memorial Stadium was the setting for the Ravens' biggest win in their first two years. Ex-Steeler TE Eric Green caught a touchdown pass and RB Bam Morris rushed for 100 yards as the Ravens stunned the defending AFC champions. Ravens 31, Steelers 17.

Team Leaders

Rushing Yards
1,511 Byron "Bam" Morris, 1996-present

Passing Yards
7,148 Vinny Testaverde, 1996-97

Passing Touchdowns
51 Vinny Testaverde, 1996-97

Receptions
145 Michael Jackson, 1996-present

Interceptions
5 Antonio Langham, 1996-97

Touchdowns
18 Michael Jackson, 1996-present
Derick Alexander, 1996-present

Points
201 Matt Stover, 1996-present

Fans' notes

On Screen

The Ravens, the NFL's oddly conceived un-expansion franchise, has no real history in images. You can catch up on their attempts to write a new history with the official team video from NFL Films Video.

Bookshelf

From Colts to Ravens: A Behind-The-Scenes Look at Baltimore Professional Football by a Writer Who Was There. John F. Steadman (Bancroft 1997).

> "I was cut when I went out for 65-pound pee-wee football when I was around seven years old. They said I had no talent. My dad was one of the coaches." — Former Ravens center Steve Everitt.

You Gotta See...

▶The only national historic site for a sports hero, this is a must for all sports fans. It's the renovated **Babe Ruth home**. See where the Babe was born as well as many mementos of his career including his 1914 rookie card in which he's wearing the uniform of his first pro team — the Baltimore Orioles.

▶Baltimore's **Inner Harbor**, just over ten minutes' walk from Camden Yards, is the nation's best-known and most successful waterfront rehabilitation project. With attractions like the National Aquarium, a waterside walk and Harborplace's host of shops and restaurants, it's the city's showpiece.

▶The **U.S.S. Constellation**, the country's first commissioned Navy ship, was launched over 200 years ago. It is currently a floating museum in the Inner Harbor.

floors in public areas. *550 Light St., (410)234-0550, (800) 824 0076. $$$$*

Omni Inner Harbor. This is Baltimore's largest hotel. It features 703 rooms and was refurbished in 1994. It has an outdoor pool and a workout room. *101 W. Fayette St., (410) 752-1100, (800) 843-6644. $$$*

Holiday Inn Inner Harbor. This 375-room hotel is convenient to the Camden Yards area and underwent a $6.5-million renovation in 1993. Children under 18 stay for free. *301 W. Lombard St, (410) 685-3500, (800) 465-4329. $$*

Against the Odds

Bennie Thompson is a special special-teams player. In 1995, the Ravens' special teams captain missed three games with a broken wrist and still finished third on the unit with 16 tackles. What made Thompson's '95 season truly remarkable is that he played the year despite personal tragedy. On February 5, Thompson's three-year-old son, Devyn, and his ex-wife were murdered in a robbery at their New Orleans home. For some time Thompson was considered a suspect by police, but his name was eventually cleared.

Buffalo Bills

I f you've watched ESPN's "NFL Primetime" through the years, you've heard the following: "No one circles the wagons like the Buffalo Bills."

This, of course, is tribute to one of the NFL 's most resilient teams ever, a Bills unit that had the moxie to advance to four straight Super Bowls in the '90's, undaunted by the previous year's loss. But if truth be known, the Bills have been circling the wagons from the very beginning.

Franchise History

Buffalo Bills (AFL)
(1960–69)
Buffalo Bills (NFL)
(1970–present)

It all started with Ralph Wilson's business decision to become a charter member of the "Foolish Club," a group of eight men who decided to challenge the NFL in 1960 by forming the AFL. The Bills began operations in one of the smallest pro football towns, but they would soon be living large, winning back-to-back AFL titles in 1964 and 1965, shutting down the high-powered San Diego Chargers both times, 20-7 and 23-0.

Those teams featured a blue-collar defense that a blue-collar town could love:

By the Numbers

(Since 1970)
Regular Season: 202-220-2
Postseason: 12-11
Division Titles: 7
Vs. Division: 108-111-1 (Playoffs: 4-0)
Playoff Appearances: 11
Home: 119-93-1
Away: 83-127-1

(Overall)
Regular Season: 267-289-8
Postseason: 14-13
Playoff Appearances: 15
Home: 153-126-4
Away: 114-163-4

Tom Sestak, Jim Dunaway, and Ron McDole up front, Butch Byrd in the secondary, and Mike Stratton at linebacker. Stratton's hit on the Chargers Keith Lincoln in the playoffs is legendary.

On offense, future congressman, cabinet member and presidential candidate Jack Kemp was at quarterback, Billy Shaw and Stew Barber headmanned the offensive line, and the playmakers were Cookie and Golden Wheels — RB Cookie Gilchrist and WR Elbert Dubenion. Buffalo had to wait until Super Bowl XXV to make it to football's ultimate game, but they were simply one year too early from making it to the very first one.

Most Revered Football Figures

Jim Kelly. A tad rough around the edges, but plenty of heart and a compulsion to rise and fight again after getting knocked on his butt. A metaphor for the city of Buffalo itself.

Darryl Talley On a team that included Bruce Smith, Thurman Thomas, Jim Kelly and Andre Reed, Talley was the spiritual leader in the golden age of Buffalo football.

Billy Shaw. Captain of the AFL champions of the mid-1960s, he retired before the league merged with the NFL. Ron Wolf, GM of the Packers, says, "He belongs in the Hall of Fame."

Rivalries

The Bills and Boston **Patriots** met in the very first AFL game, an exhibition on July 30, 1960, which the Pats won, 28-7. They have battled like siblings ever since, with the Pats holding a 40-35 lead with one tie. The most memorable game was on December 20, 1964, when they met for the championship of the AFL East. Buffalo won at Fenway Park, 24-14. The first time the Bills played the Miami **Dolphins** they scored 58 points. When Don Shula arrived, however, the Dolphins swept the '70s, winning 20 straight from the Bills despite the famous Howard Cosell line, "Miami has the oranges, but Buffalo has The Juice." In the Dan Marino-Kelly years, however, Marv Levy won 17-of-22 games from Shula, including three '90's playoff games and the great Shula's last appearance on the sidelines, narrowing the series to 41-25-1, Dolphins.

> **did you know?**
>
> Until the '90s, no Buffalo player was issued No. 31 because it was part of the team logo on its stationery.

Their bid at three straight AFL titles was stopped in 1966 by Kansas City, 31-7. As a result, the Chiefs made history, and the Bills would have to wait.

Not long afterwards, in 1968, Buffalo fell to an abysmal 1-12-1 (their only win was over the eventual Super Bowl champion New York Jets), but the wagons were circled when they earned the number 1 draft pick and selected O.J. Simpson.

Once The Juice and his "Electric Company," led by Reggie McKenzie and Joe DeLamielleure, got flowing, the sky was the limit. In 1973, on a snowy December day at Shea Stadium, Simpson became the first man to eclipse the 2,000-yard barrier, an even more impressive feat when you remember that the season was 14 games then, not 16. Alas, Simpson's Bills would make the postseason only once, the next season (1974), when they were bounced, 32-14, by eventual Super Bowl champ Pittsburgh. Undaunted, Simpson ended his Hall of Fame career with 11,236 yards rushing, which at the time stood second only to the great Jim Brown.

The Bills fell to 2-12 in 1976. But by 1980, they were back in the playoffs, as they were again in 1981 under coach Chuck Knox and quarterback Joe Ferguson. Again, the Bills fell hard, going 2-14 in 1984 and 1985. At this low point GM Bill Polian and coach Marv Levy entered the scene, and began to turn Buffalo from counterfeit Bills to the gold standard in the AFC.

A young Bruce Smith was waiting at defensive end for some help, which came when QB Jim Kelly arrived in 1986 from the USFL, LB Cornelius Bennett was acquired in a trade in 1987 and Thurman Thomas was drafted in 1988. Sprinkle in Andre Reed at receiver, Kent Hull on the line, Darryl Talley at LB, and Steve Tasker on special teams,and you have the ingredients for a playoff team eight out of nine years from 1988 to 1996. The Bills and their coach were quite a juxtaposition — a high-powered, no-huddle offense and a quiet but worldly head coach with a masters degree from Harvard. But what a combination, and, oh, how they circled the wagons.

They got everything right except the Super Bowl. Some of us feel that if the Bills had won that scintillating Super Bowl XXV instead of losing, 20-19, to the New York Giants, they could have been at least 2-2 in their Super Bowl years. But they went from 20-19, to 37-24 losers to Washington, to 52-17 and 30-13 losers to Dallas.

An odd thing happened during their fourth Super Bowl appearance, though. The jokes stopped, and the respect began, especially from within the NFL, where everyone knew that four straight Super Bowl appearances might never be seen again.

> "There's more to life than climate." — Chuck Knox, after he left Los Angeles where he won five consecutive division titles with the Rams, for Buffalo. (1978)

Nor would a 32-point comeback in the playoffs ever be seen again. Only the Bills could have pulled it off, trailing Houston, 35-3, in the third quarter of the 1992 wild card round and winning, 41-38, in overtime with backup QB Frank Reich and Reed the heroes.

As the '90's come to a close, only a few remain from Buffalo's glory years. But since those names include

The "I Was There" Game

Jamuary 3, 1992: Trailing Houston 35-3, five minutes into the second half of the AFC wild card playoff, the Bills were in deep trouble. A comeback seemed unlikley as the Oilers had thumped the Bills, 27-3, the week before. To make matters worse, QB Jim Kelly was still at the sidelines from a knee injury suffered in that loss. Jump ahead, to two minutes left in the third quarter. Back-up QB Frank Reich throws his third consecutive touchdown pass to Andre Reed, cutting the deficit to 35-31. Trading scores, the teams finished regulation knotted at 38, but Buffalo's Steve Christie kicks a field goal 3:06 into overtime, winning the game, 41-38, in the greatest comeback in NFL history.

The Paper Bag Game

September 16, 1968: Before the 1968 season, coach Joe Collier traded promising quarterback Daryl Lamonica to Oakland for veteran quarterback Tom Flores and star receiver Art Powell. In week two, the Raiders came to Buffalo and buried the Bills, 48-6. Collier was fired that night. The Bills won only once during that season, but the consolation was drafting O.J. Simpson.

Great Names

Veno Belk (TE, 1987)
Billy Joe (FB, 1965)
Julian Nunamaker (DE, 1969–71)
Todd Schlopy (K, 1987)
Marco Tongue (DB, 1984)
Mack Yoho (DE, 1960–63)

Hall of Fame

O.J. Simpson   (RB, 1985)

Our top story

`"Bills Pick the Juice"`
`Jan. 28, 1969`
After finishing 1-12-1 in 1968, the Bills used the top pick in the 1969 draft on O.J. Simpson, bringing a ray of hope to the franchise. Signing Simpson was still a dodgy prospect, though, because his agent threatened to force a trade or take O.J. to the Canadian League.

`"Bills Rock Raiders, Head`
`to Super Bowl"`
`Jan. 20, 1991`
There wasn't much doubt about the outcome of this one at half-time, when Buffalo already led, 41-3. The defense had six interceptions, Jim Kelly threw for 300 yards, and the Bills recorded their most lopsided victory ever, 51-3, earning the franchise's first trip to the Super Bowl.

`"Not Guilty"`
`October 3, 1995`
Former Bills great O.J. Simpson is acquitted of double homicide in what is arguably the most-covered court case of the century.

> **"When it's freezing cold, it's snowing and the other team wishes it were home, that's Buffalo Bills weather."**
> **— Jim Kelly**

`"Marv Levy Retires"`
`December 31, 1997`
After 12 years and 123 victories in Buffalo, the 72-year old Levy decided that it was time to do something else.

Bruce Smith, Thurman Thomas and Andre Reed, the will to win and the ability to succeed remain.

As will the reality that nobody circles the wagons like the Buffalo Bills.

— Chris Berman

Rich Stadium

Rich Stadium is 25 years old this season, yet it is still considered a jewel by the locals, probably because of the hassle it was to get it built. In 1968 the Erie County Legislature voted to build a domed stadium in Lancaster, a northern suburb. The stadium was never built. Lawsuits were filed, politicians went to jail. Ralph Wilson, the Bills' owner, actually visited Seattle, then lusting for a franchise of its own. Wilson almost had a deal with King County, Washington, when the Erie County Legislature, in a compromise move, voted to build an outdoor, 80,000-seat stadium in Orchard Park, a southern suburb. For the last eleven seasons, the Bills' attendance has ranked in the league's top seven. During the Super Bowl run they led the NFL three times. For many fans, a trip to a Bills' game is just below a pilgrimage to Lourdes. The aroma of ribs, kielbasa and various other delicacies wafts through the air a mile from the stadium on game-day morning.

While it's relatively new, one of the more popular traditions is the film of a Buffalo stampede shown on the Jumbotron as the home team is about to kick off or receive. It seems to be right out of *Dances with Wolves*, and the fans get fully stoked. Stiffened security has eased the problem of misbehaving fans, but one remaining

> **did you know?**
> Buffalo lost 4 straight Super Bowls in the 1990s to the Giants, Redskins and Cowboys (twice). In the regular season from 1990-96, the Bills were 11-1 vs. NFC East clubs.

Best of the Bills

Best Team

1990 (15-4): Quarterback Jim Kelly, RB Thurman Thomas and WR Andre Reed were the big weapons in an attack that simply outscored its opponents. Buffalo put 95 points on the board in playoff wins over the Dolphins and Raiders, but were stifled in the stunning 20-19 Super Bowl XXV loss to the ball-control Giants as the Bills defense, featuring DE Bruce Smith and LB Cornelius Bennett, couldn't get off the field.

Greatest Players by Position

Pos:	Player
QB:	Jim Kelly
RB:	O.J. Simpson
WR:	Andre Reed
TE:	Pete Metzelaars
OL:	Joe DeLamielleure
DL:	Bruce Smith
LB:	Darryl Talley
DB:	Nate Odomes
P/K:	Paul Maguire
ST:	Steve Tasker

And Don't Forget...

RB: Thurman Thomas. The epitome of the all-purpose back, Thomas redefined the statistic "Total Yards from Scrimmage."

G: Billy Shaw. Eight-time AFL all-star and one of the franchise's best players of the 1960s.

C: Kent Hull. Underrated Pro Bowl veteran equally adept at run or pass blocking and the anchor of the Bills' talented offensive lines.

LB: Mike Stratton. Consistent, hard-hitting defensive stalwart and the enforcer on Buffalo's AFL title teams.

NT: Fred Smerlas. Five-time Pro Bowler and the heart and soul of Chuck Knox's defenses in the early '80s.

G: Reggie McKenzie. The most vocal member of the Electric Company — the offensive line that "turned loose The Juice" — he was the sparkplug of the Bills' line for a decade.

Best Argument

Quarterback: Jim Kelly or Jack Kemp? True, Kelly remains the only quarterback to lose four Super Bowls, but he was the unquestioned leader of his team and did a fair amount of his own play-calling, a rarity in today's game. Kemp was a heady field general who led the Bills to back-to-back AFL championships in 1964-65, and did it with both his arm and his legs.

> **"You can't be a great quarterback in snow and thirty-mile-per-hour wind." — Jim Kelly on choosing the USFL's Houston Gamblers over the Bills, who drafted him with their first pick. (1983)**

Best Coach

Marv Levy (1986-97): A favorite of fans of NFL Films, Levy is sometimes best known for his "over-officious jerk" remark while he was the sideline leader of the Chiefs. But his real strong suit was the ability to relate to his players and adjust to their talents. Forget the fact that he's the only coach to lose four straight Super Bowls. Levy made sure the Bills got to the Big Game, and he might be the only NFL head coach who is a member of Phi Beta Kappa.

Pressbox

Who to Read...

The *Buffalo News* penetrates its circulation area deeper than any newspaper in the U.S. It provides blanket coverage of the Bills and NFL by a task force which includes beat writers Vic Carucci, Mark Gaughan, Allen Wilson and the dean of them all, Larry Felser. Coverage includes a Sunday "NFL Notes" piece. In Rochester, their name is merely "the Bills." The *Rochester Democrat* and *Chronicle/Times-Union* offers its readers daily stories and commentary by Leo Roth and Sal Maiorano.

Who to Watch...

Empire Sports Network, a cable station which reaches throughout upstate New York, has a load of Bills-related programming. Paul Maguire co-hosts the weekly coach's show and has a call-in show of his own. ESN also has a Bills postgame show, as well as programs from sports mavens Howard Simon, Jim Brinson, Mike DeGeorge and Pete Weber. New ESPN analyst Jim Kelly has a show on WGRZ–NBC, co-hosted by Ed Kilgore. The city's top sports anchors, Van Miller of WIVB–CBS and John Murphy of WKBW–ABC, do a good job covering all the Bills games.

Who to Listen To...

This season the Bills have begun aiming for a younger demographic, broadcasting games simultaneously at two spots on WGRF (96.9 FM), a classic rock station, and WEDG (103.3 FM), an alternative rock station. Both feature a pregame and a postgame show as well as the game action itself, hosted by Miller and Murphy.

---

annoyance are the large number of fans who get up to get a beer at the most tense times.

Thanks to an upcoming multi-million dollar renovation, the best seats next season will be heated, dugout-style seats ringing the center of the stadium. The bad news is that seat license fees will triple the cost of those seats. The worst seats are in the corners of the upper decks. Normal tailgating is now supplemented by a version of the NFL Experience, plus bands, alumni booths, and other attractions in the adjacent Ralph C. Wilson Fieldhouse. The Fieldhouse is a 95,000-square-foot, 12-story Astroturf field on which the team practices during bad weather.

The Bottom Line on Rich Stadium

Address: One Bills Dr., Orchard Park, NY, 14127; (716) 649-0015.

Tickets: Season ticket sales begin on February 1. You can get seats by calling the ticket office at (716) 649-0015. There used to be a discount on season tickets, but not any longer. Seats for the disabled are in section 168.

1998: $30/$35/$37

1994: $26/$34/$41

Parking: There is parking for 12,000 cars ($7 each) as well as 300 buses and 250 campers on stadium grounds. Across the street is Erie County Community

College's South Campus, where thousands of additional spots are available. Nearby satellite lots hold additional parking.

Extras: There is no local public transportation. For those coming from as far east as Albany, there is a special train on game days with shuttles from the train station to the stadium. Same for Canadian fans coming down from Toronto and Hamilton. A new station on the stadium grounds is part of the renovation.

Capacity: 80,025.

Restrooms: 46 men's and 46 women's.

did you know?
Al Cowlings, the "A.C." of the infamous slow Bronco chase, was the Bills' first draft choice in 1970, the year after his USC buddy, O.J. Simpson, was No. 1.

Where to Go . . . in Buffalo

Best Bars

Best boat drinks. A huge place, **The Pier** is very popular in the good weather when some customers arrive by boat. *Rt. 5, next to the small boat harbor on the lake. (716) 853-4000.*

Best crowd. The Barrel House is a popular meeting place on a popular street. *85 W. Chippewa, downtown Buffalo, (716) 856-4645. M-Sa 11am-4am, Su closed.*

Best non-football atmosphere. Located in the artsy Allentown section of downtown Buffalo, **Mulligan's Brick Bar** will get your mind out of the huddle. **The Pink Flamingo**, next door, pushes the envelope further. *229 Allen St. No telephone.*

Best Biff bar. Preppies of all ages gather at **Cole's** on the Elmwood strip in a tradi-

Ready For Primetime (Monday Night)

September 16, 1974: It would prove to be a typically wild Monday night affair for Oakland, only this time they found themselves on the wrong end of the scoreboard. Buffalo trailed, 13-7, with just under two minutes to play, but the teams combined for three touchdowns in the next 85 seconds, including QB Joe Ferguson's 12-yard pass to WR Ahmad Rashad with thirty-one seconds to play which proved to be the difference. (Bills 21, Raiders 20) Overall Monday night: 16-19 Overall Thursday night: 1-1 Overall Sunday night: 6-4

Think About the Weather

December 16, 1973: Snow-covered Shea Stadium was the venue for the culmination of arguably the greatest performance by a player in NFL history. Behind fullback Jim Braxton, Bills' RB O.J. Simpson carried 34 times for 200 yards and a score, wrapping up a campaign which saw him rush for 2,003 yards in a 14-game season. Those who showed up saw another Jets' loss, but an appreciative crowd was chanting "Juice" by game's end. (Bills 34, Jets 14). In Buffalo, the cold is always a factor deep in the season, but on Sept. 30, 1973, the wind blew so fiercely that Joe Namath of the Jets looked more like knuckleballer Phil Niekro. Namath and Joe Ferguson completed fewer than a half dozen passes between them and Buffalo won, 9-7.

Worst Team

1984 (2-14): It was a very long year for head coach Kay Stephenson, in his second season as Chuck Knox's replacement. The Bills didn't break into the win column until week 12, when they stunned the Cowboys behind rookie RB Greg Bell — one of the team's lone bright spots. Buffalo allowed a whopping 454 points, 30 or more in eight of their setbacks — and dropped four games by 30 or more points.

Swami Sez:

As long as Bruce Smith lines up at defensive end, the Bills will be dangerous.

Team Leaders

Rushing Yards
11,405 Thurman Thomas, 1988-97
Passing Yards
35,467 Jim Kelly, 1986-96
Passing Touchdowns
237   Jim Kelly, 1986-96
Receptions
826   Andre Reed, 1985-97
Interceptions
40   George (Butch) Byrd, 1964-70
Touchdowns
83   Thurman Thomas, 1988-97
Points
670   Scott Norwood, 1985-91

tional hangout dating back to the leather helmet days. *1104 Elmwood Ave., near Buffalo State College, (716) 886-1449. 7 days 11:30am-4am.*

did you know?

Never has one team been so totally dominated by another, as the Bills were by the Dolphins: Miami beat the Bills a record 20 consecutive times from 1970-79.

Best Restaurants

Best taste of Buffalo. Classic Buffalo joint. The owner-chef of **Billy Ogden's**, Andy DiVincenzo, annually represents the city in the "Taste of the NFL" at the Super Bowl. Informal setting, haute cuisine. *1834 William St. (at Ogden St.), Lovejoy district. (716) 896-8018. M-Th 5pm-9:45pm, F-Sa 5pm-11:45pm, Su closed. AE, MC, V. $$$$*

Best spot for kids. A family kind of place, **Ilio Di Paolo's** draws Bills coaches and players for the huge helpings. *3785 South Park, Blasdell, near Rich Stadium. (716) 825-3675. M-F 11:30am-10pm, Sa 2pm-12am, Su 1pm-10pm. AE, MC, V. $*

Best chicken wings. No Kidding. The world's most ubiquitous appetizer was created here at **Anchor Bar.** Jazz on weekends, takeout available. *1047 Main St. (716) 886-8920. M-F 11am-10pm, Sa-Su 12pm-10pm. AE, D, MC, V. $*

Best beef on weck. Anderson's, with lots of horseradish. *2235 Sheridan Dr., Kenmore, (716) 875-5952. Seven days 11am-10pm. All major credit cards. $*

Best Accommodations

Radisson Hotel and Suites. Across from Buffalo Airport. 4243 Genessee St. *(716) 634-2300. $$-$$$*
Sheraton Inn. Across from Buffalo

Fans' notes

On Screen

Bills alumni seem to appear on the news with greater frequency and impact than most any other team. Start with the 1996 vice-presidential debates, featuring former Bills quarterback Jack Kemp. Chances are we'll be seeing a lot more of him as the next election creeps closer. And then there's O.J. Best to focus on **Airplane** and **The Towering Inferno**, two classic films, and the once-omnipresent Hertz commercials. Given all that's happened since — the chase with fellow Bills alum, A.C. Cowlings, the trials, the whole thing — it's safe to say we won't see him acting again. For something more football related, try **Thunder and Destruction** from NFL Films, which features Bruce Smith as one of the hardest hitters in the league.

Fight Songs, etc.

There have been a number of song written about the Bills, but the only one to catch on is a customized version of "Shout!"

Bookshelf

Armed and Dangerous. Jim Kelly and Vic Carucci (Doubleday 1993).
Contesting the Super Bowl. Dona Schwartz (Routledge Press 1997).

Relentless: The Hard-Hitting History of Buffalo Bills Football. Sal Maiorana (Quality Sports Publications 1994).
By a Nose. Fred Smerlas and Vic Carucci (S&S 1990).
O.J.: The Education of a Rich Rookie. O.J. Simpson (Macmillan 1970).

> "We're so good, we cut Superman." — Marv Levy, after the team cut actor Dean Cain, a free agent safety from Princeton. (1988)

You Gotta See...

▸There is a famous waterfall 26 miles up I-190 which should not be missed. Canada is across from downtown Buffalo, and a scenic ride begins on the Canadian side of the Peace Bridge, east along the Niagara River to **Niagara Falls**.
▸Continue beyond along the lower Niagara, whirlpool and gorge to the mouth of **Lake Ontario** and the resort town of **Niagara-on-the-Lake**. Important battles were fought there in the French and Indian War, but the attraction now is the **George Bernard Shaw Festival**.

While You Were Eating Turkey....

On Wednesday, Nov. 26, 1975, the Bills set out for a Thanksgiving game against the Cardinals in St. Louis. Their plane had to land in Chicago because a snowstorm closed the St. Louis airport. Coach Lou Saban reacted uncoachly, retreating to the lounge of the O'Hare Hilton to socialize with the media over a few scotch Old Fashioneds. The players also let nature take its course. The Bills finally made it to Busch Stadium an hour before kickoff the next day. When the doors of their buses opened, gales of laughter were let out. The heavily-favored Cardinals were upset by their relaxed foes, 32-14.
Overall, 2-3-1

A Fan's Notes: The NFL

Bookshelf

▶ *Iron Men: Bucko, Crazylegs, and the Boys Recall the Golden Days of Pro Football*, Stuart Leuthner, Doubleday, 1988.

▶ *When the Grass Was Real: Unitas, Brown, Lombardi, Sayers, Butkus, Namath and All the Rest: The Best Ten Years of Pro Football*, Bob Carroll, Simon and Schuster, 1993.

▶ *75 Season: The Complete Story of the NFL, 1920–1995*, Will McDonough, et al, Turner Publishing Co., 1994. A beautiful and factual coffee-table book that all fans who care about the history of the NFL should have in their collection.

▶ *The Women's Armchair Guide to Pro Football*, Betsy Berns, Bvision Sportsmedia, 1996. If you want to teach the game to someone, this is a good start.

▶ *A Game of Passion: The NFL Literary Companion*, John Weisbusch and Brian Silverman (eds.), Turner Publishing, 1994.

▶ *The Armchair Quaterback*, John Thorn (ed.), Scribners, 1982. This volume contains the best in pro football reporting and reminiscence, both fact and fiction.

▶ *The Fireside Book of Pro Football*, Richard Whittingham (ed.), Simon and Schuster, 1989.

▶ *Pigskin: The Early Years of Football*, Robert W. Peterson, Oxford, 1997.

▶ *Total Football*, Bob Carroll, John Thorn, et all. (eds), HarperCollins, 1997. The official reference guide to America's favorite sport.

▶ *The Football Encyclopedia*, Tod Maher and Bob Gill (eds), Macmillan, 1997.

▶ *Super Bowl: The Game of Their Lives*, Danny Peary (ed), Macmillan, 1997. Recollections about the greatest game, by those who played in it.

▶ *The Gridiron Game*, Dick Wimmer (ed), Masters, 1997. A literary anthology of great football writing.

Against the Odds

The picture of **Joe Ferguson** (1973-1984) hobbling to the line of scrimmage in a 1980 playoff game against San Diego illustrates his gritty 12-year career. Even though the Bills lost, 20-14, Ferguson played gamely on a severely sprained ankle, completing 15 of 30 pass attempts for 147 yards and a touchdown. A tough, fiery on-field leader, he inspired the club through the good times and the bad. From 1975-83, even though the Bills posted a 58-73 record, Ferguson threw for 23,072 yards and 153 touchdowns in 152 games.

Airport, next to Walden Galleria. 2040 Walden Ave. *(716) 681-2400. $$*

Garden Place Hotel. Owned by Salvatore's Italian Gardens, a lavish nearby restaurant. Free transportation to and from airport as well as to and from restaurant. *Exit 49 off I-90, 6615 Transit Rd., Williamsville. (716) 635-9000. $$*

Carolina Panthers

"We didn't get into this for funsies." — owner Jerry Richardson, predicting a Super Bowl win within the Panthers' first 10 years.

To understand how Ericsson Stadium, the beautiful Charlotte home of the Carolina Panthers, came to be, flash back to 1959, when the Baltimore Colts beat the New York Giants for the NFL championship. Colts receiver Jerry Richardson had just played his second season, and though he could have played longer, he had a taste for business: Instead of being turned into hamburger on the field, he turned to the hamburger trade. Richardson took his $4,864 in playoff money and invested with his Wofford College pal, Charlie Bradshaw, in the Hardee's restaurant chain.

Franchise History

Carolina Panthers
(1995–present)

Thirty-five years later, their business had expanded into a variety of franchised restaurants — from Hardee's to Denny's — and Richardson was positioned to return to the NFL. But this time, he would own the club. And he had an idea. Richardson visualized a stadium built without turning to the taxpayers; instead "Permanent Seat Licenses" would be sold. With the assistance of key local businessmen, Richardson offered Carolina football fans the rights to a seat for prices ranging from $600 to $5,400.

Season tickets would still have to be purchased annually, but the idea took flight in the form of $100 million, a fair chunk of the $187-million the stadium needed for construction. On October 26, 1993, some nine years after Richardson first dreamed of an NFL team, league owners unanimously awarded him the expansion franchise which became the Carolina Panthers, to begin play in 1995. Richardson had to pay $140 million in expansion fees — and forego half the network TV revenues for three years — but he had a plan. With a stadium on the way, he assembled a savvy front office headed by Mike McCormack, who had served as general manager of the Seattle Seahawks, and former Buffalo Bills general manager Bill Polian. They stepped on some toes when they hired little-known Pittsburgh Steelers defensive coordinator Dom

By the Numbers

(Overall)
Regular Season: 26-22
Postseason: 1-1
Division Titles: 1
Vs. Division: 14-10
Playoffs Appearance: 1
Home: 15-9
Away: 11-13

Most Revered Football Figures

Sam Mills. He never missed a game in his three years with the Panthers, where the players considered him a coach on the field. In his 12 years in the NFL, he played in five Pro Bowls, before retiring after the 1997 season as the oldest position player ever to make the Pro Bowl.

Steve Beuerlein. Has played the role of backup QB well, helping to get the franchise on its feet.

Dom Capers. Named Coach of the Year in his second season, Capers's Panthers set a record in '96 by becoming the first second-year team in NFL history to win a division title and advance to the NFC Championship Game.

Bill Polian. Even though he took off for Indianapolis in 1998, locals give credit to the general manager who took advantage of the free-agent market to get the fastest results in league history.

Rivalries

With two games per season against each of their divisional rivals, that is where the action is right now for the Panthers. Dom Capers's club put special emphasis on the **49ers**. The clubs have split their six meetings to date, and home field has meant little: Visitors have a 4-2 edge. The Atlanta **Falcons** figured to be natural rivals. So far it's Panthers over the Falcons four out of six games. If the Falcons ever improve, this could be one of the better regional rivalries in the league.

> **did you know?**
> Ericsson Stadium has a rule prohibiting fans from taking off their shirts during the game.

Capers — NFL commissioner Paul Tagliabue fined the Panthers $150,000 and two draft picks for tampering. But Capers proved to be a brilliant hire — he and his coaching staff led the Panthers to a expansion-record 7-9 season as the team played its home games at Clemson University while Ericsson Stadium was under construction.

In 1996, the Reverend Billy Graham dedicated the stadium, and the Panthers had a blessed season, stunning the league with a 12-4 record and an NFC West championship over the vaunted 49ers. The "zone-blitz" defense led by linebackers Sam Mills, Kevin Greene and Lamar Lathon terrorized NFL quarterbacks. The fairy-tale season didn't end there — the Panthers beat the defending Super Bowl champion Dallas Cowboys and advanced to the NFC title game before falling to the eventual Super Bowl champion Green Bay Packers.

Trouble finally found its way to Carolina in 1997 when the Panthers fell back to 7-9. With McCormack already retired, Polian left after the season to become president of the Indianapolis Colts. Quarterback Kerry Collins had been a franchise hero after just two seasons, but stumbled on and off the field. Still, in the end, Richardson was determined to fix things. Fans had built his stadium. He said he would never forget it. And you can believe him.

—*Chris Mortensen*

Ericsson Stadium

Ericsson Stadium is one of the better arenas in the NFL. It's an open-air, natural grass stadium nestled in uptown Charlotte and was built specifically for football. The

$186 million facility covers 33 acres, including practice fields. The stadium features landscaping with indigenous flowers and trees that add color all year to a grey concrete stucture that is highlighted with the team colors of black, blue and silver. Massive arches and towers greet fans at the three main entrances, each guarded by two one-ton bronze panthers.

The stadium is a sharp mix of technology and luxury. Each extra-wide seat features cup and program holders. There are 412 concession points, with tall and wide concourses that convey an open feel. The scoreboard system has state-of-the art sound, video and lots of instant replays.

They say there's not a bad seat in the house, and that is mostly true. The endzone is only 20 feet from the field wall, and the sidelines are only 50 feet from the front row. But the top level seats are nearly 13 stories above the field.

Many games include a Carolina blue sky over the stadium, and at night, the stadium sparkles along with the uptown skyline. There is also a distinctly college flavor at Panther games, reflecting the many colleges and universities in North and South Carolina. Fans spend hours tailgating, and the smoke

> "I couldn't believe the electricity of the crowd. They really hate the Cowboys."
> — Wesley Walls on the fans during the Panthers' NFC Divisional playoff game, January 5, 1997.

of barbeque grills in many of the parking lots pervades the area with a festive aroma. Even the team song is vaguely collegiate.

Inside, you'll find regular stadium fare, as well as specialties such as both mustard- and vinegar-based barbecue, black and blue Panther Burgers, and other southeastern

The "I Was There" Game

January 5, 1997: The Panthers are the only team in NFL history to win a division title in their second year of play and advance to the NFC Championship Game. So, the Panthers had already made some history when the NFC West champs faced the highly talented defending Super Bowl Champion Dallas Cowboys. After Deion Sanders and Michael Irvin swaggered into the stadium, the Panthers pounded the Cowboys, 26-17, to advance to the championship game. Ironically, both Sanders and Irvin were knocked out with injuries.

did you know?

In their second year in the NFL and their first year at Ericsson Stadium, the Panthers joined Super Bowl winner Green Bay as one of only two NFL teams with a perfect at-home record in '96 (including playoffs).

The Paper Bag Game

November 30, 1997: The Panthers were still clinging to a playoff bid in '97 when the lowly Saints came into their house for the 13th game of the season. But costly turnovers would kill Carolina and, despite a rally led by Steve Beuerlein, the Panthers lost the game on a last-second field goal, 16-13.

Great Names

Tshimanga Biakabutuka
(RB, 1995-present)
Andre Royal (LB, 1995-97)
Mitch Running (WR, 1997)

Our Top Story

"We're In!"

October 26, 1993

At a league meeting in Chicago, NFL owners unanimously selected Carolina as the 29th franchise and the first expansion team since 1976. Owner Jerry Richardson looked into the camera and thanked the fans.

"We're Good, Too."

1996 season

The Carolina Panthers made history in their second season by going 12-4, winning the NFC West and then beating the defending Super Bowl Champion Cowboys, 26-17, at Ericsson Stadium in their first playoff game to advance to the conference championship.

"Ouch!"

August 9, 1997

Broncos' linebacker Bill Romanowski lays a helmet-to-helmet shot on quarterback Kerry Collins in the Panthers' second preseason game, breaking Collins's jaw and drawing a hefty fine from the league.

Worst Team

1997 (7-9): Much more was expected from a club that had won a division title and battled the Packers hard in the NFC title game the year before. But age and off-the-field problems proved to be major distractions as the Panthers never found their stride.

did you know?

Including postseason, through 1997, the Panthers played 50 games and place-kicker John Kasay connected on 91-of-110 field goal attempts. Meanwhile, Carolina's offense produced just 88 touchdowns.

favorites like crabcakes. There is a raw seafood bar on the club level, and fare in honor of visiting fans in the suites such as toasted ravioli for the Rams and clam chowder for the New England Patriots. Also, a local micro-brewery owned by Panthers President Mark Richardson offers "Carolina Blond" beer.

The Bottom Line on Ericsson Stadium

Address: 800 South Mint St., Charlotte, NC 28202

Tickets: There are 100 PSLs still available at $3000 each. Game tickets for PSL holders range from $19-60. For more ticket information, call 704-358-7800 or 704-358-7000.

1998: $60/$50/$45/$42/$35/$32/$26/$19
1994: N/A

Public Transportation: Several city bus routes let off within a few blocks of the stadium. Call Charlotte Transit for more information. (704) 336-3366.

Parking: Traffic is not bad, and parking is plentiful with 37,000 spaces. If you park in the parking deck at the north entrance on Mint Street, a band will greet you on the "Cat Walk" over to the stadium.

Capacity: 73,248.
Restrooms: 90.

Where to Go . . . in Charlotte

Best Bars

Best pre-game bash. A local radio station hosts a party at the **Atlantic Beer and Ice Company**, where you'll find a cock-

Best of the Panthers

Best Team

1996 (13-5): After a 7-9 debut, some thought reality would catch up with Dom Capers's club. Instead, the Panthers maintained their momentum: They dethroned the 49ers for the NFC West title, knocked the Cowboys out of the playoffs and got within a game of the Super Bowl. A veteran defense showed no signs of fatigue and QB Kerry Collins made some timely plays, but the unsung star was the offensive line.

Greatest Players by Position

Pos:	Player
QB:	Kerry Collins
RB:	Anthony Johnson
WR:	Mark Carrier
TE:	Wesley Walls
OL:	Matt Elliott
DL:	Greg Kragen
LB:	Sam Mills
DB:	Eric Davis
P/K:	John Kasay
ST:	Michael Bates

And Don't Forget...

OL: Frank Garcia. Versatile blocker who has seen his share of action at both guard and center.

DL: Mike Fox. Doesn't get a lot of sacks in the Panthers system, but can usually be found at or around the football.

DB: Brett Maxie. Aggressive, ball-hawking safety and one of the defensive standouts during Carolina's debut season in '95.

RB: Fred Lane. A free agent find from (no joke) Lane College in Tennessee, the power-runner led the Panthers with 809 yards rushing in '97.

LB: Kevin Greene. The much-traveled pass-rusher has taken the revolving-door approach to being a Panther, but he was the biggest terror in the feared 1996 defense.

> "It's a message from God!"
> — Kevin Greene on the Panthers winning the NFC West in 1996.

Best Argument

Linebacker: Sam Mills or Lamar Lathon? Mills began his pro career in the USFL, followed Jim Mora to New Orleans and, later, Dom Capers to Carolina. The Panthers' defensive leader over their first three seasons, the veteran set the tone, excelling against the run and the pass. In his first season with Carolina in '96, Lathon earned Pro Bowl honors, but was hampered by injuries in '97.

Best Coach

Dom Capers (1995-current): One of the many fathers of the "zone blitz" defense, the one-time Saints assistant honed his skills in Pittsburgh as Bill Cowher's defensive coordinator for three years before earning his shot in Carolina. Capers led his club to a division title in just their second season and came within a game of the Super Bowl, but off-the-field distractions took their toll on the club in '97.

Pressbox

Who to Read...

Charlotte has been one of the most supportive and enthusiastic NFL cities since their Panthers arrived in 1995, and the *Charlotte Observer*, the town's primary paper, offers extensive pre-game and post-game coverage. Columnists Tom Sorensen and Scott Fowler provide behind-the-scenes insight, while Charles Chandler issues the team's report card after each game.

Swami Sez:

Was 1996's title game appearance too much too fast for Carolina???

Who to Watch...

A number of Panthers players, including linebacker Lamar Lathon, have been regular guests on local TV shows. But it's head coach Dom Capers who runs the show. Thus there's "The Dom Capers Show," a weekly update on the Panthers' affairs, broadcast on local CBS affiliate WBTV.

Who to Listen To...

Panthers games are carried on the team's flagship station, WBT (1110 AM). Every year, a number of players become regular guests on local radio programs. In the past, the cast has included offensive lineman Frank Garcia and linebacker Carlton Bailey. "The Gerry V Show" on WBT (1110 AM, 99.3 FM) is a popular listen. WFNZ (610 AM) is a 24-hour sports station with hosts ranging from Billy Packer's son, Mark, to former NFL players Ethan Horton and Dino Hackett.

tail lounge, cigars and entertainment, with a Caribbean and South Florida menu. *330 N. Tryon St. (704) 339-0566. M-Th 11am-midnight, F-Sa 11am-2am, Su (game days only) 10am-8pm.*

Best place to watch the game. **Bailey's Sports Bar and Grille** has a big-screen TV, pool tables — all the trappings of a sports bar. But it's just a touch classier than the average joint. Two locations. *5873 Albemarle Rd., (704) 532-1005; 8500 Pineville-Matthews Rd., (704) 541-0794. Seven days 4pm-2am.*

The other best place to watch the game. More than one hundred televisions spread throughout **Jock 'n' Jill's** make this popular spot perfect for watching sports. *4109 South Stream Blvd. (704) 423-0001. Seven days 11am-2am.*

Best post-game bash. There's live entertainment before and after the game at the **Rainbow Cafe South End**, but after is better. *1933 South Blvd. (704) 377-8835. Seven days 11am -2pm.*

Best Restaurants

Best casual atmosphere. Grab a beer and a bite before or after the game at **Vinnie's Southside Sardine**. Features a grill and raw bar. *1714 South Blvd. (704) 332-0006. M-Sa 11 am-2pm, Su 12-11pm. Most major credit cards. $*

Best Panther sightings. A nice micro-brewery in the South End, **South End Brewery and Smokehouse** offers live entertainment. The menu revolves around a wood-burning smoker, grill and pizza oven. Panthers are often seen here after the games; the restaurant is owned by team president Mark Richardson. *2100 South Blvd. (704) 358-4677. Lunch: M-F 11:30am-4pm, Sa 11am-4pm, Su 11am-2pm; dinner: Su-Tu 4-10pm, W-Sa 4-11pm. All major credit cards. $$*

Best sports bar/restaurant. It's not near the stadium, but you can see most NFL games at **The Scoreboard Restaurant**, where the nine TV screens are complemented by a speaker at each table. There are also four giant six-by-eight-foot screens. Features Panther pints of beer. *2500 Crown Point Executive Center. (704) 847-7678. M-Th 4pm-1am, F-Sa 11am-2am, Su 12-12. All major credit cards. $*

> ## did you know?
> The unlikely became reality on November 5, 1995, when the Panthers edged the 49ers at San Francisco 13-7—the first time an expansion team had defeated a defending NFL champion.

> "We'd go to Iceland to play that game." — Pat Terrell, commenting about playing the NFC Championship game in frozen Green Bay, January 12, 1997.

Best Accommodations

Days Inn Central. A simple, economical choice with a downtown location, and there's an outdoor pool. *601 N. Tryon St. (704) 333-4733 (800) AAA-DAYS. $*

Adams Mark Hotel. Situated uptown, it's a sizable hotel with a pool, fitness center and reasonable rates. *555 S. McDowell St. (704) 372-4100, (800) 444-ADAM. $$*

Westin Hotel, Charlotte. This uptown choice is connected to the YMCA, where a small fee grants access to fitness equipment. *222 E Third St.(704) 377-6664, (800) WESTIN-1. $$-$$$.*

Ready For Primetime (Monday Night)

Dec. 8, 1997: In their first meeting since the 1996 playoffs, the struggling Panthers were supposed to be easy fodder for a proud but slumping Cowboys team that everyone figured could still make the playoffs. But Dom Capers's team came to play this night. Panthers 23, Cowboys 13.

Overall Monday night: 1-1

Overall Sunday night: 2-2

Think About the Weather

January 12, 1997: NFC Championship Game. A wind-chill factor which dipped to 25 below helped ice Carolina's playoff hopes at Lambeau Field. The Panthers struck first, but a pair of quick scores put the Packers up at halftime. The deep freeze set in, as the usually sure-handed Panthers began to miss tackles and drop the ball. (Packers 30, Panthers 13.)

Team Leaders

Rushing Yards
1,588 Anthony Johnson, 1995-97
Passing Yards
7,295 Kerry Collins, 1995-97
Passing Touchdowns
39   Kerry Collins, 1995-97
Receptions
157   Mark Carrier, 1995-97
Interceptions
10   Eric Davis, 1996-97
Touchdowns
16   Wesley Walls, 1996-97
Points
341 John Kasay, 1995-97

Fans' notes

On Screen

If you're a Carolina fan, you may have mixed feelings toward linebacker Kevin Greene, who after acting as the Panthers' defensive sparkplug in 1996 became a holdout and joined the rival 49ers in '97. Greene made his way onto TV as a result of his career in pro wrestling, where his Hulk Hogan hairdo (while he had it) was more of an asset than it was on the gridiron.

Bookshelf

The Carolina Panthers: The First Season of the Most Successful Expansion Team in NFL History. Joe Menzer and Bob Condor (Macmillan 1996).

Year of the Cat: How the Carolina Panthers Clawed Their Way to the Brink of the Super Bowl. Scott Fowler and Charles Chandler (Simon and Schuster 1997).

Carolina Panther Sunday. Wallace Sears (Pachyderm Press 1996).

You Gotta See...

▶Under normal circumstances, you might not associate fun with banks. But you'll find events with bands and food before and after the games at home offices of both major banks in Charlotte. The **Pigskin Party at First Union Plaza and Atrium** at 301 S. Tryon Street is often outside. The party at **NationsBank** is in Founders Hall at 100 N. Tryon St. and is catered by adjoining restaurant **Bistro 100.**

▶The **Hornets** are the other buzz around Charlotte in wintertime. They play at the Charlotte Coliseum, a fine basketball arena bathed in the team's blue hues and located about 20 minutes out of downtown.

▶It didn't provide the Panthers with the same home-field advantage it gives Clemson, and it's a good drive from Charlotte proper, but the imposing stadium known as **Death Valley** was the Panthers' stomping ground when they were still kittens.

Against the Odds

Matt Campbell (1995-present) was one of the 10 original free agents signed by Carolina in December 1994 — and at the end of the '97 season, the only "street" free agent remaining on the roster of either the Panthers or their sister expansion team, the Jaguars. An unheralded tight end out of South Carolina, Campbell defied odds even further when he made the difficult switch to tackle before the 1996 campaign. The experiment was a success, and Campbell was the object of a tug-of-war during the 1998 offseason when the Panthers had to ante up to match the Dolphins' three-year, $8 million offer.

Chicago Bears

C hicago is known as the city of big shoulders, and it's a good thing, too, because its football team carries the burden of a great legacy—legendary owner George Halas, Papa Bear himself, was the father of the professional game. At Ralph Hay's Hupmobile showroom in Canton, Ohio, Halas, representing the Decatur Staleys, met with representatives of 12 other clubs, each of whom paid $100 for membership in the American Professional Football Association, which later became the NFL. But football in Chicago predates even Halas. The city was still making steel and butchering hogs in 1899 when the Morgan Athletic Club started an amateur team which was two years later named the Cardinals, after the used University of Chicago jerseys they wore.

Franchise History

Decatur Staleys
(1920–1921)
Chicago Staleys
(1921–1922)
Chicago Bears
(1922–present)

Once he had bought the Bears in 1922, Halas considered calling his team the Chicago Cubs out of respect for his associates, legendary baseball pioneers Bill Veeck, Sr. and William Wrigley, but as Halas noted in his autobiography, football players were bigger than baseball players so if the latter were Cubs, then the gridiron giants must be Bears. The Cardinals (home in Comiskey Park) and Bears (in residence at Wrigley Field) enjoyed a spirited, if one-sided rivalry— the advantage was held by the Bears 47-19-6 until the Cardinals moved to St. Louis in 1960.

During Halas's 40 year tenure as head coach, the Bears won six world championships and altered the face of pro football. They signed the NFL's first marquee name, Harold "Red" Grange, to an unprecedented $100,000 deal in 1925. The Bears played the first indoor game in

By the Numbers

(Since 1970)
Regular Season: 215-208-1
Postseason: 7-9
Division Titles: 6
Vs. Division: 106-98 (Playoffs: 1-0)
Playoff Appearances: 10
Home: 127-84-1
Away: 88-124

(Overall)
Regular Season: 602-406-42
Postseason: 14-14
Playoff Appearances: 21
Home: 354-169-24
Away: 248-237-18

Most Revered Football Figures

Gale Sayers. His gracefulness and acceleration could coax tears from a Southside sausage plant worker.

Red Grange. "The Galloping Ghost" was homegrown at Illinois and emerged a Bear legend 10 days after graduation.

Dick Butkus. Could pummel opponents with a stare; confessed that his overriding life's aim was to separate a running back's head from his neck.

George Halas. Without him there is probably no NFL, definitely no Chicago Bears.

Walter Payton. Ask any Chicagoan under 40; "Sweetness" was the greatest football player—at any position—they ever saw.

Rivalries

Bears fans loathe the Green Bay **Packers** (82-67-6). This is the oldest continuous rivalry in pro football — their first game was in 1921 — and it's a doozy no matter how bad the teams are. Wisconsinites consider Bears fans to be crass and impolite; Bears fans consider Packers fans to be inbred rubes. With Chicago's ample history of despising cross-town rivals, Bears fans developed a natural and entertaining hatred for the Chicago/St. Louis/Arizona **Cardinals** (52-25-6). Longtime Thanksgiving day nemesis and ferocious blue–collar foe, the Bears make the Detroit **Lions** (76-55-5) cowardly.

> **did you know?**
> The 1997 Bears surrendered the most points (421) in team history.

1930, boasted the league's first 1,000-yard rusher in rookie Beattie Feathers in 1934, participated in the NFL's first game broadcast on radio, developed the T formation in 1940, and played the first sudden-death overtime game in 1941. Synonymous with Bears were names like Bronko Nagurski, Dick Butkus and Mike Ditka, who epitomized what became known as the Black and Blue division. Yet the fire and furor of a Butkus was countered by the grace of his draft classmate, Gale Sayers, who set a then-NFL record with 22 touchdowns as a rookie before his glorious career was cut short by a knee injury after only seven seasons.

Post-Papa Bear, the Bears drifted through 15 miserable years salvaged mainly by the presence of "Sweetness," Walter Payton, who would rush to the top of the NFL's record books. After a succession of inept coaches, Halas breathed new life into his franchise by naming Ditka as head coach in 1982. In only three years he built a championship team led by, arguably, the most dominant defense of its era, which allowed only 10 points during the playoff run to the Super Bowl. The '85 Bears were a team of character and characters, from the punky QB named Jim McMahon to the Refrigerator, William Perry. But Super Bowl glory lasted only one season and patience ran out after a 5-11 campaign in 1992, the same year Ditka suffered a heart attack. The next season he was replaced by Dave Wannstedt, and the team went from mediocre to abysmal with occasional glimpses of inspired play.

The Bulls may reign supreme these days in Chi-town, but only until the emergence of a new plan to restore the roar.

—Andrea Kremer

Soldier Field

Built virtually on top of Lake Michigan and framed by Roman pillars, Soldier Field had a storied history long before the Bears arrived in 1971. It hosted the legendary Dempsey-Tunney fight in 1927, the first ski meet ever held in a stadium, and the era's all-time largest football crowd (123,000) for Chicago's high school Prep Bowl.

Scoreboards, announcers and music are, in keeping with the Bears' blue-collar tradition, simple and effective. First-timers will notice, before anything else, the rabid loyalty of the Bears season ticket holder. Fans arrive hours early, and not necessarily to tailgate. Some simply roam the area like hyenas on the hunt, twitching, hungry and uncertain what to do with themselves before the Bears move in for the kill. Games against longtime division rivals wring every last drop of flavor from the stadium. Those who show up in enemy colors play the fool at Soldier Field. Other fools include those in the high corner seats, who get slammed by the wind. The view of the lake and the Chicago skyline don't make up for it.

For 50 years until 1971, the Bears played their games in the friendly confines of Wrigley Field. There, Ditka, Butkus, Sayers and countless other legends punished opponents as the NFL learned to associate Chicago with pain. For the first years at Soldier Field, the team stunk but the punishing tradition remained; even after lopsided losses, the other side usually left Soldier Field limping, cursing and entirely black and blue.

The food inside the stadium is not worth the money or the heartburn, but any grilled meat produced for a tailgate party

> "The Bears have no chance of being the least bit respectable until the next century." — Jay Mariotti, columnist, Chicago Sun-Times (1997)

The "I Was There" Game

January 12, 1986: The Bears' 1986 victory against the New England Patriots in Super Bowl XX is the obvious choice, but Chicagoans relish the NFC Championship game from two weeks prior, when the Bears suffocated the Los Angeles Rams, 24-0, at home; after that, the Super Bowl was locked. The 1940 NFL Championship Game, in which the Bears beat the Redskins, 73-0, is also thought of fondly, if remembered by few.

The Paper Bag Game

January 3, 1987: Favored to win it all, the Bears spend their bye week before the NFL Playoff game with the Washington Redskins already counting the days until Super Sunday. The Redskins don't cooperate, and with an entire city dumbstruck, the disaster is complete: Redskins 27, Bears 13.

did you know?
The Bears were the first team (1940) to employ the T formation.

> "I wouldn't ever set out to hurt anybody deliberately unless it was, you know, important—like in a league game or something."
> — Dick Butkus

Our Top Story

"Brian Piccolo Dies"
June 16, 1970
Popular running back Brian Piccolo dies of cancer. A month earlier, while accepting the Player of the Year award at the Pro Football Writers of America banquet, Gale Sayers delivers one of the most famous Bear quotes: "I love Brian Piccolo, and I'd like all of you to love him. When you hit your knees to pray tonight, please ask God to love him, too."

"Ditka Dumped"
January 15, 1983
He casts a larger shadow today than in 1993, when president/CEO Mike McCaskey, generally disliked by Bears fans, committed Bears sacrilege by firing Iron Mike.

"Da Bears Win! Da Bears Win!"
January 21, 1986
After the team's victory in Super Bowl XX, the citizenry of an entire city relaxed, breathed deeply and believed it could finally die contented, having waited 25 years since Chicago's last major sports championship.

Great Names

Connie Mack Berry (DE, 1942-46)
Cap Boso (TE, 1987-91)
Charlie Brown (DB, 1966-67)
Dick Butkus (LB, 1965-73)
Beattie Feathers (RB, 1934-37)
Al Hoptowit (T, 1941-45)
Bronko Nagurski (RB, 1930-37; 43)

did you know?

Sid Luckman threw seven TD passes vs. the Giants at the Polo Grounds in 1943. RB Gale Sayers scored six touchdowns vs. the 49ers in 1965. As a QB, Bobby Douglass rushed for 968 yards in 1972. All three of these feats remain NFL records.

in the South and East Soldier Field parking lots is heavenly and intended by God for Sunday football. By all means, attempt to glom onto someone's cookout by offering a few bucks and your favorite Bears memory. (If you have no favorite Bears memory, invoke the 1965 game in which running back Gale Sayers scored six touchdowns in the slop against the Niners—that's always good for a burger and a beer. Do not mention that you are a vegetarian and by no means mention Doug Flutie.)

The Bottom Line on Soldier Field

Address: 1600 S. Waldron, Chicago, IL, 60605. (847) 295-6600.

Tickets: As for season tickets, the current list is 9,500 names long, and some years not a single person moves up in line. However, every spring, the Bears release a few thousand "Orange and Blue" ticket packages to the public. You get only five games in the cheap seats (all end zone), but it's a chance to attend 5 regular season games without having to cough up tribute money for those bogus pre-season "match-ups." Send a SASE—after June 1 only—to the Bears (1000 Football Dr., Lake Forest, Illinois 60045), and they'll mail you an application. Overall, tickets range from $33 to $52.

1998: $52/$45/$35/$33
1994: $40/$35/$28

> "Halas throws nickels around like manhole covers."
> —Mike Ditka

Best of the Bears

Best Team

1985 (18-1): This squad came closer than any team to matching the Dolphins' perfect season of 1972. Their fierce defense limited the opposition to just 198 points during the regular season. They blanked the Giants and Rams on their way to overwhelming the Patriots at the Superdome in Super Bowl XX.

Greatest Players by Position

Pos:	Player
QB:	Sid Luckman
RB:	Walter Payton
WR:	Dick Gordon
TE:	Mike Ditka
OL:	Jimbo Covert
DL:	Doug Atkins
LB:	Dick Butkus
DB:	Gary Fencik
P/K:	Kevin Butler
ST:	Gale Sayers

Swami Sez:

The Bears have the greatest running back lineage in football history: Walter Payton, Gale Sayers, Red Grange, and Bronko Nagurski. Too bad none of them is playing now.

And Don't Forget...

RB: Rick Casares. When you're a running back on a franchise that includes names like Payton, Sayers, and Grange, it's easy to get overlooked.
T/LB: George Connor. During his nine seasons with the Bears, he was a premier blocker and one of the league's best run-stoppers.
RB: Neal Anderson. He quietly replaced a legend in the Chicago backfield and proved to be a productive runner and pass-catcher.
DT: Dan Hampton. For a dozen seasons, he terrorized quarterbacks and ball carriers. "Danimal" was named to four Pro Bowls.
LB: Bill George. The Hall of Famer spent 14 of his 15 pro seasons in Chicago and was the league's first middle linebacker.

Best Argument

Linebacker: Dick Butkus or Mike Singletary? Was there ever a better defensive player than #51? The mere mention of his name symbolizes toughness, and he punished every offensive opponent who ever touched the football. But Singletary is a Hall of Famer as well, his consistent play leading to 10 Pro Bowl invitations. He also led one of the best defenses in league history, something Butkus only dreamed of. And who could forget that stare?

Best Coach

George Halas (1920-29, '33-42, '46-55, '58-67): The "Papa Bear" coached his beloved franchise for a total of 40 years and won two-thirds of his games. His aggressive physical teams mirrored his tough image. His love for the game he helped make a national obsession may never be matched.

"Just breaking in a helmet, coach." — DE Doug Atkins, in response to coach Halas's demand to know what he was doing sleeping against a tree during practice.

Pressbox

Who to Read...

The *Chicago Tribune* and *Chicago Sun-Times* devote mammoth, blanket coverage to the Bears, while substantial local papers such as the *Daily Southtown* and *Daily Herald* are well-written and occasionally scoop the big boys. *Sun-Times* columnist Jay Mariotti is mandatory Monday morning reading; he says the tough things fans don't necessarily want to hear. Hometown boy made good Rick Telander is also there. Bernie Lincicome at the *Tribune* is fun when the Bears lose. Dan Pierson, also at the *Tribune*, is the dean of Chicago football writers.

Who to Watch...

Dave Wannstedt is rumored to do a show, but the Mike Ditka show was the last coach's television program anyone in Chicago can remember watching. Many Bears players show up on late night postgame programs, but the only one anyone remembers watching is the 1994 "Bears Extra" show on WMAQ–NBC, when Steve McMichael

pulled a switchblade (in jest) on his cohost. Former Bear great Johnny Morris, once a mainstay on WBBM–CBS, has been relegated to occasional fill-in duty.

Who to Listen To...

A true Chicago treat. Every football Sunday, the city mutes the television sound and turns on WMAQ (670 AM) to hear announcers Wayne Larrivee, Hub Arkush and Tom Thayer pop the veins in their foreheads rooting for the orange and blue. Larrivee's booming crescendo trademarks his touchdown calls, while Arkush and Thayer possess rare insight into the game. Best of all, none is afraid to slam the Bears as the need arises. Midday hosts Dan Jiggets and Mike North highlight Chicago's all-sports radio station WSCR (1160 AM). Try the other stations on the AM dial, including ESPN Radio WMVP (1080 AM) seven nights a week, that devote time heavily to the Bears during the nighttime hours of the NFL season.

Public Transportation: The CTA (bus and subway) and Metra (commuter trains) run special shuttles to Soldier Field (#128, Soldier Field Express) on game days; call info line (312) 836-7000 anytime for schedules.

Parking: Soldier Field parking is limited to season ticket holders. If you must drive, park in the underground Grant Park or Monroe Street garages just north of the stadium; shuttle buses whisk parkers to the game for free.

Capacity: 66,944.

Restrooms: 36.

Where To Go . . . in Chicago

Best Bars

Best local color. Blue collar and full of Bears fans before every game. People actually say "Da Coach" and "Da Bears" in **Mother Hubbard's** without cracking a smile. Just around the corner from the city's shuttle bus to Soldier Field at Kinzie and

State, which departs approximately every 10 minutes. *5 W. Hubbard St. (312) 828-0007. Seven days, 11am-4am.*

Best comedy routine. The newspaperman's joint on which John Belushi based his "Cheezbooga, no fries, cheeps!" sketch. Still owned and run by the Greek immigrants made famous by late and legendary Chicago columnist Mike Royko, **The Billy Goat Tavern** is great, and football is the subject of every conversation. Opens at 11 a.m. on Sundays, and about a 10-minute cab ride to Soldier Field. *431 N. Michigan Ave. (underground) (312) 222-1525. M-F 7am-2am, Sa 10 am-3am, Su 11am-2am.*

Best really big glasses. Pay tribute to the man who was the heart and soul of Chicago sports. **Haray Caray's** is a first-rate bar with plenty of savvy football talk to go with some terrific bar eats. The fabulous baseball memorabilia that covers the walls makes those crisp November Sundays feel like it's 78 in the shade. The city's Soldier Field shuttle, which leaves every 10 minutes, is just out the door. *33 W. Kinzie St. (312) 828-0966. M-F 11:30-3pm, M-Th 5pm-10:30pm, F 5pm-11 pm, Sa 11:30-2pm, 5pm-11pm, Su 12-2pm, 4pm-10pm. Bar Only 11:30 am-2am most nights.*

Best Restaurants

Football fanatics only. Satellite dishes galore (the Saints game is always on), mountains of Bears memorabilia and the only place in the world you can see Mike Ditka's Rookie of the Year trophy is here at **Iron Mike's Grille.** Opens at 7 a.m. on

Ready For Primetime (Monday Night)

December 2, 1985: The Bears are abysmal on Monday nights. Even in 1985, the year they dominated the NFL, the menace of Monday night kept the team from a perfect season. Dan Marino and the Dolphins dissected the vaunted Bears defense for a shocking 38-24 victory at the Orange Bowl, pulling in a 29.6 rating and 46.0 television share for ABC, still a record for a Monday Night Football broadcast. Overall Monday Night: 16-28; 5-19 on the road. Overall Thursday Night: 2-1 Overall Sunday Night: 5-4

> **did you know?**
>
> Due to a heavy snowfall in Chicago in December 1932, the Bears vs. Portsmouth Spartans game was relocated indoors to Chicago Stadium. The field was shortened to 80 yards, and the Bears broke the game open when Bronko Nagurski took a fourth down handoff, then lobbed a pass to Red Grange, who was all alone in the end zone—except for the smell of elephant dung from the circus that had just left town. Final: Bears 9, Spartans 0.

Think About the Weather

December 31, 1988: The Bears defeated the Eagles, 20-12, to advance to the 1988 NFC Title game, but almost no one saw the game. An impenetrable fog descended on Soldier Field, making the field invisible to fans, a national TV audience and even to players downfield. Despite seeing only clouds of white, Chicago television viewers stayed glued to the broadcast and still remember the game as among the most exciting they've ever watched.

Worst Team

1975 (4-10): Jack Pardee's first season as Bears' head coach was certainly forgettable despite the presence of rookie RB Walter Payton. Mistake-prone Chicago (40 turnovers in 14 games) dropped 9 of its first 11 contests and averaged less than 10 points per outing.

> "That last guy hit me pretty good." — Bronko Nagurski, after rushing for a touchdown by flattening four tacklers and then knocking himself unconscious by running into a Wrigley Field brick wall head first.

Team Leaders

Rushing Yards
16,726   Walter Payton, 1975-87

Passing Yards
14,686   Sid Luckman, 1939-50

Passing Touchdowns
137   Sid Luckman, 1939-50

Receptions
492   Walter Payton, 1975-87

Interceptions
38   Gary Fencik, 1976-87

Touchdowns
125   Walter Payton, 1975-87

Points
1,116   Kevin Butler, 1985-95

did you know?

An NFL mark that will almost certainly never be broken is owned by the 1932 Bears, who played 14 games that season and lost just once, totaling seven wins and a record six ties.

Sundays; bartenders are specially trained to comfort many of those who still can't get over the fact that the coach was fired. *100 E. Chestnut St. (312) 587-8989. M-Th 6:30am-11pm and 12pm Fr and Sa, Su 7am-11pm. All major credit cards. $$*

Best chance of seeing Cindy Crawford. Miller's Pub has long been one of the top joints in which to see and be seen by Chicago celebrities. (Gibson's, near Rush Street, is another) Generous drinks, a killer chicken sandwich and only about a mile and a half to Soldier Field. *134 S. Wabash Ave. (312) 645-5377. Seven days 11am-1am. AE, DC, MC, V. $$*

Best family bet (If you're a large German family). Berghoff, a century-old Chicago institution and just a 10-minute cab ride to Soldier Field. Everything's hearty, from the Middle-European cuisine and homemade light and dark beers to the fresh-baked soft rye breads that barely manage to keep the bratwursts and knock-wursts on the plate. *17 W. Adams St. (312) 427-3170. M-Th 11am-9pm, 9:30 on Fr, Sa 11am-10pm, Closed Su. AE, MC, DC, V. $$*

Best Italian beef. The greatest example of this local delicacy can be found here at **Al's.** Order it "extra wet" (dunked in juice) and by all means, say yes to the fries, also among Chicago's best. Hot

While You Were Eating Turkey....

The Bears are merely average on Thanksgiving since 1920 (8-6 vs. Detroit, 0-2 vs. Dallas, 7-3-2 vs. the Chicago Cardinals, including back-to-back 0-0 ties in 1925 and 1926). Most fans still baste in the thrill of the Turkey Day game vs. the Lions in 1980, when RB David Williams returned the opening overtime kickoff 95 yards for a gut-busting 23-17 victory. Overall, 15-13-2.

Fans' notes

On Screen

"Super Bowl Shuffle" — Performed by the Bears on the way to their victory in Super Bowl XX. Rerun, look out! It's worth the price to see William "The Refrigerator" Perry dance. Great Bear moments on TV include George Wendt's unembarrassed Ditka-worship on "Saturday Night Live," any of Dick Butkus's many appearances in shows from "Magnum P.I." to "Murder, She Wrote," and a young Walter Payton showing off his moves on TV's "Soul Train." Moviewise, there's the heartbreaking and unbeatable **Brian's Song**. You won't be a girly-man if you cry over this classic Billy Dee Williams/James Caan story of the friendship between teammates Gale Sayers and the dying Brian Piccolo. **The Galloping Ghost,** a thirties serial, stars Red Grange himself, and while **Gus** boasts a fieldgoal-kicking mule in the title role, this Disney flick also features Dick Butkus as a jilted football-playing boyfriend. And of course Bears quarterback Jack Concannon makes his only appearance in an Altman film in **M*A*S*H**.

Fight Songs, etc.

"Bear Down, Chicago Bears," written by Al Hoffman, who also wrote "If I Knew You Were Coming I'd Have Baked a Cake."

Bookshelf

I Am Third. Gale Sayers (Viking 1970). Moving story of Sayers's friendship with Brian Piccolo; basis for *Brian's Song.*
Brian Piccolo: A Short Season. Jeannie Morris (Bonus 1995).
Ditka: An Autobiography. Mike Ditka and Don Pierson (Bonus 1987).
Butkus: Flesh and Blood. Dick Butkus and Pat Smith (Doubleday 1997).
Calling the Shots: Inside the Chicago Bears. Mike Singletary and Armen Keteyian (Contemporary 1986).
Halas: An Autobiography. George Halas with Gwen Morgan and Arthur Veysey (Bonus 1986). Papa Bear tells how it all began.
McMahon!: The Bare Truth About Chicago's Brashest Bear. Jim McMahon and Bob Verdi (Villard 1986).
The Bears: A 75-Year Celebration. Richard Whittingham (Taylor 1994). Both *Magic* and *Wait Till Next Year* (Bantam 1998) by former Chicagoan and screenwriter William Goldman have the same, terrific scene of Bronco Nagurski's comeback in the thirties.
The Red Grange Story. Red Grange as told to Ira Morton (Putnam 1953).

You Gotta See...

▸**Wrigley Field**, at the corner of Addison and Clark, is worth a trip. As well as the hallowed home of the Cubs, it was home to five decades of Bears highlights, from 1920 to 1970.
▸Though way off the beaten track, a century ago, **the corner of Racine and 63rd** was the site of Normal Park, which was where a bunch of neighborhood guys formed a pickup team that in a few years became the Racine Cardinals, later the Chicago Cardinals, the oldest team in the NFL.
▸And if you have kids with you, just go to the **Museum of Science and Industry**. Between the coal mine, the submarine and all the other stuff provided by the good people in corporate America, there's something to keep everybody busy for an afternoon.

Hall of Fame

George Halas	(Coach/Owner 1963)
Red Grange	(HB 1963)
Bronko Nagurski	(FB 1963)
Ed Healey	(T 1964)
Roy Lyman	(T 1964)
George Trafton	(C 1964)
Paddy Driscoll	(HB 1965)
Danny Fortmann	(G 1965)
Sid Luckman	(QB 1965)
Walt Kiesling	(G/Coach 1966)
Bill McAfee	(HB 1966)
Clyde Turner	(C 1966)
Bobby Layne	(QB 1967)
Joe Stydahar	(T 1967)
Bill Hewitt	(E 1971)
Bill George	(LB 1974)
George Connor	(LB/T 1975)
Gale Sayers	(HB 1977)
Dick Butkus	(LB 1979)
George Blanda	(QB/PK 1981)
Doug Atkins	(DE 1982)
George Musso	(T 1982)
Mike Ditka	(TE 1988)
Alan Page	(DT 1988)
Stan Jones	(G 1991)
Walter Payton	(HB 1993)
Mike Singletary	(LB 1998)

Against the Odds

On a franchise with such good stories as Brian Piccolo and Gale Sayers, **Chris Zorich** (1991-1997) stands out from the crowd. It's much easier to measure this one-time Bear by the size of his body (6-1, 282) than the size of his heart. Zorich may be known as much for his passionate work off the field as on. He has dedicated his life to helping others and honoring the most important person in his life, his mother Zora, whom he found dead upon returning home from the 1991 Orange Bowl.

dogs in this town are special — fresh veggies, poppy seed roll. Al's got them, too. *169 W. Ontario St. (312) 943-3222. M-Th 10:30am-12 am, Fr and Sa until 2am, Sun until 10pm. Cash Only. $*

Best Accommodations

Chicago Hilton and Towers. A clear view of Soldier Field and a Sunday Bears Brunch ($37.95 adults; $17.50 kids) make the Chicago Hilton and Towers the prime lodging spot for any visiting football fan. Plus, the kids will love running into the Bears, who stay here before home games and are known to roam the lobbies while contemplating the game plan. Package rates are available. *720 S. Michigan Ave. (312) 922-4400. $$$*

Days Inn Lakeshore. Terrific lakefront location and about a 30-minute walk to Soldier Field. Clean and solid, and perfect for shoppers who want to graze along the shopping Mecca that is the "Magnificent Mile" on Michigan Avenue. *644 N. Lake Shore Dr. (312) 943-9200. $$-$$$*

> **"Yeah. It would have made it 73-6."**
> **—Redskins QB Sammy Baugh,** in response to a reporter's question as to whether an early dropped TD pass would have affected the outcome of the NFL championship game won by the Bears, 73-0.

Motel 6. The basics, but a whopper of a location just off the Magnificent Mile and the best rates anywhere downtown ($85 single; $91 double). Best feature: doesn't look like a Motel 6. *162 E. Ontario. (312) 787-3580. $$*

Cincinnati
Bengals

Pro football in Cincinnati does not have a long history, but few people know that the Bengals had a previous incarnation in the 1930s and early 1940s in an old American Football League which folded just before the Japanese attacked Pearl Harbor. With men going off to war, it was tough to field one pro football league, let alone two.

It would be a good twenty five years before pro football would return to Cincinnati, but it was brought by one of the greatest names in the game—Paul Brown. The disciplined approach Brown took to football created a team very much like the city in which they play; hard-working, conservative and anything but flashy or emotional. Namath or Stabler wouldn't have cut it in Cincinnati; instead think of Bengal hero Ken Anderson, who led the club to the Super Bowl with a quiet, nine-to-five intensity, or Boomer Esiason, who with Ickey Woods in the late eighties provided as much color as Cincinnati could handle.

Franchise History

Cincinnati Bengals (AFL)
(1968–69)
Cincinnati Bengals (NFL)
(1970–Present)

By the Numbers

(Since 1970)

Regular Season: 200-224-0
Postseason: 5-7
Division Titles: 5
Vs. Division: 82-90 (Playoffs: 1-0)
Playoff Appearances: 7
Home: 125-87
Away: 75-137

(Overall)

Regular Season: 207-244-1
Postseason: 5-7
Playoff Appearances: 7
Home: 131-95
Away: 76-149-1

The Bengals were born when Paul Brown finally convinced Ohio Gov. James Rhodes that the state could support a second pro football team along with Cleveland. The new AFL awarded Brown a franchise and the team played its first season in 1968. This Bengals team would have far more success far more quickly than the Browns did. After just three seasons, Cincinnati won the new AFC Central Division in 1970, the year of the NFL-AFL merger. They lost their first playoff game, but Brown's eye for talent and creative tactics allowed the Bengals to quickly shed the tag "expansion team." Still, after two more playoff losses

Most Revered Football Figures

Paul Brown. It only seems as if "PB" invented football. In truth, he only invented certain aspects of it, including the Bengals.

Anthony Munoz. The only Hall of Fame player inducted as a Bengal, the big offensive tackle was named to the NFL's 75th Anniversary All-Time Team.

Cris Collinsworth. The team's all-time leading receiver, the self-deprecating Collinsworth was a steady source of humor and locker-room commentary.

Boomer Esiason. In a buttoned-down town, this swashbuckling quarterback was much loved for his competitiveness, candor, and decency.

Rivalries

When Art Modell fired Paul Brown as coach of the Cleveland Browns, the team Brown had built, it set the stage for the most personal rivalry in pro football, Bengals vs. **Browns** (24-27). The Browns have gotten the better of it, although they have never won a title of any kind since the unceremonious departure of the man for whom the franchise was named. The rivalry is on hold while Cleveland waits for a team. Other rivals include the Pittsburgh **Steelers** (23-32), highlighted by the fact that former coaches Chuck Noll and Sam Wyche wouldn't shake hands. Wyche also had a hand in the nastiness between the Bengals and the Houston **Oilers** (29-29-1), calling former coach Jerry Glanville "the biggest phony in pro football" and whipping him once to the tune of 61-7.

— in 1973 and 1975 — Brown decided it was time to get off the sidelines. He remained as the team's general manager.

In 1981, the Bengals returned to the playoffs under head coach Forrest Gregg and landed in Super Bowl XVI against the San Francisco 49ers. Brown's protege, quarterback Ken Anderson, was outplayed by Joe Montana and his mentor, head coach Bill Walsh. The 49ers won, 26-21. In the strike-shortened year of 1982, the Bengals returned to the playoffs but were bounced out in the first round by the New York Jets, and Gregg was gone by the following year.

Enter Sam Wyche, who worked under Walsh in San Francisco. The Bengals went back to the playoffs in 1988. Facing San Francisco again in Super Bowl XXIII, Cincinnati's southpaw quarterback, Boomer Esiason, employed virtually a carbon copy of the 49ers offense to give the Bengals a late lead. But Montana engineered a flawless fourth-quarter drive, and Cincinnati again went home empty-handed, 20-16.

From there, it's been a long struggle. Wyche brought them back to the playoffs in 1990, but they have been shut out of the postseason ever since Paul Brown died at age 82 in 1991. After a brief comeback attempt, Esiason retired following the 1997 season. Under new head coach Bruce Coslet, the Bengals look like they're turning the corner toward playoff contention. The new facility will be ready for the year 2000. It will be named, as it should be, Paul Brown Stadium.

—Sal Paolantonio

Cinergy Field

The best thing about Cinergy Field is that in 2000 the Bengals won't be playing there, having moved five blocks down the river to the new Paul Brown Stadium. Actually, there isn't anything that wrong with Cinergy Field (known for most of its three-decade existence as Riverfront Stadium). It's just that there isn't much right, either. It's a colorless, concrete saucer that had the misfortune of being built when drab conformity was the rule.

Pre-game tailgating is fine, just don't open your beer. Cincinnati doesn't allow open containers of beer or liquor in public places. However, food and beer are sold at The Jungle Zone, a corporate-sponsored pre-game party on the stadium plaza. Cincinnati is a dog-and-beer town. The hotdogs go from the plain old frankfurter to the quarter-pound super-dog, mettwursts, bratwursts, and Gold Star cheese coneys (hotdogs, chili, and shredded cheese, Cincinnati style). There are several microbrews available to wash down the wieners.

> "You don't live in Cleveland! You live in Cincinnati!" —Wyche at a 1989 Seahawks-Bengals game, admonishing an unruly crowd through the field microphone after fans had thrown snowballs at the visiting Seahawks.

Despite the stale environs, Riverfront once had a atmosphere to it. In the 1980s, when the Bengals went to a couple of Super Bowls and had stars like Boomer Esiason and Ickey Woods, the Bengals actually had a little home field advantage. They called the stadium "The Jungle," and

did you know?

The Bengals rarely get off to a quick start, one reason why they haven't had a winning campaign since 1990. From 1991 through 1997, they were just 9-47 over the first half of the season.

The "I Was There" Game

December 20, 1970: Forget the result (Bengals 45, Patriots 7); this blowout of Boston in the season finale was only half the story. Paul Brown's team endured a six-game losing streak during the season and were 1-6 at the halfway point. But the club went on an incredible seven-game run and would not lose again, outscoring the opposition a combined 209-78 and capturing the newly-formed AFC Central title.

The Paper Bag Game

January 9, 1983: Coming off a Super Bowl season in 1981, the Bengals had a strong chance to win another AFC championship in 1982. They finished the strike-shortened regular season at 7-2. But while hosting a first round playoff game against a Jets team that frightened no one, they were routed, 44-17.

Great Names

Coy Bacon (DE 1976-77)
Tommy Casanova (KR 1972-77)
Boobie Clark (RB 1973-78)
Elvis Peacock (RB 1981)
Elbert "Ickey" Woods (RB 1988-91)

Hall of Fame

Paul Brown	(Coach 1967)
Forrest Gregg	(Coach 1977)
Bill Walsh	(Coach 1993)
Charlie Joiner	(WR 1996)
Anthony Munoz	(T 1998)

Our Top Story

"Brown Steps Down"
January 1, 1976
After 41 years as a head coach—eight with the Bengals—Paul Brown turned the team over to assistant Bill "Tiger" Johnson in 1976.

"Drug Suspensions"
1983
In the league's largest effort to date at handing out drug-related suspensions, defensive end Ross Browner and running back Pete Johnson were suspended for the first four games of the season.

"Super Bowl Slips Away"
January 22, 1989
The Bengals led the San Francisco 49ers, 16-13, with less than a minute to play in Super Bowl XXIII in Miami, but Joe Montana won the game by hitting John Taylor from 10 yards out with 34 seconds on the clock.

"The Stadium Tax"
March 19, 1996
Fearing that team president Mike Brown would move the Bengals to Cleveland, Hamilton County voters approved a half-cent sales tax increase to fund new stadiums for the Bengals and Cincinnati Reds.

Worst Team

1991 (3-13): After winning the AFC Central Division in 1990, Sam Wyche's club lost its first two games by a combined 75-21, and the losing streak would reach eight games before they beat the Browns in November.

the fans wore gorilla masks and shouted things like "Who Dey! Who Dey! Who dey think gonna beat dem Bengals?!" The inimitable "Ickey Shuffle" was the league's best-known end-zone celebration, and it spawned numerous inferior dance steps.

But the moment passed, and Riverfront/Cinergy is once again a 36-acre parking garage with AstroTurf and 60,000 seats. Now, the deepest tradition among Bengal fans is leaving early.

did you know?

Those tiger stripes on the side of the Bengals' helmet were Paul Brown's idea, and after he painted them on in 1981, the team immediately made it to the Super Bowl. Grr.

The Bottom Line on Cinergy Field

Address: 200 Cinergy Field, Cincinnati, OH 45202. (513) 621-3550

Tickets: The most expensive tickets ($46) are in the enclosed, club-level area, which is the closest thing Cinergy has to skyboxes. Because of the field angle, the corner seats in the green section are considered among the best in the stadium. Season and single-game tickets are available through the Bengals' ticket office or through TicketMaster (513) 749-4949 in Cincinnati, (800) 529-5353 outside Cincinnati.

1998: $46/$38/$34
1994: $43/$39/$35/$31

Public Transportation: Cincinnati's Metro bus service (513/621-4456) operates a Bengals Express shuttle from a dozen suburban locations for $5.00 (round-trip). The Transit Authority of Northern Kentucky (606/331-8265) offers a Bengal bus originating at Florence Mall and picking up at six stops along I-75.

Best of the Bengals

Best Team

1981 (14-5): After winning just 14 games the previous three seasons, little was expected from the '81 Bengals. But Forrest Gregg's team was 5-3 by mid-season and flexed its muscles during a perfect November (5-0), establishing itself as the AFC's team to beat. After upending the Bills and Chargers in the playoffs, a poor first half vs. the 49ers cost them Super Bowl XVI.

Greatest Players by Position

Pos:	Player
QB:	Ken Anderson
RB:	James Brooks
WR:	Isaac Curtis
TE:	Rodney Holman
OL:	Anthony Munoz
DL:	Tim Krumrie
LB:	Reggie Williams
DB:	Ken Riley
P/K:	Jim Breech
ST:	Lemar Parrish

And Don't Forget...

TE: Bob Trumpy. The Bengals' first tight end, Trumpy provided the team with sure hands and solid blocking for 10 seasons.

DB: David Fulcher. A hard-hitting, big-play safety, Fulcher had the size of a linebacker and the quickness to cover plenty of ground.

DT: Mike Reid. One of the Bengals' early stars on the defensive line, Reid played just five seasons before pursuing a successful musical career.

WR: Carl Pickens. One of the premier receivers of the 1990s, the former Volunteer should hold all of the Bengals' receiving records one day.

FB: Pete Johnson. A really BIG back who rolled over opposing defenses, Johnson was nearly unstoppable near the goal line.

Best Argument

Quarterback: Ken Anderson or Boomer Esiason? One of the masters of the short passing game, Anderson could pick apart the best of defenses and also had the arm to burn opponents deep. Young quarterbacks looking to perfect their ability to play-action pass need only to look at Esiason, who consistently kept defenses guessing and made the tight end a major weapon.

Swami Sez:

A great defensive draft should help this unit finally register more hits than the Bangles.

Best Coach

Paul Brown (1968-75): After making his name by building the Browns into a football powerhouse, Brown was the force who brought the Bengals into the NFL. In just their third season (1970), he led them to a division title. Brown's clubs also made two other post-season appearances in his eight seasons as head coach. The franchise has made just four trips to the playoffs in the 23 years since Brown retired.

"The game isn't worth it. There's golf to be played and tennis to be served up and other things to be done out there other than worrying about a football game." — Wyche, concerning the criticism he and his players were receiving as they struggled to a 3-13 record in 1991.

Pressbox

Who to Read...

The *Cincinnati Enquirer* is the big paper in town. Columnist Tim Sullivan has been covering the Bengals since 1977, before they had stripes, and Paul Daugherty has been around since 1988. Chris Haft and Geoff Hobson offer blanket coverage on the team beat.

Who to Watch...

In recent years, a good number of Bengals home games have been blacked out, and TV coverage of the team has lagged correspondingly. On Sunday nights, after the local news during the season, "Bengals Extra" on WLWT–NBC, hosted by George Vogel, is the show Bengals fans watch. Former Bengal Solomon Wilcots presented a popular "breakdown" segment before moving on to ESPN. Another former Bengal, perhaps Eric Thomas, will replace him. Also on WCTO is Sunday night's "Sports of All Sorts," which has a good Bengals wrap-up.

Who to Listen To...

Bengal broadcasts are now heard on WUBE (105.1 FM) and the city's new sports station, WBOB (1160 AM), which was not named for its star host, former Bengal tight end and NBC commentator Bob Trumpy. As a media guy, Trumpy made his name at WLW-AM (700), where he hosted a popular and controversial sports-talk show. Following him at WLW was Collinsworth, whose folksy opinions went over well in Cincinnati. The most trusted color man in town is former Bengal lineman Dave Lapham, who complements play-by-play radio announcer Peter Arbogast with an unpretentious expertise that the locals find charming. Lapham's voice is amplified by the fact that many Cincinnati home games are blacked out.

Parking: The garage at the stadium holds 4,500 cars, but you probably won't get in without a pre-paid pass. Not to worry. There are more than 15,000 additional parking spaces within twelve blocks. Or you can park on the other side of the river in Covington, KY, and walk across the Suspension Bridge.

Capacity: 60,000

Restrooms: 26 men's, 26 women's.

Where to Go . . . in Cincinnati

Best Bars

Best historic atmosphere. The city's oldest and all-around best tavern is **Arnold's**, and it is not to be confused with a mere sports bar. *210 E. Eighth St. (513) 421-6234. M-Sa 11am-1am, Su closed.*

Best cerveza. The **Rock Bottom Brewery and Restaurant** is a brewpub with Southwestern decor, brown ale chicken, and weekend blues. *10 Fountain Sq., (513) 621-1588. Su-Th 11am-12pm, F-Sa 11am-2am.*

Best neighborhood sports bar. Downstairs, below a Skyline Chili in St. Bernard, is **Crosley's**, a homey sports bar long on baseball but conversant in all sports. *4901*

Vine St., St. Bernard, (513) 242-3311. M-F 11am-2:30am, Sa 8am-2:30am, Su 8am-8pm.

Best Restaurants

Best chili spaghetti. The best example of Cincinnati's signature meal can be had at any of the numerous **Skyline Chili** parlors, including this one at Seventh and Vine downtown. *643 Vine St., (513) 241-2020. M-F 10:30am-7pm, Sa 11am-3pm, Su closed. Cash only. $.*

Best restaurant to actually see a Bengal. The Precinct is not cheap, but that's because it has the best steaks in town. *311 Delta Avenue, Columbia Pkwy. (U.S. 50, east out of downtown), (513) 321-5454. Su-Th 5 pm-9:30pm, F-Sa 5pm-10:30pm AE, DC, MC, V. Reservations recommended. $$$*

> "What should I say now, Paul?" — Sam Wyche, in the press conference announcing his installation as head coach, in response to a question about whether he would be a puppet for Paul Brown.

Best late-night pig-out: Beef and pork barbecue in great supply. **Louis'** is open till 2 a.m. on weekends, so you have no excuse to miss it. *131 E. 3rd St., Newport, Ky., (606) 581-3003. M-W10am-12am, Th 10am-1am, F-Sa 10am-2am. Cash only. $*

Best Accommodations

The Regal Cincinnati Hotel. The Regal is connected to the skywalk leading to major downtown shopping corridors, plus it's only seven blocks from the stadium. *150 West Fifth St., (513) 352-2100. $$$*

The Cincinnatian. Cincinnati's only four-star hotel features full concierge service and all the amenities you deserve. *601 Vine St., (513) 381-3000. $$$-$$$$*

Embassy Suites at RiverCenter The best

Ready For Primetime (Monday Night)

November 17, 1975: This key clash against the Bills turned into a duel between the arm of Bengals' QB Ken Anderson, who threw for 447 yards and a pair of touchdowns, and the legs of Bills' RB O.J. Simpson, who ran through the Bengals' defense for 197 yards and two scores on just 17 carries. (Bengals 33, Bills 24).

Overall Monday Night: 7-16
Overall Thursday Night: 3-1
Overall Sunday Night: 2-5

Think About the Weather

January 10, 1982: There's cold and there's ridiculously cold. And then there's the weather on the day the Bengals played their first-ever AFC Championship Game. One week after winning at Miami, the Chargers not only had to battle the Bengals but a temperature of minus-9 degrees and a wind-chill factor of minus-59. Bengals won, 27-7.

Team Leaders

Rushing Yards
6,447   James Brooks, 1984-91
Passing Yards
32,838   Ken Anderson, 1971-86
Passing Touchdowns
197   Ken Anderson, 1971-86
Receptions
417   Cris Collinsworth, 1981-88
Interceptions
65   Ken Riley, 1969-83
Touchdowns
70   Pete Johnson, 1977-83
Points
1,151   Jim Breech, 1980-92

Fans' notes

On Screen

Bengals alumni don't head for the silver screen; they head for the booth. Bob Trumpy, Cris Collinsworth, Sam Wyche, and Boomer Esiason are all graduates of Cincinnati.

Fight Songs, etc.

During his playing career, defensive tackle Mike Reid earned Rookie of the Year and Pro Bowl honors. Even after he retired in 1976, the accolades continued to pour in — a pair of 1985 best-songwriter Grammy awards for country hits "Stranger in My House" and "Lost in the '50s Tonight." Showing a softer side than he did on the defensive line, Reid has written hit songs for Tanya Tucker, Bonnie Raitt, the Judds and other country stars, and even released a pair of solo albums, "Turning for Home" and "Twilight Town."

Bookshelf

PB: The Paul Brown Story. Paul Brown and Jack Clary (NAL 1979)
Trump! Bob Trumpy (Donning Co. 1979).

Super Stripes: PB and the Super Bowl Bengals. Ritter Collett (Landfall Press 1981).
The Cincinnati Bengals and the Magic of Paul Brown. Dick Forbes (Prentice Hall 1973).

You Gotta See...

▶Sports bars are all over the place, but none can match **Sorrento's**. Willie DeLuca, the owner, knows the games backwards and forwards, and can also balance bar stools on his nose. Really. Pete Rose drank there.
▶The Bengals played their first few seasons at **Nippert Stadium**, on the campus of the University of Cincinnati.
▶Like it or not, football fans, Cincinnati is first and foremost a baseball town (the first all-professional team was the Reds), so if you swing that way, there's **a replica of old Crosley Field** in Blue Ash, completed in 1987, an actual field they play on in a suburb of Cincinnati.

rooms offer views of the stadium shimmering in the reflected night light of the river. Since it's the closest hotel to Cinergy Field, many of your fellow guests during a game weekend will be season ticket holders. *10 E. RiverCenter Blvd., Covington, KY., (606) 261-8400. $$$*

Against the Odds

Even though **Elbert "Ickey" Woods**' (1988-1991) career lasted just 37 games, he made his presence felt. The charismatic Woods rushed for a team-high 1,066 yards as a rookie in 1988, and created a new end zone dance sensation, "The Ickey Shuffle." His play helped the Bengals pull off one of the most impressive turnarounds in history — from 4-11 in 1987 to 12-4 and an AFC championship in 1988. After missing most of '89 with a serious knee injury, Woods returned to the club in 1990 and averaged 4.2 yards per carry, even though the league restricted his dancing to the sidelines.

Cleveland
Browns

"We're the Ben Hogans, the Joe Louises, the New York Yankees of our game, and that's the way we aim to keep it." — Paul Brown

For a couple of months in early 1996, the guts of the Cleveland Browns franchise lay packed away in cardboard boxes at the Pro Football Hall of Fame in Canton, Ohio. Records, coaching films, personnel files and championship banners had all been stored under lock and key per order of NFL Commissioner Paul Tagliabue himself. One of the greatest franchises in football history was put into mothballs.

The city of Cleveland is one of the four present at the NFL's creation that still has a team (even if they're not playing in 1998). In the formative years of the NFL they were known variously as the Tigers, Indians and Bulldogs. In 1945, Cleveland won the NFL Championship as the Rams, defeating Washington, 15-14. It was their last game in Cleveland, for in an irony that even Art Modell could appreciate, owner Dan Reeves moved the team to Los Angeles 27 days after the title victory.

The departure of the Rams NFL franchise created the opportunity for the founding of the soon-to-be-beloved Browns in Cleveland. It was the first year of the fledgling All-America Football Conference, and Cleveland embraced coach Paul Brown's team. The Browns were the only AAFC team to make a profit in 1946, drawing nearly 400,000 fans to Municipal Stadium for seven home games. Led by quarterback Otto Graham and fullback Marion Motley, the Browns won all four AAFC championships and compiled a regular-season record of 47-4-3.

In December, 1949, the NFL accepted Cleveland, Baltimore and San Francisco into the league. The question of just how well the Browns could compete in the

Franchise History

Cleveland Browns (AAFC)
(1946–49)
Cleveland Browns (NFL)
(1950–95)
Cleveland Browns Trust
(1996–present)

By the Numbers

(Since 1970)
Regular Season: 194-195-3
Postseason: 4-10
Division Titles: 6
Vs. Division: 78-78 (Playoffs: 0-2)
Playoff Appearances: 10
Home: 109-84-2
Away: 85-111-1

(Overall)
Regular Season: 374-266-10
Postseason: 11-19
Playoff Appearances: 23
Home: 202-117-5
Away: 172-149-5

Most Revered Football Figures

Paul Brown. The team's first and most successful coach and namesake. In 17 seasons Brown won four AAFC championships, three NFL championships and 11 division titles.

Jim Brown. Arguably the greatest running back of all time. He captured eight rushing titles in nine seasons, and his Browns won three division titles and one league championship (1964).

Otto Graham. The Browns first and best quarterback, and the greatest winner in pro football history. He led the Browns to 10 division titles and seven league championships (AAFC and NFL) in 10 seasons.

Rivalries

Pittsburgh and Cleveland — two blue-collar cities, two nose-to-the-grindstone football teams. It wasn't much of a contest on the field the first 20 years — the Browns won 31 of the first 40 games. But since 1970, when both teams moved to the AFC Central, the **Steelers** have narrowed the gap to 52-41, Browns, with the Steelers winning the only postseason game, in January 1995, 29-9. The fact that the Browns lost three AFC titles (in 1986, '87, and '89) to the **Broncos** (5-16) has made Denver highly unpopular. Cleveland's rivalry with the Cincinnati **Bengals** (27-24) is more naturally hate-filled. Both teams descended from Paul Brown. In the early days of the rivalry, Brown would not even shake hands with Blanton Collier, his successor in Cleveland.

NFL was a matter of strenuous debate. Their NFL debut provided a clue. Cleveland crushed the defending champion Philadelphia Eagles and went on to win the NFL title game, 30-28, over Los Angeles, the former Cleveland Rams. Powered by maybe the greatest running back ever, Jim Brown, the Browns reached the

did you know?

In 1959, Jim Brown was offered a contract to play baseball for the Cleveland Indians. He didn't accept it, but it's believed the offer helped him score a better football contract.

NFL Championship game in seven of their first eight seasons, winning three. Cleveland won its final league title in 1964, then moved to the American Football Conference in the 1970 merger. Thanks to Denver's John Elway, the Browns never reached the Super Bowl — three times in four seasons, the Broncos beat the Browns in the AFC Championship game, once in a memorable overtime. By the early '90s, the Browns were a vital aspect of life in Cleveland and to Clevelanders everywhere. The nationwide interest in the Browns was even responsible in part for the spread of satellite television game packages.

Browns owner Art Modell, seeking a better financial deal, pulled out of Cleveland, prompting the jilted city to file a lawsuit on behalf of the loyal fans. The team formerly known as the Browns, was to play the 1996 season as the "Baltimore Ravens".

In the end, Cleveland settled the lawsuit in exchange for some $11 million. More important than the settlement figure, however, the city retained the rights to the team

> "God, it's cold."
> —Banner hung out by a Browns fan at Cleveland Stadium during the January playoff game against the Raiders. (1981)

name and colors. As part of the agreement, the NFL also promised Cleveland a new team in time for the 1999 season.

Today you can find the Browns' glorious past — unshackled and uncrated, at last — and their future, too, at the team's facility in Berea, home of the Cleveland Browns Trust. It's virtually all that's left until 1999, when the Browns can begin to reclaim their very proud heritage and rebuild their team.

—*Greg Garber*

Cleveland Browns Stadium

On May 15, 1997, the city of Cleveland broke ground for the Browns' new stadium on the site of old Municipal Stadium, which had already had its appointment with the wrecking ball. The new facility is being financed with grants and loans from the city, state, county, Regional Transit Authority, Cleveland Tomorrow and the NFL — and nothing from Art Modell's pocket.

The new, concrete-and-glass stadium, designed by HOK Architects, will try to live up to the standards set by Jacobs Field, the picturesque home of the Indians. The Browns' stadium will be twelve stories tall at its highest point, with a main concourse that looks out over Lake Erie. Other planned features include a 11,950-square-foot museum and store and a restaurant with views of the playing field, museums, Lake Erie and the city skyline. Eleven elevators will make the facility accessible to the physically challenged,

did you know?
The Browns are the only team to make the playoffs twice with a non-winning record— going to the '82 Playoffs with a 4-5 mark and winning the AFC Central in '85 with an 8-8 record.

The "I Was There" Game
December 27, 1964: After a scoreless first half, Browns QB Frank Ryan hooks up with WR Gary Collins for three touchdowns and Jim Brown rushes for 114 yards to nail the NFL championship over Baltimore. Browns 27, Colts 0.

Swami Sez:
We welcome you back with open arms.

The Paper Bag Game
January 4, 1981: Cleveland's "Kardiac Kids" were trailing the Oakland Raiders 14-12 in the waning moments of this AFC Divisional Playoff. Coach Sam Rutigliano disdains a short field goal attempt on the frozen tundra of Cleveland Stadium. Instead he calls for "Red Right 88," a pass play. Quarterback Brian Sipe throws into double coverage in the end zone. Oakland's Mike Davis intercepts. The Browns watch the rest of the playoffs on TV.

Great Names
Jubilee Dunbar (WR, 1974)
Henry Ford (HB/DB, 1955)
Bob Gain (DE/DT/DG/T, 1952-64)
Chip Glass (TE, 1969-73)
Fair Hooker (WR, 1969-74)
Weldon Humble (G/LB, 1947-50)
Special Delivery Jones (HB/DB, 1946-49)
Ed Nutting (T, 1961)
Dick Shiner (QB, 1967)
Mac Speedie (E/DE, 1946-52)

Our Top Story

"Go Browns!"
September 6, 1946

The Browns debuted before a crowd of 60,135 at Cleveland Municipal Stadium, pummeling the Miami Seahawks 44-0. Paul Brown's team went on to a 12-2 record and the first of their four AAFC championships.

"Browns Pick Brown"
November 27, 1956

Looking for a quarterback in the 1957 draft, the Browns watched the Steelers choose QB Len Dawson with the third overall pick. Cleveland regrouped and used the number-four pick to select Syracuse running back Jim Brown.

"Browns fire Brown"
January, 1963

Less than two years after buying the team, Arthur B. Modell fired head coach Paul Brown. Hoping to minimize publicity, Modell chose to drop his bombshell during a newspaper strike. Inevitably, though, the move made headlines, rocking the city of Cleveland.

"Ernie Davis"
August 18, 1962

Diagnosed with leukemia and never to play pro ball, first round draft pick Ernie Davis was introduced and ran across the field under a spotlight. It was his only appearance in a Browns uniform. He died the next year.

and assisted listening devices will be available for the hearing impaired.

The new stadium will have sixteen concessions on the main concourse, eight on the upper concourse, three in the Dawg Pound area and more elaborate options on the club level. The exact nature of food at the new stadium remains to be seen, of course, but at old Municipal Stadium, the hit was not a main dish but a condiment — Cleveland's famous brown "Stadium Mustard."

Three tiers of seats, one more than Municipal had, will accommodate 72,000 fans in self-rising armchair seats. There will be 113 suites and two club lounges, but down in the end zones, the old Dawg Pound will be preserved. You might be tempted to bring a leash and scooper if you sit in the Pound. There you'll find barking fans wearing dog masks and carrying bones. They come well-armed with a supply of dog biscuits to throw at opposing players who dare to cross the

> "Jeez, they had a lot of guns."
> — Eagles coach Greasy Neale, after the Browns made their NFL debut by beating his defending NFL champion squad 35-10 in Philadelphia. (1950)

Browns' goal line. And when Mother Nature scores a ducat, the arsenal includes snowballs. When football returns to Cleveland after a three-year absence, the fans' exuberance will undoubtedly be clear.

The Bottom Line on Cleveland Browns Stadium

Tickets: The Cleveland Browns Trust should be contacted for all information concerning Permanent Seat Licenses (PSLs), which are required to purchase season tickets for the new Browns. The

Best of the Browns

Best Team

1950 (12-2): Right from the start, the Browns meant business. In their first year in the NFL after four years in the less-than-imposing AAFC, they opened the season against the two-time champion Philadelphia Eagles and promptly embarrassed the Birds, 35-10. By season's end, they would silence all doubters, and a week after narrowly besting the Giants in the playoffs, would edge the Rams for the league title.

Greatest Players by Position

Pos:	Player
QB:	Otto Graham
RB:	Jim Brown
WR:	Paul Warfield
TE:	Ozzie Newsome
OL:	Frank Gatski
DL:	Jerry Sherk
LB:	Clay Matthews
DB:	Thom Darden
P/K:	Lou Groza
ST:	Eric Metcalf

And Don't Forget...

FB: Marion Motley. One of the first big backs, he did most of his damage as part of the Browns AAFC title teams.
QB: Bernie Kosar. He rarely looked pretty while throwing and never got the Browns to a Super Bowl, but he was a winner from day one.
WR: Gary Collins. Sure-handed and with a nose for the end zone, 70 of Collins' 331 career receptions went for touchdowns.
CB: Hanford Dixon. Teamed with opportunistic Frank Minnifield, they made up one of the premier cornerback tandems of the '80s.

RB: Leroy Kelly. Second place on any team's all-time rushing list is quite an accomplishment, especially when first place is occupied by Jim Brown.

Best Argument

Wide Receiver: Paul Warfield or Dante Lavelli? One of the most graceful athletes to ever don a football uniform, Warfield spent the beginning and the end of his Hall of Fame career with the Browns and made the big plays. "Gluefingers" Lavelli was a member of the franchise during its AAFC days, and if you combine those numbers with his NFL statistics, he stacks up against the game's best.

> "We all wish Mother Teresa owned the Browns. It would be an easier sell." — Cuyahoga County Commissioner Timothy Hagan, before the 1995 vote on a sin tax extension, which could have been used for renovating the city's facilities to Art Modell's specifications.

Best Coach

Paul Brown (AAFC; 1946-49, NFL; 1950-62): In essence, he was the Browns. More importantly, the league is forever indebted to Brown for his many contributions to pro football, ranging from full-time coaching staffs to grading game films. As for his impact on the field, his club won four titles in the AAFC, then appeared in six straight NFL title games from 1950-55, winning three championships.

Pressbox

Who to Read...

While local media have been cooling their heels during the Browns' three-year hiatus from the field, sportscasters and reporters have spent their time speculating and prognosticating about the expansion Browns. For fans who want to be in the know, the person to read is the *Cleveland Plain Dealer* NFL beat reporter and columnist Tony Grossi. His "Ravens Droppings" section about the Modell organization has a tendency to remind Browns fans that they'll probably be better off when the new team arrives. Longtime Browns reporter Hal Lebovitz is also on top of things. His column can be read in *The Lake County Herald* and *The Lorain Journal*. Terry Pluto at the *Akron Beacon Journal* is another stop for serious fans.

Who to Watch...

The Browns Trust is keeping the spirit alive with TV and radio broadcasts during the football season such as "Countdown to '99." The TV show airs Sunday at 11:30am on WOIO. It's hosted by Ronnie Duncan and former Browns receiver Reggie Rucker. All of the Cleveland television stations do a solid job covering the Browns. WKYC–NBC Sports Director Jim Donovan also did occasional play-by-play for the network. WUAB–UPN Sports Director Jeff Phelps has been an "Ohio Sportscaster of the Year" and offers entertaining and in-depth perspective on the Browns. John Telich keeps tabs on the Browns for WJW–FOX. WEWS–ABC offers "Your Browns Now," hosted by Matt Underwood on Saturdays at 7pm.

Who to Listen To...

Since the untimely death of Nev Chandler, "The Voice of the Browns," in 1995, local radio coverage is limited to the local talk shows. The most-listened-to host is Mike Trivisonno, "Mr. Know-it-all" of WTAM (1100 AM), who actually began his career as a talk show caller. WTAM Sports Director Mike Snyder and John Antus of former Browns flagship station WKNR (1220 AM) lend authoritative insight. The Browns Trust "Countdown to '99" radio show airs at 10am Sundays on WKNR; Mark Kestescher and former Browns offensive tackle Doug Dieken preside.

---

only exception are the seats in the new end zone Dawg Pound. Ticket prices for 1999 have not yet been announced. More PSLs are slated to go on sale in late 1998, but at higher prices than those previously offered. For more information, contact the Cleveland Browns Trust at (440) 891-5050, or toll-free (888) 891-1999.

Public transportation: Though plans are not carved in stone, transit will include Browns special buses and a new waterfront trolley line. Both services will be provided by the Greater Cleveland Regional Transit Authority (RTA). Call (216) 621-9500 for information.

Parking: Your best bet will be at the municipal parking lots located along I-90, just east of the stadium. Most downtown parking lots operate for special events.

Capacity: 72,000
Restrooms: 31 men's, 39 women's.

Where to Go . . . in Cleveland

Best Bars

Best place to become a Browns fan. Sports Inn, which opened in 1986, is the quintessential neighborhood sports bar. There are photos and posters of Browns and Indians players and various items of memorabilia from floor to ceiling. The patrons are staunch Cleveland Browns fans, but are divided on whether the expansion team should keep the name or start fresh. Very friendly atmosphere ... and the wings have been voted Cleveland's Best! *4716 State Rd. (216)741-9625 M-Su 11am-2:30am.*

Best bathroom. Not only has this party establishment been voted Cleveland's #1 dance club, but **The Basement** is also home to a "treasured" piece of old Cleveland Stadium ... the toilet seat from Art Modell's loge box. *1078 Old River Rd. (216) 344-0001. Seven days until 2:30am.*

Best pre-game stop. Open since December 1997, **Fishbones** is one of a number of new watering holes that have popped up since the opening of Jacobs Field and Gund Arena. This is a peanut shells-on-the-floor type of place, long and narrow with a loft level on top. This bar is graced with eight TVs and boasts of 40 beers on tap and 120 bottled brands. And they have a great selection in their jukebox. *746 Prospect (216) 575-0226. M-Sa 4pm-2:30am, Su opens two hours before game time.*

Ready For Primetime (Monday Night)

September 21, 1970: This was the first ABC Monday Night game, brought to Cleveland by Art Modell, a leading member of the league's television committee. The largest crowd ever for a Browns game—85,703—saw the home team beat Joe Namath and the Jets, 31-21.

Overall Monday night: 13-11
Overall Thursday night: 2-2
Overall Sunday night: 0-3

▼

did you know?

Baseball's home run king Henry Aaron used to don a raincoat, hat and sunglasses and sit among the Browns faithful in the Dawg Pound. Aaron, who's from Mobile, Alabama and played for Milwaukee and Atlanta, says he has no idea why he even became a Browns fan.

▲

Think About the Weather

December 18, 1988: A snowy afternoon anywhere for the Oilers usually meant trouble, but here was Jerry Glanville's club having an easy time of it, ahead 23-7 in the third quarter at Cleveland. Then backup QB Don Strock, starting in place of injured Bernie Kosar and already guilty of throwing three interceptions, directed three unanswered touchdown drives and put the Browns in the playoffs. Browns 28, Oilers 23.

Worst Team

1990 (3-13): After making five consecutive trips to the playoffs—including three AFC title game appearances in four years—the bottom fell out fast in Cleveland. While a 2-3 start included a win over the Steelers and a much-awaited victory at Denver, the Bud Carson/Jim Shofner-led Browns won only one game the rest of the year and set franchise marks for losses and points allowed (462) in a season.

Team Leaders

Rushing Yards
12,312   Jim Brown (1957-65)
Passing Yards
23,713   Brian Sipe (1974-83)
Passing Touchdowns
154   Brian Sipe (1974-83)
Receptions
662   Ozzie Newsome (1978-90)
Interceptions
45   Thomas Darden (1972-74, 1976-81)
Touchdowns
126   Jim Brown (1957-65)
Points
1,349   Lou Groza (1950-59, 1961-67)

did you know?

In 1958 and '59, the Browns helmet had the player's number on its side, then it returned to plain burnt orange. In the 1964 pre-season, Art Modell joined the NFL trend and put a logo on the side of the helmet. The players disliked the interlocking "CB" so much, they ripped it off their helmets.

Best Restaurants

Best expensive meal. Located in the Omni International Hotel, **Classics** is Cleveland's finest, most romantic and expensive restaurant — and worth every cent. It has won numerous awards for its wine list and service. Ostrich skin adorns the walls; the place settings are silver and Lenox crystal. The rack of lamb and Steak Diane are house specialties. *206 E. 96th St., (216) 791-1300. M-F 11:30am-2:30pm, 5:30pm-9pm, Sa. 5pm-10pm. Saturday reservations should be made two weeks in advance. $$$$*

Best sports restaurant. He later moved to Miami, but Don Shula is from Greater Cleveland (Grand River), and he played for the Browns. At **Shula's Steak 2**, sports memorabilia is everywhere, including seats from old Muncipal Stadium. The food is terrific, the prices fair (all the kids menu items are $1.95) and the wine list extensive. In the Hilton Hotel, *6200 Quarry La., Independence, (216) 901-7852. Open for breakfast and full menu service M-Th 6:30am-10pm, F-Sa 7am-11pm, Su 7am-9pm. Reservations are suggested for Saturday night. $$*

While You Were Eating Turkey

November 23, 1989: Thanksgiving Day football is one of the only departments in which the Browns don't have a rich tradition — they have played just twice and never won. In their most recent appearance in 1989, Bud Carson's playoff-bound Browns, who had earlier that year handed the Steelers a 51-0 knuckle sandwich, faced off against the mediocre Lions and came up on the short end of a 13-10 contest. Overall, 0-2.

Fans' notes

On Screen

Jim Brown's talent as an NFL running back was unequaled. And even if he didn't turn out to be Lawrence Olivier, Brown made his contribution to the movie world as well. After leaving football in 1966, he made his way onto the big screen in **The Dirty Dozen**. Brown went on to become America's premier black action hero with movies like **100 Rifles**, **I Escaped From Devil's Island**, **Three the Hard Way** and **Kid Vengeance**. The only movie to feature the Cleveland Browns team itself is the classic Billy Wilder film **The Fortune Cookie**, starring Walter Matthau and Jack Lemmon. A few of the scenes were filmed at Municipal Stadium, as was game footgage featuring running back Leroy Kelly. Lemmon plays a photographer who's run over by a Browns player on the sideline. Matthau plays his sleazy attorney who sues the player and the Browns.

Paraphernalia

Even though the team's name and nondescript helmet don't lend themselves awfully well to merchandising, Browns fans snatch up anything that includes a reference to dogs or "The Dawg Pound." The tradition originated in 1985, when Hanford Dixon referred to the defensive backfield as the "Last Dogs of Defense." A whole canine aura developed around the team, culminating in everything from spiked collars to chew toys.

Bookshelf

Browns Memories: The 338 Most Memorable Heroes, Heartaches and Highlights from 50 Seasons of *Cleveland Browns Football.* Tim Long (Gray and Co. 1996).
Glory For Sale: Fans, Dollars and the New NFL. Jon Morgan (Bancroft 1997).
When All the World Was Browns Town: Cleveland's Browns and the Championship Season of 1964. Terry Pluto (Simon and Schuster 1997).
The Cleveland Browns: A 50-Year Tradition. Steve Byrne, et al. (Sagamore 1995).
Out of Bounds. Jim Brown and Steve Delsohn (Kensington 1989).
PB: The Paul Brown Story. Paul Brown and Jack T. Clary (Macmillan 1979).

You Gotta See...

▶The greatest off-the-field show can be found just one hour south of downtown in Canton: the **Pro Football Hall of Fame**. This is where the first game of the NFL preseason is played in late summer, right after the Hall of Fame parade and induction ceremonies. It's a wonderful time for football fans to visit Canton.

▶Cleveland has come a long way since the '70s — find out for yourself in **The Flats**, formerly a warehouse district and now home to many of the city's nightspots, restaurants, and galleries.

▶For a view of the wildlife, check out either the Cleveland **Metropark Zoo** or **Sea World of Ohio**, a short drive away in Aurora.

▶Just a field goal away from the east endzone, **The Rock and Roll Hall of Fame** features a boss collection of cool rock stuff and some most excellent multimedia jams. Rock on, Garth!

Against the Odds

Everybody loves an underdog, especially in Cleveland, home of the Dawg Pound. In 1980, no player and team played the role of underdog quite like **Brian Sipe** (1974-1983) and the Browns. Affectionately known as the "Kardiac Kids," Sipe and company finished the season 11-5, logging the club's most wins since 1965 (11-3) and ending an eight-year playoff drought. In that storied season, 13 of the Browns' 16 regular-season games were decided by a TD or less, and Sipe became only the third player (at that time) to throw for over 4,000 yards in a season (4,132). Sipe was named the league's Most Valuable Player.

Hall of Fame

Otto Graham	(QB 1965)
Paul Brown	(C 1967)
Marion Motley	(FB 1968)
Jim Brown	(FB 1971)
Lou Groza	(T, K 1974)
Dante Lavelli	(E 1975)
Len Ford	(DE 1976)
Bill Willis	(G 1977)
Willie Davis	(DE 1981)
Doug Atkins	(DE 1982)
Bobby Mitchell	(WR 1983)
Paul Warfield	(WR 1983)
Mike McCormack	(T 1984)
Frank Gatski	(C 1985)
Len Dawson	(QB 1987)
Tommy McDonald	(WR 1998)

Best sandwiches. Owned by former Brown Frank Winter, **Panini's Gateway Bar and Grille** would have become a Browns Backers hangout — if the team hadn't left town. When that happened, Winter, who also played for Green Bay, decided to make it a Packer Backer bar. Whatever its allegiance, Panini's has the most unique and best $4.50 over-stufffed sandwich in the area. All the sandwiches come stuffed with tomatoes, french fries, cole slaw and cheese. *840 Huron St., (216) 522-1510. M-F 11am-9pm (later if there's a downtown event). Sa-Su 10am-2:30am. (Closed Sunday if no downtown event). $*

Best Accommodations

The Ritz-Carlton. Cleveland's only four-star and four-diamond hotel, located adjacent to the exclusive Tower City Center shopping plaza and a short walk to the Browns stadium. *1515 East Third St., (216) 623-1300, (800) 241-3333. $$$$*

Embassy Suites. The rate is $120, but you're getting a well-furnished suite of over 800 square feet, with two televisions. In-room kitchen facilities include a wet bar, refrigerator, coffeemaker and microwave. Great for families. *1701 East 12th St., in Reserve Square, (216) 523-8000, (800) 362-2779. $$$*

Comfort Inn. This recently remodeled hotel has 130 guest rooms and 36 whirlpool suites. VCRs, microwaves, refrigerators, laundry/valet service and an exercise room are available. *1800 Euclid Ave., (216) 861-0001, (800) 228-5150. $$*

Dallas Cowboys

"I wanted to start something from scratch and build it into a success." — Tex Schramm

Texas fancies itself a larger-than-life state, and whether it's been planned all these years or just something in the water, the Dallas Cowboys have been a larger-than-life football team. The glamour of the cheerleaders, the soap opera excess of fur coats in the stands, bull-riding backs, Staubach and Aikman, run-ins with the law — the 40-year history of the 'Boys has enough hubris, color and triumph to satisfy any Texan's taste for tall tales.

Franchise History

Dallas Cowboys
(1960–present)

The story began when Clint Murchison Jr., the team's original owner, hired Tom Landry to coach his new expansion franchise in 1960. Five losing seasons could not shake Murchison's confidence in Landry. He stunned the sports world when he gave the coach a 10-year contract after the team's fourth sub-par year, and he finally struck oil in 1966 when the Cowboys made the playoffs behind quarterback Don Meredith and the "Doomsday Defense" led by Lee Roy Jordan, Bob Lilly and Chuck Howley.

Success triggered a series of events that took the Cowboys from an expansion team to "America's Team." First, Tex Schramm, the general manager, became the team's president and started to run the most innovative, fan-friendly organization in football. Second, Murchison announced plans to build Texas Stadium in suburban Irving, TX, and third, the Cowboys played in one of the NFL's most memorable games, losing to the Green Bay Packers, 21-17, in the 1967 league championship game, the famed "Ice Bowl."

Playing their first season in their new home, the Cowboys made the playoffs for the fifth straight time in 1970 and won the NFC title, only to drop a 16-13 decision to the Baltimore Colts in the

By the Numbers

(Since 1970)
Regular Season: 267-157-0
Postseason: 31-15
Division Titles: 14
Vs. Division: 142-77 (Playoffs: 2-3)
Playoff Appearances: 20
Home: 149-63
Away: 118-94

(Overall)
Regular Season: 334-222-6
Postseason: 32-19
Playoffs Appearances: 24
Home: 185-92-4
Away: 149-130-2

Most Revered Football Figures

Roger Staubach. Still so respected and worshiped, he could easily become the next governor of Texas.

Tom Landry. Say Dallas Cowboys, and the quiet man in the hat immediately comes to mind.

Troy Aikman. He's the current king, and three Super Bowl rings are enough to keep him enthroned for years to come.

Rivalries

The Washington **Redskins**-Cowboys feud actually started before the Cowboys even joined the NFL. In 1960, Washington owner George Preston Marshall attempted to block the Cowboys' entry into the NFL. Cowboys owner Clint Murchison countered by acquiring the rights to the Redskins popular fight song, "Hail to the Redskins." Murchison then informed Marshall he could not see how Washington could be allowed to play HIS song if the Redskins did not vote to add Dallas to the NFL. Murchison got his vote and Marshall got his song for $1. The Cowboys lead the series, 41-33-2. Another barometer for Cowboy success is beating the Green Bay **Packers.** This rivalry (13-11) dates way back to the Lombardi days in the late 1960's, when the Packers twice denied the Cowboys an NFL title. There's been the Ice Bowl, the Cowboys' eight consecutive victories in the '90's, including the 1995 NFC Championship, and the Cheeseheads' most recent vindication, a 45-17 victory at Lambeau Field in 1997.

Super Bowl. One year later, Landry and the Cowboys won the first of the team's five Super Bowls, as Meredith's successor, Roger Staubach, started his reign as a local hero and future Hall of Famer.

Great players continued to wear the Cowboys star—Ed "Too Tall" Jones, Mel Renfro, Randy White, and Tony Dorsett, to name a few—and helped Landry to 20 straight winning seasons. The streak was broken in 1986, though, and a year later Murchison died. Things were about to change. Jerry Jones, an Arkansas oilman bubbling with enthusiasm, purchased the team from Bum Bright on Feb. 25, 1989. Within hours, he stomped a boot on the toes of franchise history when he dismissed Landry, the team's only coach, and named Jimmy Johnson as his successor.

And so another amazing chapter in the Cowboys story began. Johnson traded the team's best player, Herschel Walker, for a slew of draft picks from the Minnesota Vikings. With that, he built a team around UCLA quarterback Troy Aikman, running back Emmitt Smith and wide receiver Michael Irvin as the Cowboys won three Super Bowl titles in the '90s. The third chapter came with former Oklahoma coach Barry Switzer on the sidelines, since Jones and Johnson had a falling out in 1993 after their second Super Bowl win. Switzer got his ring, but he was gone by 1998, replaced by Pittsburgh Steelers offensive coordinator Chan Gailey, a humble, soft-spoken man much in the mold of Tom Landry.

—*Chris Mortensen*

did you know?

The nickname "America's Team" was not a Cowboys public relations concoction, but initiated by NFL Films while putting together the team's highlight video back in the 1970's.

Texas Stadium

So after a 6-10 season in 1997, does anyone still really think the Dallas Cowboys receive heavenly intervention through the hole in the roof? If Green Bay's Lambeau Field is known for subfreezing temperatures and Chicago's Soldier Field for sitting on the lakefront, then Texas Stadium is embedded in the nation's consciousness for the partial opening over its top. And because of the Cowboys' success in late 1960s and throughout the decade of the '70s, Texas Stadium still oozes with importance, as if a national landmark, when game day approaches. The fans are a tad rowdier than in the old days, but that is not saying much since the fans in the old days were rather sedate. Don't expect hard-to-please Cowboys fans to act up if the team is not playing well. Amazingly, though, the stadium has been well preserved. If you didn't know better, you would not believe Texas Stadium is turning 27 years old this season, opening on Oct. 24, 1971, with the Cowboys beating New England, 44-21.

Due to a no-open-flame law, there is no tailgating to speak of at Cowboys games, so check out The Corral. Fans stream into this tented facility outside Texas Stadium prior and after the games for food, drink and live bands. Big-screen TVs are available to watch other

> ## did you know?
> Cowboys' LB Chuck Howley remains the only linebacker, as well as the only player on a losing team, to earn Super Bowl MVP honors, in Super Bowl V.

> "I'm not going to say worried. I'm going to say concerned." — Cornerback Deion Sanders, after the Cowboys' 3-3 start in 1997. The team would finish 6-10.

The "I Was There" Game

December 23, 1972: To this day, the image of the Cowboys is one of late-game heroics. Those heroics all started in the NFC Division Play-off with Hall of Fame QB Roger Staubach. The Cowboys trailed in San Francisco in the fourth quarter, 28-13, and Staubach brought them all the way back to win, 30-28. This game is often overshadowed because it occurred the same day as the fabled "Immaculate Reception" in Pittsburgh.

The Paper Bag Game

November 13, 1988: En route to his worst season since the winless 1960 campaign, Tom Landry saw his Cowboys drubbed by the visiting Vikings, 43-3, before a crowd of nearly 58,000 disgruntled fans. It was the Cowboys' seventh consecutive loss in a streak that would extend to 10 before a win at Washington.

Great Names

Tommie Agee (FB 1990-94)
Richmond Flowers (S 1969-71)
Buzz Guy (G 1960)
Gary Hogeboom (QB 1980-85)
Ron Howard (TE 1974-75)
Eric Hurt (CB 1980)
Ed "Too Tall" Jones (DE 1974-78, 1980-89)
Lance Poimboeuf (K 1963)
Golden Richards (WR 1973-78)
Junior Tautalatasi (RB 1989)

Our Top Story

"Switzer Caught Packing"
August 8, 1997
Head coach Barry Switzer was arrested when a .38 caliber handgun was found in his carry-on luggage at Dallas-Fort Worth Airport. The courts eventually gave him one year of probation, a $3,500 fine and 80 hours of community service. Owner Jerry Jones slapped him with a $75,000 fine.

"Hell Freezes Over"
February 25, 1989
Who would have thunk it? Not only were the Cowboys sold to an Arkansas interloper, but this oil man named Jerry Jones had the temerity to actually tell Tom Landry, the only coach in Dallas' 29-year history, he no longer would be coaching the Cowboys.

"This Year's Champs"
January 16, 1971
At long last, after losing back-to-back NFL championships to Green Bay in 1966-67 and then losing Super Bowl V to Baltimore, the Cowboys claimed Super Bowl VI, beating Miami 24-3 to forever lose their annoying moniker as "Next Year's Champs."

"How 'Bout Dem Cowboys?"
January 17, 1993
That was the cry of head coach Jimmy Johnson, when his underdog, and then still darling, Cowboys went into San Francisco and emerged 30-20 victors over the 49ers in the 1992 NFC Championship Game. This ignited the Cowboys string of back-to-back Super Bowl titles and three in four years.

games. It's a place to be seen. Maybe this is why the Cowboys fans have this annoying habit of showing up fashionably late for games.

The Bottom Line on Texas Stadium

Address: Texas Stadium, 2401 E. Airport Freeway, Irving, TX, 75062. (972) 556-9900.

Tickets: Tickets go on sale in the spring. Call (972) 579-5000 for information. Steer clear of the east end-zone seats, especially early in the season, where the direct sun is a killer. Tickets are also available at Rainbow/Ticketmaster Outlets at Blockbuster Music, Fiesta, Foley's and Tom Thumb stores or by phone (214-373-8000).
1998: $34/$35/$50/$55
1994: $30/$34/$38

Extras: Bus service via Dallas Area Rapid Transit is available to all games, picking up riders at the city's various park-and-ride facilities. Call DART (214) 979-1111 for schedule information.

Parking: Arriving at least 90 minutes to two hours prior to the game keeps you out of traffic and gets you a space in the pay lots. After that, good luck. The smart locals know the back way in on Luna Road, going south from either I-635 or Northwest Highway. The ultra-smart fan purchases a Blue coupon to park in the stadium's inner circle.

Capacity: 65,675

Restrooms: 87

did you know?
After losing Super Bowl V in their blue jerseys, the Cowboys developed a superstition about those uniforms—to this day, road opponents often force Dallas to play in blue rather than the usual visiting whites.

Best of the Cowboys

Best Team

1977 (15-2): This edition of Tom Landry's team ranked first in the NFL in offense and defense, and their demolition of the Denver offense in Super Bowl XII in New Orleans was scary. The "Doomsday Defense" featured Randy White and Harvey Martin, who earned co-MVP honors in Super Bowl XII. Rookie Tony Dorsett rushed for better than 1,000 yards on the season, and QB Roger Staubach was never better.

Greatest Players by Position

Pos:	Player
QB:	Roger Staubach
RB:	Tony Dorsett
WR:	Michael Irvin
TE:	Billy Joe DuPree
OL:	Rayfield Wright
DL:	Bob Lilly
LB:	Chuck Howley
DB:	Mel Renfro
P/K:	Rafael Septien
ST:	Bill Bates

And Don't Forget...

RB: Don Perkins. Underrated offensive weapon who was one of the most consistent runners in the league in the 1960s.

LB: Lee Roy Jordan. Five-time Pro-Bowler who anchored the middle of the Dallas defense for 14 seasons (1963-76).

WR: Drew Pearson. Clutch receiver best known for pulling down Roger Staubach's Hail Mary pass in the '75 playoffs at Minnesota.

DT: Randy White. Fourteen strong seasons and a club-record eight straight Pro-Bowl selections earned him a place in Canton.

RB: Robert Newhouse. Reliable blocker and ball-carrier and the first running back to throw a TD pass in a Super Bowl (XII vs. Broncos).

CB: Everson Walls. Undrafted free agent who totaled 44 interceptions in nine seasons in Dallas and led the league with 11 in 1981, his rookie year.

WR: "Bullet" Bob Hayes. A deep threat reputed to be the fastest man in the world, and fast enough to average 20 yards per catch for his career.

Best Argument

Running Back: Tony Dorsett or Emmitt Smith? Hall of Famer Dorsett was one of the most unique runners in the league, displaying deceptive speed and amazing toughness despite his lack of size, and he still ranks as the NFL's third-leading rusher. Smith was the workhorse for the Cowboys' 1990s Super Bowl teams, and is one of the top TD producers in NFL history, but could already be on the downside of his career.

Best Coach

Tom Landry (1960-88): He was the team's first and best sideline leader. His teams never quit on the football field. And even though each of the Cowboys' past head coaches (Jimmy Johnson, Barry Switzer) have won at least one Super Bowl, Landry put the Cowboys on the map. For a time, his fedora and stoic countenance on the sidelines stood for the NFL itself.

Pressbox

Who to Read...

Few professional sports teams get the media coverage that the Cowboys do. The *Dallas Morning News* crew presents saturation coverage of the team's comings and goings with a huge crew of beat writers and special sections. Randy Galloway is the columnist. The *Fort Worth Star-Telegram* also offers thorough coverage peppered with columns from Jim Reeves. The Cowboys' sphere of influence extends to Austin, where the *Austin-American Statesman* devotes serious attention to the team. And if all this newspaper coverage is just too impartial for you, check out the *Dallas Cowboys Weekly*, a 40-page magazine with color player pictures, coverage of roster moves, wrapups of the previous week's action, and even cheerleader centerfolds.

Who to Watch...

Not surprisingly, even the owner has his own show. "Special Edition" features Jerry Jones and Babe Laufenberg — yes, the former quarterback. It airs locally on KDFW-TV at 9:30am, Sundays. Mike Doocy and Mickey Spagnola host the pregame "Countdown to Kickoff" and the postgame show on KDFW. "The Daryl Johnston Show" airs Sundays on KXAS-TV, with the popular Cowboys fullback and Scott Murray for a half-hour.

Who to Listen To...

Darren Woodson, Emmitt Smith, Troy Aikman, and Daryl Johnston all have shows on AM radio. Try KRLD (1080 AM) for Aikman and Johnston. For the hardcore, there is "The Coach Joe Show" with Cowboys special teams coach Joe Avezzano and co-host Mickey Spagnola on KTCK (1310 AM), 7pm-8pm, Thursdays, from a remote location. There are seven other pre- or post-game radio shows. One of the better sports radio shows is "Dunham & Miller," with George Dunham and Craig Miller. They offer sports talk laced with witty skits and off-beat subjects during the morning drive on KTCK, better known as The Ticket. Two more good ones are Norm Hitzges on KLIF (570AM) weekday mornings and Randy Galloway on WBAP (820 AM).

Where to Go . . . in Dallas

Best Bars

Best joint in town. Louie's serves the stiffest drink and conversation in the city of Dallas, sans ferns, bands, valet parking and meat market, if you catch the drift. The joint of joints, with some of the city's best thin-crust pizza pies. Get them with the homemade Italian sausage and a handshake from Louie. *1839 N. Henderson. (214)826-0505. M-F 3pm-2am, Sa 7pm-2am, Su 4-10pm*

Best behavior. During the hell-raising Barry Switzer era, Jerry Jones put the **Cowboys Cafe** off-limits to players for a while. There's an outstanding collection of Cowboys memorabilia, and if you're lucky you might catch any number of former or current Cowboys on the premises. *9450 N. MacArthur, Irving. (972) 401-3939. Seven days 11am-2 am.*

Best boisterous bar The Las Colinas location of **Humperdinks** is normally packed after games, as the yuppies who did not have enough revelry at the game and those without game tickets gather to party into the night. This is where the boys go to meet girls, and where some players will show up after the game. *4959 N. O'Connor, Irving. (972) 717-5515. Seven days 11am-2am.*

The in crowd. The place to see and be seen, especially on weekend nights, is **Champps Americana** — if you don't mind elbow-to-elbow capacity crowds in the bar area. Several big-screen TVs, along with numerous televisions spread throughout the bar and restaurant area, make the watching of any number of games possible from any number of positions. *4951 Belt Line, Addison. (972)991-3335. M-Th 11am-1am, F-Sa 11am-2 am, Su 10am-12am.*

> "Don't bother reading that. Everyone dies in the end." — Wide receiver Pete Gent to a rookie holding the Cowboys' playbook.

Best Restaurants

Best Mex. For real, interior Mexican food, and not the popular Texas knock-off known as Tex-Mex, **Nuevo Leon** is the place to be. Don't let the original Farmers Branch location in a strip shopping center dull your enthusiasm. Once inside, the food, helpful staff, homey entertainment and festive atmoshere will be a pleasant surprise. *12895 Josey Lane, Farmers Branch. (972)488-1984. M-Th 11am-9pm, Sa 10am-10pm, Su 10:30am-2:30pm. All major credit cards. $-$$.*

Ready For Primetime (Monday Night)

September 5, 1983: The Cowboys had lost the 1982 NFC title game to the Redskins at Washington, and this opening night affair at RFK Stadium saw them trailing Joe Theismann and company, 23-3, at halftime. But QB Danny White and WR Tony Hill did their thing, and the Boys came away with a big win, 31-30, over the defending Super Bowl champs.

Overall on Monday night: 31-25
Overall on Thursday night: 0-1
Overall on Sunday night: 9-6

> **did you know?**
> Former Cowboys President Tex Schramm still owns a luxury suite at Texas Stadium. He still attends nearly all the home games. Schramm is the franchise's only Hall of Fame member who has not been inducted into Texas Stadium's Ring of Honor.

Think About the Weather

December 31, 1967: Baby, it was cold outside. When the Cowboys and Packers met in the infamous Ice Bowl for the 1967 NFL Championship, the temperatures dipped to 13-below at Lambeau Field. The Cowboys' 21-17 loss on Bart Starr's last-second quarterback sneak was the only thing to hurt worse than the post-game frostbite.

Worst Team

1988 (3-13): The final year of the storied Tom Landry Era saw the team get old in a hurry. After splitting their first four games, the Cowboys dropped 11 out of 12, although that lone victory in the final three months came at RFK Stadium against the defending Super Bowl champion Redskins. The Jimmy Johnson Era began a year later with a 1-15 mark, but youth was being served.

Swami Sez:

Sure they fell from grace in '97, but were it not for a great effort in 1994 by the 49ers, the Cowboys would have won 4 straight Super Bowls. How 'bout 'dem Cowboys, indeed.

Team Leaders

Rushing Yards
12,036   Tony Dorsett, 1977-87
Passing Yards
26,016   Troy Aikman, 1989-present
Passing Touchdowns
155   Danny White, 1976-88
Receptions
666   Michael Irvin, 1988-present
Interceptions
52   Mel Renfro, 1964-77
Touchdowns
119   Emmitt Smith, 1990-present
Points
874   Rafael Septien, 1978-86

---

did you know?

During training camp and practice sessions, all rookies and first-year players dress in the team's old metallic silver-blue colored game pants while veterans wear practice whites.

Best blackened anything. For the most authentic Cajun dishes and New Orleans-type atmosphere, the very casual **Dodie's Seafood Cafe** is a must. Owner Charlie McGuinness and his family recipes have a way of turning Dallas's hustle and bustle into a Big Easy dining experience. The po' boys are good as they get. And there may be a little lagniappe on the right nights. *2129 Greenville Ave. (214) 821-8890. M-Th 11am-10pm, F-Sa 11am-11 pm, Su 12:00pm-8pm. All major credit cards. $$.*

Best western spaghetti. There are fancier Italian restaurants in Dallas, but for the absolute best food at a reasonable price, you must make the trek out to **Salerno's** in Flower Mound to taste the dishes of renowned area chef Morris Salerno. No one does basic Italian better, and the creative dishes will wow you. *3407 Long Prairie Rd., Flower Mound, (972) 539-9534. M-Th 11am-10pm, F 11am-11pm, Sa 4pm-11pm, Sun 11am-9pm. $$.*

Best steak house. Want a steak just the way you like it? Let the folks at **Del Frisco's** pamper you with hearty portions and attentive service. But phone ahead. Del's serves almost nightly to a capacity crowd that comes dressed as nicely or casually as it likes. *5251 Spring Valley. (972) 490-9000. M-Th 5pm-10pm, F-Sa 5pm-11pm. All major credit cards. $$$-$$$$.*

"Cover the one they throw the ball to." — Head coach Tom Landry explaining to All-Pro safety Cliff Harris how to choose whether to cover the fullback or halfback on a blitz.

Fans' notes

On Screen

Semi-Tough is loosely based on the Cowboys but, thankfully, strictly based on the acclaimed novel of the same name by Dan Jenkins. **North Dallas Forty**, an above-average sports movie, is based on Pete Gent's novel and takes a hard look at the way football players are used up and thrown away by the league and owners. **Black Sunday** is also based on a novel, this one by Thomas Harris. Terrorists attempt to blow up the stadium hosting a game between the Steelers and Cowboys. Definitely not based on a novel is the **Dallas Cowboy Cheerleaders** starring Lauren Tewes. For something a little more realistic, NFL Films has compiled **The Greatest Moments in Dallas Cowboy History**. Despite his nickname, Thomas "Hollywood" Henderson never really hit the big screen, not even to the extent that Ed "Too Tall" Jones did in 1979's **The Double McGuffin**, with Lyle Alzado.

Bookshelf

Time Enough to Win. Roger Staubach with Frank Luksa (Word 1980).
Cowboys Have Always Been My Heroes: The Definitive Oral History of America's Team. Peter Golenbock (Warner 1997).
Dallas Cowboys: The Authorized Pictorial History. Jeff Guinn (Summitt 1996). A must for Cowboy fans.
The Dallas Cowboys Encyclopedia: The Ultimate Guide to America's Team. Jim Donovan, et al. (Citadel Press 1996). The title says it all.
Hell-bent: The Crazy Truth About the 'Win or Else' Dallas Cowboys. Skip Bayless (Harper Collins 1996).

The Ice-Bowl: The Green Bay Packers and Dallas Cowboys Season of 1967. Mike Shropshire (Donald I. Fine 1997). A great season that ended with one of the NFL's greatest games.
Duane Thomas and the Fall of America's Team. Duane Thomas and Paul Zimmerman (Warner 1989).
God's Coach: The Hymns, Hype, and Hypocrisy of Tom Landry's Cowboys. Skip Bayless (Simon and Schuster 1990).
Semi-Tough. Dan Jenkins (Scribner 1972). Perhaps the best, funniest and most profane novel ever written about football. Very loosely based on the Cowboys.
North Dallas Forty. Pete Gent (Morrow 1973). A breakthrough football book. Written by former Cowboy Gent, the novel offered one of the first tough looks inside the pro game,
The Texas Celebrity Turkey Trot. Pete Gent (Morrow 1978). More top notch football fiction.

You gotta see...

▶ The **Sixth Floor Window of the Texas Book Depository**, adjacent to the infamous **Grassy Knoll** where President John F. Kennedy was assassinated. Not something Dallasites are proud of, but is one of those must-sees if you are visiting for the first time.
▶ Dallas may be the birthplace of the chicken fajita, but it's also the birthplace of the **Neiman-Marcus** retail empire. Check out a piece of retail history and visit the store's original location in downtown Dallas.
▶ The **Exposition Park** area, once the site of Texas's State Fair, has been transformed from a dangerous wasteland to a fringy punker mecca full of bookstores, tattoo parlors and the like.

Hall of Fame

Bob Lilly	(DT 1980)
Roger Staubach	(QB 1985)
Tom Landry	(Coach 1990)
Tex Schramm	(Owner 1991)
Tony Dorsett	(RB 1994)
Randy White	(DT 1994)
Tommy McDonald	(WR 1998)

Against the Odds

Chuck Howley (1961-73) originally retired before the Cowboys even came into existence, but he returned from a serious knee injury suffered in 1959 to play an integral role in the growth of Dallas' fledgling franchise. A big-play linebacker with great speed and instincts, the six-time All-Pro was one of the leaders of Dallas' Doomsday Defense. He is also the only player in Super Bowl history to be named Most Valuable Player for a losing team, when he registered two interceptions and forced a fumble in the Cowboys' 16-13 loss to the Colts in error-plagued Super Bowl V.

> **did you know?**
> Through 1997, the Cowboys had just three head coaches in 38 seasons—Tom Landry, Jimmy Johnson and Barry Switzer—none of whom owns a losing career record with the franchise.

Best Accommodations

Radisson. A short hop from the Love Field Airport, this Mockingbird Lane location is central to the city, suburbs, and stadium and is known to attract Cowboys fans in town for the game, making for a nice game-day atmosphere. Reserve early; out-of-towners know about this place. *1893 W. Mockingbird Lane, Dallas. (214) 634-8850. $-$$.*

Airport Marriott. If you just have to stay where the Cowboys stay, this has been one of the places the past few seasons where the team actually bunks the night before the game. You might catch a glimpse of a player or three in the lobby in the early evening, or walking out to the buses on game day. But reserve early. Hard-core fans know about this place, too. *8440 Freeport Pkwy., Irving. (972) 929-8800. $$-$$$.*

Four Seasons Resort and Club. This galaxy of stars hotel adjacent to two golf courses used for the Byron Nelson stop on the PGA Tour has a full health club and tennis club. Don't be surprised if you see the Madden Cruiser parked here on game weekends. *4150 N. MacArthur Blvd., Irving. (972) 717-0700. $$$$-$$$$$*

While You Were Eating Turkey....

November 28, 1974. The Cowboys have become Thanksgiving Day dressing around America, having played 30 games on Turkey Day. And no Cowboy has more deeply etched his name in Thanksgiving Day lore than QB Clint Longley, better known as the "Mad Bomber," who spoiled many meals in the nation's capital when he led the Cowboys to a frenetic 24-23 victory over Washington. Longley's comeback heroics, constituting the bulk of his NFL career, prompted former Cowboys president Tex Schramm to say "One of those angels was sitting on Clint's shoulder." Overall, 20-9-1.

Denver Broncos

From the moment the Broncos organization was created in 1960 as a charter member of the AFL, it was more than just a football team to Denver. For all the wonderful things about this jewel of a city set among the Rocky Mountains, many people in the '60s and '70s knew little about the place other than that the Broncos played here. It wasn't easy for the Broncos at first, and it wasn't easy for awhile after that either: The team struggled through 13 non-winning seasons from 1960 to 1972 before they finally broke .500 in 1973. But the people of Denver never stopped rooting for the Broncos. During those losing seasons, the Denver Broncos sold out every single Sunday.

Franchise History

Denver Broncos (AFL)
(1960–69)
Denver Broncos (NFL)
(1970–present)

The Broncos took the first step toward their winning tradition at the end of the '60s, when a wave of great players came aboard. Rich Jackson, Lyle Alzado, Billy Thompson and perennial Pro-Bowler Paul Smith were joined by RB Floyd Little, who became the team's first franchise player. The nucleus was now in place for the ball club that would finally start winning games in 1973 behind coach John Ralston and Charlie Johnson, a genuinely wise quarterback with a doctorate in engineering. With Little, they led the Broncos to respectability.

By the Numbers

(Since 1970)

Regular Season: 242-176-6
Postseason: 13-11
Division Titles: 8
Vs. Division: 113-93-2 (Playoffs: 2-2)
Playoff Appearances: 12
Home: 150-59-4
Away: 92-117-2

(Overall)

Regular Season: 281-273-10
Postseason: 13-11
Playoff Appearances: 12
Home: 174-102-7
Away: 107-171-3

From 1973 to 1980, the identity of the Broncos was wrapped up with the "Orange Crush" defense, led by greats such as Randy Gradishar, Rubin Carter, Louis Wright and Alzado. QB Steve Ramsey, RB Otis Armstrong, Haven Moses at WR and All-Pro Riley Odoms at TE provided support on offense. The first taste of real success came in 1977, when the

87

Most Revered Football Figures

John Elway. He got the Broncos close many times and then, in Super Bowl XXXII, he took them all the way. Essentially, a god in Colorado.

Tom Jackson. Voted Denver's most inspirational player six straight years, Jackson was huge in Denver before he ever became huge on ESPN.

Floyd Little. The franchise's first round pick in 1967, he was a captain each of his nine seasons.

Rivalries

Unlike the Chiefs, who spent most of their AFL days battling the **Raiders** (25-50-2) for league supremacy, Denver was often a doormat for the league's former Bad Boys, and perhaps the Men From Mile High still haven't earned the Raiders' respect. In recent seasons, the Broncos biggest rival has been the Kansas City **Chiefs** (33-43). The Chiefs' rivalry with the Broncos really got nasty in 1967, when Kansas City attempted an onside kick in the fourth quarter of a game which they won, 52-9. And these teams don't like each other any better now. In 1997, Chiefs coach Marty Schottenheimer allegedly offered to pay any fines his players incurred for breaking any Bronco's jaw. No Bronco jaws were broken. But wide receiver Ed McCaffrey's face was ripped open on a vicious shot from Chiefs safety Jerome Woods, who was fined $10,000. No word on whether Schottenheimer paid the fine.

did you know?
While the Broncos are the sixth team to go to at least five Super Bowls, they are the only club in that group to meet a different foe (Cowboys, Giants, Redskins, 49ers, Packers) in each contest.

Broncos made it to Super Bowl XII, only to lose to the Cowboys. Their success continued through 1980, either as division champs or as wild card winners, but the fact that the team hadn't made it back to the Super Bowl began to haunt the organization. Early owners Gerald and Allan Phipps sold the team to Edgar Kaiser Jr. in 1981, and new coach Dan Reeves instilled a sense of discipline into the team and the organization. But the Broncos still lacked that one key player who would take them back to the Super Bowl.

He finally showed up in 1983. When John Elway attended his first Broncos minicamp, half the team came to watch him throw. Elway proved to be a marvelous leader. His natural ability to handle pressure broke through, and the Broncos were back in the playoffs by his second year. By 1986, the Broncos returned to the Super Bowl against the Giants. As timing would have it, the once-great defense had aged and gave up 39 points. Denver lost again. On the sidelines, I told Elway, "Remember what losing this game feels like, because you'll be back here again."

John took the advice to heart, and he continued his unmatched leadership. The Broncos made it back to two more Super Bowls — XXII and XXIV — but they lost each time. Those losses, despite all the success, became what the organization was known for until 1997, when the Broncos made their march through the playoffs behind Elway and RB Terrell Davis. For most Broncos and their fans, much of their self-image had hinged on winning the

Super Bowl. By beating the Packers in Super Bowl XXXII, Elway put to rest the ghosts that had haunted the Broncos and coach Mike Shanahan proved that he's one of the finest coaches in the game. One Super Bowl win makes you a good coach; more than one makes you great. Shanahan will prove to be great. In the locker room prior to the game, he said, "Men, let's go out and show the world what kind of football team we have." All of Denver is glad that the world finally knows just how good the Broncos are.

—Tom Jackson

Mile High Stadium

It's pretty amazing to think that the Broncos are so desperate to take a wrecking ball to the home that has been so good to them. Mile High Stadium has provided them with one of the top home-field advantages in all of football. Since 1974, no team has posted a better home record than Denver's 139-45-1 mark. And under Mike Shanahan, who took over the Broncos in January 1995, Denver has been just about unbeatable in Mile High: Shanahan has a 22-2 record at home and has not lost a regular season game there since December 1995. What makes Mile High such a tough place to play is an assortment of factors, not the least of which is the problem opponents have in breathing Denver's thin air late in the game. Then there's the crowd. The fans come all the time, as 222 straight sellouts

> **"It's Terrell's team."**
> —John Elway in 1997, on running back Terrell Davis's emergence to superstar status.

did you know?

In 1974, Denver hosted the NFL's first regular-season overtime game. So much for rules changes — after five quarters, the Broncos and Steelers stayed tied, 35-35.

The "I Was There" Game

January 11, 1987: AFC Championship Game: Now that John Elway has his Super Bowl ring, will this game for the ages take a back seat? Trailing 20-13 with 5:43 to play and 98 yards of real estate ahead of him, Elway drove the Broncos down the field to tie the score with :37 left in regulation (a five-yard TD toss to WR Mark Jackson), and PK Rich Karlis's 33-yard field goal in OT would win it. The game-tying scoring march became known simply as "The Drive." Broncos 23, Browns 20.

The Paper Bag Game

September 18, 1994: By the third quarter of the most embarrassing loss in franchise history, Mile High Stadium was half empty, as strange a sight as the figures on the scoreboard. This loss to the Raiders paved the way for the departure of Wade Phillips and the arrival of Mike Shanahan. Raiders 48, Broncos 16.

Great Names

Larry Canada (FB, 1978-79, 1981)
Billy Corgan (CB, 1970)
Mike Current (T, 1967-75)
John Denvir (G, 1962)
Glenn Glass (DB, 1966)
Darryl Hall (S, 1993-94)
Le-Lo Lang (CB, 1990-93)
Robert McNamara (HB, 1960-61)
Goldie Sellers (DB, 1966-67)
Mac Speedie (Coach, 1964-66)

Our Top Story

"First in the Win Column"
September 9, 1960
After losing all five of their preseason games, the first-year Broncos became the first AFL team to register a win, beating the Boston Patriots, 13-10, on a Friday. Denver went on to register a 4-9-1 record.

"Elway Heads Our Way"
May 2, 1983
In the biggest trade in franchise history, the Broncos sent quarterback Mark Herrmann, offensive lineman Chris Hinton and a 1984 No. 1 choice to Baltimore for quarterback John Elway, who didn't want to play for the Colts. From a Colts fan perspective, it is simply one of the worst trades in sports history.

"Bowlen Buys Broncos"
March 23, 1984
Less than a year after the team traded for Elway, a group led by Pat Bowlen bought the Broncos. Bowlen was introduced as the team's majority owner. And with his aggressive approach and carefree spending, Bowlen helped introduce the Broncos to consistent winning.

"Superb!"
January 25, 1998
After four Super Bowl losses, the Broncos took the fifth. The Broncos beat the Packers, 31-24, in Super Bowl XXXII. All asterisks are removed from the team's history and John Elway's resume.

of 76,273 fans testify. Any empty seats are actually booed. And it also doesn't help that the stadium is a noise factory, producing decibel levels that can harm one's hearing. And when it gets loud, the fans stomp their feet and the stands shake and Mile High becomes one of the most intimidating stadiums in the league. It is not the prettiest place in the league, though. The concourses are grimy, the restrooms are crowded. But the fans don't come for aesthetics. They come for the hard-core football experience. Maybe the Broncos figure that the fans are the main reason they do so well at home, and a new stadium is the least they can do in return for so much support over the years.

▼

did you know?

You can debate about which was better, the old orange or the new navy uniforms, but the Broncos' original yellow-and-brown uniforms were among the ugliest ever in sports — especially with those infamous vertically striped socks.

▲

The Bottom Line on Mile High Stadium

Address: 1900 Eliot St., Denver, CO 80204. (303) 649-9000.

Tickets: Generally a high-drawing team, the Broncos are sure to sell out their single game tickets even more quickly after their Super Bowl win. Even with the Lombardi trophy in Denver, season tickets can be had in this lifetime. The waiting list runs about 10,000 names deep, which means anywhere from two to five years. Call (303) 433-7466 for ticket information.

1998: $42/$36/$34/$25/$20
1994: $38/$30/$19

Public Transportation: Denver's RTD buses stop at Federal Boulevard, right

Best of the Broncos

Best Team

1997 (16-4): Most felt Mike Shanahan's club would be in Super Bowl XXXII, but the Broncos failed to win the AFC West—putting John Elway and company on the road for most of the playoffs. After avenging their '96 loss to the Jaguars, Denver rode the legs of RB Terrell Davis to wins at Kansas City and Pittsburgh, then capped the year with a very Super 31-24 surprise of the defending champion Packers.

Greatest Players by Position

Pos:	Player
QB:	John Elway
RB:	Terrell Davis
WR:	Lionel Taylor
TE:	Shannon Sharpe
OL:	Keith Bishop
DL:	Rich Jackson
LB:	Tom Jackson
DB:	Dennis Smith
P/K:	Rich Karlis
ST:	Rick Upchurch

And Don't Forget...

RB: Otis Armstrong. In just his second season (1974), he led the NFL in rushing—the last Bronco to accomplish that feat.

RB: Floyd Little. The Broncos' "franchise" during his nine seasons, Floyd was a star on offense and also excelled as a return artist.

DB: Austin "Goose" Gonsoulin. One of the original Broncos, this ball-hawk picked off 43 passes during his seven years in Denver.

CB: Louis Wright. A five-time Pro Bowler with a nose for the ball (37 takeaways), he was a star in the Denver secondary for 12 years.

LB/DE: Karl Mecklenburg. A twelfth-round draft choice who made the most of his abilities, Mecklenburg was named to six Pro Bowls.

DL: Simon Fletcher. One of the great sack artists of the '80s and '90s, he never went to the Pro Bowl.

Best Argument

Linebacker: Tom Jackson or Randy Gradishar? In today's game, there are linebackers who can get to the opposing quarterback on a consistent basis, or out-muscle a tight end down the field. The versatile Jackson could do both well. He was complemented by the relentless Gradishar, who never missed a game in 10 seasons and is the franchise's all-time leader in tackles.

> "Half a loaf is better than none at all." — Head coach Lou Saban in 1971, after his unpopular decision to run out the clock on a 10-10 tie with Miami rather than go for the win.

Best Coach

Dan Reeves (1981-92): Best remembered for three Super Bowl losses and his rocky relationship with John Elway, Reeves probably doesn't get enough credit for making the Broncos a consistent playoff contender during his tenure. Criticized for his stubborn nature, the one-time Cowboys assistant did plenty without an abundance of on-field talent, but the lack of talent eventually proved his undoing.

Pressbox

Who to Read...

Colorado's biggest newspaper is the *Denver Post*, where Broncos fans will find everything they need, including expansive Sunday football coverage. The city's most popular writer is *Post* columnist Woody Paige, who has been around Denver longer than any other sports columnist. "Expansive" is probably an understatement; exhaustive may be more like it. The *Post's* sports section on gamedays gets into every nook and cranny of Broncodom, with Adam Schefter and Joe Sanchez leading the way. Clay Latimer and Bob Kravitz at the *Rocky Mountain News* do a good job, too, but they just can't match the *Post* for the sheer amount.

Who to Watch...

KCNC–CBS is televising the Broncos games in 1998. But some would say the Broncos TV station is KUSA–NBC. "The Mike Shanahan Show," a weekly team update after the usual model, is aired on KUSA. KUSA also televises "One on One with John Elway" Sundays at 10:35 pm and "Broncos Tonight" at 10:45 pm, hosted by Kevin Corke.

Who to Listen To...

For sports talk radio, tune into KOA (850 AM), the Broncos flagship station. It is home to talk-show hosts Dave Logan, Scott Hastings and Lou from Littleton, three personalities whose sphere of influence extends over the entire Denver area. KOA also broadcasts a three-hour pre-game show on game days. KTLK (760 AM), a sister station of KOA, features sport talk show hosts Irv Brown and Joe Williams.

by the stadium. Call (303) 299-6000 for more information.

Parking: The stadium has 10,000 spaces. Eight dollars for cars and $16 for RVs. There is additional parking at Auraria College, within walking distance of the stadium.

Capacity: 76,078.

Restrooms: 37 men's, 39 women's.

Where to Go . . . in Denver

Best Bars

Best sports bar. Within walking distance of McNichols Arena and Mile High Stadium, **Brooklyn's** is known for its half-pound burgers. It gets a big crowd for the Avalanche, Broncos and every sporting event except the Denver Nuggets. *2644 W. Colfax Ave. (303) 572-3999. Seven days 11am-11pm, open later on game nights.*

Best sports bar II. Jackson's All American Sports Rock is known as the best place to view sporting events because it has 60 small-screen TVs and 10 big screens. And it's located right across from home plate at Coors Field. *1520 20th St. (303) 298-7625. M, Tu, Th 11am-midnight, W, F, Sa 11am-2am, Su 11am-10:30pm.*

Best bar in a cool old building. Another popular sports bar, **Zang's Brewing Company** is housed in a brick building from the mid-19th century. Also not far from Mile High Stadium, Zang's has lots of memorabilia, televisions and the occasional visit from a jock. *2301 Seventh St. (303) 455-2500. M-Sa 11-2am, Su 11am-10pm.*

Best single malt selection. Denver's original brewpub, **Wynkoop Brewing Company**, sits in the heart of lower downtown. It serves eclectic food and features the state's biggest single-malt scotch selection. Not a big TV place, but there is an upstairs with more pool tables than football fans could ever want. *1634 18th St., (303) 297-2700. M-Sa 11am-2am, Su 10am-midnight.*

did you know?

Broncos quarterback Marlin Briscoe became the first African-American to play quarterback on a regular basis in pro football.

Swami Sez:

To John Elway, Terrell Davis, and all of the Denver Broncos...from all of your friends in the AFC..."Thank you."

Best Restaurants

Best basic fare. Always packed for Broncos games, **Sports Column** is a gathering place for sporting events. On Super Bowl Sunday '98, it opened its doors at 11 am, but there was a line at 8:30 am. There's basic bar fare, with some pastas and burritos. *1930 Blake St. (303) 296-1930. Seven days 11am-2am. All major credit cards. $*

Best Bronco sighting. For after the game, folks in search of a hearty hot meal can find it at **Carmine's on Penn.** They serve

Ready For Primetime (Monday Night)

October, 15 1984: Another snowy evening in Denver as a storm made it interesting from the get-go. The Broncos bolted to a 14-0 lead just thirty-seven seconds into the game as a pair of fumbles on Green Bay's first two plays from scrimmage were returned for scores by Broncos DBs Steve Foley and Louis Wright. The rest of the night belonged to the Packers offense, which racked up the yards but never enough points. Broncos 17, Packers 14.

Overall Monday night: 16-20-1
Overall Thursday night: 0-1
Overall Sunday night: 10-8

Think About the Weather

November 11, 1979: Mile High Stadium was engulfed by a blizzard, but it was the Patriots who got snowed under early on as Red Miller's Broncos bolted to a 24-0 first-quarter advantage and owned a 38-7 lead at halftime. Rumor has it that a groggy Steve Grogan, under heavy fire from the Broncos' defense, returned to the huddle and started calling plays dating back to his college days. Broncos 45, Patriots 10.

Worst Team

1963 (2-11-1): Though the season got off to an ominous start with a 59-7 loss to the Chiefs, the team evened its mark at 2-2. But a 50-34 win over San Diego in the first week of October would be the team's last taste of victory for more than a year. Coach Jack Faulkner not only failed to win the rest of the way, but his painful streak only ended due to his dismissal just four games into the '64 season.

Hall of Fame

Willie Brown	(DB 1984)
Doak Walker	(HB 1986)
Stan Jones	(G 1991)
Fred Gerkhe	(GM 1972)

Team Leaders

Rushing Yards
6,323   Floyd Little, 1967-75

Passing Yards
48,669   John Elway, 1983-present

Passing Touchdowns
278   John Elway, 1983-present

Receptions
543   Lionel Taylor, 1960-65

Interceptions
44   Steve Foley, 1976-86

Touchdowns
54   Floyd Little, 1967-75

Points
742   Jim Turner, 1971-79

pasta, chicken, veal and seafood in enormous portions. Some of the Broncos players like to eat here after the game. *92 S. Pennsylvania. (303) 777-6443. Tu-Su 5:30-10:30 pm. All major credit cards. $$*

did you know?

The first of John Elway's many fourth-quarter comeback performances came on December 11, 1983, against the Colts, the team that had originally drafted him. Elway threw three touchdown passes in the final period, the last of which came with forty-four seconds remaining, to earn a 21-19 win.

Best brunch. Take a drive out to Golden, where the **Briarwood Inn** offers a fine Continental menu and one of the area's best brunches. The pastries are excellent, as is the view. *1630 Eighth St., Golden. (303) 279-3121. Lunch: M-F 11am-2pm, Su 10:30am-2:30pm, dinner: Seven days 5-11pm. AE, DC, MC, V. $$$*

Best buffalo. Denver is definitely where the buffalo roam, especially at **Denver Buffalo Co.**, where you can chow down on all sorts of buffalo dishes, from steaks to chili. *1109 Lincoln St. (303) 832-0880. M-Th 10am-9pm, F-Sa 10am-10pm, Su 4-9pm. All major credit cards. $$$*

Best Accommodations

Ramada Inn Mile High Stadium. Not the most glamorous hotel, but the location cannot be beat. It's right across from Mile High Stadium. *1975 Bryant. (303) 433-8331. $*

While You Were Eating Turkey

Before Thanksgiving day games became fixtures in Detroit and Dallas, the Broncos played the New York Titans on November 22, 1962, at what was then Bears Stadium in Denver. The crowd size guaranteed that no Thanksgiving tradition would emerge in the Mile High City. In front of 15,776, the Titans beat the Broncos, 46-45.
Overall, 1-6

Fans' notes

On Screen

For all the on-the-field excitement the Broncos have provided in recent years, they have made few appearances in the world of film and national television, aside from John Elway's public-service announcements promoting reading. In animated form, however, the team was featured in an episode of TV's **The Simpsons**: As a token of his gratitude toward clueless henchman Homer Simpson, Goldfinger-style villain Hank Scorpio gives him a football franchise. Upon finding the Broncos playing on his front lawn, Homer expresses his disappointment — a sentiment now dated by Denver's Super Bowl XXXII victory.

Fight Song, Etc.

Football fans should note that Gary Glitter's "Rock and Roll Part II," now a sports anthem around the country, was first played at Mile High Stadium in the mid '80s. Yeah, it's dumb, but a first is a first.

Bookshelf

Broncos: Three Decades of Football. Joseph Hession and Michael Spence (PGW, 1987).
Meck for the Defense: A Championship Season with the Denver Broncos. Karl Mecklenburg (McGraw-Hill, 1987).
Mile High: The Story of Lyle Alzado and the Amazing Denver Broncos. Lyle Alzado with Paul Zimmerman (Macmillan, 1978).
Orange Madness: The Incredible Odyssey of the Denver Broncos. Woodrow Paige (Ty Crowell Co., 1978).

John Elway: Armed and Dangerous. Clay Latimer (Addax Publishing Group, 1997).
Reeves: An Autobiography. Dan Reeves and Dick Connor (Bonus Books, 1988).

> "I'm sure people will believe I'm crazy. But if you're asking me who's going to win this Super Bowl, I say Denver wins. I think we will this time."
> — Broncos owner Pat Bowlen the week before Denver played Green Bay in Super Bowl XXXII. (1998)

You Gotta See...

▶Nearby **Coors Field**, one of the proud new additions to the major-league circuit, is the home of the homer-happy Colorado Rockies. If you can't get enough beer there, you can tour the **Coors factory**, a short drive away in Golden.

▶The stadium may be a mile high, but it's flat. The Rocky Mountain scenery is breathtaking and the skiing world class in places like **Vail**, **Breckenridge**, **Beaver Creek** and **Copper Mountain**, less than a two-hour drive from Denver.

▶In the heart of Denver, the **16th Street Mall** is the city's main shopping attraction. The picturesque, pedestrian-friendly street is lined with shops and restaurants and culminates in **Larimer Square** on one end. It's easy to get around the area; a free bus runs the length of the strip.

Against the Odds

Not much is ever expected out of a player selected in the twelfth and final round of the draft. And not even the Broncos could have imagined that **Karl Mecklenburg** (1983-1994) would provide such a high level of play for over a decade. The durable LB/DE appeared in 184 games, finishing his career second in team history with 79 sacks and 1,145 tackles. A consistent presence in Denver's defense, the 12-year veteran failed to surpass the 100-tackle total only once from 1986-92.

Loews Giorgio Hotel. The most glamorous hotel in Denver, though its location on the outskirts of the city can be beat. *4150 E. Mississippi Ave. (303) 782-9300. $$-$$$*

Westin Hotel Tabor Center. Located one block from Denver's historic Larimer Square and a short trip away from Mile High Stadium. Sometimes, opposing teams even stay here. *1672 Lawrence St. (303) 572-9100. $$$*

> **"I can't keep the shelves full."**
> **—The Denver area distributor of Orange Crush soft drink in 1977, after local sportscaster Bob Kurtz nick-named the Broncos' defense "The Orange Crush."**

Detroit Lions

The owner of the Detroit Lions, William Clay Ford, is married to Martha Firestone. No wonder Barry Sanders's motor is always running and his wheels never seem to wear out. The Lions running back is one of the truly electrifying performers in NFL history. In nine NFL seasons, Sanders has set the standard for both durability and likability. His record-breaking career will ultimately define what NFL fans remember about Detroit's pro football franchise in the last quarter-century. In fact, Sanders could be remembered as the Walter Payton of the Motor City if he accomplishes one more elusive feat—carrying the Lions to a Super Bowl title.

Franchise History

Portsmouth Spartans
(1930–33)
Detroit Lions
(1934–present)

Lions fans, some of the most loyal in pro football, have been waiting more than four decades for a championship season. In the 1950s, the Lions dominated pro football, winning four division titles and three NFL championships. Under head coach Buddy Parker, Detroit won back-to-back championships in 1952 and 1953.

By the Numbers

(Since 1970)

Regular Season: 193-227-4
Postseason: 1-8
Division Titles: 3
Vs. Division: 97-107-2 (Playoffs: 0-3)
Playoff Appearances: 8
Home: 123-88-1
Away: 70-139-3

(Overall)

Regular Season: 435-446-32
Postseason: 7-9
Playoff Appearances: 13
Home: 268-185-14
Away: 167-261-18

The core of those teams landed in the Hall of Fame, including defensive back Jack Christiansen, running back Doak Walker and quarterback Bobby Layne. Four years later, the Lions won their third NFL crown of the decade with another stellar class of Hall of Famers, including Joe Schmidt, the terrifying linebacker who led the Lions' stingy defense.

Lions fans had come to expect excellence. Detroit won the NFL championship in 1935, its second year in the league. It's no wonder the Lions, after two unsuccessful incarnations as the Wolverines and Panthers, caught on

Most Revered Football Figures

Bobby Layne. He could drink in the morning and lead a comeback in the afternoon. Some say the Lions haven't had a quarterback since he left.
Joe Schmidt. New York had Huff and Chicago had Butkus. In Detroit, Schmidt was the middle linebacker and still is.
Barry Sanders. If he isn't the best running back of all time, he's definitely among the most fun to watch.

Rivalries

Some of the Lions' most memorable games have come against the Green Bay **Packers**, but two were heartbreaking. The Lions lost, 9-7, at Green Bay in 1962 when Herb Adderley intercepted a Milt Plum pass. After the game, Alex Karras threw his helmet at Plum's head in the locker room. In 1993, the Lions lost, 28-24, in a playoff game when Brett Favre found Sterling Sharpe all alone in the end zone with 55 seconds left. The Packers lead the series, 71-59-7. Beginning in the late '60s, the Lions lost 24 games straight to the **Vikings** that didn't let up until 1979. Minnesota's advantage came down a notch after they moved to the Metrodome, but they still lead the series, 44-27-2. The Lions' match-up with the **Bears** is the longest continuous rivalry in the NFL. Plenty of Bears fans make the five-hour trip to Silverdome every year. The Bears lead this series, 76-55-5, although the Lions have fared better in recent years.

did you know?

The Lions lost both the highest scoring post-season tilt in NFL history — 58-37 to the Eagles in the '95 wild card game — and the lowest scoring, 5-0, to Dallas in the 1970 NFC divisional playoffs.

quickly. Another reason they became popular was the marketing genius of the team's first owner, G.A. Richards. In 1934, realizing his newly acquired team was a poor cousin to the baseball Tigers in Detroit, Richards staged a Thanksgiving Day game against the undefeated, defending champion Chicago Bears. Richards convinced NBC Radio to carry the game on its 94-station national network, and 26,000 fans jammed into the University of Detroit Stadium to see the game. Many thousands more were turned away at the gate. The Bears won, 19-16, but pro football on Thanksgiving Day became an American birthright. For the Lions it became more than just a publicity stunt. Between Bobby Layne and Barry Sanders, playing football on Thanksgiving defined the Lions more than anything else.

Swami Sez:

In 1997, Barry Sanders leapt over Marcus Allen, Franco Harris, Jim Brown, Tony Dorsett and Eric Dickerson. The only ones left are Walter Payton and the moon.

In 1975, the Lions came in from the cold, coarse Michigan winter and started playing in the Silverdome, about 30 miles north of Detroit. Indoor football was perfectly suited for a new kind of Lions team, featuring a quick-strike aerial assault. But Detroit could not settle on a reliable quarterback. The list of starting signal callers over a 12-year period reads like a Who's Who of backups: Joe Reed, Greg Landry,

Jeff Komlo, Eric Hipple, Chuck Long, Rusty Hilger, Rodney Peete, Erik Kramer and Dave Krieg.

In 1989, head coach Wayne Fontes drafted Sanders. Down the road, the Lions added wide receivers Herman Moore and Brett Perriman, and signed a slingshot-armed quarterback named Scott Mitchell in 1994. The top-rated offense put the Lions in the playoffs for the third straight year in 1995. But in Fontes' 10 years at the helm, the Lions only won one playoff game. He was replaced by former San Diego Chargers head coach Bobby Ross. In 1997, Sanders ran for an historic 2,053 yards, capturing his second straight NFL rushing title, but, once again the Lions were bounced from the playoffs in the first round. This time the culprits were the upstart Tampa Bay Buccaneers, division rivals who have overtaken Detroit as heirs to the NFC Central crown — unless Sanders can come to the rescue again.

—Sal Paloantonio

The Silverdome

Located in Pontiac, about a half-hour north of Detroit, the Silverdome was built for football in 1975. It has 80,311 seats and an air-supported, Teflon-fiberglass dome. There's not a bad seat in the place, and it gets loud when the Lions have a sellout crowd, but it really doesn't have a unique atmosphere to call its own. Although there's nothing wrong with the stadium, the Lions plan to move into a new stadium being built in downtown Detroit sometime in the early 21st century. Unlike Tiger

did you know?

The last eight Lions former head coaches — Harry Gilmer, Joe Schmidt, Don McCafferty, Rick Forzano, Tommy Hudspeth, Monte Clark, Darryl Rogers and Wayne Fontes — never held a head coaching job in the NFL after leaving the Lions. The last to get another job after leaving Detroit was George Wilson, the coach of the expansion Miami Dolphins.

The "I Was There" Game

December 22, 1957: The Lions trailed San Francisco, 27-7, in the third quarter of this Western Conference Playoff contest. Fired up by the fact that the Niners were whooping it up at halftime in their locker room, the Lions' rallied, sparked by a pair of second-half TD runs by RB Tom Tracy. They went on to win, 31-27. This comeback was a postseason NFL record until 1992, when the Bills erased a 32-point lead against the Oilers, also in a playoff game.

The Paper Bag Game

December 26, 1970: The Lions went to Dallas as a wild-card team riding a five-game winning streak with visions of greatness. They lost, 5-0, and it took them a decade to recover.

Great Names

Anthony Arena (C 1942-46)
Cloyce Box (WR 1949-50, 1952-54)
Dan Bunz (LB 1985)
Howard "Hopalong" Cassady (HB/FL, 1956-61, 63)
John Ford (WR 1989)
Joe Don Looney (RB 1965-66)
Willie McGee (WR 1978)
Eddie Murray (K 1980-91)
Jon Staggers (WR 1975)
Altie Taylor (RB 1969-75)

Our Top Story

"Lions Pound Browns for Title"

Dec. 29, 1957

Three years after coming up on the short end of a 56-10 title game drubbing at Cleveland's hands, the Lions returned the favor with a 59-14 walloping in Detroit. A broken ankle sidelined quarterback Bobby Layne for the game, so it was back-up Tobin Rote who led the charge for Detroit.

"Wayne's World"

Dec. 23, 1995

With a 37-10 road win over the Buccaneers, the Lions completed a turnaround which brought them from 2-5 to 10-6 and a wild-card berth. Head coach Wayne Fontes, whose job was in danger while the team struggled, had earned himself another season at the helm. The party didn't last long, though: the Lions were eliminated by the Eagles the next week, and Fontes departed after a 5-11 campaign in 1996.

"Bittersweet Victory"

Dec. 21, 1997

The Lions and their fans were not able to fully enjoy what should have been a great day for the franchise. In a season-ending game against the New York Jets, Barry Sanders became the third running back in NFL history to rush for 2,000 yards in a single season. The victory also put the team in the playoffs. Sadly, second-year linebacker Reggie Brown was injured while making a tackle and nearly died on the field. Brown retained limited use of his arms and legs but his football career was over.

did you know?

Eight Heisman Trophy winners have played for the Lions: Frank Sinkwich, Doak Walker, Leon Hart, Howard "Hopalong" Cassady, Steve Owens, Billy Sims, Barry Sanders and Andre Ware. Alas, another Heisman winner, Gino Torretta, was on the practice squad but never played.

Stadium, fans aren't really sad about Silverdome's passing because they were never truly attached to it.

There aren't any bad seats, but there are a few La-Z-Boy style recliners in the south end zone that make for either comfy viewing or sleeping, depending on how the Lions are doing. Detroit fans are quick to voice their displeasure when things aren't going well, and quarterback Scott Mitchell has been a frequent target of the boo-birds. In 1976, the fans actually cheered a Tampa Bay touchdown when the Bucs were still winless, but the Lions won the crowd back with a late rally to win. Unfortunately, Detroit is one of the few places on earth where The Wave is still hip — fans always try to get one going, and they sometimes succeed. Their timing isn't always the best, though. Last season, some fans did The Wave while safety Harry Colon was lying on the Silverdome turf, having sustained a career-ending neck injury. At least one fight — and sometimes several — usually erupts in the stands during every home game. There was a media outcry after the Silverdome security staff

> "I'm Billy Sims from Oklahoma and I'm the reason you guys didn't get any raises this year." — Billy Sims, on his first day of training camp as a highly paid rookie. (1980)

allegedly took its sweet time responding to a fight at one game, but there are times when the action off the field is better than what's taking place on it.

Best of the Lions

Best Team

1952 (11-3): Buddy Parker's team hardly looked like championship material after dropping two of their first three games, including a 28-0 loss at home to the 49ers. But the Lions were nearly unstoppable the rest of the year, dropping only a one-point decision in Chicago. They scored more than 40 points in each of their last three regular-season contests before besting the Rams and Browns in the postseason.

Greatest Players by Position

Pos:	Player
QB:	Bobby Layne
RB:	Barry Sanders
WR:	Herman Moore
TE:	Charlie Sanders
OL:	Lou Creekmur
DL:	Alex Karras
LB:	Joe Schmidt
DB:	Lem Barney
P/K:	Eddie Murray
ST:	Yale Lary

And Don't Forget...

DB/KR: Jack Christiansen. He played in 89 games for the Lions and not only picked off 46 passes but returned eight punts for scores. The best among many great Lions kick returners, including Mel Gray.
LB: Mike Lucci. A hard-nosed defender who began his career with the Browns but made his biggest impact in the Motor City.
RB: Billy Sims. He took the league by storm as a rookie in 1980, and who knows what his legacy would have been had he stayed healthy.
DT: Doug English. Four-time all-star and an underrated force up front for the Lions' defense in the mid 1970s and early '80s.
C/DB: Alex Wojciechowicz. One of the league's early iron men, who played both ways during most of his nine seasons with the Lions.
CB: Dick LeBeau. These days he's the defensive coordinator for the Bengals, but for 14 seasons he was the Lions' "other" corner, first opposite Dick "Night Train" Lane, then Lem Barney.
LB: Wayne Walker. Steady performer at outside linebacker for 14 years, many alongside Joe Schmidt. He was also the placekicker for a couple of years.
DE: Al "Bubba" Baker. A great pass rushing force on some not-so-great Lions teams.

Best Argument

Linebacker: Joe Schmidt or Chris Spielman? Schmidt was a seventh-round pick in 1953, was named All-Pro eight times in 13 seasons, team MVP four times and is a member of the Hall of Fame. Spielman was a star at Ohio State, but some thought he wasn't suited for the pro game. All he did was lead the Lions in tackles in each of his eight years with the club.

Best Coach

Raymond "Buddy" Parker (1951-56): Though his stay in the Motor City lasted but six years (Parker resigned just before the start of the '57 season), he would make the most of his days with the franchise. Parker led a talented Lions squad to consecutive NFL titles in 1952 and '53 and a total of three straight championship game appearances.

Pressbox

Who to Read...

Three daily newspapers cover the Lions — the *Detroit Free Press*, *Detroit News* and *Oakland (County) Press*. Booth Newspapers, a six-newspaper group in southern Michigan, also provide Lions news and game coverage. The best-known Detroit writer is Mitch Albom of the *Free Press*. Another of the Detroit area's top columnists is Keith Langlois of the *Oakland Press*, whose knowledgeable and insightful columns stand out. Of the beat writers, Mike O'Hara of the *News* and Curt Sylvester of the *Free Press* are the Siskel and Ebert of pro football.

Who to Watch...

Booth Newspapers writer Tom Kowalski also works for WJBK-TV, the Fox station that carries most of the Lions' games. Even though Coach Ross has no TV show at the moment, there are a half-dozen players who make regular TV or radio appearances.

Who to Listen To...

Tom Kowalski also works for WDFN (1130 AM), a station known as The Fan. Quarterback Scott Mitchell has a show on WDFN. Coach Ross has a radio show on WXYT (1270 AM), the Lions' flagship station. He bristles at times when he is reminded of the Lions' sorry history, something he wasn't part of. Other Lions of the airwaves have included Luther Elliss, Robert Porcher, Tommy Vardell, and Herman Moore, who has a show Mondays at 7 pm on WXYT. The station also has a three hour pre-game show on game day as well as a two hour post game show.

> **"If you want a messenger, call Western Union." — FB Joe Don Looney**, in response to coach Harry Gilmer's request that he bring in a play. Looney was released soon after his remark.

The Silverdome isn't known for its great cuisine. The nachos aren't bad, but the hot dogs are boiled and usually undercooked. The best advice is to load up on junk food, then eat after the game. All 38 concession stands have TV sets. Fans can also view the game from The Main Event, the Silverdome's restaurant in the north end of the stadium.

Tailgating and touch football are a staple of the Lions' parking lot, but there's not a lot of flair, possibly because it pales in comparison to the tailgating that takes place in Ann Arbor and East Lansing the day before. With the Tigers, Red Wings, Pistons, Michigan Wolverines and Michigan State Spartans in the area, the Lions might face more competition for the sports entertainment dollar than any other NFL team.

The Bottom Line on The Silverdome

Address: 1200 Featherstone Rd, Pontiac, MI 48342

Tickets: Since it's the NFL's biggest stadium, there's never a rush for season or individual-game tickets. The Lions restricted out-of-town orders this past season after Green Bay fans snapped up 40,000 tickets for the 1996 game, making the Lions' 31-3 loss seem like a Packers home game. The stadium is wheelchair accessible, with ramps leading to entrances and special seating arrangements. For information, call (248) 335-4151.

did you know?

Be it in D.C. proper or simply near the nation's capital, Detroit's 30-7 loss to the Redskins at Jack Kent Cooke Stadium in '97 dropped the Lions' lifetime record in Washington (including playoffs) to a perfect 0-19.

1998: $35/$20/$15/$12.50

1994: $37/$30/$12.50

Public Transportation: This is auto country, so just about the only public transportation you'll find is the shuttle bus service that runs between Phoenix Plaza in downtown Pontiac and the stadium.

Parking: Since the Lions rarely sell out, traffic usually isn't a problem, but it is advisable to get to the Silverdome at least 90 minutes before game time. The stadium is surrounded by a 100-acre pre-paid lot which holds 10,500 cars and 500 buses; prices are $10 for regular parking, $20 for reserved.

Capacity: 80,368.

Restrooms: 44.

Where to Go . . . in Detroit

Best Bars

Best place to B. Beer, Barca-Loungers and big-screen TVs fill **Mr. B's Spectadium**, making it a great place to watch a game. *2511 Livernois, Troy. (248) 362-4030. M-Sa, 11am-2am, Su, 12pm-12am.*

Ready For Primetime (Monday Night)

October 19, 1981: In the season's seventh week, injuries forced Lions' head coach Monte Clark to start little-used Eric Hipple at quarterback, and the second-year pro made quite a splash. Hipple finished the evening with 336 yards and four touchdowns, as well as two rushing TDs. Lions 48, Bears 17. In 1994 and 1995, the Lions beat the defending Super Bowl champions on Monday night. The Cowboys gave up 194 yards to Barry Sanders and went down in overtime, 20-17, and the next year the 49ers lost, 27-24.

Overall Monday night: 10-11-1

Overall Thursday night: 0-1

Overall Sunday night: 3-6

Think About the Weather

December 15, 1991: In the Silverdome era, the Lions have proven to be a formidable opponent at home and less-than-imposing in the elements. In the season's next-to-last game, Wayne Fontes's club had yet to win outdoors all year, and the windchill at Lambeau Field this day would reach negative 18 degrees. A big goalline stand by the Lions' defense preserved the victory. Lions 21, Packers 17. Before the Silverdome, the worst game was probably the Mud Bowl, the 1968 Thanksgiving Day game played in an all-day downpour. Sam Baker kicked four field goals for Philadelphia, which won 12-0.

Worst Team

1942 (0-11): No matter how good your defense may be, it's hard to win when you can't find the end zone or even manage a field goal. These Lions tallied a paltry 38 points (tied for the second-fewest in one season in NFL history), never more than seven in a game and were shut out five times. It's worth noting that just one year later (1943), Detroit scored 35 points on opening day in a win over the Cardinals.

> ### did you know?
> Former Supreme Court justice Byron "Whizzer" White was an All-League selection in 1940, leading the Lions in passing, rushing and scoring. He also played for Detroit in 1941 before retiring.

> "Yes, I have bet on ballgames."
> — Alex Karas on the *Huntley-Brinkley Report*.

Team Leaders

Rushing Yards
13,778   Barry Sanders, 1989-present
Passing Yards
15,710   Bobby Layne, 1950-1958
Passing Touchdowns
118   Bobby Layne, 1950-1958
Receptions
528   Herman Moore, 1991-1997
Interceptions
62   Dick LeBeau, 1959-1972
Touchdowns
105   Barry Sanders, 1989-present
Points
1,113   Eddie Murray, 1980-1991

Best place to get crabs. A seafood tavern run by a former pro football player, **Fran O'Brien's Maryland Crabhouse** serves Maryland blue crabs and stone crab claws in season. The other food is good, too, and it's close to the Dome. *621 S. Opdyke Rd., Auburn Hills. (248) 332-7744. M-F, 11am-10pm, Sa, 3pm-11pm, Su, 3pm-9:30pm.*

Best basics. Bo's Brewery and Bistro offers steaks, ribs, pasta, fish and home-brewed beer. *51 N. Saginaw, Pontiac. (248) 338-6200. M-F, 11am-2am, Sa-Su 12pm-2am.*

Best Restaurants

Best riverside eats. There are other good restaurants scenically located along the Detroit River, but the surf-and-turf and sandwiches at **Sindbads** are just a little bit more reasonable. *100 St. Clair St. (313) 822-7817. Winter hours: 7 days 11am-2am. Summer hours: Su-Th 11am-12am, F-Sa 11am-2am. All major credit cards. $$*

Best apres-ski. At the **Big Buck Brewery and Steak House**, you'll get big beer and big steaks in a big room with the atmosphere of a ski lodge. *2550 Takata Dr., Auburn Hills. (248) 276-2337. M-F 11am-11pm, Sa 12pm-11pm, Su 12pm-10pm. All major credit cards. $$$.*

Best expense account spot. If you like thick steaks, big cigars and high prices, head to **Don Shula's Steakhouse** in the Troy Marriott. *200 W. Big Beaver Rd., Troy. (248) 680-9797. M-Th 5:30-10:30pm, F-Sa*

> "Every man is entitled to one mistake in a lifetime. I made mine when I left the Lions." — Buddy Parker, in 1958.

Fans' notes

On Screen

The Lions were immortalized in the 1968 movie **Paper Lion,** starring a pre-M*A*S*H Alan Alda as George Plimpton. Plimpton had spent a training camp with the Lions, an experience which culminated in one truly ugly series as quarterback in a preseason game. The movie launched the film career of Alex Karras, who might be the best player who isn't in the Hall of Fame — his yearlong suspension for his role in a gambling scandal even kept the Lions from retiring his number. After his playing career ended, Karras went on to such work as Monday Night Football, the TV sitcom **Webster** and movies such as **Blazing Saddles,** **Victor/Victoria** and **Porky's**.

Fight Song, Etc.

Even if championships have been hard to come by in the last several decades, the Lions have had their heroes. It seems significant these days that "Gridiron Heroes: The Victory Song of the Detroit Lions" focuses on offense rather than on defense. "Forward down the field/A charging team that will not yield," the song goes.

Bookshelf

Lions' Pride: 60 Years of Detroit Lions Football. Edited by Mike Murray (Taylor Publishing 1993).
Detroit Lions. Jerry Green (Macmillan 1975).
Paper Lion. George Plimpton (Harper 1966). Participatory journalism at its best, this was one of the first books to prove that sport was a worthy subject for literature. Professional dilettante Plimpton learned that football is even harder than it looks.
Even Big Guys Cry. Alex Karras with Herb Glade. (HRW 1977). The playing memoirs of one of the biggest guys ever.
Tuesday Night Football: A Novel. Alex Karras and Douglas Graham (Birch Lane Press, 1991).

Paraphernalia

The Lions are one of the lowest-grossing teams in terms of logoed merchandise. Red Wings car flags and Michigan T-shirts far outnumber Barry Sanders jerseys in Motown.

You Gotta See...

▸The **Lindell AC**, on the corner of Cass and Michigan in downtown Detroit, was the Lions' hangout in the team's heyday. It's the place where Karras got into a fight with pro wrestler Dick the Bruiser, setting up a wrestling match during Karras's suspension in 1963. (The Bruiser sacked Karras easily.) It's also the place where Billy Martin got into a fight with pitcher Dave Boswell when both were with the Minnesota Twins. Plenty of nifty pictures, jerseys and other memorabilia adorn the walls.

▸It is the Motor City, so it's fitting that you can find the **Motorsports Museum and Hall of Fame America** near Detroit. It's located in Novi, a western suburb. Appropriately enough, you have to drive there.

▸Along with Boston's Fenway Park, Detroit's **Tiger Stadium** is the oldest baseball stadium in the majors. In season, it's a good place to catch a homer (if not a home team victory).

Hall of Fame

Earl "Dutch" Clark	(QB 1963)
Bill Dudley	(HB 1966)
Bobby Layne	(QB 1967)
Alex Wojciechowicz	(C 1968)
Jack Christiansen	(DB 1970)
Hugh McElhenny	(HB 1970)
Ollie Matson	(HB 1972)
Joe Schmidt	(LB 1973)
Dick Lane	(DB 1974)
Yale Lary	(DB 1979)
Frank Gatski	(C 1985)
Doak Walker	(HB 1986)
John Henry Johnson	(FB 1987)
Lem Barney	(DB 1992)
Lou Creekmur	(T/G 1996)

Against the Odds

It was a triumph over tragedy after **Mike Utley** (1989-91) suffered a paralyzing neck injury during a Nov. 17, 1991 victory over the Los Angeles Rams. As he was being carried off the field, Utley flashed a "Thumbs Up" sign which became not only the inspiration for the foundation he later started, but also gave his teammates the emotional lift that spurred them on to a franchise-record 12 victories and a surprising trip to the NFC championship game.

5:30-11pm, Su 5:30-10pm. All major credit cards. $$$$.

> **"If I had been to all the places and done all the things I'm supposed to have done, I'd have to be Superman."**
> **— Bobby Layne, on his reputation for fast living.**

Best Accommodations

Shorecrest Motor Inn. It's small, but it's affordable and within walking distance of the Renaissance Center and downtown Detroit. *1316 E. Jefferson Ave. (313) 568-3000. $*

Doubletree Guest Suites. Less than fifteen minutes from the Silverdome, this is where many visiting teams stay. *850 Tower Dr., Troy. (248) 879-2100. $$-$$$*

Townsend Hotel. Located in downtown Birmingham, about 20 miles south of Silverdome, this is the place to go stargazing. Barbra Streisand, Bruce Springsteen and Elton John, among others, have stayed here when they perform at the Silverdome. It's ritzy, posh and *tres* expensive. *100 Townsend St., Birmingham. (248) 642-7900. $$$$-$$$$$*

While You Were Eating Turkey

November 22, 1962: Lions 26, Packers 14. The Thanksgiving Day game is a grand Detroit tradition which began in 1934. Since then, the Lions' greatest Turkey Day glory came in 1962, when the undefeated Packers came to town. The 8-2 Lions reared up and sacked Bart Starr 11 times, sending that year's eventual NFL champs to an inglorious defeat. Detroit had a less grand Thanksgiving day against the Bears in 1980: Chicago's Vince Evans tied the game on the final play of regulation with a quarterback sneak, and Dave Williams returned the opening kickoff in overtime for a touchdown, giving the Bears a 23-17 victory.
Overall, 29-27-2.

Green Bay
Packers

At first glance, Mike Holmgren and Vince Lombardi couldn't appear more different. Lombardi was East Coast, old school, run the power sweep until they stop you. Holmgren is West Coast, with an innovative, quick-to-change offense. Yet their inner gyroscopes are very similar, powered by a fierce competitive drive and uncanny ability to judge character and talent. How did two men from such different traditions and different generations translate their unique skills into championship seasons?

The answer lies in the people of Green Bay, the stockholders of the most storied franchise in professional football. The Packers, the NFL 's only publicly owned franchise, play in the league's smallest market. Yet they have won more championships — 12 — than any other team in NFL history.

The Packers are also the only team in NFL history to win three titles in succession—they did it twice. The first dynasty was led by Earl L. (Curly) Lambeau, who in 1919 founded the Packers, named for the Indian Packing Company, which put up money for the team's first equipment. Lambeau, who preferred to play halfback, pioneered the forward pass in the NFL, making a star out of split end Don Hutson, whose record of 99 touchdown receptions stood for more than five decades. Under Lambeau, the Packers won six NFL titles — in 1929-31, 1936, 1939 and 1944.

A long drought followed. In 1957, the city fathers built a new state-of-the art stadium and, two years later, hired a coach who could fill it — Lombardi. By 1961, the Packers were back on top. This time, the passing game and its low-key leader, quarterback Bart Starr, played a

Franchise History

Green Bay Packers
(1921–present)

By the Numbers

(Since 1970)
Regular Season: 196-220-8
Postseason: 10-6
Division Titles: 4
Vs. Division: 100-99-4 (Playoffs: 3-0)
Playoff Appearances: 7
Home: 120-87-5
Away: 76-133-3

(Overall)
Regular Season: 540-440-36
Postseason: 22-9
Playoff Appearances: 18
Home: 311-180-6
Away: 229-260-20

Most Revered Football Figures

Vince Lombardi. Guided the Packers to five NFL championships in his final seven years, including Super Bowls I and II. In Lombardi's nine seasons in Green Bay, his teams posted a 98-30-4 record. The street on which Lambeau Field stands and the Super Bowl trophy both bear his name.

Brett Favre. The three-time MVP doesn't have a street named after him yet, but at his current rate, the people of Wisconsin may name an entire city after him.

Ray Nitschke. The tough man in the middle of Lombardi's great teams made Green Bay his home and the town loved him for it.

Rivalries

No two teams in NFL history have played each other more than the Packers and the Chicago **Bears** (81-68-6). The Illinois-Wisconsin border war dates back to 1921, when the Bears were known as the Chicago Staleys. The Bears went 13-2 from 1985-92; the Packers have returned the favor by going 10-1 since '92. Although the rivalry has simmered recently due to this one-sidedness, the mutual disdain remains. A fierce Packer rivalry has taken shape with the **Dallas Cowboys** (11-13). Both teams have enjoyed great success in the '90s with Dallas knocking Green Bay out of the playoffs three consecutive years (1993-95).

cameo role in an offense led by running backs Paul Hornung and Jim Taylor. World titles followed in 1962 and 1965-67, including the first two Super Bowl championships. Lombardi reached demigod status in Green Bay, but in 1965, in the midst of his championship run, the caretakers of the franchise elected to name the stadium after Lambeau. Then they refused to give Lombardi part ownership of the team, and he left for the Washington Redskins.

It would take nearly 30 years for the Packers to return to the Super Bowl. Many think the hiring of Holmgren was the turning point. However, it was really the June 5, 1989, decision by the stockholders at their annual meeting to hire Bob Harlan as president which allowed the Packers to enter the NFL's money era. Harlan immediately recognized that the small-market Packers could not compete against the Cowboys and 49ers on the field unless he could generate enough cash to compete with them in the free agent market. In August 1989, Harlan announced plans to build 1,920 club seats — an historic first at Lambeau — and 36 new sky boxes. Sales of those seats allowed the Packers to pay big money to big-money players—in particular, a free agent defensive end named Reggie White, who arrived in Green Bay in 1993. Harlan also hired personnel guru Ron Wolf, a longtime disci-

> ### did you know?
> The Packers are 12-0 in the postseason at home, with two of those wins in Milwaukee. They've outscored the opposition by a combined 329-128 in those dozen victories.

> "He's like a coach. But after a while you'd say, 'Ray, you got to stop smackin' me.'"
> — Reggie White, on Ray Nitschke's visits to the Packers locker room.

ple of the Raiders Al Davis, and Wolf hired Holmgren in 1992. That same year Wolf traded for three-time league MVP Brett Favre, who is fast becoming the most prolific quarterback in franchise history.

The result was two Super Bowl appearances — a victory in Super Bowl XXXI and a bitter loss in Super Bowl XXXII. Are there more championship seasons to come? White is near retirement. Holmgren, like Lombardi, wants more power and control. So keeping this group together to replicate the Lambeau and Lombardi dynasties won't be easy.

—Sal Paolantonio

Lambeau Field

What Fenway Park or Wrigley Field is to major league baseball, Lambeau Field is to professional football: the ultimate stadium.

did you know?

While no club has ever won three consecutive Super Bowls, the Packers are the only NFL team to win three straight championships. They turned the trick twice, 1929-31 and 1965-67.

Over the years, the Green Bay Packers organization has done a tremendous job of preserving the best of yesteryear, while also keeping pace with the modern state-of-the-art facilities being constructed across the country. In many ways, Lambeau's sidelines are just the way they were when Lombardi paced them.

Displayed prominently on the green iron siding between the floors of the stadium's private boxes are the names of the 19 Packer players and coaches who have been enshrined in Canton. Adding to the hallowed aura of the league's premier venue are the team's 12 championship years on

The "I Was There" Game

Jan. 14, 1968: The sight of Vince Lombardi being carried off the field at the Orange Bowl following Green Bay's methodical conquest of Oakland in Super Bowl II is one of football's great images. In his final game with the Pack, the legendary sideline boss watched and smiled as Bart Starr (Super Bowl MVP for a second straight year) and the defense came up big and wrapped up another world championship. Packers 33, Raiders 14.

The Paper Bag Game

January 14, 1996: Three years; three playoff trips to Irving, Texas; three disappointments. Unlike the 35-9 playoff drubbing administered by Dallas a year earlier, in this NFC Championship Game, the Packers came back to take a 27-24 lead on Brett Favre's third touchdown pass of the game. But during the fourth quarter, two Emmitt Smith touchdowns and Larry Brown's interception of a Favre pass sent Green Bay packing. Cowboys 38, Packers 27.

Great Names

Tony Bennett (LB 1990-93)
Johnny Blood (HB/DB/TB 1929-33, 1935-36)
Boob Darling (C 1927-31)
Charles "Buckets" Goldenberg (G/LB/BB/DB/FB 1933-45)
Clyde Goodnight (OE/DB 1945-49)
Baby Ray (T 1938-48)
Clarence Self (DB/HB 1952-55)
Joe Shield (QB 1986)
Jim Weatherwax (DT 1966-69)
Lyle "Cowboy" Wheeler (E 1921-23)

Our Top Story

`"Packers Survive"`

`1933`

After hard times and lawsuits nearly bankrupted the franchise, local residents came up with $15,000 to help save their team. The ownership of the Packers was divided into 600 shares, and the team survived its most serious brush with extinction.

`"Lombardi Comes to`
`Green Bay"`

`January 1959`

Faced with the prospect of abandoning the Packers franchise if its fortunes didn't turn around, league commissioner Bert Bell and Browns head coach Paul Brown suggest that the Packers hire Giants assistant coach Vince Lombardi. Green Bay went 7-5 in 1959, and Lombardi was a unanimous choice for Coach of the Year.

`"Starr Returns"`

`December 21, 1974`

Looking for a lift after several sluggish campaigns, the Packers turned over the responsibilities of head coach and general manager to local hero Bart Starr. But even the Pack's heroic quarterback proved unable to turn the team's fortunes completely around in the following decade.

`"Titletown USA, 1997"`

`January 27, 1997.`

The fine-tuned machine that Ron Wolf built and Mike Holmgren oiled brought the Vince Lombardi Trophy back to its home after 29 years. The Packers beat the Patriots 35-21.

did you know?

Hall-of-Fame running back Gale Sayers, of the much-hated Chicago Bears, is a Green Bay Packers shareholder.

display above the club seats in the south end-zone.

Tailgating here is the best in the league, hands down. Packers fans will pretty much invite anyone, with the exception of a Bears or Cowboys fan, to enjoy a beer and a brat. America's Pack, the team's official fan club, offers its members an all-you-can-eat-and-drink fiesta across the street from the stadium.

All seats have unobstructed views. However, Lambeau Field is all bench seating, though you can rent a seat-back for a couple of dollars. The worst seats are actually in the first ten rows behind each bench. These seats are so close to the playing surface that it's difficult to see over the players.

As for food, the cuisine at Lambeau is a lot like the modern touches. The brats are either the best or worst thing about the place. It's a subjective thing.

Still, Lambeau Field—at least certain aspects of it—has evolved into the type of stadium that Lombardi would have probably despised: Sony Jumbotrons. Luxury boxes. Hip-hop music and Michael Buffer during player introductions. Lombardi would enjoy these things about as much as he'd tolerate an Antonio Freeman end-zone dance.

The place is still special, though. Packers' President Bob Harlan sums up the affection many fans have for this gridiron landmark when he tells the story of a motor-home arriving from Kansas. "I was leaving the stadium one day and I stopped to watch

> "If I owned Green Bay, I'd dome the whole town."
> — Cowboys owner Clint Murchison in 1967, the year of the Ice Bowl.

Best of the Packers

Best Team

1962 (14-1): While the '96 edition of the Packers was the NFL's best team from start to finish that year, even they would be hard-pressed to outdo Vince Lombardi's second championship club, which opened the season with 10 straight victories and were tripped up just once all year—a memorable 26-14 loss at Detroit on Thanksgiving Day. Green Bay's staunch defense stifled the Giants 16-7 in the NFL title game.

Greatest Players by Position

Pos:	Player
QB:	Brett Favre
RB:	Jim Taylor
WR:	Don Hutson
TE:	Paul Coffman
OL:	Forrest Gregg
DL:	Willie Davis
LB:	Ray Nitschke
DB:	Herb Adderley
P/K:	Don Chandler
ST:	Desmond Howard

And Don't Forget...

RB: Paul Hornung. He literally did it all, and his 176 points scored in a season (1960) remains an NFL record that may never be broken.

WR: Sterling Sharpe. One of the game's most reliable and productive receivers, totaling 595 catches (65 TDs) in just seven seasons before a neck injury forced him to retire.

C: Jim Ringo. An anchor for Vince Lombardi's early title teams, seven of his 10 Pro Bowl appearances came while he was a Packer.

"He treated us all alike. Like dogs." — Henry Jordan on Vince Lombardi.

DB: Willie Wood. Eight-time Pro Bowler and a Hall of Famer, he was a key defender on Green Bay's five title teams of the 1960s.

WR: James Lofton. Caught 530 passes during his nine years with the Pack, and was one of the premier deep threats of his era.

Best Argument

Quarterback: Brett Favre or Bart Starr? From unwanted slacker in Atlanta to three straight league MVP awards, Favre has become the game's premier quarterback and perhaps its best player. Who knows where today's Pack would be without him? Starr was the right man in the right place and the field general for Vince Lombardi's title teams, playing his absolute best in the big games.

Swami Sez:

Despite the Super Bowl stunner, the Packers remain the heavies in the NFC. There aren't many (any???) better than their quarterback , their coach, or their fans on the frozen tundra.

Best Coach

Vince Lombardi (1959-67): The man who turned a small Wisconsin city into "Titletown," Lombardi came to Green Bay in 1959 and turned the Packers into the "Team of the '60s." He never suffered through a losing season, won five NFL titles during his nine-year stay with the club, and lost just one of ten postseason games.

Pressbox

Who to Read...

On the print side, the *Milwaukee Journal Sentinel* boasts perhaps the league's finest in-depth coverage. Bob McGinn, Tom Silverstein, and the rest of the convoy from Milwaukee intelligently dissect every aspect of the Packers. McGinn's most interesting tactic is getting feedback from opposing NFL scouts after each game. *Green Bay Press-Gazette* writers Chris Havel and Pete Dougherty also do a fine job covering the Packer beat. Havel, who co-authored Brett Favre's autobiography, is never afraid to follow a lead. The Packers are one of the few teams to boast multiple team newspapers. *Packer Plus* (published by the *Journal Sentinel*) and *Packer Report* are the best.

Who to Watch...

Although Green Bay weighs in as the 70th biggest media market in the country, the Packers are covered as extensively and thoroughly as any team in the league. Even so, no amount of television coverage would be considered exhaustive by the flannel-clad fanatics in northeast Wisconsin. WFRV–CBS's one-two punch of Larry McCarren (former Packer center in the late '70's and early '80's) and local media veteran John Maino provides Packer fans with probably the most entertaining analysis. Sports Director Bill Jartz and the rest of the crew at WBAY–ABC give solid all-around coverage and programs like "Monday Night Kickoff" with selected Packer guest hosts every season. Players regularly host their own shows as well—those who have recently include Mark Chmura, Antonio Freeman, Edgar Bennett, Brett Favre and LeRoy Butler.

Who to Listen To...

Many players have their own radio shows as well, and more appear as guests. Shows are carried on Green Bay's local all-sports station, WDUZ (1400 AM), as well as WNFL (1440 AM), WGEE (1360 AM) and WHBY (1150 AM) in nearby Appleton. The schedules change frequently, but recent hosts have included Packers trench soldiers Adam Timmerman and Bob Kubersky. Fans in Milwaukee listen to WTMJ (620 AM) and Jim Irwin, voice of the Packers, and Steve "The Homer" True on WISN (1130 AM). True is not really a homer, but his nightly sports talk show is heavy on the Packers during the season

because I like to see what their reaction will be. So the driver gets out — he's in his 50s — and the guy drops to his knees and starts bowing to the stadium."

The Bottom Line on Lambeau Field

Address: Green Bay Packers, 1265 Lombardi Ave., Green Bay, WI 54304. (920) 496-5700.

Tickets: Don't bother. If you must, the number is (920) 496-5719.

1998: $90/$44/$39/$36/$32

1994: $81/$33/$28/$24

Parking: Packers fans come early and stay late. Parking is plentiful at and around the stadium. Some of the best places for parking are in the driveways of neighborhood residents. They may charge you $10-$15, but that covers all the food and drink you can consume.

Extras: Besides shuttle buses from hotels, public transit is almost nonexistent.

Capacity: 60,790

Restrooms: 173 men's, 356 women's

Where to Go . . . in Green Bay

Best Bars

Best place to watch the game other than Lambeau. Take your pick between the **Stadium View** and the **50-Yard Line**. Each is located within a Lambeau Leap of the stadium. The Stadium View has more paraphernalia than Gilbert Brown has girth; both have beer, burgers, and more beer. What more could a Packers fan ask for? *Stadium View, 1963 Holmgren Way. (920) 498-1989, bar: M-Th, Su 10am-2am, F-Sa 10am-2:30am, kitchen: Seven days 11am-11pm. 50-Yard Line, 1049 Lombardi Access Rd. (920) 496-5857, bar: Seven days 11am-2am, kitchen: T-Sa 11am-11pm, Su-M 11am-10pm.*

Best place to hang with a guy named Fuzzy. Shenanigan's, a local establishment owned and operated by former Packer offensive lineman Fuzzy Thurston, is a nostalgic old joint where regulars meet to talk football and Lombardi's Packers come to reunite. *1261 S. Monroe Ave. (920) 432-9556. Seven days 11am-2am*

did you know?

Wide receiver Don Hutson caught a staggering 99 touchdown passes in only 117 games. The record stood until the Seahawks' Steve Largent, who played in 200 games, broke it in 1989. In 1945, Hutson scored 29 points (4 TDs, 5 PATs) in one quarter against the Detroit Lions.

Ready For Primetime (Monday Night)

October 17, 1983: It remains the highest scoring game in Monday Night Football history as the defending champion Skins—on their way to a second straight Super Bowl—had their hands full at Lambeau Field. Lynn Dickey and Joe Theismann threw for nearly 400 yards apiece, but a missed 39-yard field goal by Redskins' PK Mark Moseley in the final seconds preserved the Packers' victory. Packers 48, Redskins 47.

Overall Monday night: 14-21-1

Overall Thursday night: 0-2

Overall Sunday night: 6-2

Think About the Weather

December 31, 1967: Obviously, a candidate for the "I Was There" Game too, this contest would have gone down as one of the best games ever even if the conditions were ideal. But the temperature at kickoff read minus-13 degrees for this "Ice Bowl," a contest which saw Green Bay jump out to a 14-0 lead, fall behind by three, then win it on Bart Starr's one-yard sneak—with help from guard Jerry Kramer—in the final seconds. It was the coldest game in NFL history, bottoming out at 46 degrees below zero. Green Bay 21, Dallas 17.

Worst Team

1977 (4-10): In his third season, Packers' head coach Bart Starr was still looking for his first winning campaign. The team opened with a 24-20 victory at New Orleans (the club's highest scoring output of the year) and closed with a 16-14 triumph over the 49ers. In between, they won just twice (including a shutout of the then-winless Buccaneers) and managed a mere 84 points over the other dozen contests.

Hall of Fame

Cal Hubbard	(T/E 1963)
Don Hutson	(E 1963)
Earl Lambeau	(Coach 1963)
Johnny McNally	(HB 1963)
Clarke Hinkle	(FB 1964)
Mike Michalske	(G 1966)
Arnie Herber	(HB 1966)
Walt Kiesling	(G/C 1966)
Emlen Tunnell	(DB 1967)
Vince Lombardi	(Coach 1971)
Tony Canadeo	(HB 1974)
Len Ford	(DE 1976)
Jim Taylor	(FB 1976)
Forrest Gregg	(T 1977)
Bart Starr	(QB 1977)
Ray Nitschke	(LB 1978)
Herb Adderley	(DB 1980)
Willie Davis	(DE 1981)
Jim Ringo	(C 1981)
Paul Hornung	(HB 1986)
Willie Wood	(DB 1989)
Ted Hendricks	(LB 1990)
Jan Stenerud	(K 1991)
Henry Jordan	(DT 1995)

Best place to see Packers. Located in the southeast of Green Bay in DePere, **Nicky's** is a small bar which serves as a watering hole for players during training camp. Test your dart skills against Brett Favre. *331 Main Ave, DePere. (920) 336-9850. bar: M-Sa 4pm-2:30am, Su 5pm-1am, lunch: M-Sa 11am-2pm.*

did you know?

Even though they didn't pull in the big bucks as players back then, twelve of Vince Lombardi's Packers made themselves millionaires after their playing days were over, in such ventures as restaurants (Max McGee), radio stations (Willie Davis), and commercial development (Bart Starr).

Best Restaurants

Greasiest greasy spoon. Local diner **Kroll's** surely helped the state of Wisconsin earn the nation's highest obesity rate in 1997. Stroll over before the game to pick up one of their famous hamburgers (prepared in butter). You may need an angioplasty when you're finished, but your taste buds will thank you. *1990 S. Ridge Rd. (920) 497-1111. Seven days 10:30am-midnight. Cash only. $*

Best place to be seen Housed in the city's old train station, the **Titletown Brewing Co.** is Green Bay's newest hot spot. Pick from one of many house microbrews, including the Johnny "Blood" Red, named after Packers Hall-of-Famer Johnny "Blood" McNally. The diverse menu offers many great seafood, pasta and chicken entrees. *200 Dousman St. (920) 437-2337. M-Sa 11am-2:30am, Su 9am-1am. All major credit cards. $$*

Most elegant meal. Take a step back in time at the **Union Hotel**, a historical DePere restaurant. This is as elegant and romantic as dining gets in the Green

Fans' notes

On Screen

Outside of Wisconsin, few people have heard of **Reggie's Prayer** starring, you guessed it, Reggie White. Despite its limited, underground cult following, this was a breakout film for aspiring actors Brett Favre, Keith Jackson, and Mike Holmgren. The Minister of Defense stars as a high school teacher/coach trying to influence youngsters in a positive direction. When it comes to the team itself, there's no shortage of offerings from NFL Films Video. **Green Bay Packers: Super Bowl XXXI Champions** chronicles the title-winning team from 1996, and **The NFL's Greatest Games: The Ice Bowl** is an account of the 1967 NFL Championship duel between the Packers and Cowboys.

Fight Song, Etc.

Robert Brooks is credited with inventing the Lambeau Leap, and he even wrote a song about it. But "Jump in the Stands," a lyrical celebration of Brooks's touchdown celebration, never really took off in the music world.

Bookshelf

Brett Favre: Huck Finn Grows Up. Steve Camerson (Masters Press 1996).
Favre: For the Record. Brett Favre and Chris Havel (Doubleday 1997).
The Glory of Titletown: The Classic Green Bay Packers Photography of Vernon J. Biever. Peter Strupp (Ed.) (Taylor Publishing Co. 1997).
Packers. Steve Cameron (Taylor Publishing Co. 1996).
Instant Replay. Jerry Kramer and Dick Schaap (NAL 1986). Kramer's memoir of the Lombardi years is one of the classics in sports literature.
Distant Replay. Jerry Kramer and Dick Schaap (Jove 1987). A return to Green Bay to see where the old Packers are now.
Green Bay Replay: The Packers' Return to Glory. Dick Schaap (Avon Books 1997).
Run to Daylight! Vince Lombardi (Simon and Schuster 1989). The coach's diary sits next to the Bible on many Green Bay shelves.
Starr: My Life in Football. Bart Starr and Murray Olderman (William Morrow and Co. 1987).
Lombardi. John Wiebusch (Ed.) (Triumph Books 1997).

Paraphernalia

It began as a tribute to the state of Wisconsin's main industry, but the Cheesehead has since spawned numerous other products — the cheese baseball cap, cheese necktie, cheese cowboy hat, cheese earrings, cheese cheeks (the ones you sit on). There's even a mutant offspring, the Brat-Topper, a huge bratwurst link to don atop one's melon.

You Gotta See...

▶Green Bay is the only team in the league with its own **Hall of Fame**. Movies, displays, and a replica locker room provide a history of the franchise from its earliest beginnings.
▶**Green Bay's National Railroad Museum** houses everything from General Eisenhower's World War II command train to General Motors's futuristic "Aerotrain."
▶Make like the locals and go **bowling**. Nearby Oshkosh has one of the highest per-capita bowling alley populations of any American city, and the rest of the area isn't far off the pace.

Team Leaders

Rushing Yards
8,207   Jim Taylor, 1958-66

Passing Yards
24,718   Bart Starr, 1956-71

Passing Touchdowns
182   Brett Favre, 1992-97

Receptions
595   Sterling Sharpe, 1988-94

Interceptions
52   Bobby Dillon, 1952-59

Touchdowns
105   Don Hutson, 1935-45

Points
823   Don Hutson, 1935-45

Against the Odds

On a Packers team known for its tough, gritty players, **Bobby Dillon** (1952-59) stands apart. Dillon lost his left eye in an accident at the age of 10, but he went on to become an All-American at Texas and one of the best corners in Packers history. He compensated for his handicap by remaining close to his target, and he often made quarterbacks pay for throwing in his direction. Dillon played one year for Lombardi before unexpectedly retiring, but he still holds the Packers' mark for interceptions with 52 in his eight-year career.

Bay area. Select from an extensive wine list to complement one of the Union's tasty steak or seafood offerings. *200 N. Broadway, DePere. (920) 336-6131. lunch: M-F 11:30am-1:30pm, dinner: M-Th 5:30-9pm, F-Sa 5:30-9:30pm, Su 5-8:30pm. AE, MC, V. $$$*

> "The Packers overwhelmed one opponent, underwhelmed ten and whelmed one." — Green Bay native and legendary sportswriter Red Smith, on the Packers' 1-10-1 record in 1958.

Best Accommodations

Regency Suites. Each of the 223 suites contains a private bedroom and a separate living room with a sofa bed and dining/work area. A host of amenities are included, from health club to free drinks. *333 Main St. (920) 432-4555 or (800) 236-3330. $$-$$$*

Radisson Inn Green Bay. The ultimate place for cheeseheads to stay, as this is where the Packers stay before all home games. *2040 Airport Dr., Green Bay, WI 54313; (920) 494-7300 or (800) 333-3333. $$$*

PaperValley Inn. Often serves as the visiting team's headquarters and only 30 minutes from Green Bay. Indoor pool and mini-golf course are great for kids. The PaperValley boasts two restaurants and sports bars on site. *333 W. College Ave., Appleton. (920) 733-8000. $$-$$$*

While You Were Eating Turkey

November 24, 1949: The Packers played the most important game in franchise history, and ironically, it wasn't even registered as an official game. Under newly assigned head coach Gene Ronzani, the franchise found itself in a financial crisis. The Packers solved their dire need for capital by holding an intra-squad scrimmage at the old City Stadium on the town's east side. In an unprecedented gesture, Packer legend Don Hutson came out of his four-year retirement to help boost ticket sales. The organization raised $50,000 to stay afloat for another season. Other than that, though, the Packers haven't had much to be thankful for on this holiday. More than half of their wins came against perennial juggernauts like the Frankford Yellowjackets, Hammond Pros, and Brooklyn Dodgers. Overall, 10-17-2.

Indianapolis Colts

"...The cynic becomes a true believer/
When caught in the grip of that old Colt fever." — Ogden Nash

Dazzling. Breathtaking. Greatest ever. These are words often used to describe three NFL games played in three different decades, and all three have one common element — the Colts. Given the recent disappointments with this franchise, it's easy to overlook the fact that the history of the Colts, first in Baltimore and now in Indianapolis, is replete with superb performances, last-minute heroics and spectacular near-misses.

Start with the December 28, 1958 NFL Championship game at Yankee Stadium. With night falling in the bitterly cold Bronx, the Colts beat the New York Giants, 23-17, in sudden-death overtime. Hall of Fame quarterback Johnny Unitas engineered the game-winning 80-yard drive, culminating in Alan Ameche's one-yard dive into the end zone. The game was called "the greatest ever" and established Unitas's mythic status, which was solidified in 1959 by a second straight NFL championship. Again, the Colts beat the Giants — this time, 31-16, in Baltimore's beloved Memorial Stadium. The Colts of Unitas, Raymond Berry, Lenny Moore, Art Donovan and Gino Marchetti put an exclamation point on a decade which established pro football as a game made for television, and which would soon challenge baseball for the hearts and minds of America's sports fans.

In 1968, the Colts won a third NFL title and went to the Orange Bowl in Miami for Super Bowl III. This time, however, the heroics were provided by Joe

Franchise History

Miami Seahawks
(1946)
Baltimore Colts
(1946-49)
Baltimore Colts (NFL)
(1950)
Dallas Texans (NFL)
(1952)
Baltimore Colts (NFL)
(1953-1983)
Indianapolis Colts
(1984-present)

By the Numbers

(Since 1970)
Regular Season: 177-245-2
Postseason: 6-7
Division Titles: 5
Vs. Division: 97-123-1 (Playoffs: 0-1)
Playoff Appearances: 8
Home: 93-117-2
Away: 84-128

(Overall)
Regular Season: 310-329-7
Postseason: 10-10
Playoff Appearances: 13
Home: 168-151-5
Away: 142-178-2

Most Revered Football Figures

Johnny Unitas. Best quarterback of all time? Well, it's either Joe Montana or immortal number 19 of the Colts.
Jim Harbaugh. In just three seasons, "Captain Comeback" endeared himself to Colts fans with his gritty play and remarkable resiliency. Gone but not forgotten.

Rivalries

The New England **Patriots** have made for convenient opponents, for seemingly both clubs have been bad simultaneously, as well as being playoff contenders the same years. Since '88, 13 of the teams' 20 meetings have been decided by six or fewer points. Old wounds still ache when the Colts face the division rival **Jets** (33-23-0). The score will never be settled for Super Bowl III. In 1991 the Colts won only one game — against the Jets.

> ▼
> **did you know?**
> Perhaps the Mayflower vans should have headed to New Jersey. The Colts own an 11-5 lifetime record at the Meadowlands (10-4 vs. Jets, 1-1 vs. Giants).
> ▲

Hall of Fame

Raymond Berry	(WR 1973)
Art Donovan	(DT 1968)
Weeb Ewbank	(Coach 1978)
Ted Hendricks	(LB 1990)
John Mackey	(TE 1992)
Gino Marchetti	(DE 1972)
Lenny Moore	(RB 1975)
Jim Parker	(G 1973)
Johnny Unitas	(QB 1979)

Namath and his upstart New York Jets. In perhaps the greatest upset in pro football history, the Colts lost, 16-7. But again Baltimore had a big part in pro football history. Super Bowl III gave the junior league credibility, and it transformed the Super Bowl into an international extravaganza. Two years later, the Colts were back at it. In Super Bowl V, rookie kicker Jim O'Brien booted a 32-yard field goal with five seconds left for a breathtaking 16-13 win over the Dallas Cowboys.

The 1970s and '80s, however, were an embarrassing time for this storied franchise. Moved to the AFC, the Colts were overshadowed by the Miami Dolphins, Oakland Raiders and Pittsburgh Steelers. So bad were the Colts — they didn't win a game in the strike-shortened season of 1982 — that Stanford's John Elway, the highest rated quarterback prospect, refused to play for them after they selected him first in the 1983 college draft. So the Colts traded Elway's rights to the Denver Broncos. The next year, the Irsay family spirited the team out of Baltimore in the middle of the night and moved it to Indianapolis.

Swami Sez:

> The best part about having a new quarterback, a new GM, and a new coach is that all of them know what they're doing.

Mediocrity followed until the 1995 season, when the Colts entered the playoffs as a wild card and nearly went to the Super Bowl. In a dazzling finish at the AFC Championship game in Pittsburgh, quarterback Jim Harbaugh's "Hail Mary" pass dropped off the fingertips of wide receiver Aaron Bailey in the end zone as time expired — Steelers 20, Colts 16. The disappointment of that loss lingered through the next two seasons: The Colts finished 3-13 in 1997. Bill Tobin, their longtime personnel guru, was fired. With the first pick in the 1998 college draft, team owner Jim Irsay wanted a new crew, so in came general manager Bill Polian and veteran coach Jim Mora. Fans hope these two veteran football minds along with rookie quarterback Payton Manning can put words like "dazzling" and "breathtaking" in front of the word "Colts" once again.

—Sal Paolantonio

RCA Dome

The RCA Dome is a cavernous setting for a football game. That it's at all passable can be attributed to the Midwestern friendliness of Indiana. In the Dome's defense, the Colts haven't given fans here too many reasons to transform the place into anything more than a big enclosed space in which to watch a football game. Mostly the fans come to watch the game and get out of the house. If you want passion in Hoosier Country, go to a high school basketball game. The fans don't come early, either. No one really knows why, but the art of talgating has not really caught on in Indianapolis. What little there is takes place at the south lot. It's hard to picture the RCA Dome ever becoming a hallowed site in sports history.

Completed in 1984, the $77.5 million stadium is also the site of other major events such as concerts and conventions.

---

did you know?

The hard-luck Colts drafted QB John Elway with the first pick in the 1983 draft, and LB Cornelius Bennett with the second choice in '87. Neither ever played for the organization.

The "I Was There" Game

1958 NFL Championship game. Referred to as "The Greatest Game Ever Played," this tilt at Yankee Stadium was the tonic pro football was looking for. With New York holding a 17-14 lead with 1:56 remaining, Colts' QB Johnny Unitas drove his team to a tying field goal with seven seconds to play. Unitas then led the march which ended with Alan Ameche's fabled one-yard TD plunge in overtime. (Colts 23, Giants 17, OT)

> "The rest of life was easily eclipsed when Johnny U stepped into the sunlight on a Sunday afternoon."
> — Author William Gildea.

The Paper Bag Game

December 20, 1981. Sometimes winning isn't enough. The Colts opened the season by beating the Pats, 29-28, and closed it in similar fashion. Between the two encounters they went 0-14. The Pats finished 2-14, as well. Only 17,000 and change attended this low point in Baltimore football. (Colts 23, Patriots 21)

Great Names

Dextor Clinkscale (S 1986)
Joe Don Looney (RB 1964)
Zefross Moss (OT 1989-94)
Irv Pankey (OT 1991-92)
Royce Womble (RB 1954-57)

Our Top Story

"Turnaround,"
Dec. 21, 1975
The Colts complete one of the greatest turnarounds in NFL history with their ninth straight win, defeating New England, 34-21, at Memorial Stadium to finish 10-4 and win the AFC East title.

"We're Outta Here"
March 31, 1984
A convoy of moving vans crept into Indianapolis during the early morning hours, bringing the late Baltimore Colts and professional status to Indianapolis. While they loved him in Indiana, back in Balitmore, they wanted owner Robert Irsay's head on a stick.

"The Trade"
October 31, 1987
A three-way trade between the Colts, the Bills and the Rams brings RB Eric Dickerson to Indianapolis.

Team Leaders

Rushing Yards
5,487   Lydell Mitchell (1972-77)
Passing Yards
39,768   Johnny Unitas (1956-72)
Passing Touchdowns
287   Johnny Unitas (1956-72)
Receptions
631   Raymond Berry (1955-67)
Interceptions
57   Bobby Boyd (1960-68)
Touchdowns
113   Lenny Moore (1956-67)
Points
783   Dean Biasucci (1984, 1986-94)

ventions. The RCA Dome has a 19-story-high fiberglass roof and is one of only six major air-supported domed stadiums in the world. Which is something.

did you know?
Johnny Unitas' first pass for the Colts was intercepted by the Bears J.C. Caroline and returned for a touchdown in a 58-27 rout by Chicago.

The Bottom Line on RCA Dome

Address: RCA Dome 100 S. Capitol Ave., Indianapolis, IN
Tickets: Not that hard to come by. Fill out a form and season tickets are yours. Pick up a phone and single game tickets can be had. (317) 197-7000.
Parking: There are 10,000 parking spaces within a one mile radius of the Dome, and 54,000 parking spaces in downtown Indianapolis, providing lots of options for fans.
Public Transportation: A host of city buses run past the Dome on Capital Avenue. Call (317) 635-3344 for information.
Extras: RCA Dome tours depart from the Indianapolis City Center and include a high-tech, multi-sensory presentation as well as a look at the Indianapolis Colts locker rooms, the owner's suite, the press box and the stadium floor. For tour information, call (317) 237-5200.
Capacity: 60,500.
Restrooms: 124.

Where to Go . . . in Indianapolis

Best Bars
Best Sports Bar: Sports fans congregate on the fourth level of the Circle Centre

Best of the Colts

Best Team

1968 (15-2): Don Shula's Colts were as dominant as any team in the league in any era, rolling over nearly every opponent with ease. Their only loss during the regular season was a 30-20 setback to the Browns, whom they routed in the NFL title game in Cleveland (34-0). They could have and should have won a world championship, but weren't prepared for a confident Jets squad in Super Bowl III.

> ...When hearing tales of Bubba Smith
> You wonder is he man or myth.
> He's like a hoodoo, like a hex.
> He's like Tyrannosaurus Rex."
> — Ogden Nash

Greatest Players by Position

Pos:	Player
QB:	Johnny Unitas
RB:	Lenny Moore
WR:	Raymond Berry
TE:	John Mackey
OL:	Jim Parker
DL:	Gino Marchetti
LB:	Mike Curtis
DB:	Bobby Boyd
P/K:	Rohn Stark
ST:	Clarence Verdin

And Don't Forget...

RB: Lydell Mitchell. One of the most versatile offensive players of the '70s, the former Nittany Lion made life easier for QB Bert Jones.

DE: Art Donovan. Known more today for his legendary stories and poking fun at himself, he was no laughing matter on the football field.

WR: Roger Carr. Deceptive speed and sure hands made Carr one of the most dangerous deep threats of his decade.

QB: Bert Jones. Strong-armed, productive passer who flourished under Ted Marchibroda, although injuries plagued his career.

C: Ray Donaldson. When the going was tough, Donaldson anchored the middle for some less-than-scintillating Colts' squads.

Best Argument

Line backer: Mike Curtis or Stan White? For 11 seasons, most of those in the middle, the hard-hitting Curtis made Sunday afternoons miserable for opposing teams. White was one of the most underrated players of the 1970s — never named to a Pro Bowl — and totaled an incredible 25 interceptions during his eight seasons with the franchise.

> "You can't go to New York or L.A. and play for those teams and end up in somebody's living room like you can in Baltimore." — Joe Ehrmann, defensive tackle, on the booster mentality of Colt fans.

Best coach

Weeb Ewbank (1954-62): Perhaps more heralded for his days with the Jets, Ewbank's first three seasons in Baltimore produced a combined 13 victories. But the Colts became winners in 1957 and followed that breakthrough season with NFL championships in 1958 and '59 — both at the expense of the Giants. Don Shula may have won more games with the Colts, but never a world title.

Pressbox

Who to Read...

Robin Miller of *The Indianapolis Star*, offers commentary on all things sports-related in town and has a lot to say on just about everything and everyone. He appears on local sports television talk shows, and everyone reads his column. Other reporters at the *Star* providing extensive coverage of the Colts include Mike Chappell, Conrad Brunner and Bill Benner.

Who to Watch...

WISH–CBS features "Sports Locker," on Saturdays from 11:30 pm to midnight, hosted by Will Hampton and on Sundays from 11:30 pm to midnight hosted by Mark Patrick. Two more strong shows are WTRV-ABC's "Sports Extra," which airs Saturdays at 11:30 pm with Rob Powers, and Sundays at 11:30 pm there's Ed Sorenson's show.

Who to Listen To...

In the past, if you couldn't make it to the game or it was sold out, you could always count on Bob Lamey's play-by play coverage on WIBC (1070 AM). But beginning with the '98 season, those games will move to WFBQ (95 FM) and, thankfully, Lamey's going with them. When the Colts organization switched radio station affiliation, they made Lamey an offer he couldn't refuse. Now an employee of the Colts, Lamey will call the games on the FM dial.

Mall, where **Brewski's Sport and Wing Shack** offers two big screens and 15 TV monitors. Brewski's fare includes 15 styles of chicken wings and more than 120 beers, as well as sandwiches and salads. *49 W. Maryland. All major credit cards. (317) 630-5483. $*

Best Young Crowd. An extremely popular bar and restaurant with the recently 21- year-old crowd, **Ike and Jonesy's**, is casual with daily tasty specials like breaded tenderloin and other sandwiches. *17 W. Jackson St., (317) 632-4553. All major credit cards. $.*

> "I'm a B and B man — booze and broads."
> — Big Daddy Lipscomb.

Best Bar Name in America. The best blues bar in town features live entertainment nightly. The music is the draw at **The Slippery Noodle Inn**, but not while the game is on. Steaks, ribs, soup and sandwiches are the fare. Comfortable, casual. *372 S. Meridian St., (317) 631-6974. All major credit cards. $$.*

Best Restaurants

Best Romantic Dinner. Atop the Hyatt Regency Hotel, the **Eagle's Nest** offers beautiful views as the restaurant slowly rotates. Prime rib, filet mignon and salmon are the favorites. *1 South Capitol Ave., (317) 632-1234. $$$$*

Best Bogart Joint. One block from the RCA Dome, **Rick's Cafe Americain** offers an extensive menu with lots of appetizers, salads, sandwiches and entrees. Also features live jazz. Nice and cozy atmosphere. *39 West Jackson Pl. (317) 634-6666. $$*

Best Steak. Locals have been coming to **St. Elmo's** for nearly a century to eat big slabs of meat. The feel is old Indianapolis, with old photos of sports and entertainers on the walls. *127 S. Illinois St., (317) 635-0636. All major credit cards. $$$$.*

Best accommodations

Days Inn Downtown. An easy walk to the RCA Dome and across the street from Market Square Arena, where the Pacers play. *401 E. Washington St., 800-325-2525. $*

Embassy Suites Downtown. Three hundred sixty suites just two blocks from the Dome. Amenities include an exercise room and an indoor pool. *110 Washington St. 800-362-2779. $$*

Omni Severin Hotel. Near the Dome as well as the many downtown attractions. Thirty eight suites, a fitness center and indoor pool. *40 West Jackson Pl. Indianapolis, 800-843-6664. $$$*

> **"I didn't give a damn about the clock. It was our pace to set." — Johnny Unitas** on the sudden-death period of the '58 title game.

Against the Odds

Even in 1972, a 6'1", 224-pound linebacker was considered undersized. That explains why **Stan White** (1972-1980), an All-Big Ten player, was selected in the 17th round in 1972. In 1975, the Colts (10-4) had a superb year, giving up their fewest points in three seasons (269). That season, White had a team-high 109 unassisted tackles, seven sacks, eight deflected passes and broke Jack Ham's record for interceptions by a linebacker (seven in 1972) with eight. The player so many people thought was too small for the big time averaged 16.9 yards per interception return, including a 22-yard TD.

did you know?

Weeb Ewbank is the only coach in NFL history to lead teams in each league to the championships — the NFL Colts in 1958 and 1959 and the AFL New York Jets in 1969, against his old team, the Colts.

Ready For Primetime (Monday Night)

October 31, 1988; Colts 55, Broncos 23: Ron Meyer's Colts set a Monday Night Football record for scoring thanks to RB Eric Dickerson. The one-time Ram rushed for 124 yards and four touchdowns in the first half (finishing with 159) as a shoddy Broncos defense provided little opposition.

Overall on Monday night, 10-8

Overall Thursday: 1-0

Overall Sunday night: 2-8

Think About the Weather

September 18, 1978; Colts 34, Patriots 27: It rained on everyone this night, especially the Patriots defense and special teams. The Colts had dropped their first two games of the season by a combined 80-0 score, so it was up to RB Joe Washington to take matters into his own hands, throwing for a score, catching a touchdown pass and then breaking a 27-all tie with a 90-yard kickoff return (all in the fourth quarter) to stun the Pats.

Worst Team

1981 (2-14): This tale of ineptitude featuring a plethora of lopsided defeats (averaging a margin of nearly 20 points per loss) can be mainly blamed on a defensive unit that allowed the most yards in a season in league history. This edition of the Colts also gave up an NFL-record 533 points.

Fans' notes

On Screen

This is exactly where the Baltimore/Indianapolis/Cleveland thing gets tough. Although **Diner** takes place in Baltimore, and the quiz Steve Guttenberg forces upon his fiancée concerns Baltimore football, it still feels fundamentally like a Colts movie. All-pro defensive end Bubba Smith went the beer commercial route after retiring, and appeared in **Stroker Ace** and **Police Academy**, both in 1983. You can get a glimpse of Johnny Unitas in the Disney film **Gus**, about a place-kicking mule. Art Donovan has done some pretty terrific ads himself.

Bookshelf

When the Colts Belonged to Baltimore: A Father, and a Son, a Team and a Time. William Gildea (Johns Hopkins U. Press 1996). A must-read personal memoir of Baltimore football in the 1950s and 1960s.
From Colts to Ravens: A Behind-the-Scenes Look at Baltimore Professional Football by a Writer Who Was There. John F. Steadman (Tidewater 1997).
Sundays at 2:00 with the Baltimore Colts. Vince Bagli, et al. (Tidewater 1995).
Let 'er Rip: The Colts in Indianapolis; A Look Back, A Look Ahead. Terry Hutchens (Masters 1996)
Fatso: The Football Follies of Artie Donovan. Arthur J. Donovan, Jr. and Bob Drury (Morrow 1987).
Mad Ducks and Bears. George Plimpton. (Random House 1973). The sequel to **Paper Lion**, Plimpton tries his hand again at quarterback, and fares no better.

> "Some of the players had even spent their winnings before the game." — Steve Rosenbloom, son of Carroll Rosenbloom on the Colts team before Super Bowl III.

You Gotta See...

▶"Gentlemen, start your engines." The most famous sports venue in town is the **Indianapolis Motor Speedway**, home of the Indy 500. You'll find the Brickyard in Speedway, IN, about seven miles west of Indianapolis.
▶The **Eiteljorg Museum of American Indians and Western Art** is an adobe-style building with collections of native American art (pottery, basketry and clothing) and American Western paintings and bronzes by such artists as Frederic Remington and Georgia O'Keeffe.
▶Located in the RCA Dome, the **National Track & Field Hall of Fame Museum** honors American track and field greats such as Jim Thorpe, Jesse Owens and Bruce Jenner. The history of track and field is chronicled through the display of photos and early track equipment.
▶The **Children's Museum of Indianapolis** houses 100,000 artifacts in 10 major galleries that explore the physical and natural sciences, history, foreign cultures and the arts.

Jacksonville
Jaguars

Jacksonville an NFL city? Many didn't believe the city belonged in the same league as New York, Chicago, Dallas and the other strongholds of the game. But the dreams of this vast city in northern Florida became reality on November 30, 1993, when shoe magnate Wayne Weaver secured an expansion franchise for the NFL's 30th team. And even more remarkably, Weaver assembled an organization that has become one of the NFL's most progressive and successful almost overnight. Many experts project the Jaguars as a Super Bowl contender through the next three seasons.

Franchise History
Jacksonville Jaguars
(1995–present)

Of all Weaver's early acts as owner, none was as critical as the hiring of Boston College coach Tom Coughlin to be the team's coach and general manager more than a full year before the team would begin play in 1995. From the start, Coughlin created the team and organization he wanted. He set up a scouting staff and mapped out a plan that would take full advantage of the team's array of expansion draft picks. The team's forays into free agency always put youth first, a plan forged by Weaver, Coughlin and Michael Huyghue, the vice president of football operations. The result was a Jaguars team that bore the very strong mark of Tom Coughlin.

On the eve of the team's first draft, Coughlin made what many consider a cornerstone move: He traded for Mark Brunell, a quarterback who had backed up Brett Favre with the Green Bay Packers. With his first pick the next day, he selected left tackle Tony Boselli, who quickly emerged as one of the game's great blockers. While the Jaguars struggled with a 4-12 record in their inaugural season, the community defied the "small market" syndrome by selling out every home game to the tune of 73,000 a pop.

It started to come together in the second season when the young Jaguars began to mature. A five-game winning streak marked the end of a 9-7 regular

By the Numbers
(Overall)
Regular Season: 24-24
Postseason: 2-2
Division Titles: 0
Vs. Division: 15-9
Playoff Appearances: 2
Home: 16-8
Away: 8-16

Most Revered Football Figures

Tom Coughlin. He may act like he's in the military, but the fans love his work ethic.

Mark Brunell. His No. 8 jersey is the hottest-selling item in town. Brunell's scrambling and playmaking ability are the signatures of the Jags' style of play.

Tony Boselli. The team's first draft pick, Boselli may be the most-loved lineman in the league.

Rivalries

The Jags have established a suitably nasty relationship with the Pittsburgh **Steelers** (3-3). The Jaguars' 20-16 victory over them in 1995 was the first time an expansion team beat an eventual Super Bowl team in the regular season. Since then, there have been several fights in the series, and even an incident in 1997 involving Jaguars wide receiver Keenan McCardell and Steelers linebacker Greg Lloyd that bordered on the bizarre. In the Steelers 23-17 overtime win, Lloyd cheapshotted McCardell and then said he did so because McCardell phoned his home and threatened his family. The league investigated and never substantiated Lloyd's claim, but it added to an already nasty rivalry. Another solid source of antagonism is the Carolina **Panthers** (1-0). They have only met once in the regular season, but in a 1997 preseason game the Panthers objected to the Jags' use of an overly aggressive, blitzing defense.

season, but that was just a preview of things to come. The Jaguars became the first team to win a playoff game against the Buffalo Bills in Buffalo's Rich Stadium. And then Brunell, with battering Natrone Means at running back, pulled an even bigger upset by defeating the AFC favorite Denver Broncos, 30-27, at Mile High Stadium. The Broncos got their revenge in 1997, but the Jaguars still finished with an 11-5 record, again sold out every game, and appear to be on a march that could wear out a good pair of Weaver's shoes.

—Chris Mortensen

ALLTEL Stadium

When Jacksonville was awarded the Jaguars in November of 1993, the Gator Bowl was a dump. But by the time the Jaguars kicked off in their first game in August of 1995, a major renovation had rendered the stadium state-of-the-art. It had luxury suites, club seats and great sight-lines for fans. Tickets sold out immediately. On game days, the fan passion which helped Jacksonville win the franchise is very much in evidence. The stadium is now called ALLTEL Stadium, and it's become one of the toughest places in the league for visitors to play. The Jaguars were 7-1 at home last season, playing to sold-out crowds. As the team has improved, so have the fans. In the first season, a lot of fans were just learning when and how to cheer. Since then, they have become much more sophisticated,

> **did you know?**
> The Jaguars had three different uniform designs in their first three seasons.

> "This is training camp. This isn't Club Med."
> — Coach Tom Coughlin on his tough 1995 training camp.

much more understanding of their role. Players appreciate the improvement. "Coming into our home is anything but easy," said guard Ben Coleman. "Our fans make it hell for opposing teams. And that's the way we like it."

Swami Sez:

The only problem with this team is its sense of geography. Central Division??? The last time we checked, Jacksonville was rather close to the Atlantic Ocean.

Not all of the fans have gotten with the program, however. The best seats in ALL-TEL are the expensive club seats. Unfortunately, the corporate types who inhabit this section on occasion do not return to their seats after halftime on a hot day. Why come to the stadium if you're only going to watch the game on screen from the air-conditioned club area? Well, the team is only three years old. Maybe they'll figure it out.

The Bottom Line on ALLTEL Stadium

Address: One ALLTEL Stadium Place, Jacksonville, FL 32202. (904) 633-6100.

Tickets: There are some season tickets available, but not many. The team sold out all of their games in the first three seasons, but there are tickets to be had each week. The average ticket price is $35. For more information call 904-633-2000.

1998: $20-$150

1994: N/A

Parking: Spots go for $20 a pop, but the catch is that you have to pay ahead for the whole season. If you don't pay

The "I Was There" Game

December 22, 1996: All the Jaguars needed to make the playoffs in only their second season was to beat a bad Atlanta team at home. But instead of rolling to an easy victory, they labored, and they needed a miracle to clinch it. That miracle came when Atlanta's Morten Andersen, one of the game's top kickers, missed a 30-yard field goal with four seconds remaining to give the Jaguars a surprising victory. Jacksonville 19, Atlanta 17.

The Paper Bag Game

Dec. 17, 1995: By far the team's worst loss. The Lions so humiliated the Jaguars this day at the Silverdome that they actually took a knee midway through the fourth quarter to prevent the score from getting worse. Detroit 44, Jacksonville 0.

did you know?

The Jaguars are the only expansion team to make the playoffs in two of their first three seasons.

Great Names

Natrone Means (RB, 1996-97)
Darren Studstill (S, 1995-97)

Worst Team

1995 (4-12): The Jags started winless in September, and after managing a 3-5 mark at midseason, they suffered seven straight losses—giving up a whopping 221 points in those games.

Our Top Story

"The NFL in Jacksonville?"
August 17, 1989
Tom Petway, Jeb Bush, Hamilton Jordan and Arthur "Chick" Sherrer (Wayne Weaver joined on later) announce the formation of Touchdown Jacksonville!, an organization devoted to bringing an NFL team to Jacksonville, where WFL and USFL teams once resided.

"Jags Upend Broncos"
January 4, 1997
After stunning the aging Bills, 30-27, in the wild card game, Jacksonville faced a well-rested Broncos squad at Mile High Stadium, where Denver had gone undefeated on the season. But after falling behind, 12-0, in the first quarter, Mark Brunell and the Jags came back to stun the Broncos, 30-27, behind 140 yards rushing from Natrone Means. It was easily the biggest win for the young Jaguars franchise.

did you know?

Through the 1997 season, the Jaguars defeated the Cleveland Browns/Baltimore Ravens franchises all six times the teams met.

"Brunell Suspected Out for Season"
September 7, 1997
In a preseason game, Giants linebacker Jessie Armstead rolled into Mark Brunell's leg, seemingly causing severe damage to his knee. The Jags packed the knee in ice and prayed that the ACL (anterior cruciate ligament) wasn't torn, and that Brunell wouldn't be lost for the season. Amazingly, the damage was minor, and Brunell returned to action after missing just two regular-season games.

ahead, you'll be left looking around the stadium for a space, which is not a pleasant alternative.

Public Transportation: One of the best ways to get to the stadium is a river taxi which will take a fan from the opposite bank of the St. Johns River to the stadium. Jacksonville Transportation Authority buses run from throughout the city to the stadium. Call (904) 630-3100 for more information.

Capacity: 73,000.

Restrooms: 24 men's, 24 women's.

Where to Go . . . in Jacksonville

Best Bars

Best sports bar. Jaguars tackle Tony Boselli once owned a piece of **Sneakers Sports Grille**, and it's still a favorite of some players after games. The bar is located 15 minutes from the stadium, where it plays host to a big after-game crowd. While food is served, this is essentially a drinking place. Some nights you may find a Jaguar playing celebrity bartender. *10750 Atlantic Blvd., (904) 641-4263. Seven days 11am-2am.*

"It's not raising someone from the dead or anything like that. But God has done those things, so why can't he heal a knee?" — Linebacker Bryan Schwartz in 1997, after discovering that Mark Brunell's ACL was not torn.

Best pre- and post-game party. Located across the river from the stadium, the **River City Brewing Company** is the

Best of the Jaguars

Best Team

1997 (11-6): After coming within a game of a Super Bowl in '96, the Jaguars picked up where they left off and showed their tenacity despite health problems. A 3-0 start came via three different quarterbacks (Rob Johnson, Steve Matthews and starter Mark Brunell), but just when it appeared the Jags were getting healthy, injuries did in the defensive line, and there would be no playoff upset in Denver.

Greatest Players by Position

Pos:	Player
QB:	Mark Brunell
RB:	Natrone Means
WR:	Keenan McCardell
TE:	Pete Mitchell
OL:	Tony Boselli
DL:	Tony Brackens
LB:	Bryan Schwartz
DB:	Mickey Washington
P/K:	Mike Hollis
ST:	Chris Hudson

And Don't Forget...

LB: Kevin Hardy. The Jaguars' first-round pick in '96, the former Illini 'backer is a budding star and is a certain Pro Bowler down the road.

DE: Clyde Simmons. Discarded by the Cardinals, the wizened veteran was a pass-rushing force for the Jags and even made a huge impact blocking kicks.

T: Leon Searcy. No one gets much attention playing opposite Pro Bowler Tony Boselli, but this one-time Miami Hurricane just does his job.

WR: Willie Jackson. You could always find the one-time Florida Gator speedster contributing on offense and on kick returns.

P: Bryan Barker. The pride of coach Larry Pasquale's well-schooled special teams, he was rewarded with a Pro Bowl invitation in '97.

RB: James Stewart. His team-leading numbers in rushing and touchdowns prove that his five-touchdown game in 1997 was no fluke.

Best Argument

Wide Receiver: Keenan McCardell or Jimmy Smith? A former 12th-round pick of the Redskins, McCardell has proven to be one of the most dependable receivers in the league. Smith has been the Jaguars' big-play machine and continues to improve. Talk about cohesion. When McCardell was voted to the Pro Bowl in 1996, he took Smith as his guest. Smith returned the favor in '97.

> "There's no love. It's like we're scared." — WR Andre Rison in October 1996, on playing for Tom Coughlin.

Best Coach

Tom Coughlin (1995-present): During his first season on the job, the former Boston College sideline leader was criticized for his regimented and disciplined ways, and it was assumed he could not make the adjustment to the pro game. So much for opinion. Two straight postseason appearances, including road playoff upsets at Buffalo and at Denver in '96, put Coughlin and his team on the map.

Pressbox

Who to Read...

The Jaguars are one of the most poorly reported teams in the NFL. Only one full-time beat writer, Pete Prisco of *The Florida Times-Union*, covers the team. Several other Florida newspapers follow the Jaguars on a limited basis, but the *Times-Union* more than fills in what the other papers lack. There, Jaguars news — such as a major injury — is routinely front-page material.

Who to Watch...

The local television stations, on the other hand, cover the Jaguars intensely. A rotating schedule of Jaguars players hosts a weekly wrap-up show on WTLV–NBC, the Jaguars' flagship station. Saturdays from 6:30 to 7pm during the season, on the same station, head coach Tom Coughlin has a weekly show co-hosted by team broadcaster Matt Robinson. And Jeff

Lageman has hosted a weekly half-hour called "The End Zone" on WJXT–CBS.

Who to Listen To...

Jacksonville radio has embraced the Jaguars at least as warmly as television, especially the two all-sports radio stations, WBWL (600 AM) and WNZS (930 AM). WBWL, known as "The Ball," has more Jaguars talk than does WNZS, which focuses more on college football. Jaguar tackle Tony Boselli has a show on The Ball, as do linebacker Bryan Schwartz and guard Ben Coleman. The *Times-Union*'s Pete Prisco also hosts a two-hour show on the same station, focusing almost entirely on the Jaguars. Tom Coughlin's weekly radio show, from 6 to 7pm on Thursdays, is carried on WOKV (690 AM) and a network of affiliated regional stations.

meeting place for a lot of Jaguars fans. After the game, you may see a few players enjoying a meal — if they won. The restaurant offers a river taxi to the game, and has a dock for any boaters who would like to stop over before going to the game. *835 Museum Circle, (904) 398-2299. Su-Th 5-10pm, F-Sa 5-11pm.*

Oldest bar. The Palace Saloon is believed to be the oldest bar in Florida. They've changed the kegs a number of times since it was built in 1878, but there's plenty of memorabilia to remind you of the place's past. On weekend nights there's live music, too. *113 Centre St., Fernandina Beach. (904) 261-6320. Seven days 11:30am-2am.*

> "As far as sheer talent, I think we have an awful lot." — QB Steve Beuerlein, before the Jaguars' inaugural season. (1995)

Best Restaurants

Best cheap beach eats. Celebs and ordinary beachgoers alike stop in at the **Beach Hut Cafe**, located in the South Beaches strip mall, for inexpensive home-cooking. Breakfast and lunch are served, just a stone's throw from the ocean. *1986*

San Marco Blvd. (904) 249-3156. Seven days 6am-3pm. DC, MC, V. $

Best late-night dinner. Stylish **Café Carmon** serves a surprisingly inexpensive menu of fresh pastas, steak, chicken and fish. For game days, there's a Sunday brunch. *1281 S. 3rd St. (904) 399-4488. M-Th 11am-11pm, F-Sa 11am-midnight, Su 9am-9pm. All major credit cards. $$*

did you know?

The Jaguars have never had a 1,000-yard rusher in three seasons, but have had a 4,000-yard passer (Mark Brunell in 1996) and four 1,000-yard receiving seasons (Jimmy Smith and Keenan McCardell in both 1996 and 1997).

Best place to splurge. Located in the Hilton Hotel downtown, **Ruth's Chris Steakhouse** is a high-class favorite for wealthier Jaguars fans after the game. Located across the river from the stadium, it has quickly established itself as one of the leading restaurants in the city. *1201 Riverplace Blvd. (904) 396-6200. M-Th 5-10:30pm, F-Sa 5-11pm, Su 5-10pm. All major credit cards. $$$*

Best Accommodations

Sea Horse Oceanfront Inn. Close to much of Jacksonville's nightlife and right on the beach, this inexpensive choice has ocean views in every room. *120 Atlantic Blvd. (904) 246-2175. $-$$*

Marriott at Sawgrass. Golfers will want to consider this hotel, connected with the TPC at Sawgrass course. Golf packages are available. *1000 PGA Tour Blvd. (904) 285-7777. $$-$$$*

Omni. If you're pulling out all the stops on your trip, you can indulge in a stay at this luxurious downtown hotel. *245 Water St. (904) 355-6664. $$$$-$$$$$*

Ready For Primetime (Monday Night)

Sept. 22, 1997: A seesaw tilt had the Jaguars ahead, 23-21, but Steelers K Norm Johnson was lining up for a 40-yard field goal in the final seconds. A bad snap, the block by DB Travis Davis and a return for a score by S Chris Hudson preserved the win. The most memorable image was that of Pittsburgh coach Bill Cowher barely resisting the impulse to tackle Hudson as he streaked by. Jaguars 30, Steelers 21.

Overall Monday night: 1-0
Overall Sunday night: 1-1

Think About the Weather

December 1, 1996: Jaguars 30, Bengals 27. Playing at home in a steady rain, the Jaguars used all facets of their game to pull out a win. It was the second of five straight wins in the Jags' last five games, a streak which put them in the playoffs.

Team Leaders

Rushing Yards
1,803   James Stewart, 1995-present
Passing Yards
9,816   Mark Brunell, 1995-present
Passing Touchdowns
52   Mark Brunell, 1995-present
Receptions
187   Jimmy Smith, 1995-present
Interceptions
5   Chris Hudson, 1995-present
5   Deon Figures, 1997-present
Touchdowns
22   James Stewart, 1995-present
Points
338   Mike Hollis, 1995-present

Fans' notes

On Screen

Jacksonville used to be the preferred location for warm-weather movie shoots, back before the biz left New York City for Hollywood, but the Jaguars have yet to create an illustrious filmography for themselves. Fans need not despair, though; NFL Films still offers the annual team video.

Bookshelf

Jags to Riches: The Cinderella Season of the Jacksonville Jaguars. Pete Prisco and John Oehser (St. Martin's 1997). These two Times-Union beat writers wrote a book chronicling the team's road to the AFC Championship game. The book not only offers a peek into the 1996 season, but also traces the city's pursuit of an NFL franchise.

Paraphernalia

Two really bad bits of paraphernalia have popped up in the team's first few seasons. There are a lot of Jaguars fans who also are Florida Gators fans. That led to some awful T-shirts with an ugly logo depicting a Jag-Gator. And in the team's first season, somebody had the bright idea to sell dye which could color your tongue teal — to match the cat's tongue on the Jags' helmets. It made fans look dangerously close to death. Open up and say "Arrgghh."

You Gotta See...

▶Jacksonville's **Riverwalk** zigzags 1.2 miles along the St. John's River. From the Friendship Fountain at the western end, it runs past the Maritime Museum, Jacksonville Historical Society and other sights. It's a favorite spot for jogging, walking, or just looking at the river's reflection of the downtown skyline.

▶Who would be your top draught pick? The **Anheuser-Busch Brewery**, near the airport, offers guided and self-guided tours, as well as a tasting room.

▶All manner of animals make their home on the grounds of the **Jacksonville Zoological Gardens,** which includes an aviary, an 18-acre veldt and a natural wetlands.

Against the Odds

If anyone ever wanted to write a book about **Jimmy Smith**'s (1995-present) NFL career, it could be titled "The Long and Winding Road." The 36th player drafted overall in 1992, Smith spent two seasons with Dallas, sitting out the entire 1993 season. Smith was out of football in 1994, but he was the first receiver signed by the expansion Jaguars. After a mediocre inaugural season with the Jags (22-288-3), Smith finally put all the pieces together in '96, coming up with 83 receptions for 1,244 yards and seven touchdowns. In '97, Smith earned a trip to the Pro Bowl. And he's no longer hampered by injuries — he has played in all of the franchise's 52 games (including playoffs).

Kansas City
Chiefs

For 35 seasons now, Kansas City has lived to love its Chiefs. The rugged Chiefs reflect the best qualities of their Middle American fans: They're honest, hard-working and successful. And do not underestimate the value of that success.

"The great support we've received probably relates to the fact that we've had nine consecutive winning seasons," says owner Lamar Hunt. "We really work at it, and I think the fans appreciate it."

Indeed, the Chiefs have not merely won, they've won in style. Fueled by an aggressive free agency plan, six of those winning seasons have included double-digit victory totals. Going into the 1998 season, Kansas City's nine-year streak is first among AFC teams and second in the league to the San Francisco 49ers (15).

Hunt, a member of the Pro Football Hall of Fame, is the main reason. It was Hunt who saw the possibilities back in 1960, when he organized the American Football League. His Dallas Texans came into being the same year the NFL added the Dallas Cowboys to its roster. In 1962 coach Hank Stram brought in a journeyman quarterback named Len Dawson, and the Texans won the AFL championship over the Houston Oilers in double overtime.

In 1963, Hunt moved the Texans to Kansas City and renamed them the Chiefs. "It was an attractive place to play for many reasons," Hunt says. "We were one of only two major teams there, along with baseball's Kansas City Athletics. And there was no college football in town. Lawrence [the University of

Franchise History
Dallas Texans (AFL)
(1959–62)
Kansas City Chiefs (AFL)
(1963–70)
Kansas City Chiefs (NFL)
(1970–present)

By the Numbers
(Since 1970)
Regular Season: 212-205-7
Postseason: 3-9
Division Titles: 4
Vs. Division: 107-96-2 (Playoffs: 1-2)
Playoffs Appearances: 9
Home: 126-82-3
Away: 86-123-4

(Overall)
Regular Season: 299-253-12
Postseason: 8-11
Playoffs Appearances: 13
Home: 174-103-4
Away: 125-150-8

Most Revered Football Figures

Len Dawson. The stature of the Super Bowl-winning QB turned local sportscaster only grows with time.

Hank Stram. Some locals still rue the day in 1974 when the Chiefs' Super Bowl coach was fired.

Bobby Bell. One of the best linebackers of all time, Bell turned restaurateur and is still a fixture of Kansas City culture.

Willie Lanier. Beside Bell and Jim Lynch, this prototypical middle linebacker anchored one of football's best linebacking corps ever.

Rivalries

For some, there is no better rivalry in football than Chiefs-**Raiders** (39-37-2). In the 1990s, it hasn't been much of a contest as the Chiefs have prevailed in 15 of the last 17 encounters, including a 10-6 win in the first round of the playoffs in 1991. In the early days, there was usually much more on the line, like supremacy of the AFL. Don't worry; the franchises still hate each other. Just as heated but much more relevant recently is the Chiefs and Denver **Broncos** series, which the Chiefs lead 43-32. Amid accusations of dirty play and unjustified whining, this previously civilized rivalry has turned nasty. The Chiefs or Broncos won the division in each of the past three seasons and five of the last seven, only adding to the drama. The Broncos' 14-10 playoff win at Arrowhead Stadium last season spilled fuel onto an already raging fire.

did you know?
The Chiefs had seven players, more than any other club, selected to the all-time All-AFL team.

Kansas] and Columbia [the University of Missouri] were not direct competitors. Plus, the Mayor (H. Roe Bartle) was very supportive." The mayor, whose nickname was "Chief," promised to expand Municipal Stadium and guaranteed Hunt three times the season ticket base he'd had in Dallas.

Still led by Stram and Dawson, the Chiefs won the AFL Championship game again in 1966 and 1969, and Kansas City had the honor of representing the league in the first Super Bowl, losing to Green Bay, 35-10. In January, 1970, the Chiefs won their first and only Super Bowl (IV) over Minnesota, 23-7, in New Orleans. The AFL merged with the NFL in 1970, thanks in large part to Hunt, and the new conference expressed its gratitude by naming the AFC championship trophy after him.

In 1972, the Chiefs moved into Arrowhead Stadium, a state-of-the-art venue that remains fan-friendly today. Fans have always been a priority of the Chiefs. The cover of the 1997 media guide didn't feature coach Marty Schottenheimer or quarterback Elvis Grbac; it showed fans at Arrowhead cheering for the Chiefs. Kansas City could easily have the NFL's largest season-ticket base; Arrowhead seats 79,451. But the Chiefs set aside some 7,000 tickets for every home game to provide greater access. And so, with a waiting list of 20,000 for season tickets, they settle for 72,000 regulars — third in the league behind the two New York teams.

> "The Chiefs' defensive line looked like a redwood forest."
> — Vikings quarterback Joe Kapp, after a 23-7 loss to Kansas City in Super Bowl IV. (1970)

"The fans," Hunt says, "they're important to us."

The feeling is mutual in Kansas City.

—Greg Garber

Arrowhead Stadium

A trip to a Kansas City Chiefs game combines the city's two true passions, football and barbecue. Arrowhead and its vast parking lots are enveloped in smoke emanating from grills hours before kickoff. Some fans head to Arrowhead without tickets, and no intention of getting any. They just want to be part of the pre- and post-game atmosphere. They'll set up tailgate shop in the parking lot and stay there at kickoff, watching the action on portable TV sets and hearing the roars from the stadium.

The only rule concerning tailgating is that everybody does it. From tuxedo-clad patrons and their catered meals, white tablecloths and candelabra (it's true) to the guy toting around his own 12-pack and having a liquid meal, you see it all in the Arrowhead Stadium parking lots. The Chiefs, who encourage their fans to come early and tailgate, furnish bins for used charcoal briquets. That doesn't mean there isn't the occasional accident. A few years back, one fan slid a grill full of simmering coals under his car and headed for the stadium. He returned after the game to find four wheels and a charred mess.

Inside, the Chiefs enjoy one of the NFL's better home field advantages, going undefeated at Arrowhead in two of the last three years. The Chiefs have led the NFL in attendance the past four seasons and virtually all of the 79,000 fans who fill the place

did you know?
The original plans for Arrowhead Stadium and its companion baseball stadium called for a sliding roof that would cover one of the buildings at a time.

The "I Was There" Game

January 4, 1970: In this AFL Championship Game — the final game played by the American Football League, it was only fitting that the two clubs who represented the AFL in the first two Super Bowls be around to decide who would play in the fourth. Three weeks earlier at Oakland, the Chiefs were stifled, 10-6. But it was their defense that stood tall this time around as they silenced the Raiders' fans. (Chiefs 17, Raiders 7).

The Paper Bag Game

December 22, 1996: The Chiefs had taken great pride in their ability to make the playoffs in every season in the 1990s. That streak came to an inglorious end courtesy of this ugly 20-9 defeat in Buffalo's Rich Stadium. The loss did nothing for the reputation of coach Marty Schottenheimer who is still dogged by a "can't win the big one" reputation.

Great Names

Zenon Andrusyshyn (P, 1978)
Jitter Fields (KR, 1987)
R.B. Nunnery (DT, 1960)
George Shorthose (WR, 1985)
Barry Word (RB, 1990-92)

Hall of Fame

Lamar Hunt	(Owner 1972)
Bobby Bell	(LB 1983)
Willie Lanier	(LB 1986)
Len Dawson	(QB 1987)
Buck Buchanan	(DT 1990)
Jan Stenerud	(PK 1991)

Our Top Story

"Stram Is Fired"
December 27, 1974
An era closes as Hank Stram, head coach since the franchise's early days in Dallas and leader of the Super Bowl IV champion squad, is fired at the end of a 5-9 campaign.

"Death of a Hero"
June 29, 1983
Young running back Joe Delaney drowned while trying to rescue two children in a Monroe, LA, park pond. The 24-year-old Delaney appeared destined to become one of the best runners in club history. He gained 1,121 yards as a rookie in 1981.

"Mr. Smith Goes to Denver"
April 14, 1997
As a free agent, Neil Smith decided to take his services elsewhere, opting to join the Broncos for a lower figure than the Chiefs' offer.

Team Leaders

Rushing Yards
4,897   Christian Okoye, 1987-1992
Passing Yards
28,507   Len Dawson, 1962-75
Passing Touchdowns
237   Len Dawson, 1962-75
Receptions
416   Henry Marshall, 1976-87
Interceptions
58   Emmitt Thomas, 1966-78
Touchdowns
60   Otis Taylor, 1965-75
Points
1,466   Nick Lowery, 1980-93

are wearing red. Arrowhead is one of the better football-viewing stadiums in the country, despite being nearly thirty years old. The third and upper decks are rather steep, however, which means you are close to the action but need to be in decent shape simply to get to your seat. An upper deck tip: Get seats on the stadium's north or east side. That will put you in the warmth of the sun for late season games.

The Bottom Line on Arrowhead Stadium

Address: Truman Sports Complex, Kansas City, MO 64129 (816)924-9300.

Tickets: Most of the 79,000 seats are sold on a seasonal basis. Roughly 6,700 single-game tickets are available, and they are put on sale for groups and individuals each summer and sell out in minutes. The average price is $42.
1998: $37-$49.50
1994: $20-$35

Public Transportation: Bus service is available on game day from suburban locations and is a good way to beat the crowd. Call Metro Bus (816) 221-0660 for more information.

Parking: The parking lots can handle more than 20,000 cars, but that means quite a hike to the stadium for late-arriving fans.

did you know?
The Chiefs' final game at Municipal Stadium was the double over-time, 27-24 loss to the Dolphins in the 1971 playoffs. Kansas City opened Arrowhead Stadium in 1972 with a 20-10 loss to Miami.

While You Were Eating Turkey....
Perhaps Chiefs-Patriots should be a regular Turkey Day game. In any case, the Chiefs have played on Thanksgiving Day twice in the 1990s, beating Detroit, 28-24, in 1996, their most recent appearance.
Overall, 4-5.

Best of the Chiefs

Best Team

1969 (14-3): The Chiefs were the most successful team in the AFL, and their win over the Raiders in the 1969 title game at Oakland gave them a league-best three championships. Despite it being their second Super Bowl appearance, Hank Stram's club was a huge underdog to Minnesota in New Orleans. But DE Buck Buchanan and friends beat up the Vikings' QB Joe Kapp and the rest of the offense, securing the Chiefs' place in history.

Greatest Players by Position

Pos:	Player
QB:	Len Dawson
RB:	Christian Okoye
WR:	Otis Taylor
TE:	Fred Arbanas
OL:	Ed Budde
DL:	Buck Buchanan
LB:	Bobby Bell
DB:	Emmitt Thomas
P/K:	Jan Stenerud
ST:	Albert Lewis

And Don't Forget...

S: Johnny Robinson. A member of the American Football League's all-time team, totaling 57 interceptions in 11 seasons.

RB: Ed Podolak. All-purpose runner who was a one-man show (350 total yards) in the '71 playoff loss to the Dolphins.

DE: Art Still. The former Kentucky star totaled 72.5 sacks with the Chiefs, and came to play every week and every down.

DB: Deron Cherry. Six-time Pro Bowler who stole 50 passes during his 11 seasons in Kansas City.

T: John Alt. A stalwart on the offensive line, playing 13 seasons for the Chiefs and earning two trips to the Pro Bowl.

NT: Bill Maas. Versatile defensive lineman who could play inside or out, earning a pair of Pro Bowl berths at nose tackle.

Best Argument

Linebacker: Bobby Bell or Willie Lanier? Teamed with Jim Lynch, they made up one of the most formidable linebacking trios in pro football annals. Bell was a big-play performer, with the size of a defensive end and the agility of a cat. Lanier was a hard-nosed rock in the middle and the leader of the defense. Both are deserved members of the Pro Football Hall of Fame.

> **"We moved by bus. Now we travel by jet."**
> **— Hank Stram, after the signing of Heisman Trophy winning running back Mike Garrett. The speedy Garrett averaged 5.4 yards per carry in 1966, his rookie season, and rushed for over 1,000 yards in 1967.**

Best Coach

Hank Stram (1960-74): A notable omission from the Pro Football Hall of Fame, Stram turned the Chiefs into the AFL's most successful team, amassing an impressive 129-79-10 mark in 15 seasons with the club. His multi-faceted attack kept defenses off-balance, but he's best known for his colorful sideline chatter during Super Bowl IV as "65 Toss Power Trap" led to a Chiefs' touchdown.

Pressbox

Who to Read...

The *Kansas City Star* prints special Chiefs sections each Sunday and Monday during the season — that's in addition to its voluminous coverage during the rest of the week. With a recent redesign and some new, more opinionated writers, the *Star* gets higher marks now from fans than in past years.

Who to Watch...

Most of the TV stations in the area have special Chiefs shows during the season. Many are hosted by players, most notably Marcus Allen, whose show airs Sundays at 11am on KCTV–CBS. Former Chiefs great Len Dawson is the sports anchor on KMBC–ABC. Chiefs games appear on KCTV. A local favorite is cable station Metro Sports, which features Chiefs Pellom McDaniels and Will Shields. WDAF–FOX carries Chiefs Update.

Who to Listen To...

An unofficial count last season turned up 11 players with TV and/or radio shows. That's not counting Carl Peterson, the club's president and general manager, who also has his own show on KCFX Radio (101 FM) on Monday. Games are broadcast on KCFX, with Mitch Holthius and Len Dawson announcing. Dawson's not afraid to speak his mind, and Chiefs fans love him for it. KPRS (103.3 FM) also has a Monday night show; past hosts have included Chiefs Danan Hughes and Donnell Bennett.

Capacity: 79,101.
Restrooms: 48.

Where To Go . . . in Kansas City

Best Bars

Best beer and burger. Good place for cold beer, pub food and football watching. Hanging on each of several television sets scattered around the bar at **Tanners** is a sign listing the game shown on that particular set at a particular time. There are several locations in Kansas City — downtown is a personal favorite. *1000 Broadway. (816) 471-8687. M-Th 10am-1:30am, F-Sa 10am-3am, Su 11am-1:30am.*

Best sports bar. Fuzzy's is the all-around most popular place outside Arrowhead to watch the Chiefs play. *1227 W. 103rd St. (816) 941-7702. Seven days 11am-3am.*

Best old-fashioned drinks. The place downtown is smoky, loud and beloved **Quaff**. The perfect mix of rowdy fun and comfortable dive, real fans go here. *1010 Broadway. (816) 471-1918. M-Sa 6pm-3am.*

Best Restaurants

Best barbecue. Calvin Trillin called **Arthur Bryant's** the greatest restaurant in America. What more do you want to know? You haven't been to Kansas City if you haven't eaten a massive pile of beautiful Bryant's barbecue. If you're not tailgating, pick up a sandwich to go. *Two locations. 3200 North Station Dr. (816) 414-*

7474. *Su-Th 11am-10pm, F-Sa 11am-1am. 1727 Brooklyn, (816) 231-1123, M-Th 10am-9:30pm, F-Sa 10am-10pm, Su 11am-8pm. AE, DC, MC, V. $*

Best Italian. Many folks in Kansas City (including Derrick Thomas, who's a regular) love Garozzo's for Italian, but **Figlio's Country Club Plaza** has its own following. It's a classy but unpretentious Italian eatery with a great outdoor dining deck in warm weather. The atmosphere is warm and inviting, with service to match. *209 W. 46th Terr. (816) 561-0505. M-Th 11am-10pm, F-Sa 11am-11pm, Su 10:30am-10pm. All major credit cards. $$*

Best fiesta. Reasonably priced and popular, **Margarita's** offers Mexican fare, with burgers, too. *2829 Southwest Blvd. (816) 931-4849. Su-Th 10am-10pm, F-Sa 10am-11pm. All major credit cards. $*

> "In my mind, it does not stick out as a great football game. It will stick out as a personal disaster." — Placekicker Jan Stenerud, who missed a 32-yard field-goal attempt in the closing minute of regulation, on the Chiefs' dramatic 1971 double-overtime playoff loss to the Dolphins.

Best Accommodations

Adam's Mark. Across the street from the stadium; occasionally the visiting team stays here. Package deals, including passes to postgame parties, are available. *9103 E. 39th St. (816) 737-0200. $$*

Holiday Inn Sports Complex. Right off I-

---

did you know?

In 1993, Derrick Thomas delivered the keynote address at the Vietnam Veterans Memorial in Washington. When he was five years old, the airplane carrying his father, Air Force Captain Robert Thomas back from a mission in Vietnam had been shot down. The mission's name: "Operation Linebacker Two."

Ready For Primetime (Monday Night)

September 8, 1997: Few games in the history of Monday Night Football are more memorable than this contest between the Chiefs and Raiders at Oakland Coliseum. The Chiefs drove 80 yards in 55 seconds without the aid of a timeout, scoring when Andre Rison inexplicably got behind the secondary and caught a 32-yard TD pass with three seconds left to give the Chiefs a 28-27 win. Overall Monday Night: 16-10 Overall Thursday night: 3-0 Overall Sunday night: 4-2

Think About the Weather

January 7, 1996: Despite sporting an NFL-best 13-3 mark (8-0 at home) and a decisive homefield advantage considering the temperature (11 degrees) and wind-chill factor (minus-9), the Chiefs were the team that couldn't handle the conditions. The Colts, more suited to the climate-controlled atmosphere of the RCA Dome, did just enough to pull off a huge 10-7 upset in this AFC divisional playoff.

Worst Team

1977 (2-12): Losers of their first five games, the Chiefs were 1-6 at the halfway point when head coach Paul Wiggin was dismissed and replaced by Tom Bettis, who prevailed in his debut (a 20-10 win over the Packers) but then dropped his final six contests.

Fans' notes

On Screen

Cornerback Fred "The Hammer" Williamson may have been on the losing side with the Chiefs in the first Super Bowl, but two years later he helped lead the boys of the 4077th to victory on the gridiron in **"M*A*S*H"**. Williamson made his home on the '70s screen, with perhaps no appearance more memorable than his starring role in the 1972 boxing flick **Hammer.** In comparison, running back Marcus Allen generally keeps a low profile. Allen did join the supporting cast behind Mario Van Peebles for the 1991 TV movie **A Triumph of the Heart: The Ricky Bell Story,** about the tragic illness and death of Buccaneers running back Bell.

Bookshelf

Winning It All: The Chiefs of the AFL. Joe McGuff (Doubleday 1970).
Arrowhead: Home of the Chiefs. Michael McKenzie (Addax Publishing Group 1997).
Hail to the Chiefs. Bob Gretz (Sagamore Publishing Co. 1994).
Marcus: The Autobiography of Marcus Allen. Marcus Allen and Carlton Stowers (St. Martin's Press 1997).

You Gotta See...

▸**Old Municipal Stadium** no longer stands. A community garden sits where the greatest Chiefs teams played at the corner of 22nd Street and Brooklyn Avenue.
▸A long-overlooked piece of sports history which is finally receiving proper attention, baseball's Negro Leagues, is documented and commemorated at the **Negro Leagues Hall of Fame** in Kansas City.
▸The **NCAA Hall of Champions,** located in Overland Park, just over the Kansas state line, pays tribute to the greats of college athletics — football, basketball, you name it.

Swami Sez:

Nobody is trying harder than the Chiefs to put their owner's name on the Lamar Hunt trophy, awarded annually to the AFC champion.

70, within walking distance of the Truman Sports Complex. There's an indoor pool, exercise facility, restaurant and lounge. *4011 Blue Ridge Cutoff. (816) 353-5300. $$*

Drury Inn by the Stadium. Also right off the highway, it's just a few blocks to Arrowhead. Free continental breakfast. *3830 Blue Ridge Cutoff. (816) 923-3000. $-$$*

Against the Odds

The promising career of **Mack Lee Hill** (1964-1965) was tragically cut short when he died on the operating table undergoing routine knee surgery late in the 1965 season. (In less than two seasons, Hill rushed 230 times for 1,194 yards and six TDs.) Each year, Chiefs veterans award a trophy to the first-year player who "best exemplifies the spirit of the late Mack Lee Hill ... the man with the giant heart and quiet way." His number (36) is one of only eight that the team has ever retired.

Miami Dolphins

Once upon a time, Florida was known primarily for oranges, rockets, water skiing and retirees. Professional sports had made few inroads amid the citrus groves until the Dolphins came to Miami and gave America something other than Jackie Gleason to remember the city by. In 1972, the Dolphins played a perfect 17-0 season, a display of brilliant football and distinguished management, and while so much about Florida has changed since the sixties, that unbeaten season still stands as the only one in NFL annals. That benchmark, a defining aspect of the team's identity, is also a tough standard to meet.

Franchise History

Miami Dolphins (AFL)
(1966–69)
Miami Dolphins (NFL)
(1970–present)

To the Dolphins credit, the team has come close. Since the 1970 merger of the National and American Football Leagues, the Dolphins are the winningest team in professional football. Any of the 25,188 who were in attendance at the very first game played at Miami's Orange Bowl should not be surprised at the team's success. Although Oakland came out a winner, 23-14, Joe Auer returned the opening kickoff 95 yards for a Dolphin touchdown, with one of the ownership partners, entertainer Danny Thomas, sprinting down the sideline trailing Auer into the end zone.

The first head coach was George Wilson, who compiled a 15-39-2 record in his four years, and the first training camp was conducted on a rocky practice field in St. Petersburg Beach. The cuisine served up at the training table came from the Chinese restaurant in the team hotel. Ultimately, the camp moved to St. Andrews School in Boca Raton.

During those years of futility, though, general manager Joe Thomas was per-

By the Numbers

(Since 1970)

Regular Season: 274-148-2
Postseason: 17-15
Division Titles: 11
Vs. Division: 142-80-1 (Playoffs: 3-5)
Playoff Appearances: 17
Home: 156-54-1
Away: 118-94-1

(Overall)

Regular Season: 289-187-4
Postseason: 17-15
Playoff Appearances: 17
Home: 165-71-3
Away: 124-116-1

Most Revered Football Figures

Don Shula. The NFL's winningest coach of all-time brought championship football to Miami.

Dan Marino. Set records with 5,084 yards and 48 TD passes in 1984, and didn't stop there — he captured the imagination of fans by redefining the passing game.

Bob Griese. Not pyrotechnic like Marino, but a ball-control quarterback who led the Dolphins during their era of dominance.

Dwight Stephenson. Had his career not been cut short by a knee injury in 1987, he might have been the best center ever.

Rivalries

Miami-**Buffalo** has mattered a lot recently because the teams have battled at every level of the playoffs. The Dolphins used to have their way in this match-up, beating the **Bills** a record 20 straight times during the 1970s. How the tables have turned. From 1987-97 (including playoffs), the 'Fins are just 7-18 in this rivalry, but they still lead the series 41-25-1. With the emergence of **New England** as one of the top teams in the AFC, the rivalry that brewed in the mid-1980s has been rekindled. It was the **Patriots** who twice foiled Dan Marino's attempts to get back to the Super Bowl, and now they are the team that the Dolphins must deal with if Marino is to ever get back there. New England thumped Miami in back-to-back, season-ending meetings in 1997, narrowing the Dolphins series lead to 38-27.

forming some astute drafting and trading. In 1967, Bob Griese, a Purdue quarterback was the fourth player selected in the common draft. Next year's draft produced fullback Larry Csonka and safety Dick Anderson along with Zonk's partner in the backfield, Jim Kiick. In 1969, Bill Stanfill, who would become a Pro Bowl defensive end, and the speedy Mercury Morris were tabbed by Thomas, who also made three sensational deals which brought all-time AFL middle linebacker Nick Buoniconti and future Hall of Famers guard Larry Little and wide receiver Paul Warfield.

The man who would lead them to glory, Don Shula, was hired on February 18, 1970, after seven years with the Baltimore Colts. He established his style quickly. "I'm just a guy who rolls up his sleeves and goes to work, " he said at his first press conference. In successive years, the Dolphins went to three Super Bowls, winning in 1972 and '73. The '72 win capped a 17-0 season, the only perfect season in NFL history. The 26-year Shula era saw him become the all-time winningest coach at 347-173-6 (.665). His 328 regular season wins is also a record. He would also take the Dolphins to Super Bowls in 1982 and '84, losing to Washington and San Francisco.

It was after the loss in Super Bowl XVII that Shula looked to replace quarterback David Woodley. With the 27th pick in the 1983 draft, he selected Dan Marino, who, in 1984, led the Dolphins to a 14-2 record, and set records for passing yards (5,084) and TD passes (48). With the Marks Brothers, Duper

did you know?

In 1972, teammates Larry Csonka and Mercury Morris both ran for 1,000-plus yards during the season, an NFL first. From 1979-97, Karim Abdul-Jabbar was the 'Fins' lone 1,000-yard runner (1996).

and Clayton, as his keys early on, and a variety of strong receivers since, Marino's career has brought him every imaginable passing record.

Dolphins patriarch Joe Robbie died in 1990 at the age of 73, and by 1994, H. Wayne Huizenga had acquired ownership of the franchise. But the changing of the guard wasn't over yet in Miami. Don Shula retired after the 1995 season, and Jimmy Johnson, who had led both the Dallas Cowboys and Miami Hurricanes to championships, came to town. The Dolphins met with mixed success in Johnson's first two seasons at the helm, and there was friction as he began to mold the club to his own vision. More changes certainly lie ahead for the Dolphins: Johnson wants to stress the running game, and the great Marino must eventually retire. No matter how things change in Miami (and change they do—Anita Bryant was the most visible woman in Florida in 1972; now it's Madonna), a small gleam of perfection will always light on the Dolphins.

—Hank Goldberg

Pro Player Stadium

Located between Miami and Fort Lauderdale, Pro Player Stadium (formerly Joe Robbie Stadium) was the first sports complex in South Florida to cater to both Miami-Dade and Broward counties. Former Dolphins owner Robbie built the stadium with his own money after he battled the city of Miami for improvements to the Orange Bowl. The stadium was opened in 1987

> "Don Shula can take his'n and beat you'n, and he could take you'n and beat his'n." — Oilers head coach "Bum" Phillips

did you know?
The Dolphins hold the NFL record for consecutive victories at home with 27, from 1971 to 1974.

The "I Was There" Game

January 14, 1973: Super Bowl VII: It might not have been the most exciting Super Bowl, but the image of Don Shula being carried off the field at the L.A. Coliseum on the shoulders of his players remains a special moment. In a contest dominated by the Dolphins on the field but not on the scoreboard, Shula's club was one crazy play (Garo Yepremian's pass attempt on a blocked field goal) away from a Super Bowl shutout. The Dolphins won 14-7. The win put the cap on a 17-0 season.

The Paper Bag Game

December 30, 1995: AFC Wild Card Game: Having finished the regular season as a 9-7 wild card, the Dolphins had the unenviable task of visiting Orchard Park, New York, in the winter. The Bills rushed for 341 yards, the second-best total in NFL playoff history, forcing out Don Shula as coach and ending the most controversial season in Dolphins history. (Buffalo 37, Dolphins 22)

Great Names

Sinatausilinuu (Nuu) Faaola (FB, 1989)
African Grant (S, 1990)
Jim Kiick (RB, 1968-74)
Larry Little (G/T, 1969-80)
Edward "Wahoo" McDaniel (LB, 1966-68)
Mercury Morris (RB, 1969-75)
Uwe Von Schamann (K, 1979-84)
Irving Spikes (RB, 1994-present)

Our Top Story

"Perfect"

January 14, 1973

The Dolphins finished the only undefeated season in NFL history, going 17-0 with a 14-7 win over Washington in Super Bowl VII. The perfect record came in only the third season after the team joined the NFL in the merger with the AFL, and in only the third season under coach Don Shula.

"WFL Hobbles Dolphins"

September 22, 1975

The Dolphins open their 1975 campaign without three of their biggest offensive weapons — running backs Larry Csonka and Jim Kiick and receiver Paul Warfield. All three played in the World Football League that season. Miami fell to the Raiders in their first game, 31-21, and went on to miss the playoffs for the first time since 1969 despite a 10-4 record.

"Mercury Fallen"

August 18, 1982

Former Dolphin great Mercury Morris was arrested for allegedly selling cocaine. He spent nearly three years in a prison located within sight of the Orange Bowl before his trial was declared unfair on March 6, 1986, and he was released.

"Don Shula Resigns"

January 6, 1996

Shula, the winningest coach in NFL history, stepped down after a season in which he lost control of his team and was embarrassed in a playoff loss at Buffalo.

did you know?

Despite having had players selected to the Pro Bowl 126 times, the Dolphins have never had a cornerback make it.

and was renovated in 1992 to provide a home for the baseball Marlins.

The facility, which has played host to two Super Bowls and will host a third after the 1998 season, is a state-of-the-art stadium with an extensive club level featuring indoor bars and dining, entertainment and a ring of luxury boxes with a prime view of the field. The facility's design has been a model for other stadiums in towns such as Charlotte, Jacksonville and Nashville. Like South Florida itself, the atmosphere at a Dolphins game is unique. While Florida is a hotbed for football, Dolphins fans tend to be a little more laid back about their team. Even though crowds tend to be young, there are a lot of transplants in the Miami area, and fans here are not as rabid as their counterparts in Pittsburgh, Oakland, Chicago or New England.

Unlike some older stadiums not built especially for football, there are no quirky seats at Pro Player Stadium. That is, there are none located behind poles and the like. All of the seats face the field at the correct angle and there is no bench seating anywhere. Unlike many NFL cities, there is no strong tailgating tradition among Dolphins fans. There are plenty of other pre-game activities available at the stadium, such as Sportstown, where fans can participate in football-related activities and other sports such as basketball.

The Bottom Line on Pro Player Stadium

Address: 2269 NW 199th Street, Miami, FL 33056. (305) 620-2578.

Tickets: Surprisingly, tickets are available

Best of the Dolphins

Best Team

1973 (15-2): Better than undefeated? One year after posting their legendary 17-0 campaign of '72, Don Shula's Dolphins had meshed into a well-oiled machine and dominated on a weekly basis. A disciplined defense made life easier for Bob Griese and company as Miami limited 15 of its 17 foes to 17 or fewer points, and outscored the Bengals, Raiders and Vikings a combined 85-33 in the postseason.

Greatest Players by Position

Pos:	Player
QB:	Dan Marino
RB:	Larry Csonka
WR:	Mark Clayton
TE:	Keith Jackson
OL:	Larry Little
DL:	Manny Fernandez
LB:	Nick Buoniconti
DB:	Dick Anderson
P/K:	Reggie Roby
ST:	Duriel Harris

And Don't Forget...

WR: Nat Moore. A reliable, big-play receiver who thrived during the ball-control days and into the wide-open Dan Marino Era alongside Marks Brothers Duper and Clayton.

G: Bob Kuechenberg. One of the well-schooled blockers on Don Shula's dominating offensive fronts.

LB: John Offerdahl. Always around the football, the five-time Pro Bowler enjoyed a productive but injury-plagued career.

LB: A.J. Duhe. A versatile defender who could line up at a number of spots, he was magnificent during the Dolphins Super Bowl run in 1982.

WR: Paul Warfield. Played just five seasons in Miami, but averaged 21.5 yards per reception and caught 33 TD passes.

LB: Bob Matheson. Rarely missed a game in nine years with the team's "No-Name Defense."

Best Argument

Quarterback: Dan Marino or Bob Griese? One has all the numbers, the other owns a pair of championship rings. We may never see another Marino, but he mostly played on teams that lacked a running game and, for the most part, a reliable defense. Griese was the smart field general and wasn't called on to carry the load, totaling just 41 pass attempts in three Super Bowl appearances.

> "The Dolphins haven't been able to run the football for a long time before I got here. And so I don't think it's just personnel." — Jimmy Johnson, speculating about the Dolphins' rushing woes.

Best Coach

Don Shula (1970-95): Duh. Shula has more victories than any coach in NFL history. Shula's detractors point to the fact that he went 22 seasons without a championship after winning Super Bowls VII and VIII, but that's nonsense. This Hall of Famer saw it all during his days with the 'Fins, and usually defeated it.

Pressbox

Who to Read...

The Dolphins are covered daily by three major newspapers, *The Miami Herald*, the *Fort Lauderdale Sun-Sentinel* and the *Palm Beach Post*. Each paper has a regular beat writer on the team. Armando Salguero of the *Herald* and Jason Cole of the *Sun-Sentinel* both provide in-depth coverage, and each has covered the team for nearly a decade. In addition, award-winning writers Dave Hyde *(Sun-Sentinel)*, Edwin Pope *(Herald)*, Dan LeBatard *(Herald)* and Dave George *(Post)* regularly weigh in with their commentary. *El Herald* provides Spanish language coverage.

Who to Watch...

During the season, coach Jimmy Johnson has his own television show, co-hosted by Tony Segreto and Joe Rose of WTVJ–NBC. In addition, Rose (the for-mer Dolphins' TE who caught Dan Marino's first touchdown) and radio color man Jim Mandich are the regular hosts on WQAM-Radio in the morning and afternoon, respectively. Former Dolphins wide receiver Jim Cefalo is the lead sports anchor on WPLG–ABC. Pre-season games can be seen on WFOR–CBS.

Who to Listen To...

This is Miami, so football is a bilingual affair. Games are broadcast in English on WQAM (560 AM) Sports Radio, the Dolphins flagship station, with Bill Zimpher and Jim Mandich, and in Spanish on WQBA (1140 AM) with Rene Giraldo. Although no Dolphins' players host a radio show, it should come as no surprise that Jimmy Johnson has a weekly program with Hank Goldberg on WQAM.

every year by calling the Dolphins ticket office. The team holds several promotional activities where seats are sold and fans can pick out exactly what they want from the available spots. Getting the premium season tickets between the 30-yard lines takes many years. In addition to the six-tiered seating plan, from the lower sideline to the upper deck, there are club-level seats available in the luxury boxes. Luxury boxes are available on a long-term basis only.

1998: $45/$38/$37/$24

1994: $33/$28/$20

Public Transportation: Mass transit stops right at the stadium; there are buses available from all sections of South Florida. Dade Transit: (305) 638-6700. Browards Transit (954) 357-8400. Palm Beach County Transportation Authority (561) 233-1114.

Parking: There are ample parking lots directly around and across the street from the stadium. For big games (such as on Monday night), nearby Calder Race Course provides public parking and a shuttle service. Traffic can be heavy on the surface streets, but the Florida Turnpike runs adjacent to the stadium, and there is an exit from it to the stadium parking lots. There are also a number of designated Park-and-Ride spots nearby.

Capacity: 74,916.

Restrooms 40 men's, 40 women's.

Where to Go . . . in Miami

Best Bars

Best spot for the single fan. In South Beach, the **Clevelander Hotel** provides the definition of the Art Deco district. With a poolside bar, reasonable drink prices and great views of all sorts of natural (and not-so-natural) beauty, this is the place to be. *1020 Ocean Dr., Miami Beach, (305) 531-3485. Seven days 11am-5am.*

Best place to go nuts. Centrally located in Coconut Grove and outdoors, **Fat Tuesday's** is one of the many, many, many spots in Coco Walk where a very good time is had by all. *3015 Grand Ave., Miami, (305) 441-2992. Mon-Wed 11am-12:00am, Th-Su 11am-2am.*

Best burger-and-beer joint in the Florida tradition—Tucked along the Intercoastal in Hollywood is **Le Tub**, a small, open-air bar where the drinks come in plastic cups and the food is served on picnic-ware. Still, it's a great place to just hang out and get away from the fast pace of the beaches and the rest of South Florida. *1100 North Ocean Dr., Hollywood, (954) 921-9425. Seven days 11am-4am.*

> "When you've had two coaches like Don Shula and Jimmy Johnson with this team, there's no question about what the goal is. You're expected to win."
> — Cornerback Terrell Buckley

Best Restaurants

Best family spot: Dave & Busters provides the perfect backdrop for a day of watching football and entertaining the kids.

Ready For Primetime (Monday Night)

December 2, 1985: The Dolphins protected the legacy of their undefeated 1972 team with a 38-24 victory over Chicago, 12-0 at the time. It was the Bears' only loss that season. Indicative of the record's stature, many of the '72 Dolphins were on the sidelines. Marino threw for three touchdowns in a game that he and former coach Don Shula count among their favorites of all-time.

Overall Monday Night: 33-24
Overall Sunday Night: 12-3
Overall Thursday Night: 3-1

Think About the Weather

November 26, 1989: The humid heat of South Florida is a problem for opposing teams, but on this day the humidity became rain in a 34-14 loss to Pittsburgh. The downpour created a sheet of water on the field and Dan Marino came out of the game because effective passing was impossible. He finished by completing only eight of 16 passes for 128 yards.

Worst Team

1967 (4-10): There's never been a really horrendous Dolphins team, unless you go back to the team's second year of existence during the waning years of the AFL. Rookie QB Bob Griese was the biggest name on the roster, but it was an infamous Miami defense that garnered attention, allowing 407 points (still a team record)—31 or more points in half of their games. Talk about a lack of support.

Hall of Fame

Paul Warfield	(WR 1983)
Larry Csonka	(FB 1987)
Jim Langer	(C 1987)
Bob Griese	(QB 1990)
Larry Little	(G 1993)
Don Shula	(Coach 1997)
Dwight Stephenson	(C 1998)

Swami Sez:

If there really is a football god, He (or She) will follow up John Elway's Super Bowl win with one by Dan Marino.

Team Leaders

Rushing Yards
6,737   Larry Csonka, 1968-74, 1979
Passing Yards
55,416   Dan Marino, 1983-
Passing Touchdowns
385   Dan Marino, 1983-
Receptions
550   Mark Clayton, 1983-92
Interceptions
35   Jake Scott, 1970-75
Touchdowns
82   Mark Clayton, 1982-92
Points
830   Garo Yepremian, 1970-78

With a restaurant, a bar with televisions and an array of video games and other activities, this has the right balance for everyone until 10pm, after which you must be 21. *3000 Oakwood Blvd., Hollywood, (954) 923-5505. M-Th 11am-1am, F 11am-2am, Sa 11:30am-2am, Su 11:30am-1am. All major credit cards. $*

Classic Miami fare. Located at the end of South Beach, **Joe's Stone Crab** is the standard for great food, particularly when the crabs are in season. That happens to coincide with the football season, so get crackin'. *227 Biscayne St., Miami Beach, (305) 673-0365. Open Oct. 15 to May 15, M 5pm-10pm, Tu-Th 11:30am-2pm, 5pm-10pm, F-Sa 11:30am-2pm, 5pm-11pm, Su 5pm-11pm. All major credit cards. $$$*

"Jacksonville and Tampa Bay have football, but when you grow up in Florida, there is only one team that you really want to play for because of all the history and the tradition. That's the Dolphins." — Former Dolphins safety Louis Oliver.

Best place to catch the coach. Full of TVs and ex-jocks, **Jimmy Johnson's Three Rings Bar & Grill** in the Eden Roc Hotel is a burgers-and-beers kind of place which pays tribute to the coach's winning ways. *4525 Collins Ave., Miami Beach, (305) 672-6224. M-Sa 11:30-1am, Su 10:30-midnight. All major credit cards. $$*

Best atmosphere/local fare. Lario's On The Beach, a South Beach staple, is reasonably priced, provides huge portions and has a great selection of Cuban food to go with other items. Co-owned by singer Gloria Estefan, this is a favorite of locals and tourists alike. Its clientele include notables such as Florida Marlins pitch-

Fans' notes

On Screen

Alrighty, then! Marino, Shula and several other Dolphins were featured in **Ace Ventura: Pet Detective** (the first one, in 1993) starring actor-comedian Jim Carrey. The plot revolves around an attempt to kidnap the Dolphins aquatic mascot. Marino may be better known for "taking care of the hands that take care of him" (i.e., his offensive line) in holiday-season TV ads for gloves. **Miami Dolphins 25th Anniversary: Days of Victory, Years of Glory**, an NFL Films video release, is an hour-long journey from the team's AFL roots through their rise to NFL prominence.

Bookshelf

Shark Among the Dolphins. Inside Jimmy Johnson's Transformation of the Miami Dolphins. Steve Hubbard (Ballantine 1997).
Marino: On the Record. Dan Marino (HarperCollins 1996).
The Miami Dolphins: Football's Greatest Team. Al Levine (Prentice-Hall 1973).
The Miami Dolphins: Winning Them All. Steve Perkins (Putnam 1973).
Marino! Dan Marino and Steve Delsohn (Contemporary 1986).

Against the Grain. Eugene "Mercury" Morris and Steve Fiffer (McGraw-Hill 1988).

You Gotta See...

▶If you're making a long trip to South Florida (six days or more), the **Florida Keys and Key West**, in particular, are must-sees. Time hasn't changed the relaxed nature of the Keys, where everything from diving and snorkeling to good food, to raucous partying are available. If you're in town for just a weekend, the **beach** is a must and taking a boat ride on **Biscayne Bay** is the ultimate in relaxation.
▶**Little Havana**, centered around **Calle Ocho** (SW 8th Street), provides a full-on immersion in food, shopping and recreation Cuban style.
▶To get a full dose of sun-drenched, scantily clad, Art Deco, outrageous Miami, head to **South Beach**. During the day, you can find volleyball, rollerblading, surfing and tanning, for participation or just for watching. At night, the neighborhood shelters a variety of clubs, bars and late-night eateries, as well as a diverse cast of characters.

While You Were Eating Turkey....

November 25, 1993. The Dolphins are 3-0 all-time on Thanksgiving Day and played one of the most memorable Turkey day games ever. During an ice storm, they beat Dallas 16-14 on a gaffe by Cowboys defensive tackle Leon Lett. After Dallas blocked a last-second field goal attempt by Pete Stoyanovich, Lett thought he had to down the ball and went sliding across the snow-and-ice-covered turf. When he touched the ball, it became live. The Dolphins recovered and were allowed to kick another field goal for the victory. Overall, 3-0.

Against the Odds

Of the seven Dolphins inducted into the Hall of Fame, not one played defense, proving that it truly was a "No-Name Defense." Notoriety or none, **Nick Buoniconti** (1969-1976) anchored a unit which in the team's perfect 1972 season limited 14 of 17 opponents to 17 points or less. Buoniconti helped preserve the club's undefeated season by intercepting a Terry Bradshaw pass with 2:30 remaining in the '72 AFC Championship. He was named Miami's most valuable linebacker, an honor he earned five times in seven years with the team.

> "When you walk around this city, I think there's a different sense of pride about being a Dolphin. You really feel like you're part of what happens and what has happened."
> — Former Dolphins linebacker Nick Buoniconti.

did you know?

Since 1970, the Dolphins have yet to suffer back-to-back losing seasons, finishing under .500 just twice (1976 and '88) since the merger.

er and Cuba native Livan Hernandez. *820 Ocean Dr., Miami Beach, (305) 532-9577. Su-Th 11:30am-12:00am, F-Sa 11:30am-2am. All major credit cards. $$*

Best Accommodations

The Fort Lauderdale Marina Marriott. Centrally located in Fort Lauderdale, The Marina Marriott is close to the beach, the airport, numerous restaurants and the city's main shopping district. *1881 SE 17th St., (954) 463-4000. $99 and up, call for more information. All major credit cards.*

The Boca Resort. A little out of the way, but well worth the drive. Has golf and tennis and is located in a gorgeous, restored building in one of South Florida's more fashionable areas. *501 E. Camino Real, Boca Raton, (561) 395-3000. $130 (villas), $145-160 (main resort), $225 (beach club). All major credit cards.*

Delano. Situated at Miami's fashion ground zero in South Beach. Swimming pool, David Barton Gym, the Blue Door restaurant: All are celebrity-friendly and acclaimed for their design. The rooms aren't huge, but it's only a walk to local restaurants and nightlife. *1685 Collins Ave. Miami Beach, (305) 672-2000. Peak Season: $335-$415; Off-peak $205-$265.*

Minnesota Vikings

U p in the Land of Ten Thousand Lakes, giants once walked the tundra. Page, Eller, Marshall and Tarkenton were some of their names. They were Vikings; Purple People Eaters, the most fearsome defense in the Black and Blue Division. They played on a frozen field called Metropolitan Stadium and established there a rule of the Upper Midwest that has held, with the occasional challenge, since the '70s.

Founded in 1961, the Vikings were placed in the NFL's Central Division, where they would have to joust with the league's perennial powerhouse, Green Bay. But when those Packers began to get old, the Vikings developed into a dominant team under former Canadian Football League coach Bud Grant, whose stoic sideline manner was a perfect fit for the snow-covered flatlands of Minnesota. In 1968, the Vikings won the first of 10 divisional crowns in 11 years. During that era, the Vikings sent Carl Eller, Alan Page, Ron Yary, Chuck Foreman and many others to the Pro Bowl. The "Purple People Eaters" swallowed opposing quarterbacks in a way that few teams have ever imitated, but as tough as they were on defense, the Vikes rolled up the yards with Tarkenton passing to a series of talented receivers such as Ahmad Rahshad and Sammy White. Tarkenton retired with the NFL record for passing yards (47,003).

But the Vikings also failed to win an NFL championship. Their four Super Bowl losses are the most for an NFC team. Grant would be inducted into the Pro Football Hall of Fame, but never got his hands around the Lombardi Trophy. Grant finally retired after the 1985 season, and the Vikings have yet to go back

Franchise History

Minnesota Vikings
(1961–present)

By the Numbers

(Since 1970)
Regular Season: 246-176-2
Postseason: 12-18
Division Titles: 12
Vs. Division: 127-77-1 (Playoffs: 0-1)
Playoff Appearances: 18
Home: 141-71-1
Away: 105-105-1

(Overall)
Regular Season: 298-243-9
Postseason: 14-20
Playoffs Appearances: 20
Home: 168-104-4
Away: 130-139-5

Most Revered Football Figures

Fran Tarkenton. To prepare for his legendary role as co-host of television's "That's Incredible," he bypassed acting classes and opted to play the tundra's movie-star quarterback for 13 of his 18 seasons.

Bud Grant. The original Bud Man, he's the only one who ever led the Vikes to the Big Show — four times, as a matter of fact. His low-key personality shone under Scandinavian skies.

Alan Page. The Honorable Purple People Eater. The nine-time Pro Bowler went on to become a justice of the Minnesota Supreme Court.

> **did you know?**
> Kicker Fred Cox (1963-77) has the patent for the Nerf football.

Rivalries

The Vikes and Green Bay **Packers** are 36-36-1 since the conference neighbors started bumping heads in 1961. Cheeseheads have been known to make even more noise than the home fans at the Metrodome. While Green Bay may be the NFC Central's current glamour team, there was a time that the division belonged to the **Bears** (6) or Vikings (12). These two teams have combined to collect 18 of the 27 crowns awarded since 1970. Defense had been the hallmark of the rivalry with the Bears in the early days, but the current Minnesota-Chicago series would make old followers of the "Black and Blue" division a bit red-faced.

to the Super Bowl. And then the Vikings moved indoors to the Metrodome. No more clumps of sod hanging off the helmet of a frostbitten tackle. No more plumes of steam. No more snowmobile suits. The very nature of the team seemed to change; to some, soften. The change did no good. Grant's replacements, Les Steckel, Jerry Burns and Dennis Green, went to the playoffs eight times after that, but the promise of a championship remained unfulfilled. Years of frustration took their toll. The Vikings ownership group thought of moving the team, then — with prodding from the league — decided late in 1997 to sell. Bestselling author Tom Clancy tried to put together a group to buy the team.

"Why buy the Vikings?" said Clancy. "Why not? It's a good team, a lovely area. Minneapolis is one of the nicest cities in the country. And they were available."

Even though Clancy's efforts to buy the team fell through, it wasn't the first time the team had played a major role in his life's work. In "The Sum of All Fears," his 1991 techno-thriller, Clancy devises a nasty but critical scene at a fictional Super Bowl in Denver. During the game, Syrian terrorists detonate a 120-kiloton bomb, leveling Mile High Stadium, the city of Denver and the surrounding environs — in all, 250,000 people dead. Of course, both teams are incinerated in the hideous mayhem. One of those teams is the Minnesota Vikings.

Oops.

> **"I'm glad the bars close at 1 am here. If I'd been drafted by New York, I'd be dead."**
> **— Tommy Kramer to Inside Sports (1981).**

With Clancy out of the picture, Vikings fans continue to look for someone to keep the Vikes in Minnesota and to write the next chapter in the team's history.

—Sal Paolantonio

The Metrodome

What if you built it — and nobody wanted to come? In 1997, 15 years after the Hubert H. Humphrey Metrodome was inflated, the Vikes and the Minnesota Twins were threatening to leave unless they got some new digs. For die-hard fans, it's a far cry from Metropolitan Stadium which now lies, metaphorically, under the Mall of America. Fans have been abandoning the Dome in droves. Even though the Vikings were good enough to make the playoffs in 1997, low attendance meant that most of the home games were blacked out.

The Dome, which cost $68 million and is covered by more than 10 acres of Teflon-coated fiberglass, has all the character of a marshmallow. The atmosphere inside can be sterile and extremely loud, especially during the commercials frequently shown on the scoreboards. The food is unspectacular, although the Dome recently tried to add some new flavors by setting up an outdoor

▼

did you know?

The Vikings can take credit for creating terms on both sides of the ball. Sportwriters came up with the term "scramble" after watching quarterback Fran Tarkenton dance around in the pocket. Coach Bud Grant coined the term "the hurry," which later became a recorded statistic, as a way of describing the way Alan Page threatened quarterbacks to throw.

carnival atmosphere before games, with rock music, games and different snacks. On the sidelines Ragnar, the team's mascot, rallies the Viking faithful in his animal skin outfit

The "I Was There" Games

December 14, 1980: The Vikes trailed the Cleveland Browns, 23-22, with five seconds on the clock, when Two-Minute Tommy Kramer sent up the Queen of Hail Marys. The ball was tipped and Ahmad Rashad snagged it with one hand, then stepped into the end zone, assuring the team a playoff spot. (Vikings 28, Browns 23).

Swami Sez:

With the talent they have at the skill positions, they might have the most exciting offense in football. They have Jake Reed and Cris Carter at wide receiver and have added Randy Moss there. Robert Smith is solid at running back. I really like a healthy Brad Johnson at quarterback.

The Paper Bag Game

December 28, 1975: With about a half minute to go, Roger Staubach sent up a ball that flopped in the wind and landed awkwardly aside Drew Pearson's hip, giving the Dallas Cowboys a 17-14 win. Vikings fans insisted that Pearson pushed off against Nate Wright, and an on-field squabble ensued in which one ref got bonked on the head with a whisky bottle. Fran Tarkenton's father died of a heart attack watching the game on TV. Despite the heartbreak, some Vikings fans claim this as their favorite squad.

Our Top Story

`"Domes-day"`
`August 21, 1982`
The Vikings came in from the cold when the Metrodome opened, forever transforming rough 'n' tumble Minnesota football into a parlor game.

`"Bud is Back"`
`December 18, 1984`
Just when he thought he was out, they sucked him back in. After resigning as head coach in January 1984, Bud Grant returned two days after the Vikings ended the '84 season at 3-13. Apparently, fishing season was over. Grant coached the 1985 team to a 7-9 record before returning to the wild.

`"Everybody for Walker"`
`October 12, 1989`
It was the most lopsided trade since Manhattan was had for a string of beads. GM Mike Lynn decided the Vikings needed a superstar, and the price ended up being the team's future. Lynn traded away five Vikings, eight draft choices and a partridge in a pear tree to the Cowboys, all in exchange for Herschel Walker, who went on to accomplish pretty much nothing. The Cowboys used the deal to build a dynasty.

Great Names

Amp Lee (RB, 1994-96)
Ed Marinaro (RB, 1972-75)
Billy Martin (TE, 1968)
Mike Mullarkey (TE, 1983-88)
Buster Rhymes (WR, 1985-87)
Steve Stonebreaker (LB/E, 1962-63)
Mick Tingelhoff (C, 1962-78)

and sword. Joe Juranitch has been portraying the head Norseman for the past few seasons, replacing the more generic horned plunderer who preceded him.

On the upside, most of the seats inside are excellent, and there are almost no seats with blocked views. And even the bravest fans must say a silent prayer of thanks every time the temperature dips below ten degrees and they can cheer under shelter. Weather is never a factor, save for the two times in 1983 the Dome collapsed under the weight of snow. The only element you'll have to fight is the whoosh of air that pushes you in and out of the revolving doors.

> "We're gonna keep coming back until we can find an AFC team we can beat." — Fran Tarkenton on losing his third Super Bowl in four seasons (1977).

The Bottom Line on Hubert H. Humphrey Metrodome

Address: 34 Kirby Puckett Place, Minneapolis, MN 55415; (612) 338-4537.

Tickets: Season tickets, which ranged from $450 to $150 in 1997, are available by calling (612) 33-VIKES. Single tickets go from $23 to $45. For information on one of the 115 luxury suites, call (612) 478-4837. The best seats, on the first deck behind the benches, are reserved for season-ticket holders. Because of the lack of interest in the last few years, tickets are rarely hard to come by, except for Packers games, in which rival fans help to fill the Dome.

1998: $23/$28/$38/$45
1994: $19/$27/$31/$34

did you know?
The Vikings cheerleaders were originally known as the St. Louis Parkettes.

Best of the Vikings

Best Team

1969 (14-3): Sure, Bud Grant's team came up short in the Super Bowl loss to Kansas City, but this Vikings squad made easy work of nearly every opponent during the regular season, outscoring the opposition nearly three to one (379-133) and limiting 13 of those foes to 14 or fewer points. Postseason conquests of the Rams and Browns put Joe Kapp and company in New Orleans, where they were humbled by the Chiefs.

> "It's hard to pick out our stars. It would have to be an awfully dark night to find them."
> —Bud Grant

Greatest Players by Position

Pos:	Player
QB:	Fran Tarkenton
RB:	Chuck Foreman
WR:	Cris Carter
TE:	Steve Jordan
OL:	Ron Yary
DL:	Alan Page
LB:	Matt Blair
DB:	Paul Krause
P/K:	Fred Cox
ST:	Bill Brown

And Don't Forget...

DE: Carl Eller. While Alan Page dominated foes from his inside spot, the nasty Eller made a meal out of opposing quarterbacks.

DE: Jim Marshall. Known best for "going the wrong way" with an opponent's fumble, it's hard to believe Marshall isn't in Canton.

WR: Sammy White. A consensus Rookie of the Year selection in 1976, he emerged as one of the Vikings' most reliable receivers.

LB: Jeff Siemon. Always around the football, this four-time Pro Bowler was one Viking who made his share of key plays in the big games.

G: Ed White. A key to the running game and a reliable pass blocker, White was a member of all four of the Vikings' Super Bowl squads.

RB: Bill Brown. He played with blood on his pants and steel in his heart. Nothing stopped bowlegged "Boom Boom." Legend has it that the NFL moved the goal posts further back in the end zone primarily because Brown got three concussions by running into them.

Best Argument

Wide Receiver: Cris Carter or Anthony Carter? It's hard to believe that Cris, one of the top offensive players in the game in the 1990s, had his share of off-the-field problems, hence his release from Philadelphia. The Eagles' loss was certainly the Vikings' gain. There were few more exciting than the speedy Anthony, who frustrated defenses and kick coverage units with his big-play abilities.

Best Coach

Bud Grant (1967-83, '85): A successful veteran of the CFL coaching ranks, Grant arrived in the Twin Cities in '67 and suffered through a 3-8-3 campaign. He would not endure another losing season for more than a decade, and over an 11-year stretch (1968-78) won 10 division titles and made four trips to the Super Bowl, where his Vikings fell to four of the best teams of their era.

Pressbox

Who to Read...

Both the *Minneapolis Star Tribune* and the *St. Paul Pioneer Press* agressively cover the team. Star Tribune columnist and WCCO-AM radio personality Sid Hartman is the "King of All Sports" in the Twin Cities, building up a huge stable of "close, personal" friends over the years. The beat writers are Dan Banks at the *Star Tribune* and Jeff Seidel at the *Pioneer Press*.

> "That surface also appears to be exceptionally safe for fans in the upper deck. If they fall out of the stands, they have a good chance of bouncing right back up to their seats." — Ron Luciano, baseball umpire on the Dome's artificial turf in "The Fall of the Roman Umpire." (1986).

Who to Watch...

For Sunday night post-mortems, Viking fans tune into Mark Rosen's show, "Rosen Sports Sunday" on WCCO–CBS and Joe Schmit's "Sports Rap" on KSTP–ABC.

Who to Listen To...

WCCO (830 AM) is the flagship station for Vikings games, with Dan Rowe and Stu Voight in the booth. KFAN (1130 AM) is the area's only all-sports station. The big names to listen for are Dan Bariero and Chad Hartman. Dark Star is another local favorite with a nightly call-in show on WCCO.

Public Transportation: Along Fourth Street, there's the 16A bus. Chicago Avenue is the stop nearest the Dome.

Parking: Lots of lots around the Dome, but the lots aren't attached to it, so there's not much tailgating. Don't bother coming early and expect to pay more than $10. If you've got the energy, you might be better off parking at one of the many downtown ramps, grabbing lunch or a drink in that area, then walking the eight or ten blocks to the Dome.

> "The best plan is for us to meet at the quarterback." —Jim Marshall

Capacity: 64,152 for football games.

Restrooms: 32

Where to go . . . in Minneapolis

Best Bars

Best cheap, stiff drink. Ask for a double at the **Mill Inn**, an irresistible blue-collar dive just a couple blocks from the Dome, and the server will just cackle "Honey, everything here is a double!" You've been warned. *515 Washington Ave. S. (612) 332-3241. Seven days, 10am-1am.*

Best impression of a roadhouse. Once a hangout for factory workers, **Lee's Liquor Bar** has transformed itself into a hot rockabilly club that often has shows on Sunday nights. *101 Glenwood Ave. N. (612) 338-9491. Seven days, 9 am-1 am.*

Best place to sing away your sorrow. Lou Snider, longtime pianist at **Nye's Polanaise Room**, attracts an odd mix of old-timers who love to croon the big-band classics and college students drawn to the kitsch and Polish beer. Come early for a stool around the piano. *112 Hennepin Ave. E. (612) 379-2021. M-Sa 11am-1 am, Su 5pm-1 am.*

Best place to see the scores and seat the kids. **Champp's** has lots of TV sets and big tables to accommodate families. Screaming children are no problem. *100 N. 6th St. (612) 335-5050. M-Sa 11 am-1 am, Su 10am-10pm (game days).*

Funkiest martinis. The Lounge is the closest thing to swank in the Twin Cities, with couch seating, R&B music and pricey drinks. One of the few clubs around where sports caps and sneakers are frowned upon. *411 2nd Ave. (612) 333-8800. M-Th 5pm-1am, F 4pm-1am, Sa 6pm-1am. Often closed on Sundays, so call first.*

> **"All those Super Bowls kind of blend in. The only reason they stand out in my memory is that we lost all of them." — Alan Page,** on his four Super Bowl losses, to the San Francisco Examiner in 1981

Best Restaurants

Best steak. Manny's Steakhouse has a mouth-watering selection of cuts, lobster and desserts that'll make you feel like

> **did you know?**
> Bud Grant delayed an NFL career to play for the Minneapolis Lakers basketball team for the 1950-51 season. He earned varsity letters in numerous sports at the University of Minnesota. On his first day on campus, he met soon-to-be-legend Sid Hartman on campus. It was Hartman's first day as a sportswriter.

Ready For Primetime (Monday Night)

January 3, 1983: Thanks to some necessary scheduling, Dallas and Minnesota would battle in the final regular-season contest of the strike-shortened 1982 campaign. Both teams would wind up in the 16-team Super Bowl Tournament, but this night would be best remembered for Cowboys' RB Tony Dorsett's 99-yard touchdown run. Forgotten was the fact that the host Vikings won. Vikings 31, Cowboys 27.

Overall Monday night: 16-17
Overall Thursday night: 4-4
Overall Sunday night: 9-5

Think About the Weather

December 26, 1977. NFC divisional playoffs. Chuck Knox's team had to endure its share of playoff games at frigid Metropolitan Stadium amid snowmobile suits and smuggled-in flasks of schnapps, so when his Rams finally got a chance to play host to the Purple Gang, there was revenge in the air. But rain had turned the L.A. Coliseum into a mud-wrestling pit, and the Vikings (minus an injured Fran Tarkenton) handed Knox's club another frustrating setback (Vikings 14, Rams 7).

Coldest game temperature at Metropolitan Stadium: -2° (Dec. 3, 1972)
Warmest: 82° (Oct. 6, 1963)

Worst Team

1984 (3-13): With the departure of future Hall of Famer Bud Grant in 1983 came the arrival of Les Steckel, who quickly became known for his regimented ways, that apparently didn't sit well with his players. Perhaps it was best said late that season, when the Vikings fell behind, 31-0, to the Redskins in the second quarter on a Thursday night at the Metrodome. A sign in the stands read "Les Steckel, More Bud."

Team Leaders

Rushing Yards
5,879   Chuck Foreman, 1973-79
Passing Yards
33,098   Fran Tarkenton, 1961-66,
         1972-78
Passing Touchdowns
239   Fran Tarkenton, 1961-66,
         1972-78
Receptions
667   Cris Carter, 1990-91
Interceptions
53   Paul Krause
Touchdowns
76   Bill Brown, 1962-74
Points
1,365   Fred Cox, 1963-77

you just swallowed a football. *1300 Nicollet Mall. (612) 339-9900. M-Sa 5:30-10pm, Su 5:3 0-9pm. All major credit cards. $$$$*

Best chili. For a winter warmer, it's hard to beat the chicken chili at **Pickled Parrot**, also known for its sandwiches and ribs. *26 N. 5th St. (612) 332-00673. M 11am-10pm, Tu-Th 11am-10:30 pm, F-Sa 11am-11:30 pm, Su 10am-10pm. All major credit cards. $$$*

Cheap eats. The pasta at **The Old Spaghetti Factory** won't make you feel like you're in Italy, but it can't be beat for the price. (Minnesotans love a good value.) Besides, it's just two blocks from the Dome. *233 Park Avenue. (612) 341-0949. M-Th Lunch: 11:30-2pm, dinner: 5-9:30 pm; F Lunch: 11:30-2 pm, dinner: 5-11pm; Sa 5-11pm; Su 4-9:30 pm. DC, DIS, MC, V. $$*

did you know?

The original drawing of the Viking logo was created by Los Angeles Times cartoonist Karl Hubenthal. He had been contracted by the team's first general manager, Bert Rose, who also insisted on the team's name, because it connoted the region and a will to win.

Best Accommodations

Whitney Hotel. Located on the mighty Mississippi, this is where the celebrities often stay when they're in town. They probably won't hoof it to the game from here, but you can. *150 Portland Ave. (612) 339-9300. $$$*

Holiday Inn. It's a long walk to the Dome from here, but there's plenty of cheap

While You Were Eating Turkey....

November 27, 1969: The Vikes shut out Detroit, 27-0, at Tiger Stadium to clinch the team's second division title and rack up the 10th of a 12-game winning streak. They finished the season at 12-2.
Overall, 4-4.

Fans' notes

On Screen

Hollywood has not fallen for the Vikings, although Fran Tarkenton has enjoyed some TV success with **That's Incredible** and those Tony Robbins commercials, as well as a cameo in **M*A*S*H**. Wide receiver Ahmad Rashad ended up marrying actress Phylicia Rashad of "Cosby" fame after his playing days, and defensive end Carl Eller appeared in the B-biker movie **The Black Six** with, among others, Joe Greene and Mercury Morris. And of course John Amos's character, Gordy, on "The Mary Tyler Moore Show" was supposed to have been a retired Vike. Does that count?

Fight Songs, etc.

The Vikings' fight song, "Skol Vikings," was written by "Red" McCloud. The term "skol" comes from the rather unpleasant ritual practiced by victorious Norsemen in the Viking age, in which the winners celebrated by drinking ale from the craniums of their enemies. This explains why the word sounds so much like skull.

Bookshelf

No Room for Crybabies. Dennis Green (Sagamore 1997). Coach Denny Green made his mark in the publishing world by including a blueprint on how he might sue the team.
No Time for Losing. Fran Tarkenton (Ballantine 1976). The scrambler's playing memoirs.
Rashad: Vikes, Mikes and Something in the Backside. Ahmad Rashad and Peter Bodo (Viking 1988).
Purple Hearts and Golden

Memories: 35 Years with the Minnesota Vikings. Jim Klobuchar (Quality Sports 1996).
Bud: The Other Side of the Glacier. Bill McGrane (HarperCollins 1986).
Minnesota's Vikings: the Scrambler and the Purple Gang. Bob Rubin (Prentice Hall 1975).

You Gotta See...

▶Tight end Joe Senser has opened two successful sports bars. **Joe Senser's Sports Grill & Bars** are located at 4217 W. 80th St., Bloomington, and 2350 Cleveland Ave., Roseville. Sports anchor Mark Rosen, WCCO–CBS, has his name on the downtown sports bar, **Rosen's**, 430 1st Avenue, Minneapolis.
▶Northern fans should check out **The Nordic Inn,** a bed and breakfast in Crosby, MN, just ten miles from Brainerd, where rabid fan Rick Schmidthuber provides Norsemen entertainment and five rooms, including one dedicated totally to the Minnesota Vikings. The floor is covered in Astroturf and, instead of a closet, you hang up your clothes in a locker. Call (218) 546-8299 for reservations.
▶Pay homage to the old Vikings and Twins home by visiting the **Mall of America.** Not only can you pick up souvenirs, but there's a plaque in Camp Snoopy, the kiddie amusement park, that marks the site where home plate used to be.

> "We're not big, but we sure are slow."
> —Line coach Stan West, on the first-year Vikings (1961).

Hall of Fame

Hugh McElhenny	(HB 1970)
Fran Tarkenton	(QB 1986)
Jim Langer	(C 1987)
Alan Page	(DT 1988)
Jan Stenerud	(PK 1991)
Bud Grant	(Coach 1994)
Paul Krause	(DB 1998)

Against the Odds

In the late '60s and early '70s, **Jim Marshall** (1961-79) joined Carl Eller, Alan Page and Gary Larsen in a Vikings defensive front that earned the name the "Purple People Eaters" for its ability to dominate a game. And Marshall never missed a game. He was the NFL's greatest iron man, playing in a record 282 consecutive contests, 302 including postseason. There were occasions when he had to leave the hospital in order to keep his streak alive. But for all the gutty performances that Marshall delivered, he may be best remembered for his most embarrassing one: his wrong-way return of a fumble in 1964 which resulted in a safety.

did you know?

The Pittsburgh Steelers defeated the Vikes, 16-6, in Super Bowl IX, and the MVP might have been the equipment manager. In the middle of the game, a cold rain came down on Tulane Stadium in New Orleans, making the ground very slick. At halftime, the Steelers switched from typical artificial turf shoes to white Canadian shoes with spiral cleats that had been brought along. The change kept the team from sliding around and helped them post a victory.

parking in the ramp and the hotel is near the University of Minnesota, which means lots of interesting bars and restaurants. *1500 Washington Ave. S. (612) 333-4646, $$$*

Super 8. The Palace of cheap sleeps. There are not a lot of bargain hotels anywhere near the Dome. This one is only five miles away. *2401 Prior Ave. N. Roseville, 1-800-800-8000. $50-$60. $*

New England Patriots

On Nov. 16, 1959, the American Football League's eighth and final franchise was awarded to Billy Sullivan, owner of the Boston Patriots — even though his team didn't have a stadium to play in. The Patriots have been one of pro football's sorrowful stepchildren ever since.

It's tough when your siblings in the old AFL and now in the AFC East have been overachievers. The Buffalo Bills won two early AFL championships and appeared in the Super Bowl four straight times. The New York Jets made history with Joe Namath in Super Bowl III. The Miami Dolphins hired Don Shula, reached perfection, then drafted quarterback Dan Marino — the Patriots passed on Marino, taking Tony Eason instead. In 1963, in their only appearance in the AFL championship game, the Patriots were trounced, 51-10, by the San Diego Chargers. Twenty-two years later, the Chicago Bears humiliated New England, 46-10, in Super Bowl XX.

Franchise History

Boston Patriots (AFL)
(1960–69)
Boston Patriots (NFL)
(1970)
New England Patriots (NFL)
(1971–present)

By the Numbers

(Since 1970)

Regular Season: 195-229
Postseason: 6-8
Division Titles: 4
Vs. Division: 110-110 (Playoffs: 3-1)
Playoff Appearances: 8
Home: 114-98
Away: 81-131

(Overall)

Regular Season: 258-297-9
Postseason: 7-9
Playoff Appearances: 9
Home: 147-128-6
Away: 111-169-3

After a particularly bitter stretch of losing seasons that included a 2-14 record in 1992, the Patriots were nearly sold and moved to St. Louis. But Robert K. Kraft, a Boston businessman and season ticket-holder since 1972, rescued the team for New England. Kraft purchased the team, its home, Foxboro Stadium (built in 1969) and two-time Super Bowl champion head coach Bill Parcells, who had been brought on board by the previous owner James Orthwein. Parcells drafted a tall, strong-armed quarterback named Drew Bledsoe with the first pick in the 1993 college draft.

Parcells took a team devoid of talent

Most Revered Football Figures

John Hannah. Not only the most talented player in Patriots history, but the toughest, meanest and grittiest. Hannah was named to the NFL's 75th Anniversary team.

Robert Kraft. Popular Patriots owner saved the franchise from moving to St. Louis and stabilized a vagabond franchise.

Drew Bledsoe. He's the most exciting quarterback in the team's history, and thus the most popular.

Rivalries

An already good rivalry got better when Bill Parcells left the Patriots to coach the New York Jets (35-40-1). Now an excellent New York-Boston rivalry has the intrigue of one team's owner hating the other team's coach and vice-versa. The **Dolphins** own a 38-27 advantage over the Patriots. Even in the Patriots' good years in the '70s, they couldn't beat the Dolphins in Miami. Don Shula dominated the Pats, but so far the Patriots have had the upper hand on Jimmy Johnson. The **Bills** (40-35-1) and Patriots had great battles in the old AFL days when Babe Parilli and Jack Kemp locked up in shootouts. The Bills dominated in the early '70s winning nine straight games against the Pats, but since then the teams have gone back and forth. Jack Tatum's literally crippling hit on Darryl Stingley and Patriots owner-GM Pat Sullivan's fight with Howie Long and Matt Millen during a playoff game in 1985 have always made any game against the **Raiders** worth watching.

> **did you know?**
>
> From 1989 through 1997, the Pats were 13-5 vs. the division rival Colts and a horrid 46-86 vs. the rest of NFL, including playoff games. New England is also 10-4 lifetime at Indianapolis's Hoosier/RCA Dome.

and rebuilt it, and by 1996, four Patriots went to the Pro Bowl — Bledsoe, running back Curtis Martin, tight end Ben Coates and offensive lineman Bruce Armstrong. The Patriots' defense, built around speedy pass rushers Willie McGinest and Chris Slade, became one of the most feared in the league. And, in year four of the Kraft-Parcells-Bledsoe era, the Patriots returned to the Super Bowl, falling short of knocking off the Green Bay Packers in Super Bowl XXXI, 35-21.

Parcells, who had complained for years that he didn't have enough control over personnel decisions, asked out of his five-year contract a year early and left the Patriots, joining the Jets as head coach.

It was a bitter divorce. After Parcells's departure, Bledsoe complained that he had felt tormented by the big Tuna's special sideline concoction of sarcasm, hostility and tough love. And Parcells snarled at the thought of Kraft — a man who made his millions selling paper products — having the nerve to tell him how to run a football team.

To replace Parcells, Kraft hired the far more malleable Pete Carroll, who, ironically, was a former head coach of the Jets. If you think that's the end of it, fuhgetaboutit. Parcells has already stolen one of his former players: Curtis Martin signed a free agent contract with the Jets, forcing the Patriots to scramble to find a running back in the 1998 draft. And no doubt as other Patriots reach free agency status, Parcells will begin grabbing them, too.

Nevertheless, as long as Bledsoe is wearing a Patriots uniform, New England will have a franchise-level quarterback capable of taking a team to the Super Bowl and keeping the Jets at bay. Maybe the stepchildren have finally come into their own.

—Sal Paolantonio

Foxboro Stadium

If the red tape is cut in time, the Patriots will build a new Foxboro Stadium at the current site by the year 2001. Owner Robert Kraft will spend about $200 million of his own money, while the state is slated to approve slightly more than $70 million for infrastructure.

In the meantime, fans have come to accept Foxboro Stadium as their home, though it took more than 25 years to develop that feeling. Over the years, slight improvements such as better restrooms and the alleviation of major traffic along Route 1, where the Stadium sits, have made it a less agonizing venture for loyal fans.

The Kraft family has attempted to make the Patriots' home a much more family-oriented stadium by beefing up security and having virtually no tolerance for rowdy behavior, with a consistent policy of bouncing patrons who have abused alcohol and disrupted other fans. The stadium also has non-smoking and family sections. New ramps make it easy for handicapped fans to get in and out of their seats, and plenty of ushers have been added to help fans find their seats.

> "A friend told me if you're going to cook the meal, they ought to let you shop for the groceries." — Bill Parcells, frustrated at not having the final word on personnel moves during the 1996 season.

The "I Was There" Game

January 12, 1986: The numbers before this AFC Championship Game all pointed to a Miami win. Including playoffs, the Pats had lost 18 straight games at the Orange Bowl, the Dolphins hadn't lost at home all year and the 'Fins were a perfect 5-0 in AFC title games. But the numbers that counted this day were six Miami turnovers and 255 yards rushing from New England's Craig James and pals. Patriots 31, Dolphins 14.

The Paper Bag Game

December 18, 1976: This controversial AFC divisional playoff game ended in a 24-21 Oakland Raiders' victory over the Patriots, a decision that altered Patriots' history for the worse. With less than a minute remaining in the game, a controversial roughing-the-passer call on Patriots' defensive end Ray Hamilton was called on a third and 18 after Ken Stabler's pass fell incomplete. The call, to this day disputed by Hamilton, gave the Raiders life with a first and 10 from the Patriots' 13. Five plays later, with 14 seconds left in regulation, Stabler ran around left end for the winning score.

Great Names

Sam Adams (G, 1972-80)
Tom Beer (TE, 1970-72)
Ferric Collons (DE, 1995-present)
John Outlaw (DB, 1969-72)
Mosi Tatupu (RB, 1978-90)
Dick Felt (DB, 1962-66)
Joe Sweet (WR, 1974)

Our Top Story

"Fairbanks Flees"
December 17, 1978
Coach Chuck Fairbanks quit a team that was 11-4 right before a big Monday night game against the Dolphins, to coach the University of Colorado football team. Ron Ehrhardt and Hank Bullough, the offensive and defensive coordinators, co-coached the team for the final regular season game and a first-round playoff loss to Houston, 31-14.

"Trouble in the Locker Room"
September 17, 1990
Boston Herald writer Lisa Olson sued the Patriots, then owned by Victor Kiam, the CEO of Remington Products, claiming that tight end Zeke Mowatt was waving his private parts in her face while she was trying to conduct locker room interviews. Long, drawn-out depositions and suits followed before the matter was finally settled.

"Kraft Buys Pats"
January 21, 1994
Patriots owner James B. Orthwein was close to selling the team to a St. Louis bidder when Boston businessman Bob Kraft came to the rescue and bought the struggling franchise.

"The Tuna Swims South"
February 12, 1997
Just days after the Patriots lost to the Green Bay Packers in Super Bowl XXXI, Parcells was heading to New York to coach the Jets. The Patriots received four draft choices over a three-year period, including the Jets' No. 1 pick in 1999, as compensation.

While it isn't outstanding, the food at Foxboro Stadium certainly outstrips the setting. Fans are usually pleased with the culinary options, which were upgraded a few years ago to include major items from D'Angelo's Sub Shops, Papa Gino's Pizza, Kayem Franks, soft pretzels and Häagen-Dazs ice cream. The best stuff is at Giovanni's Sausage carts, located at several spots around the stadium, offering a popular hot and mild sausage with condiments. Anna's Fried Dough isn't bad either.

It's still a very uncomfortable concrete-and-aluminum stadium — as you might expect from its $7 million price tag and the 326 days it took to build in 1970-71. Adding to the discomfort is the seating, the majority of which consists of aluminum benches with no backs — they're absolutely brutal on cold winter days. The new place has to be better. Still, Patriots fans are as rabid as you will find in the NFL, and they definitely give their guys a distinct home field advantage.

did you know?
The Patriots' road to Super Bowl XX included playoff road wins against the Jets, Raiders and Dolphins, making them the only team to win three road playoff games in the same season.

The Bottom Line on Foxboro Stadium

Address: Foxboro Stadium, 60 Washington St., Route One, Foxboro, MA

Tickets: There's currently a waiting list of about 3,000 for season tickets. The best seats are the 100-level seats on either sideline. The worst are the 300-level seats in the corners of the end zones, but despite the fact that this stadium is one of the NFL's worst facilities, the

Best of the Patriots

Best Team

1976 (11-4): After a dismal 3-11 season which ended with a six-game losing streak, a 27-13 loss at home to the Colts in week one proved to be an aberration. In the next three weeks, Chuck Fairbanks's young club shocked AFC powers Miami, Pittsburgh and Oakland on consecutive Sundays. New England had the Raiders on the ropes in the divisional playoffs, but let a 21-10 third-quarter lead slip away.

Greatest Players by Position

Pos:	Player
QB:	Steve Grogan
RB:	Sam Cunningham
WR:	Stanley Morgan
TE:	Ben Coates
OL:	John Hannah
DL:	Julius Adams
LB:	Andre Tippett
DB:	Mike Haynes
P/K:	John Smith
ST:	Mosi Tatupu

And Don't Forget...

LB: Nick Buoniconti. Best known for his days with the Dolphins' No-Name defense, he's a member of the Patriots Hall of Fame.

TE: Russ Francis. He enjoyed two separate stints in New England, and earned three straight Pro Bowl invitations in the late 1970s.

LB: Steve Nelson. Three-time Pro Bowler who anchored the middle of the Patriots defense for 14 very productive seasons.

CB: Raymond Clayborn. The franchise's all-time interception leader with 36 thefts, he started a team-record 161 straight games.

T: Bruce Armstrong. The former Louisville standout is one of the league's premier tackles, named to his sixth Pro Bowl in '97.

Swami Sez:

Reading the Boston and New York papers when the Patriots are about to play the Jets, or when Bill Parcells is discussed, must be like reading the French and German papers discussing the same battle in World War II.

Best Argument

Wide Receiver: Stanley Morgan or Gino Cappelletti? One of the most consistent and reliable deep threats of the 1980s, Morgan was often the lone shining star on some sub-par Patriots' squads. Cappelletti was not only a consistent pass catcher—ranking fourth on the Patriots' all-time list with 292 receptions—but an excellent place-kicker as well, and he remains the franchise's scoring leader.

Best Coach

Raymond Berry (1984-89): From 1978-81, Berry served as New England's receivers coach. On October 25, 1984, he replaced Ron Meyer as the sideline leader and after splitting his final eight games that year, led New England to Super Bowl XX followed by an AFC East title in 1986. His lone losing campaign with the club proved to be his last as the Patriots managed only five wins.

Pressbox

Who to Read...

The Pats get many inches in the *Boston Globe*, nearly year-round. The big-name columnist, Will McDonough, is plugged into the NFL as well as anyone. Patriots fans get terrific material from Ron Borges's "On Football" column, a definite must-read, and Nick Cafardo, who covers the Pats beat. The *Boston Herald* is the town's tabloid; look for Kevin Mannix, who is doing a first-rate job on the Pats. In Providence, it's Ed Duckworth for the *Journal-Bulletin*; at the *Quincy Patriot Ledger*, read Ron Hobson.

> "All I know about grocery shopping is when I go with my wife I push the cart." — Pete Carroll, upon replacing Parcells as head coach in 1997.

Who to Watch...

"Patriots Preview," hosted by Mike Lynch, is seen on WCVB. Sunday nights, Pats fans watch "Sports Final," which features astute game film analysis by former NFL linebacker Steve DeOssie, on WBZ.

Who to Listen To...

Pats games are heard on WBCN (104.1 FM), with Gil Santos and Gino Cappelletti in the broadcast booth. WEEI (850 AM) is the sports talk station, with Eddie Andelman and Dale Arnold from noon to 3 on "The A-Team," and Glen Ordway from 3 to 6pm. Andelman has been around for a long time and has lots of opinions and a loyal following. The same can be said of Ordway, who also has a Monday afternoon post-mortem show with Drew Bledsoe. John Dennis and Gerry Callahan come on after "Imus in the Morning" with an intelligent, even-handed show. Former All-Pro and Boston College alum Fred Smerlas brings experience to his many duties, from guesting on Ordway's show to helping out on the preview show on Sundays.

view is surprisingly good overall. The Krafts have kept ticket prices the same the past two years.

1998: $60/$42/$39/$28/$26

1994: $50/$38/$35/$32/$25/$23

Public Transportation: Commuter trains take fans from Boston's South Station and points in between to and from Foxboro. The trains stop at the former racetrack, a short walk from the stadium. Call the MBTA for information. (617) 722-3200.

Parking: There is parking available for 16,000 cars. Traffic problems haven't been completly alleviated, but they're better than ever. Fans who arrive prior to 11am for a 1pm game have a short wait to get a parking spot. After 11,

> "Am I going to be all right?" —WR Darryl Stingley, after being hit by Jack Tatum in a 1978 exhibition game. Stingley was permanently paralyzed from the neck down.

traffic backs up on either side of Route 1 until game time. Most patrons find that they spend about 90 minutes in traffic after a game before they can break through to I-95 north or south. Most of the lots along Route 1 average about $15 to park.

Capacity: 60, 292.

Restrooms: 30.

Where to Go . . . in Boston/Providence

Best Bars

Best local joint. The Endzone is the average Joe's kind of place. It's a combination bar-motel-eatery, and it caters to Patriot fans. Beer and a variety of finger foods are popular. *5835 Post Rd., E. Greenwich, RI, (401) 885-8226. Seven days 11:30am-1am.*

Best brew pub. At the casual **Union Station Brewery**, a typical beer pub, there are lots of home-brewed beers to choose from. There's also excellent pizza. *36 Exchange Terr., Providence, RI. (401) 274-2739. Su-Th 11:30am-10pm, F-Sa 11:30am-11pm.*

Best post-game bash. Nearby the stadium, the **Ground Round** is a big gathering place after Patriots games. It has a good bar atmosphere and quality, quick food. *670 Providence Highway (Route 1), Walpole, MA (508) 668-7990. M-Sa 11am-12:30am, Su 12pm-12:30am.*

Where everyone will know your name. If you're visiting the area, the **Bull and Finch Pub** (the infamous "Cheers" bar) is a touristy must. It's about 40 minutes from the stadium. *84 Beacon St., Boston, (617) 227-9605. Seven days 11am-2am.*

Best Restaurants

Best pub grub. Because it's located about three miles from the stadium but off congested Route 1, **The Piccadilly Pub**

Ready For Primetime (Sunday Night)

Don't ask. The Pats have rarely been ready for prime time. And it is somehow fitting that Howard Cosell informed a national audience of the death of John Lennon while the Patriots blew their playoff chances with an overtime loss to the Dolphins in a 1980 Monday night game. But Tuna Bowl I, Sept. 14, 1997, which was played on a Sunday night at Foxboro Stadium, perhaps was the biggest game in Patriots history. The Patriots beat Bill Parcells, 27-24, in overtime, upon his return to Foxboro Stadium. Never has a regular season game seen so much emotion, enough so that it rattled Drew Bledsoe, but inspired Curtis Martin to run for 199 yards on 40 carries, one of the best individual rushing performances in Patriots history.

Overall Monday night: 6-14

Overall Sunday night: 5-9

Overall Thursday night: 1-1

Think About the Weather

December 12, 1982: In a blinding snowstorm at Schaefer Stadium, kicker John Smith was about to enter the game in the final minutes of a 0-0 tie, when coach Ron Meyer ordered staff snowplow driver Mark Henderson to clear a spot for a favorable placement for Smith. Miami coach Don Shula was popping a blood vessel on the opposite sideline, arguing that this was an illegal act. But while Shula moaned, Henderson plowed. Smith came on and booted the game-winning field goal. Patriots 3, Dolphins 0.

Worst Team

1990 (1-15): After dropping a tough 27-24 decision to the Dolphins at Foxboro on opening day, the Pats rebounded with a two-point win at Indianapolis. That would be New England's only taste of victory the entire season as Rod Rust's lone campaign as head coach proved to be a disaster. An anemic offensive unit managed only 18 touchdowns all season, while the defense allowed a whopping 446 points.

did you know?
Between 1987 and 1996, the Patriots ranked dead last in the AFC in turnover differential with a minus-44.

Hall of Fame

John Hannah   (G, 1991)
Mike Haynes   (DB, 1997)

Team Leaders

Rushing Yards
5,453   Sam Cunningham, 1973-79, 1981-82
Passing Yards
26,886 Steve Grogan, 1975-90
Passing Touchdowns
182   Steve Grogan, 1975-90
Receptions
534   Stanley Morgan, 1977-89
Interceptions
36   Raymond Clayborn, 1977-89
Touchdowns
68   Stanley Morgan, 1977-89
Points
1,130   Gino Cappelletti, 1960-70

has become a popular gathering spot for post-game meals and drink. *25 Foxboro Blvd., Foxboro, MA (508) 543-0535. M-Sa 11am-11pm, Su 12pm-10pm. All major credit cards. $*

Best seafood. If you are in New England, you have to eat some seafood. It's excellent at **Hemenway's Seafood Grill and Oyster Bar** — the oyster bar is especially good. *1 Old Stone Sq., Providence, RI, (401) 351-8570. M-Th 11:30am-9:30pm, F-Sa 11:30am-11pm, Su 12pm-9:30pm. All major credit cards. $$*

Best seafood (rustic division). If you're operating out of Boston, **Ye Olde Union Oyster House** has great chowder and will more than satisfy any history jones you may have come down with here—It claims to be the oldest continuously serving restaurant in the United States. *41 Union St. (617) 227-2750. M-F 11am-9:30pm, Sa-Su 11am-10pm. All major credit cards. $$$$*

> **"We gave it everything we had."**
> **— Head coach Raymond Berry after the Pats' 46-10 loss to Chicago in Super Bowl XX. (1986)**

Best Italian. Capriccio's serves upscale, formal Italian food on the edge of downtown Providence. *2 Pine St., Providence, RI (401) 421-1320. Su-F 11:30am-10:30pm, Sa 5-11pm. All major credit cards. $$$*

Best Accommodations

The Marriott. This moderately priced hotel draws a lot of out-of-state fans. It's usually the home of the opposing team. *1 Orms St., Providence, RI, (401) 272-2400. $$*

The Westin. Considered the most upscale of the local hotels, the Westin Providence was the site of the NFL's

Fans' notes

On Screen

Maybe it's their star-crossed history, but the Patriots just haven't taken the world of film and television by storm. They do have their share of highlight reel material, of course, all documented on the official team video from NFL Films.

> "The Jewish people have a word for it. It's called chutzpah." — Owner Billy Sullivan, on the timing of Chuck Fairbanks's 1978 announcement — right after the Pats had clinched the AFC East — that he would leave the team at the end of the season.

Fight Song, Etc.

Music has played a tangential role in the Patriots' recent fortunes. While he was making his rushing totals high, former Pats running back Curtis Martin dated pop/R&B singer Toni Braxton. And Drew Bledsoe, Scott Zolak and Max Lane (weighing 233, 235 and 305 pounds respectively) were reportedly stage-diving at a 1997 concert by the alternative-rock band Everclear when a young woman was injured. They were not linked to the woman's injury, but the publicity didn't do anyone any good — except for maybe Everclear.

Bookshelf

The Road to the Super Bowl. Bob Ryan (Masters Press, 1997).
The New England Patriots. Larry Fox (Macmillan, 1977).
Happy To Be Alive. Darryl Stingley (Beaufort Books, 1983).

You Gotta See...

▶The old Boston Garden is gone, but you can still find a piece of living sports history in **Fenway Park**, rivaled only by Chicago's Wrigley Field when it comes to that old-time baseball feel.

▶Boston is riddled with historic attractions such as the **U.S.S. Constitution**, the **John F. Kennedy Library and Museum** and the three-mile-long **Freedom Trail**, a walking tour of 18th-century landmarks. Also don't miss Faneuil Hall Marketplace, a picturesque collection of restaurants and shops near Government Center.

▶In and near downtown Providence, R.I., you'll find the **Arcade** (the oldest indoor mall in the United States), a paradise of Italian restaurants on **Federal Hill** and the newly landscaped **Waterplace Park**.

While You Were Eating Turkey

November 22, 1984: Riding high after a 50-17 trouncing of the Colts in Indianapolis, the Patriots came into Dallas trying to improve on their 8-4 record. But their Thanksgiving was spoiled by a three-point Dallas victory. Cowboys 20, Patriots 17. The Patriots went on to lose their next two games and miss the playoffs with a 9-7 mark.
Overall, 0-1

A Fan's Notes: The NFL

Radio

The NFL on ESPN Radio — Radio's most comprehensive NFL show, better than being at the game, you're at EVERY game. Live, up to the second reports, scoring and big plays as they happen. Plus after the game, the best post game show on radio. Interviews with stars of the games, plus analysis from Chris Berman, Chris Mortensen, Tom Jackson and John Clayton.

Websites

Get online for the fastest, most complete, you-are-there football coverage. You'll find extensive, always updated game material, as well statistics, interviews, and more, at ESPN.com and NFL.com.

Against the Odds

What separated **John Hannah** (1973-1985) from all other offensive guards was neither his size (6-3, 265) nor his ability to quickly and smoothly pull out to block outside. It was his consistently high level of play and dependabilty; that led many to consider the 10-time All-Pro the best lineman of his era. In a 13-year career, "Hog" Hannah was an iron man at a heavy-wear position, starting 183 of a possible 191 games, including eight seasons during which he never missed a start. In 1978, with Hannah starting all 16 contests, the Patriots established an NFL record with 3,165 yards rushing, a 197.8-per-game average.

AFC championship party — much to the dismay of Boston hoteliers. *1 W. Exchange St., Providence, RI, (401) 598-8000. $$$*

Motel 6. Simple, budget accommodations conveniently located for trips to Foxboro. *60 Forbes St., Mansfield, MA, (508) 339-2323. $*

> "It's bad enough to get beat up, but to get beat up by a flag!"
> —TE Don Hasselbeck, who needed three stitches in his lip after being hit by a penalty flag. (1979)

New Orleans Saints

Jim Taylor and Earl Campbell, a pair of NFL Hall of Famers, have run the football for the New Orleans Saints. Ken Stabler once was the quarterback. Coaches who have passed through town read like a Who's Who: Hank Stram, Bum Phillips, Jim Mora and Mike Ditka have all marched the sidelines. The franchise has a colorful history, but it's one that mostly sends fans out to Bourbon Street to drown their miseries, because the Saints have come to define mediocrity in the NFL.

Franchise History

New Orleans Saints (NFL)
(1967–present)

New Orleans was awarded the NFL's 16th franchise on Nov. 1, 1966, which happened to be "All Saints Day." John Mecom Jr. was the owner and Tom Fears the first coach. Tulane Stadium was the original home field and the site of Tom Dempsey's legendary 63-yard field goal that beat the Detroit Lions, 19-17, in 1970.

There were local heroes, for sure. Ole Miss quarterback Archie Manning was the No. 1 draft pick in 1971 and endured one of the most courageous careers of any NFL player. As a rookie, Manning led the Saints to a 24-20 upset over the Dallas Cowboys before 83,000 fans — the Cowboys went on to win the Super Bowl. The Saints, as they did in each of their first 20 years of existence, watched the playoffs. By then, the greatest goal of the Saints and their fans was not a ticker tape parade down Bourbon Street, Lombardi Trophy in tow, but simply to make the playoffs. That meager goal remains the New Orleans dream.

The Lousiana Superdome, which would become site of numerous Super Bowls, opened in 1975. Manning was named the NFL's MVP in '78 and led the

By the Numbers

(Since 1970)
Regular Season: 171-249-4
Postseason: 0-4
Division Titles: 1
Vs. Division: 64-105-2 (Playoffs: 0-1)
Playoff Appearances: 4
Home: 95-116-1
Away: 76-133-3

(Overall)
Regular Season: 183-278-5
Postseason: 0-4
Playoff Appearances: 4
Home: 103-129-1
Away: 80-149-4

Most Revered Football Figures

Archie Manning. Saints history begins and ends with the carrot-topped No. 8, probably the greatest quarterback never to lead a winning team.

Rickey Jackson. A stalwart at outside linebacker for 13 years. Only longtime Saint with a legit shot at the Hall of Fame.

Eric Martin. The "possession" guy from LSU holds every Saints career receiving record. His incredible hands and physical play made up for a stunning lack of speed.

Morten Andersen. Even though he wound up in Atlanta, fans still love Andersen and his All-Pro leg, which bailed the Saints out of many a jam.

Rivalries

Being geographically isolated from the rest of the NFL, the Saints have not developed many neighborhood rivalries. The Atlanta **Falcons** (24-34) are the exception. The animosity between the Saints and Falcons has subsided in recent years as both teams sank to the bottom of the NFC West, but the twice-yearly games bring extra excitement to two half-empty stadiums. In the late '90s, however, the series has become a showcase for former Saints to shine against their old team. Former New Orleans place-kicker Morten Andersen has used his lethal left leg to deflate the Saints on a couple of occasions. Quarterback Bobby Hebert, a native of nearby Cut Off, LA, is now reviled for his "swooping falcon" celebrations after throwing touchdown passes in the Superdome.

team to its first .500 season in '79. But dreams fell short, until local car dealer Tom Benson bought the franchise for $70 million in 1985. A few months later, in January 1986, Benson placed Jim Finks in charge of the franchise as president and general manager. Finks hired Mora, who had dominated the upstart USFL as a coach, and the two men embarked on the most successful stretch in the team's history. The Saints made four playoff appearances, gave the San Francisco 49ers fits in several meetings but fell short of the Super Bowl despite an army of loyal "Who Dat" fans.

> **did you know?**
> Of the 30 clubs New Orleans played between 1967 and 1997, the Saints logged winning records against only five, and none are division opponents: the Bengals (5-4), Lions (8-6-1), Jaguars (1-0), Seahawks (3-2) and Buccaneers (12-5).

Ultimately, the Saints tripped again as Finks fell ill to cancer. The Saints never got the leadership they needed in the new salary-cap era. Mora resigned abruptly in the middle of the 1996 season. Benson and new president-GM Bill Kuharich tabbed Ditka, the ex-Hall of Famer, to lead the team in 1997. Ditka soon discovered what many men who have coached the Saints have realized — it's a job that will either drive you to drink or to quit. Iron Mike decided to hang on, promising good times were around the corner. They always are in New Orleans.

—*Chris Mortensen*

The Louisiana Superdome

It's an ironic but altogether fitting tribute to the New Orleans Saints' historic mediocrity that while the Superdome has hosted more Super Bowls (five) than any other facility, the team has never played in one.

The Superdome itself is an awesome site in downtown New Orleans, and fans marvel at the 23-year-old facility every time they enter. Its clean lines and optimal layout make for perfect game-viewing, and it remains one of the city's primary economic engines. The Superdome truly lives up to its name. A local economist has called it "the most usable public building ever designed in the history of man." There are no truly bad seats; the worst ones are in the upper sideline sections near the top of the dome.

Superdome patrons must settle for concourse-type food like hot dogs, nachos, Bloody Marys and beers. Of course, in this city, most people do their eating before or after the game at one of New Orleans's renowned restaurants. The concourse concessions can get pretty crowded when the Dome is full, but of late, long lines have been virtually non-existent.

> **did you know?**
>
> In the Saints' very first regular-season game against the Los Angeles Rams, on September 17, 1967, at Tulane Stadium, Saints rookie wide receiver John Gilliam returned the opening kickoff 94 yards for a touchdown. New Orleans went on to lose, 27-13.

> **"I think I've seen worse teams perform better by accident on offense."**
> **— Head coach Mike Ditka in 1997, on his team's inept attack.**

Unlike the fans who attend LSU games just up the river in Baton Rouge, Saints fans are not known for their tailgating ways. One reason is the dearth of outdoor parking lots like the ones found in the Midwest and up North. If anything, Saints fans are known for showing up just for the games, making sure they get their drinking and eating done before and after the game.

The "I Was There" Game

November 29, 1987: The Saints first 20 seasons in the NFL (1967-86) had yet to produce a winning campaign, but Jim Mora's team sported a 7-3 mark and knew a victory in this game against the Steelers would ensure the club of its first-ever winning season. New Orleans got just enough offense from Bobby Hebert and company, and a fourth-quarter goal-line stand gave the Saints the much-awaited tag of "winners." Saints 20, Steelers 16.

The Paper Bag Game

January 3, 1993: There are so many to choose from, but one game stands out for its devastating impact. After building a 20-7 third quarter lead at home in a first-round playoff game against Philadelphia, the Saints gave up 29 unanswered points — 26 points in the fourth quarter. Bobby Hebert threw three second-half interceptions, hastening his departure from New Orleans. The 36-20 loss solidifed the Saints' reputation for choking in big games, and the team hasn't posted a winning record since.

Great Names

Charlie Brown (RB, 1967-68)
Jubilee Dunbar (WR, 1973)
Happy Feller (K, 1972-73)
King Hill (Coach, 1981-85)
Bivian Lee (CB, 1971-75)
Louis Lipps (WR, 1992)
Don Shy (RB, 1969)
James Taylor (T, 1978-81)
Wimpy Winther (C, 1972)

Our Top Story

"Mecom Hands Off to Benson"
May 31, 1985.
John W. Mecom Jr. gives up ownership of the Saints after 19 seasons, selling the team for $70.2 million to auto dealer and banker Tom Benson. Benson orchestrated the franchise's emergence from mediocrity by hiring general manager Jim Finks, who in turn brought in head coach Jim Mora.

"Saints Go Marching into First Place"
December 22, 1991.
The Saints defeat the Phoenix Cardinals, 27-3, to earn the franchise's first-ever division title. The Saints won the NFC West over arch-rivals Atlanta and San Francisco.

"No Mora"
October 21, 1996.
Mora, frustrated by his players' apparent lack of effort, quits halfway through a 3-13 season after a disheartening loss at Carolina.

Hall of Fame

Jim Taylor   (FB 1976)
Doug Atkins   (DE 1982)
Earl Campbell   (HB 1991)

Worst Team

1980 (1-15): It began innocently enough, with a 26-23 loss to the 49ers. But soon the Saints became the 'Aints. The low point was a 38-35 overtime loss at San Francisco as the team blew a NFL-record 28-point lead. Only a one-point win over the Jets at Shea Stadium kept the Saints from "perfection."

The Bottom Line on The Louisiana Superdome

Address: Louisiana Superdome, Super Bowl Drive, New Orleans, LA 70112. (504) 587-3663.

Tickets: Season tickets are readily available, as are single game tickets. Selling out the Dome is a big job, unless a team like the Cowboys is visiting. Tickets can be bought at a variety of locations in and around New Orleans. Call (504)-731-1700 for more information.
1998: $56/$53/$43/$40/$37/$33/$27/$18
1994: $34/$31/$23

Public Transportation: The Superdome is serviced by taxi companies and by the Clayborn and Galvez lines of the Regional Transit Authority's bus service. Call (504) 242-2600 for more information.

did you know?
In 1997, it seemed like the Saints never had the football—they committed a team-record 55 turnovers, including a franchise-worst 33 interceptions tossed by New Orleans' passers.

Parking: Dome parking is limited to only 5,000 spaces, and there is little on-street parking around the stadium. Expect to pay at least $10 for close parking at private lots. Fans staying downtown are better off just walking. Traffic gets pretty bad around the Dome, especially after the game.

> "I'd like to rush for 1,500 or 2,000 yards — whichever comes first."
> — RB George Rogers, after his record-setting 1981 rookie season.

Extras: A 45 minute tour of the Superdome takes visitors to the main arena, locker rooms, press box, private suites, terrace level and meeting rooms. A 20-minute mini-tour is also available. Prices range

Best of the Saints

Best Team

1992 (12-5): A year after winning their first NFC West title, the Saints were one of the league's most consistent teams. Their four regular-season losses were by six points or less, dropping tough decisions to the playoff-bound Eagles, Bills and 49ers (twice). New Orleans owned a 20-7 third-quarter lead over Philadelphia in the playoffs, but another inexplicable collapse saw them give up 29 unanswered points.

Swami Sez:

Even Iron Mike knows it will take a hall of fame coaching performance to get the Saints to march into the playoffs.

Greatest Players by Position

Pos:	Player
QB:	Archie Manning
RB:	Dalton Hilliard
WR:	Eric Martin
TE:	Hoby Brenner
OL:	William Roaf
DL:	Wayne Martin
LB:	Rickey Jackson
DB:	Dave Waymer
P/K:	Morten Andersen
ST:	Tyrone Hughes

And Don't Forget...

LB: Sam Mills. The NFL's Browns and the CFL didn't want him, but Jim Finks and Jim Mora turned him into the leader of the defense.
WR: Danny Abramowicz. Sure-handed wideout and one of the team's best players in the early days of the franchise.

DB: Tommy Myers. Ball-hawking, instinctive safety who picked off 36 passes in his days with the Cajuns.
RB: George Rogers. Former Heisman Trophy winner who led the Saints in rushing his first four years in the league.
C: Joel Hilgenberg. A Pro Bowl center who anchored the middle of Jim Mora's playoff teams.

Best Argument

Linebacker: Rickey Jackson or Pat Swilling? Teamed with inside backers Vaughan Johnson and Sam Mills, the Saints' quartet was as formidable as any in recent memory. Jackson was not only a standout pass-rusher, but solid against the run and had a nose for the football (team-record 26 opponent fumble recoveries). Swilling could bring the heat and simply ran past offensive tackles.

Best Coach

Jim Mora (1986-96): When the former Saint was recently hired by the Indianapolis Colts, the skeptics kept reminding us that Mora had an 0-4 record in the playoffs. But there would have been no postseason opportunity without him and general manager Jim Finks. Mora's record in New Orleans reads 93-78. The team's record without him (including 1997) is 90-204-5. Enough said.

Pressbox

Who to Read...

The only paper in town is the *Times-Picayune*. Peter Finney's column is the one to read; Brian Allee-Walsh, Mike Strom, and John DeShazier are the beat writers. The *Baton Rouge Advocate* sends Sheldon Mickles down to cover the Saints.

Who to Watch...

Since Jan. 28, 1997, when Saints owner Tom Benson introduced Mike Ditka as the team's eleventh head coach, local media have been all over Da Coach like red beans on rice. Ditka has no fewer than three weekly Ditka and Da Saints television shows— Sunday Wrap Up, "Tuesday Magazine" and "Thursday Live" — on WVUE–FOX. Other television outlets covering the Saints include WWL–CBS, WDSU–NBC and WGNO–ABC.

Who to Listen To...

The Saints' flagship radio station is WWL (870 AM). Veteran WWL-TV sports director Jim Henderson handles the play-by-play. Saints legend Archie Manning, Henderson's partner for more than a decade, recently announced his departure from the booth. Stan Brock will replace him. Mike Ditka also has a weekly Tuesday night radio show on WWL. His partner is longtime Saints wag Buddy Diliberto (known locally as Buddy D). Ditka and Diliberto go back a few years to a weekly radio show they hosted together at a riverboat casino in Mississippi (a big Saints market), when Ditka still worked as a studio analyst for NBC. Despite that friendship, Buddy D has remained impartial about the team, and his are the most sought-after comments following every Saints game. Everyone who leaves the Dome after a game turns on his show, and his callers provide as much color as he does.

from $3 to $6. Call (504) 587-3810 or (504) 587-3808.

Capacity: 72,348.

Rest rooms: 52 men's and 52 women's.

Where to Go . . . in New Orleans

Best Bars

Best place to spot Saints players after the game. After Saints games, **Hyttops** at the Hyatt Hotel kicks. There's plenty of sports memorabilia, seven big-screen TVs and 11 monitors tuned to all sorts of sports via satellite. Wednesday night is $2 pint night, and happy hour is 4pm to 6pm daily. *Hyatt Hotel, 500 Poydras Plaza. (504) 561-1234. Su-Th 11am-midnight, F-Sa 11am-1am.*

Best shrine to Marilyn Monroe. Oscar's boasts the third-largest collection of Marilyn Monroe memorabilia in the South and the largest in these parts. Once you're finished checking that out, fix your eyes upon one of 10 televisions showing sports events. *2027 Metairie Rd., Metairie. (504) 831-9540. Su-M 4pm-4am, Tu-Sa 11am-4am.*

Best place you'll probably end up at no matter what. All must go to **Pat O'Briens**, one of the biggest party spots in the French Quarter, for a massive Hurricane (made of rum and fruit juices); some must be helped out. *718 St. Pete St. (504) 525-4823. Seven days 10am-2 or 3am.*

Best Restaurants

Best bucket of food. Spanky's is a big, bustling spot with a wide selection of draft beers and finger foods like onion rings served in buckets, as well as steak specials. Coach Ditka does a weekly radio show from Spanky's during the season. *5243 Canal Blvd. (504) 488-0100. Su-W 11am-10pm, Th-Sa 11am-3am. All major credit cards. $$*

> "It's like winning the Masters with a 390-yard hole-in-one on the last shot."
> — Coach Joe Schmidt in 1970, on Tom Dempsey's game winning 63-yard field goal.

Best Saints brunch. Among the attractions at **Allegro Bistro** are forty single malt scotches at the bar and a selection of cigars available from the humidor. Saints brunches here let you keep your mind on something other than that losing team. *1100 Poydras St. (Energy Center). (504) 582-2350. Lunch only M-F 11am-2:30pm. All major credit cards. $$$*

Best Jukebox. If that New Orleans party mood has your family in its grip, try the **West End Cafe.** The jukebox is loud and there's lots of downhome food. *8536 Pontchartrain Blvd. (504) 288-0711.*

Best Accommodations

Marriott on Canal. Located about a mile from the Superdome, this is a reasonable choice. There's a restaurant and a

Ready For Primetime (Monday Night)

December 31, 1990: The Rams invaded the Superdome hoping to spoil New Year's Eve for the Saints, who needed a victory to qualify for the playoffs. A nip-and-tuck affair saw the score tied at 17 until Morten Andersen hit a 24-yard field goal with two seconds to play, sending the Saints to the wild card game. Saints 20, Rams 17.

Overall Monday night:, 6-12
Overall Thursday night: 6-5
Overall Sunday night: 5-7

Think About the Weather

December 10, 1989: It was a snowy day in Orchard Park, and it looked like it would be a long day for the Saints, who turned to QB John Fourcade — making his first NFL start in a non-replacement game. He riddled the Buffalo secondary, and Jim Mora's club came away with the 22-19 upset of the Bills.

Team Leaders

Rushing Yards
4,267   George Rogers (1981-84)
Passing Yards
21,734   Archie Manning (1971-82)
Passing Touchdowns
115 Archie Manning (1971-82)
Receptions
532 Eric Martin (1985-93)
Interceptions
37 Dave Waymer (1980-89)
Touchdowns
53 Dalton Hilliard (1986-93)
Points
1,318   Morten Andersen (1982-94)

Fans' notes

On Screen

Long before the Saints had fully established their reputation for futility, they were featured in a downer of a Hollywood tale. In **Number One**, Charlton Heston stars as Ron "Cat" Catlan, an aging Saints quarterback trying to fend off a rookie challenger while recovering from a severe knee injury. Heston triumphantly leads the Saints to a crucial touchdown, but by the end, he is flattened by the defense and left immobile on the turf. That'll teach those Saints to win.

Bookshelf

New Orleans Saints Book I. Christian Serpas (Acadian House 1991).
New Orleans Saints: 25 Years of Heroic Effort. Christian Serpas (Acadian House 1992).
The Saga of the Saints: An Illustrated History of the First 25 Seasons. Wayne Mack (Arthur Hardy 1992).

Paraphernalia

Don't be caught dead in the Holy Halo, a Styrofoam construction that fits around your head and supports a halo. Despite their best efforts, Superdome vendors just can't seem to sell any.

You Gotta See...

▶Bourbon Street isn't all there is to see in New Orleans, but no trip to the Big Easy is complete without a visit to the **French Quarter**. Make like everyone else: Eat, drink, and be merry.
▶Dying to solve the mystery of the Saints' woes? The **New Orleans Historic Voodoo Museum** doesn't really focus on football, but hey, a jinx is a jinx.
▶No one has to tell you about Mardi Gras, but the real party of the spring is the **Jazz and Heritage Festival**, a celebration of jazz, zydeco, gospel, Acadian, R&B and all the other roots music that makes New Orleans special.

heated outdoor pool. *555 Canal St. (504) 584-1000, (800) 654-3990. $$*

Hyatt Regency. This hotel is a part of the hotel/business/retail complex adjoining the Superdome, so you can wake up at 11:45 in the morning and still make it to the game. *500 Poydras Plaza. (504) 561-1234, (800) 233-1234. $$$*

Windsor Court Hotel. The only five-star hotel in the city features the Polo Club lounge and world-renowned Grill Room restaurant, as well as a health club and pool. *300 Gravier St. (504) 523-6000. $$$$*

Against the Odds

Tom Dempsey (1969-70) wasn't the best kicker in Saints history. He wasn't the longest-tenured one either. But Dempsey owns an unmistakable place in NFL lore and hearts nonetheless. Born with only half a right foot and no right hand, Dempsey overcame all odds to boot his way into the league record books with the longest kick in history, a 63-yard field goal that beat Detroit, 19-17, on November 8, 1970. No one else has been able to do it better.

New York Giants

The next two National Football League expansion franchises, we are told, could fetch as much as $500 million each, which is kind of funny when you consider it from the New York Giants' perspective. In 1925, when the world was a more innocent place, Tim Mara purchased that NFL franchise for exactly $500. Inflation? You do the math.

Safe to say, the Giants, who have won six league championships, were a terrific investment. At the time, Mara couldn't have dreamed the New York Football Giants — so named because they played at the Polo Grounds, along with the New York Giants baseball team — would become such a business.

Franchise History

New York Giants
(1925–present)

"You have to remember that pro football wasn't such a big deal back then," says Wellington Mara, Tim's son and today the Giants' venerable president. "It was more like professional wrestling." The Giants won their first title in their third season, 1927, by finishing with the league's best record, 11-1-1. While the Green Bay Packers and Chicago Bears were right behind them, there were also teams in the league named the Providence Steam Rollers, the Pottsville Maroons and the Duluth Eskimos. In 1934, the Giants scored 27 points in the fourth quarter to defeat the Bears 30-13 in the second NFL Championship game. They won their third title in 1938, their second under coach Steve Owen, beating the Packers, 23-17, before a crowd of 48,120 at the Polo Grounds.

By now, the Giants were beginning to make an impression on metropolitan-area fans. In 1956, their first season at Yankee Stadium, the Giants reached the

By the Numbers

(Since 1970)
Regular Season: 199-222-3
Postseason: 10-6
Division Titles: 4
Vs. Division: 99-119-3 (Playoffs: 2-0)
Playoff Appearances: 8
Home: 113-99-1
Away: 86-123-2

(Overall)
Regular Season: 523-429-33
Postseason: 14-19
Playoff Appearances: 24
Home: 296-198-16
Away: 227-231-17

Most Revered Football Figures

Lawrence Taylor. His number 56 jersey still appears in the crowd at the Meadowlands, and for good reason — LT was the single most dominant defensive player of the 1980s.

Frank Gifford. Believe it or not, he played football before his broadcasting career and was one of the league's early superstars.

Roosevelt "Rosey" Brown. Ever since his stellar career as an offensive lineman ended for medical reasons, Brown has stayed on with the team as a coach and scout.

Rivalries

When you play in the world's most famous city and you keep taking a back seat to "America's Team," it can rub you the wrong way. While the Big Blue has broken through occasionally— including their surprising division championship in 1997, the Giants always seem to be in the Cowboys' rear view mirror. The Philadelphia **Eagles** (67-58-2) have also provided Giants' fans with a team to boo. From New York's 56-0 win in the teams' first encounter in 1933 to the "Fumble Game" (known to Eagles fans as the "Miracle of the Meadowlands"), this matchup has been extremely physical. The Washington **Redskins** (73-53-4) defeated the Giants 11 straight times during the 1970s, but the latest chapter in this saga was written in 1997, when the Giants stole the division title from former Giant Jeff Hostetler and the 'Skins with a 30-10 victory.

> **did you know?**
>
> Vince Lombardi was a Giants assistant coach from 1954 to 1958, and so was Tom Landry from 1954 to 1959. Allie Sherman was also an assistant on these teams, and it was Sherman who eventually became the Giants' head coach.

title game against the Bears. With stars like Frank Gifford, Sam Huff, Andy Robustelli and Rosie Brown, the Giants routed Chicago, 47-7 for their fourth championship. Their heart-wrenching loss in the 1958 championship, 23-17, to the Baltimore Colts in overtime, may have been the most important game in league history. A national television audience watched, and the NFL, for the first time, was embraced widely as a legitimate and entertaining enterprise.

There were four appearances in the NFL title game over the next five seasons, but the Giants could not quite prevail. The Giants fell out of contention. They moved to the Meadowlands complex in East Rutherford, N.J., in 1976. On Valentine's Day, 1979, they hired a Don Shula disciple and former Baltimore high school history teacher named George Young as general manager. The Giants had not been to the playoffs for 15 years, but Young would get them there eight times during his 19-year tenure as GM. He drafted quarterback Phil Simms in 1979 and linebacker Lawrence Taylor in 1981, and he hired Bill Parcells as head coach in 1983.

> "The Quakers thought we were pushovers, but we kicked the bleep out of them." — **Giants tackle Babe Parnell, after a 31-0 victory over the AFL's Philadelphia Quakers (1926).**

Those three principals led the team back to the playoffs in 1984, and in January 1987, authored a victory in Super Bowl

XXI. The Giants marked the return to glory of one of the league's great franchises when they decimated the Denver Broncos 39-20 at the Rose Bowl in Pasadena. Four seasons later, the Giants brought home another title in one of the most dramatic Super Bowls in history. With seconds remaining, Buffalo's Scott Norwood missed a 47-yard field goal wide right, rendering the Giants 20-19 winners in Super Bowl XXV at Tampa Stadium.

Swami Sez:

The Giants ate up a fifth place schedule in 1997. If they can continue to munch on tougher slates, Jim Fassell could qualify as a Renaissance man.

In 1997, after several years back in the pack, the Giants did something no team had ever done: they went undefeated (7-0-1) in NFC East play. Defying the critics, most of whom predicted a last-place finish, the Giants won 10 games and returned to playoff form. Despite a dispiriting playoff loss to the Vikings, the future, under coach Jim Fassell and new general manager Ernie Accorsi, looks bright —just like the past.

—*Greg Garber*

The Meadowlands

Giants Stadium was baptized on October 10, 1976, with a loss to the Cowboys, and with many more losing seasons thereafter. Even though the Giants have since earned a pair of Super Bowl titles and contender status, the legacy of the team's Dark Ages helps enrich this otherwise unspectacular concrete bowl with an underdog spirit. Fans come to the game with an enthusiasm tempered by age-old premonitions of disaster — and

The "I Was There" Games

December 28, 1958: A turning point in all of pro football history. This was the first NFL Championship game to go into overtime, and it was well-timed—before a live television audience. Alan "The Horse" Ameche's one yard TD plunge capped the game that made America begin to love football. (Colts 23, Giants 17).

January 4, 1987: The Giants exact revenge for their playoff ouster a year earlier by obliterating Bill Walsh's 49ers in the NFC Divisional Playoffs. Joe Morris runs for 159 yards and two touchdowns, Phil Simms throws four touchdown passes, Lawrence Taylor returns an interception for a touchdown, Jim Burt knocks Joe Montana unconscious — the whole enchilada. (Giants 49, 49ers 3).

The Paper Bag Game

November 19, 1978: With New York leading Philadelphia 17-12 and running out the clock at Giants Stadium, quarterback Joe Pisarcik and running back Larry Csonka botch the exchange on a routine handoff. The ball bounces its way into the hands of the Eagles' Herman Edwards, who returns "The Fumble" for a touchdown and a stunning road victory. (Eagles 19, Giants 17).

did you know?

When Lawrence Taylor first reported to Giants camp in 1981, he wore not the number 56 which would eventually be retired in his name, but rather 98, now worn by All-Pro linebacker Jessie Armstead.

Our Top Story

"Go Elis! Go Giants."
1973
With the Meadowlands under construction and Yankee Stadium in the middle of renovation, the Giants are forced to play at the Yale Bowl in New Haven, CT. Since it will be nearly impossible for Giants' fans to see their team, an understanding President Nixon signs a bill that lifts the TV blackout on home games sold out 72 hours prior to kickoff.

"LT Gets Clean"
March 20, 1986
Lawrence Taylor goes into treatment for substance abuse and makes it work—he would end up Player of the Year and lead the Giants to a Super Bowl victory over the Broncos.

"Wide Right!"
January 27, 1991
Super Bowl XXV goes down as the closest ever, as a 47-yard field-goal attempt from Buffalo's Scott Norwood sails wide right while the clock runs out.

Great Names

Leon Bright (ST-RB, 1981-83)
Glen Campbell (E, 1929-33)
Art Carney (G, 1925-26)
Erwin "Tiny" Feather (B, 1929-30, 32-33)
Ken Strong (B, 1933-35, 39-47)
Charlie Toogood (DT, 1958)
Amani Toomer (WR, 1996-)

---

did you know?

Starting in 1932, a New York Giant—Ray Flaherty ('32), Red Badgro ('34), Tod Goodwin ('35)—paced the league in receptions three times in four years. No Giant has led the NFL in catches since.

---

they aren't shy about sharing their negative energy. Ask Phil Simms. Frankly, the downbeat, skeptical fans can be something of a downer. So, call them fickle, but don't call them fair-weather: They show, and volubly so, for every game — only in the strike season of 1987 has average attendance dipped below the 64,000 mark.

The stadium itself is a rather muted facility. A pair of average-sized Sony Jumbotrons satisfies the need for instant replays, and after each play, the dignified voice of public-address announcer Bob Shepard, who also works the mike at Yankee Stadium, clarifies the action to the crowd ("Carry by Barber ... tackled by Patton"). The focus stays on the game.

Like the entire New York City area, Giants Stadium gets too hot in the summer and too cold in the winter. While balmy early-season weather can feel picknicky, no one bothers putting ice in the cooler for a December game. The best seats in the house are near midfield, about 15 or 20 rows back in the lower level, where you can sit with employees in good standing at profitable New York corporations. Seats at the rear of the upper deck are too far away and can be bitterly cold. Don't bother.

> "We try to hurt everybody. We hit each other as hard as we can. This is a man's game."
> — Linebacker Sam Huff in 1959.

Blue-collar tailgating is alive and well at the Meadowlands. Arrive three or four hours before game time to revel or commiserate over burgers with some hard-core Giants fans. And if you have Harry Carson's number-53 jersey tucked away somewhere, wear it.

Best of the Giants

Best Team

1986 (17-2): In his first three seasons, coach Bill Parcells nurtured a team that had the ingredients to win a title. In year four, the pieces came together. Some point to Phil Simms' 22-yard completion to WR Bobby Johnson (on fourth-and-17) in a comeback win at Minnesota in mid-November as a sign of destiny. Later, New York simply pounded the 49ers, Redskins and Super Bowl XXI foe Denver in the postseason.

Greatest Players by Position

Pos:	Player
QB:	Phil Simms
RB:	Joe Morris
WR:	Del Shofner
TE:	Mark Bavaro
OL:	Roosevelt Brown
DL:	Andy Robustelli
LB:	Lawrence Taylor
DB:	Emlen Tunnell
P/K:	Pete Gogolak
ST:	Dave Meggett

And Don't Forget...

LB: Harry Carson. The yang to L.T.'s yin, Carson was a hard worker and as consistent as they come —a nine-time Pro Bowler and the heart and soul of many Giants' defenses. He also was the first man to dump Gatorade on his coach.

QB: Charlie Conerly. He led the Giants in passing 12 straight years (1948-59) and the team to a championship in 1956.

C/LB: Mel Hein. A two-way player who never missed a game during his 15 seasons with the Giants, Hein earned MVP honors in 1938.

RB: Alex Webster. Still ranked among the team's leaders in rushing and receiving, "Big Red" sparked the Giants' offense for many seasons.

LB: Sam Huff. The one-on-one battles between this Hall of Fame linebacker and running back Jim Brown are legendary.

RB: Rodney Hampton. The Giants have always had a legacy of solid running backs; Hampton leads the franchise in rushing. Ron Johnson was another backfield great.

Best Argument

Quarterback: Phil Simms or Y.A. Tittle? Simms was never appreciated by the fans in the Big Apple until he turned in a record-setting performance and won MVP honors in Super Bowl XXI. When he was in the lineup, he was the leader of the offense. Tittle was a blood-and guts legend who got the Giants within a game of a title three times during his four years with the franchise.

Best Coach

Bill Parcells (1983-90): With apologies to Steve Owen, who owns the franchise mark for victories (155), and Allie Sherman, who compiled a 33-6-1 record in his first three seasons. Parcells' eight-year stay with the Big Blue began with a dismal 3-12-1 debut, but would end with two Super Bowl titles in a five-year period. In between, the Giants were known as one of the league's most physical squads and could never be taken lightly, thanks to their master motivator.

Pressbox

Who to Read...

The New York press runs the gamut on its attitude toward the team. The *New York Times'* Mike Freeman went out on a limb with his preseason prediction in 1997 that the Giants "could be the surprise team of the league," when almost everyone else had them ranked much lower. Freeman also offers more depth about personnel than the average reporter. The *Daily News'* Ian O'Connor can be relied upon to point out just what's wrong with the Giants. Stepping back for more perspective, the *Times* venerable columnist Dave Anderson looks periodically at recent team developments and extrudes from them a vision of the state of sport today.

Who to Watch...

For years, head coach Allie Sherman had a weekly TV show, a tradition carried on by coaches through Bill Parcells. Coaches Ray Handley and Dan Reeves didn't really have the profile or personality to fill Parcells's shoes on a weekly half-hour show. But starting in 1998, head coach and new local hero Jim Fassel will appear on "Gameday New York", a weekly pregame show on WNBC co-hosted by Mike Breen. Veteran local sportscasters include

WCBS's Warner Wolf and his trademark "Let's go to the videotape"; WNBC's Len Berman, who can seem more authoritative on the Jets than on the Boys in Blue; and sweater-clad Russ Salzberg of WWOR, who plays up a kind of New Yawkah appeal. In the city proper, cable station NY1 provides "Sports on 1" a nightly call-in show that provides total immersion in the New York sports fan zeitgeist. WNYW–FOX has a loyal Giant following for sportscaster Curt Menafee and the "Sports Extra" show Sunday nights at 10:30 with Tom McDonald.

Who to Listen To...

Fassel made do in his rookie season with a weekly radio appearance on Monday evenings on local sports station WFAN (660 AM). WFAN also features Mike Francesa and Chris "Mad Dog" Russo in the afternoon. Francesa's know-it-all tone, bearable because he is quite knowledgable, blends nicely with the antic Russo. Like most sports radio shows, one theme or bit of news can dominate for hours. The name that Giants fans remember, though, is Marty Glickman, the longtime announcer who set the standard for broadcasting football.

The Bottom Line on Giants Stadium

Address: Giants Stadium, East Rutherford, NJ 07073. (201) 935-8111.

Tickets: Season tickets are out of the question—like Packers tickets or the British crown, they are passed down from generation to generation. The ticket office is still processing requests from 1976. Scalpers abound in the parking lot, however, especially by Gate D, where the New Jersey Transit buses let out. You can also try the local ticket agencies, but you'll pay. The real prices aren't that bad, with lower and upper levels at $40 and $45 for the mezzanine. Call the box office for information: (201) 935-8222, M-F 9-5.

1998: $45/$40

1994: $40/$35

Public Transportation: New Jersey Transit runs buses from New York City's Port Authority Bus Terminal to the game and back. (973) 762-5100.

Parking: Ample parking is available in the Meadowlands Sports Complex for a $10 fee, but the march along an enclosed walkway to the stadium can be a long one. The good news: The further you go on foot, the closer you are to the lot exit, which is a bottleneck at game's end.

Capacity: 78,148

Restrooms: 70.

Where to go . . . in New York City

Best Bars

Most complete sports bar. The mother of all New York City sports bars, **The Sporting Club** in downtown Manhattan comes complete with an electronic scoreboard covering all the day's sporting events. On big game days (including any NFL Sunday), call ahead to reserve a table within your rooting section. *99 Hudson St., New York, NY, (212) 219-0900. Seven days, 12:00pm-1am.*

Best raucous roadhouse. If you're a woman who wants to add her bra to the collection hanging behind the bar (like Julia Roberts did), or if you just want to meet such an individual while drinking a can of Pabst, **Hogs and Heifers** in the meatpacking district might be your kind of place. *859 Washington St., New York, NY, (212) 929-0655. M-F 11am-4am, Sa 1pm-4am, Su 2pm-4am.*

Ready For Primetime (Monday Night)

December 1, 1986: For the first fifteen years of MNF, the Giants were not even close to being ready for prime time (3-10-1). Another long night seemed in store for Bill Parcells' club as Joe Montana led his team to a 17-0 lead by intermission. But New York scored on its first three possessions of the third quarter to take the lead for good. The shot from this game of TE Mark Bavaro dragging 49er defenders down the middle of the field following a reception is one of the all-time great NFL highlights. (Giants 21, 49ers 17).

Overall Monday Night: 14-21-1

Overall Thursday Night: 1-0

Overall Sunday Night: 6-6-1

Think About the Weather

January 11, 1987: After winning the coin toss in the NFC Championship Game against the Redskins, the Giants chose not to receive the kickoff, but rather to defend a particular end zone. Why? Thirty-five mile-per-hour winds turned even a routine pass into an adventure. New York scored 10 points with the wind at their backs in the opening quarter, and an overpowering defense helped them walk away with the NFC title, 17-0.

did you know?

Following both of their Super Bowl championship campaigns (XXI and XXV), the Giants failed to make the playoffs—the only franchise to manage that feat twice.

Worst Team

1966 (1-12-1):Twenty years before L.T. and company won the Super Bowl, New York featured one of the worst defenses to ever take the field. The Giants gave up an astounding 501 points — a record for a 14-game season and the second-most in NFL history. Indicative of their troubles was the fact that in consecutive weeks, the Giants scored 41, 40 and 28 points, and lost all three games.

> "I was just saying 'Miss it, miss it.'" — Giants safety Everson Walls, on anticipating the last-second field goal attempt from Buffalo's Scott Norwood in Super Bowl XXV.

Team Leaders

Rushing Yards
6,897   Rodney Hampton, 1990-97
Passing Yards
33,462   Phil Simms, 1979-93
Passing Touchdowns
199   Phil Simms, 1979-93
Receptions
395   Joe Morrison, 1959-72
Interceptions
74   Emlen Tunnell, 1948-58
Touchdowns
78   Frank Gifford, 1952-60, 1962-64
Points
646   Pete Gogolak, 1966-74

Best view to the bridge. Proximity to highways might not be the best draw for a drinking establishment, but that's the hook for **Siggy's at the Bridge**, situated in the shadow of the George Washington Bridge. *Bridge Plaza, Fort Lee, NJ, (201) 592-6969. M-Sa 11am-3am, Su 5pm-3am.*

Best Restaurants

Best chance of dining with coaches. Bill Parcells used to plump up at **Manny's**, a real meat-and-potatoes joint. Show off your Giants knowledge here beneath signed glossies featuring the likes of Larry Csonka and Troy Archer. *110 Moonachie Ave., Moonachie, NJ, (201) 939-1244. M-Sa 11am-10pm, Su closes "a little earlier." AE, MC, V. $*

Best conga line. Not far from the Lincoln Tunnel, **Mangia e Bevi** is a good mid-range Italian restaurant which turns into a no-holds-barred party on weekend nights. If you prefer a quiet meal to a tango with your waitperson, try Julian's next door, where the ambience is mellower and the food a shade better. *800 9th Ave., New York, NY, (212) 956-3976. M-Sa 12:30-3:30pm (lunch), 3:30-midnight (dinner), Su 12:30pm-11pm Sun. All major credit cards. $$*

Best view of the Meadowlands. Sample fine, if not underpriced, fare at the highest-altitude restaurant in Gotham, which is home to a great prix-fixe brunch on Sundays, starting at 11am. **Windows on the World**, *1 World Trade Center, New York, NY, (212) 524-7011. M-Th 5pm-10:30pm, F-Sa11:30pm, Su 11am-2:30pm (brunch), 5pm-10pm (dinner). Call for reservations. Jacket required for men. All major credit cards. $$$$.*

Fans' notes

On Screen

In 1994, there was **Little Giants**, a kind of Bad News Bears on the gridiron, but only the logo shows up—Emmitt Smith and John Madden make the star cameos. There's a 1972 version of Frederick Exley's **A Fan's Notes** starring Jerry Orbach, and if you just can't get enough of The Giff, look for **The All American** for young Frank and **Two Minute Warning** for older—yet still pre-Kathie Lee—Frank. Defensive tackle Rosey Grier stepped onto the silver screen for flicks like **The Thing with Two Heads** and **The Gong Show Movie**. The Giants' top draft pick in 1969, Fred Dryer, went on to star in TV's **Hunter** during the 1980s. There's an entire NFL Films video about Lawrence Taylor called **LT**, as well as **Giants Forever: A History of the New York Giants** which only goes up to the 1986 season, but that's still 61 years worth. And if you're still thinking about Cody's dad, there's the **25th Anniversary of ABC's Monday Night Football** tape.

Bookshelf

The Game of Their Lives. Dave Klein (Random House 1976). Describes "The Game," the Giant-Colt overtime championship game of 1958.
No Medals for Trying: A Week in the Life of a Pro Football Team. Jerry Izenberg (Macmillan 1990).
Once a Giant, Always...My Two Lives with the New York Giants. Andy Robustelli (Quinlan 1987)
Parcells: Autobiography of the Biggest Giant of Them All. Bill Parcells and Mike Lupica. (Bonus 1987)
Simms to McConkey: Blood Sweat and Gatorade. Phil McConkey, et al (Crown 1987).
Giants and Heroes: A Daughter's Memories of Y.A. Tittle. Dianne Tittle deLaet (Steerforth 1995).
LT: Living on the Edge. Lawrence Taylor and David Falkner (Times 1987).
Giants: 70 Seasons of Championship Football. John Steinbreder (Taylor 1994).
A Fan's Notes. Frederic Exley (Random House 1997). A classic novel about an alcoholic who uses the Giants to keep anchored and go forward with his life.
Wait Til Next Year. Mike Lupica and William Goldman (Bantam 1988). An overlooked book about a year in New York sports, including pieces on the Giants during the 1987 strike season.
On Courage. Frank Gifford (M. Evans 1976). Sort of a football version of JFK's *Profiles in Courage.*

You Gotta See...

▶If you're in town to see football, it's Autumn in New York, a time so nice they wrote a song about it. So go to **Central Park**, watch the polar bears, take out a rowboat, go for a run. The only thing that will get you mugged is asking a New Yorker if it's safe there.
▶The **American Museum of Natural History** has nothing to do with football, but many think it's the best museum in town. Dinosaurs, massive stuffed animals, a whale hanging from the ceiling; perfect if the weather stinks.
▶The best deal in town is the **Staten Island Ferry**. You get a ride through New York Harbor past the Statue of Liberty and a great view of the skyline. How much? For you—nothing. Yep, it's free.

Hall of Fame

Mel Hein	(C 1963)
Wilber Henry	(T 1963)
Cal Hubbard	(T 1963)
Tim Mara	(Founder 1963)
Jim Thorpe	(HB 1963)
Joe Guyon	(HB 1966)
Arnie Herber	(QB 1966)
Steve Owen	(Coach 1966)
Ken Strong	(HB 1967)
Emlen Tunnell	(DB 1967)
Hugh McElhenny	(HB 1970)
Vince Lombardi	(Coach 1971)
Andy Robustelli	(DE 1971)
Y.A. Tittle	(QB 1971)
Roosevelt Brown	(T 1975)
Ray Flaherty	(E/Coach 1976)
Frank Gifford	(HB/F 1977)
Alphonse Leemans	(RB 1978)
Morris Badgro	(E 1981)
Sam Huff	(LB 1982)
Arnie Weinmeister	(DT 1984)
Fran Tarkenton	(QB 1986)
Larry Csonka	(FB 1987)
Don Maynard	(WR 1987)
Tom Landry	(Coach 1990)
Wellington Mara	(Owner 1997)

Against the Odds

It wasn't that **Frank Gifford** (1952-60, 1962-64) wasn't expected to succeed. He was, after all, an All-American at USC and the Giants' first-round draft choice in 1952. But a head-ringing tackle by the Eagles' Chuck Bednarik in 1960 put the Giants' halfback in a hospital for a week with a serious concussion, and seemingly ended his career. After sitting out the following season, however, Gifford gave it another try, returning in 1962 to a new position (flanker), where he emerged as a dynamic star and leader once again.

Best Accommodations

Econolodge. Budget accommodations located just a quarter mile from the sports complex. *395 Washington Ave., Carlstadt, NJ. (201) 935-4600, (800) 553-2666. $*

Sheraton Meadowlands. Just down the block from the arena; skilled Frogger players can walk to the game. *2 Meadowlands Plaza, East Rutherford, NJ. (201) 896-0500, (800) 325-3535. $$-$$$*

New York Hilton and Towers at Rockefeller Center. Luxury everything, and the NFL holds a number of its meetings and seminars in the conference rooms here. *1335 Avenue of the Americas, New York, NY. (212) 586-7000, (800) 445-8667. $$$$$*

did you know?
According to the Milwaukee *Journal,* in 1926, the Giants' Al Nesser played an entire game in a bathing suit.

While You Were Eating Turkey....
November 25, 1982. While there certainly was just cause for celebration on this Thanksgiving Day as the league returned to action following a bitter 57-day players strike, the 64,348 fans at the Silverdome were hardly in a festive mood. The Giants and Lions combined for four field goals after three quarters of play, but Detroit looked like they were going to break a 6-6 tie with the ball on the New York four-yard line. But Giants' LB Lawrence Taylor stepped in front of a Gary Danielson pass intended for RB Horace King, and raced 97 yards down the sidelines for the only touchdown of the game. Giants 13, Lions 6. Overall, 7-3-3.

New York Jets

Those mavericks from the AFL charted a brave course in 1960. Go into the big cities head to head with the well-established NFL.

The Rams owned Los Angeles, so the Chargers moved down the road to San Diego after one year. The Cowboys and Texans arrived in Dallas at the same time. The Cowboys are still in Big D, while the Texans after three years became the Kansas City Chiefs.

The Giants owned New York football, and still do in terms of fan loyalty. The Jets might not have survived if not for the financial failure of original owner Harry Wismer. His bankruptcy allowed Sonny Werblin to buy the team, and then shock pro football by giving Joe Namath a $400,000 contract. Bigger than life, on and off the field, Namath not only led the Jets to a Super Bowl III title over the Colts, he paved the way for the merger between the leagues by proving that a second professional football league was viable.

Franchise History

New York Titans (AFL)
(1960–62)
New York Jets (AFL)
(1963–69)
New York Jets (NFL)
(1970–present)

By The Numbers

(Since 1970)

Regular Season: 171-251-2
Postseason: 3-5
Division Titles: 0
Vs. Division: 93-126-1 (Playoffs: 0-3)
Playoff Appearances: 5
Home: 91-119-1
Away: 80-132-1

(Overall)

Regular Season: 240-316-8
Postseason: 5-6
Playoff Appearances: 7
Home: 132-144-5
Away: 108-172-3

That was 30 years ago. Not much has happened since. The Jets are still the only team around since the merger (1970) not to win their division. After a playoff-less '70s, things improved in the early '80s. Led by QB Richard Todd and defensive sack specialists Mark Gastineau and Joe Klecko, the Jets returned to the playoffs.

It's fitting that the Jets best season since 1969 was the 1982 strike season. The Jets won two road playoff games, only to lose the AFC title game when Dolphin A.J. Duhe intercepted Todd three times on an Orange Bowl field that was not covered during an all-night rain.

Remember 1986? Vintage Jets. NFL

Most Revered Football Figures

Joe Namath. Super Bowl III. His charisma and talent gave credibility to not only the Jets, but the entire AFL. When you think Jets, you think #12, Broadway Joe.

Weeb Ewbank. The fact that the greatest coach in team history has a losing record says more about the franchise than the coach.

Joe Klecko. Leader of the 1980's "Sack Exchange," he is the only defensive player in history to make the Pro Bowl at three different positions.

Rivalries

The Jets–Buffalo **Bills** rivalry (31-43) features many milestones, including New York's first league game on September 11, 1960, Joe Namath's first start as a Jet on September 26, 1965, and the 1973 game in snowy Shea Stadium that put O.J. Simpson over 2,000 yards for the season. That game was also the last one Weeb Ewbank coached for the Jets. The New England **Patriots** (39-33-1) are one of only five teams that New York has a winning record against. Conversely, the Patriots are responsible for the most lopsided loss in Jets history, beating them 56-3 in 1979. Bill Parcells left the Patriots to join the Jets in 1997, adding to the tension. The Jets–**Dolphins** (29-35-1) series is best remembered by many high-scoring thrillers and the infamous "fake spike" play by Miami QB Dan Marino in 1994 that went for a touchdown. After that bit of chicanery, the Jets went on to lose 32 of their next 36 games.

fans remember that season for Elway's drive in Cleveland or the Giants' Super Bowl victory. But ask a Jets fan, and he will tell you that '86 should have been their season in New York. The Jets started 10-and-1, stumbled to the finish and lost a double-OT playoff game to the Browns, helping set the stage for the Drive.

did you know?

The Jets changed their name from Titans in 1963 because as America entered the new "Space" or "Jet" Age, their new home, Shea Stadium, was situated between LaGuardia and Kennedy (then Idlewild) airports.

In the ensuing eleven years the Jets were simply laughable. New York appeared in just one playoff game and compiled an embarassing record of 54-104-1, a pathetic 50 games under .500. Most of this happened in GIANTS stadium.

> "What do the Jets and the Pope have in common? They're the only people who can put 80,000 people in the Meadowlands and make them all say 'Jesus Christ!' " — Jets quarterback Boomer Esiason in 1995.

Perhaps one reason the franchise has long searched for an identity is that it has never had a home of its own. The AFL Titans debuted at the Polo Grounds, a vacated baseball stadium. Then the Jets moved to the brand spanking new Shea Stadium, but a September of mostly road games and the dirt baseball infield always served as a reminder: the Jets were the second tenant at the Mets facility. Finally there was the move to New Jersey and the Meadowlands.

This year marks season 15 with the green bunting covering up the Giants colors for Jets home games. Perhaps it is only appropriate that the Jets, for the first time since the Sack Exchange, are finally developing a new personality, thanks to an ex-Giants coach.

Owner Leon Hess, loved by all who have worked for him, wanted to see one more title run in his time and brought in New York's most popular football coach, Bill Parcells.

In the first year of Tuna's tenure he gave Jets fans an eight-game positive turnaround and brought the Jets from one win in '96 to within one missed officials' call of the playoffs in '97.

It's been 12 years since a playoff win (1986), 29 years since a division win (1969), and the league in which they won it doesn't exist anymore. So now you understand why Jets fans start this season with two strange words: real optimism.

—Mike Tirico

The Meadowlands

On October 6 1983, citing Shea Stadium as "the NFL's poorest facilities for players and spectators alike," Jets owner Leon Hess announced his team would play their future games at The Meadowlands in New Jersey. So, for the past fourteen seasons the New York Jets have called Giants Stadium in East Rutherford, New Jersey, their home. There is no more telling fact about the identity-starved Jets than that they play their "home" games at Giants Stadium.

For all the charm, bleacher seats, brass bands and natural grass of Shea Stadium, Hess was correct when he called the place "run-down and neglected." Though Hess did get his expanded parking, increased seating and cleaner bathrooms, he sacrificed the team's character and soul. While Jets fans may be more comfortable in their

The "I Was There" Game

January 12, 1969: In Super Bowl III against the Baltimore Colts, a game that QB Joe Namath guaranteed the Jets would win, the 18-point underdog Jets pulled off the greatest upset in NFL history, beating the Colts 16-7.

The Paper Bag Game

January 3, 1987: Trailing 20-10 with 4:14 to play, the Browns rallied to win this AFC Divisional Playoff Game, the third-longest game in league history. Facing a 2nd and 24 from his own 18-yard line, Browns QB Bernie Kosar threw incomplete. However, true to form, the Jets were charged with a 15-yard penalty when Mark Gastineau hit Kosar too late. Four plays later the Browns were in the end zone en route to an improbable 23-20 double-OT win. The Jets have played one playoff game since. They lost.

did you know?

Because the Mets were competing in the World Series, the Jets were forced to play the first six games of the 1973 season on the road.

Great Names

Verlon Biggs (DE, 1965-70)
Emerson Boozer (RB, 1966-75)
Weeb Ewbank (Coach, 1963-1973)
Nuu Faaola (FB, 1986-89)
Foge Fazio (Asst. Coach, 1990-94)
Cosmo Iacavazzi (FB, 1965)
Siupeli Malamala (T, 1992-97)
Shafer Suggs (DB, 1976-80)
JoJo Townsell (WR, 1985-90)
Charley Winner (Coach, 1974-75)

Our Top Story

"Oh, Grandfather!"
November 17, 1968
With the Jets up 32-29 over the Raiders with 65 seconds to go, NBC switches to their scheduled broadcast of "Heidi." The Raiders score twice in the final minute to win 43-32. Jets fans are unable to decide who they hate most: NBC, the Raiders, or the Swiss.

"Super Bowl Shocker"
January 12, 1969
Led by the swagger and right arm of Joe Namath, the nine-year-old New York Jets stun the football world by winning Super Bowl III over the heavily favored Baltimore Colts.

"Come-and-Go Joe"
June 6-July 18, 1969
Embroiled in a dispute with league officials over his ownership of the New York bar Bachelors III, Joe Namath announces that he is retiring from football. Fortunately for the Jets, it takes him just over a month to change his mind, sell the bar and return to the team.

"Tuna Returns to Jersey"
February 10, 1997
Following weeks of speculation and denial, the New York Jets finally land the big one when NFL Commissioner Paul Tagliabue rules that Bill Parcells can break his contract with the New England Patriots and take over the Jets football operation, in exchange for cash and draft picks.

> **did you know?**
> His Majesty Emperor Hirohito of Japan attended the Jets home-opener against the Pats in 1975.

full-amenity, all-football stadium, they've seen only four winning seasons and two home playoff games since 1984.

At the Meadowlands, it is difficult to avoid feeling that the Jets are merely visitors in the place they call home. On game days, green coverings are draped over the stadium's blue trim, Jets banners pop up on the stadium's exterior, and the jerseys of Joe Namath and Don Maynard appear between levels of the stands, allowing the place to take on a certain "Jets" personality. Pregame tailgating parties take place throughout the stadium parking lots, though they're nothing out of the ordinary.

The chant of "J-E-T-S, Jets! Jets! Jets!" is usually led by Fireman Ed in a Jets firefighter's hat and an old #42 Bruce Harper jersey. Though simple, it is the most uniquely "Jets" aspect of attending a home game at Giants Stadium. See the Giants' chapter for details regarding the weather and location of the better seats. (Even in this book, the Jets get no respect at home.)

The Bottom Line on Giants Stadium

Address: Exit 16W, NJ Turnpike, East Rutherford, NJ 07073. (201) 935-8500.

Tickets: Although all games are sold out, (there is an 11,000-person waiting list for season tickets) the recent past indicates that scalping the $35 tickets is no problem for anyone willing to make the trip. Call the ticket office at (516) 560-8200 for information.

1998: $40/$35

1994: $35/$25

Public Transportation: New Jersey Transit offers buses from the Port Authority Bus

Best of the Jets

Best Team

1968 (13-3): As big a role as QB Joe Namath played in the Super Bowl upset of the Colts, not enough accolades go to an opportunistic Jets' defense that totaled five takeaways that afternoon. And that was the story for much of the year in the AFL as Weeb Ewbank's champions were far from a one-man show. New York's defense led the league in fewest yards allowed and consistently shut down the run.

Swami Sez:

The Jets have returned to the old uniforms with the old logos, which means the white shoes are next.

Greatest Players by Position

Pos.	Player
QB:	Joe Namath
RB:	Freeman McNeil
WR	Don Maynard
TE:	Mickey Shuler
OL:	Marvin Powell
DL:	Joe Klecko
LB:	Kyle Clifton
DB:	Erik McMillan
P/K:	Pat Leahy
ST:	Bruce Harper

And Don't Forget...

T: Winston Hill. An eight-time all-star and a reliable blocker, Hill started 174 straight games up front for the Jets.
WR: Wesley Walker. Legally blind in one eye, this sure-handed speedster stood out on a club which has had quality WRs like George Sauer and Al Toon.

RB: Emerson Boozer. The Jets got a steal with this former sixth-round pick, who knew his way to the end zone.
TE: Richard Caster. He spent his first eight years in the league in New York, and gave Jets' quarterbacks a big target.
LB Ralph Baker. A typically consistent player out of Penn State, he played 11 seasons with the Jets.

Best Argument

Running Back: Freeman McNeil or Matt Snell? Former UCLA standout McNeil led the Jets in rushing eight times during his 12-year career, posting a pair of 1,000-yard campaigns in 1984 and '85 and leading the NFL in rushing during the strike-shortened 1982 season. Snell was an unsung runner and a reliable receiver in the pass-happy AFL, making three trips to the league's all-star game.

"[Neil] O'Donnell has been nothing but a stiff puppet back there." — Wide receiver Keyshawn Johnson, well known for rubbing teammates the wrong way, before the 1997 season.

Best Coach

Weeb Ewbank (1963-73): While this space may some day belong to Bill Parcells, Ewbank gets the nod despite failing to post a winning season eight times in 11 years, including his final four years on the job. Still, the likable coach delivered the Jets' lone championship, which means a lot to a franchise whose shining moments have been few and far between.

Pressbox

Who to Read...

Gerald Eskenazi covers the team for *The New York Times*, while Mark Cannizzaro and Jay Greenberg can be found in *The New York Post*. Rich Cimini and Ian O'Connor cover the beat for *The New York Daily News*. New Yorkers tend to get the locker room dirt from the *Post* and the *News*. The *Times* has the occasional gem of a column by Ira Berkow and the estimable talents of writers such as Eskenazi, George Vecsey, Dave Anderson, Michael Freeman, and Harvey Araton. On the other hand, *Daily News* columnist Mike Lupica, also of ESPN's "Sports Reporters," exemplifies the raw, critical tone you'll find among New York natives. If you pass a weekend without reading, seeing, or hearing Lupica somewhere, you probably just haven't been paying attention. Richard Oliver follows the team for *Newsday*, along with Joe Gergen and Steve Jacobson, all of whom deftly tread the line between tabloid and the serious stuff. Fans in New Jersey read Dave Hutchinsen in the *Newark Star Ledger*.

Who to Watch...

The nation's media capital offers no shortage of information, insight and, oh yes, opinions. Games can be seen locally on WCBS. Sunday mornings during the season, WNBC offers "Jets Game Day" with hosts Mike Francesa and former Jets punter Dave Jennings. The former Jets Game Day tandem of Bill Parcells and Phil Simms has moved their operation over to WCBS for the 1998 season. Sundays on WCBS will also feature a show with WFAN's Chris Russo and John Riggins. For those who just can't get enough "Gang Green," cable channel MSG provides the weekly "Jets Journal," hosted by Al Trautwig and former Jet Marty Lyons.

> "This business is about winning. This is a great situation!"
> — Rich Kotite in 1996, en route to compiling a 4-28 record as Jets head coach.

Who to Listen To...

For those who prefer listening to reading, "The Mike and The Mad Dog Show," with Mike Francesa and Chris Russo, airs weekdays from 1pm-6pm on WFAN (660 AM) to help keep fans on top of the entire New York football scene. Francesa's close friendship with Parcells makes the Jet talk necessary for die-hard Jet fans. Games are heard on either WFAN or WXRK (92.3 FM) with Howard David and former Jets punter Dave Jennings offering play-by-play and analysis.

Terminal in Manhattan. Call (973) 762-5100 for information.

Parking: Consider arriving early enough to avoid parking by the neighboring Continental Airlines Arena and subjecting yourself to the long walk and "cattle call" experience of the elevated tunnel that connects the two venues. On the other hand, parking at such a distance provides an easier escape, especially to Route 3, with its clean shot to the Lincoln Tunnel and midtown Manhattan.

Capacity: 78,148.

Restrooms: 70.

Where to Go . . . in New York City

Best Bars

Best Jets atmosphere. Named for and founded by former Jets QB Boomer Esiason, **Boomer's Sports Club** is probably the best place in Manhattan to take in a game with like-minded fans. Plenty of TVs and beer allow for good angles and a way to forget the outcome. *349 Amsterdam Ave., (212) 362-5400. M-F 5pm-4am, Sa-Su11am-4am.*

Best libation selection. A neighborhood brewpub, **D.B.A.** offers one of the largest selection of microbrewed beers and single-malt scotches in the city. *41 First Ave. (at 4th St.) (212) 475-5097. Seven days 1pm-4am.*

Best literary haunt. One of NYC's oldest taverns, O. Henry wrote his classic Christmas short story "The Gift of the Magi" here at **Pete's Tavern**. Which is appropriate, since the Jets have provided their fans with plenty of reasons over the years to forget the game and open a book. Still, the food is good, and the atmosphere befits its longevity. *129 E. 18th St. (at Irving Place) (212) 473-7676. Su-Tu 10:30am-12pm bar until 1:30am. W-Sa 10am-1:30am, Bar until 3am.*

> "Since World War II, the Jets are the most famous bad team in sports."
> — New York sportswriter Gerald Eskenazi.

Best old bar. You might recognize this place from the old credits on the

> **did you know?**
> Hall of Famer "Slingin'" Sammy Baugh was the franchise's first head coach when the Jets (then Titans) played their home games in the Polo Grounds.

Ready For Primetime (Monday Night)

On September 21, 1970, the first MNF game ever played resulted in a 31-21 loss by the Jets to the Browns. In 1979 the first MNF game broadcast from New York saw the Jets beat the Minnesota Vikings 14-7 at Shea Stadium. Ten years later the Jets-Raiders game featured the debut of Art Shell, the first African-American head coach in the modern era of the NFL. The October 17, 1988, loss to the Bills was marred by fans setting fires in the stands. Fifty-six fans were ejected for unruly behavior while 15 more were arrested.

Overall Monday Night: 9-16
Overall Thursday Nights: 0-2
Overall Sunday Nights: 2-7

Think About the Weather

January 23, 1983: AFC Championship, Miami Orange Bowl, Miami 14, New York 0. This AFC Championship Game was played under vehement protest by the Jets because Miami's groundskeepers did not cover the field despite days of steady rain. A.J. Duhe's three interceptions led the Dolphins to a 14-0 victory and the Super Bowl. The teams combined for 12 turnovers and just over 300 total yards of offense. The scoreless tie at halftime was a first in NFL playoff history.

Worst Team

1996 (1-15): Could it get any worse for coach Rich Kotite? Retained following a 3-13 campaign, he was ridiculed throughout the season as his Jets found new and interesting ways to lose games. The team blew double-digit leads in five of their setbacks—including a pair of 14-0 advantages to the hated Dolphins—and ineptitude on defense and special teams saw the Jets allow 30-plus points in 10 contests.

Team Leaders

Rushing Yards

8,074   Freeman McNeil, 1981-92

Passing Yards

27,057   Joe Namath, 1965-76

Passing Touchdowns

170   Joe Namath, 1965-76

Receptions

627   Don Maynard, 1960-72

Interceptions

34   Bill Baird, 1963-69

Touchdowns

88   Don Maynard, 1960-72

Points

1,470   Pat Leahy, 1974-91

Letterman show when he was on NBC. Not far from Pete's, the **Old Town Bar** is mangy enough to feel comfortable. *45 E. 18th St. (212) 529-6732. M-Sa 12-11:30pm, Su 12-10pm.*

Best Restaurants

Best burger. There may be classier burgers, fancier burgers, burgers that pass as cuisine, but if you're just looking for a great tasting patty, a pile of fries, cold beer and lots of napkins to wipe your chin, **The Corner Bistro** down in the West Village is what you want. Everyone who's moved to New York thinks they discovered it. *351 W. 4th (212) 242-9502. Seven days 11:30am-4am. Cash only. $*

did you know?

The Jets lost their last game at Shea Stadium to the Pittsburgh Steelers on December 10, 1983. The Steelers also defeated the Jets in their first home game at Giants Stadium, September 6, 1984.

Best place to see a media czar. Power media types still flock to **P.J. Clarke's**, in an old holdout building on Third Avenue, to smoke cigars and eat unremarkable bar food with fellow workers. *915 Third Ave. 212-759-1650. Seven days 10am-4pm. V, MC,AX. $$*

Best mounds of garlicky Italian. If there's more than a couple of you in town and you're thinking Italian, try **Carmine's**, famous for vast, family-style servings of flavorful pastas and meat dishes. There

While You Were Eating Turkey

The Jets/Titans won their first ever Thanksgiving Day game, 21-14 over the Bills at the Polo Grounds, November 23, 1961. A year later, they beat the Broncos in Denver, in an old fashioned, 46-45 AFL shoot-out. The Jets are 0-2 on Thanksgiving Day against the Detroit Lions.
Overall, 2-2

Fans' notes

On Screen

For proof that, for a brief time, Joe Namath was the coolest guy on earth, check out his motorcycle-ridin', Ann Margret-lovin' performance in 1970's **C.C. and Company**, and his role as Glen Campbell's fellow veteran pal in **Norwood**, adapted from the novel by Charles (*True Grit*) Portis. Joe Willie also made some pretty memorable appearances on "The Flip Wilson Show," once with Muhammad Ali. If Broadway Joe was the coolest guy on earth, then a fictional Jet quarterback by the name of Flash Gordon held the honor in outer space — not in the old black-and-whites, but in the 1980 release **Flash Gordon**. The film's hero is proud of his day job, repeatedly identifying himself as "Flash Gordon, Quarterback, New York Jets." Joe Klecko went Hollywood in road movies **Smokey and the Bandit II** and **The Cannonball Run**. Speaking of the Jets' defensive line, you also may have seen the former Mrs. Mark Gastineau (aka Brigitte Neilsen) in **Red Sonja**. Jets fans can get their own copy of Namath's "I guarantee it" game from NFL Films; it's called **The NFL's Greatest Games: Super Bowl III**.

Bookshelf

Countdown to Super Bowl. Dave Anderson, with sketches by LeRoy Neiman (Random House 1969).
Broadway Joe and his Super Jets. Larry Fox (Coward-McCann 1969).
Goal To Go. Weeb Ewbank (Hawthorne Books 1972).
Joe Namath, and the Other Guys. Rick Telander (Holt, Rinehart and Winston 1976).
Football For Young Players and

Parents. Joe Namath with Bob Oates (Simon and Schuster 1986).
I Can't Wait Until Tomorrow... 'Cause I Get Better Looking Every Day. Joe Namath (Random House 1969).
The Game that Changed Pro Football. Stephen Hanks (Birch Lane Press 1989).
Nose to Nose: Survival in the Trenches of the NFL. Joe Klecko, Joe Fields and Greg Logan. (William Morrow 1988).
Rise and Walk: The Trial and Triumph of Dennis Byrd. Dennis Byrd and Michael D'Orso (Harper Collins 1993).
Just Give Me the Damn Ball! Keyshawn Johnson and Shelley Smith (Warner 1997).

You Gotta See...

▶**The Heisman trophy** lives at the Downtown Athletic Club, 19 West St. Jay Berwanger of the University of Chicago was the first winner of the award, and legend has it, the model for it. The club is open 24 hours a day and the trophy is in the lobby.

▶Not far away is the **New York Stock Exchange**, where you can watch your pension fund churn away. On November 24, 1981, the New York Sack Exchange of Klecko, Gastineau, Marty Lyons, and Abdul Salaam came through to cheers of "Defense! Defense!" Tours are available, but don't wait to get cheered.

▶If you're serious about the Jets, hop on the #7 train and ride out to **Shea Stadium** to remember what once was. Most of the team's happy moments took place in this orange and blue pile in Queens. Hurry—the Mets are looking for new real estate.

Hall of Fame

Weeb Ewbank   (Coach 1978)
Joe Namath   (QB 1985)
Don Maynard   (WR 1987)
John Riggins   (FB 1992)

> **"I just want to thank all the broads in New York." — Joe Namath, at the banquet celebrating the Jets' 1968 AFL championship.**

Against the Odds

The fact that a player's career could end on a single play was never as painfully apparent as when **Dennis Byrd** collided with a teammate on November 29, 1995, against Kansas City. Byrd was partially paralyzed after suffering a severe neck injury. He was taken off the field on a stretcher before a hushed crowd of 57,375. One week later, with Byrd's number 90 emblazoned on their helmets, the Jets ended a 10-game losing streak against division opponents by upsetting the Bills 24-17 at Rich Stadium. Amazingly, on February 12, 1996, less than three months after his injury, Byrd walked into a crowded press room under his own power.

did you know?

The Jets have made four uniform changes since their original Titans days. In 1998, Bill Parcells brought back the uniforms the Jets used from 1963-1977, saying that he identified with the Jets from that era. Joe Namath and Weeb Ewbank attended the unveiling ceremony.

are two; try this one in Times Square for the convenience. *200 W. 44th St. (212) 221-3800. Su-M 11:30am-11pm, T-Sa 11:30-midnight. AE. $$$*

Best old-time New York atmosphere. A former speakeasy which has been around since 1927, **Gallagher's** has long been a favored hangout of sports types. It's part steakhouse, part time capsule of New York sporting history, with a room full of old photographs upstairs. *228 W. 52nd St. (212) 245-5336. Seven days 12:00pm-12:00am. All major credit cards. $$$.*

Best Accommodations

The Gershwin. This Chelsea establishment has great rates for plain, no-frill rooms, some without bathrooms. Check out the nearby Flatiron Building. *7 E. 27th St. (212) 545-8000. $-$$*

The Paramount. Affordable, high-style rooms. Trendy decor, looks more expensive than it is. Dean and DeLuca, the classic, upscale Manhattan deli, has a satellite store on premises. The hotel's bar is fashionable and always full. *235 W.46th Street (212) 764-5500. Weekend rates may apply. Call ahead for information. $$$*

The Four Seasons. An overwhelming lobby is only the beginning. The beautiful rooms are lushly appointed and have bathtubs that fill in a moment. Visit the "5757" restaurant for a delicious feast. Work off those calories in the fitness spa. Super-cool and expensive. *57 W. 57th St. (212) 758-5700. $$$$$.*

Oakland Raiders

No team in any sport has ever lived up its name as well as the Oakland Raiders. The knife-chomping, one-eyed pirate has come to life over the decades in men such as Ben Davidson, Ted Hendricks, Ken Stabler and Jack Tatum; outlaws and outcasts all from the more "normal" NFL teams. Where else but in Oakland could a quarterback soon eligible for Social Security named George Blanda become a hero? Throw in people like Fred Biletnikoff, a spindly receiver covered in stickum; Ray Guy, a punter worth paying to see; and big, voluble John Madden, one of the greatest players' coaches ever, and you've got the best cast of characters any NFL team has ever handed uniforms to. These are the bad boys; the ones who wear leather jackets and hit people in the parking lot. There are the guys you don't want hanging around your daughter. At least they used to be.

Franchise History

Oakland Raiders (AFL)
(1960–69)
Oakland Raiders (NFL)
(1970–81)
Los Angeles Raiders (NFL)
(1982–94)
Oakland Raiders (NFL)
(1995–present)

By the Numbers

(Since 1970)
Regular Season: 255-163-6
Postseason: 18-12
Division Titles: 9
Vs. Division: 118-84-5 (Playoffs: 3-3)
Playoff Appearances: 15
Home: 140-70-2
Away: 115-93-4

(Overall)
Regular Season: 332-221-11
Postseason: 21-15
Playoff Appearances: 18
Home: 184-95-3
Away: 148-126-8

The man behind the culture of silver and black is Al Davis. Spanning four decades of football, Davis has never changed his motto — "Commitment to Excellence." But the cold reality is that in the twilight of his career, Davis's teams no longer live up to his slogans. After compiling the top winning percentage (.644) of any professional sports franchise from 1963 to 1996, including 16 straight winning seasons and three Super Bowl championships, the Raiders made the playoffs just three times between 1986 and 1997.

Losing can't be easy for a man who created a cult from three little words:

Most Revered Football Figures

George Blanda. "Old Folks" miraculous 1970 season did more for America's elderly than Geritol and dentures.

Ken Stabler. This whiskey-drinking, touchdown-flinging country boy sometimes played hung over, but led Oakland to its first Super Bowl victory.

Jim Otto. He can barely walk today after 30 surgeries, but has no regrets. No Raider ever gave more to the franchise than Double O.

Rivalries

Although they've been a patsy in this heated series throughout most of the 1990s, the Raiders never go down without a fight in their always interesting battle with the **Chiefs**. This remains one of the most physical rivalries in the league, and it's been enhanced in recent years by the fact that coaches (Art Shell, etc.) and players (Marcus Allen, etc.) alike have seen both sides of this fabled feud. The Chiefs lead, 37-36-2, which makes the Raiders hate them even more. Other Raider rivalries are slightly less intense. While they don't play the **Steelers** often — Oakland leads the series, 7-5 — there's a lot of history, some of it ugly. What other NFL franchises have battled each other in court, after Chuck Noll's memorable "criminal element" comment about Oakland? There was **Chargers** coach Harland Svare eyeing a light bulb in the visitor's locker room at the Oakland Coliseum. Believing the bulb was bugged, Svare cried out: "Damn you, Al Davis!" Davis later replied: "It wasn't the bulb." Bugs or no bugs, the Raiders lead this series, 45-29-2.

"Just win, baby." Born on the Fourth of July in 1929, Davis grew up in Brooklyn and, like many of his generation, found opportunity in California, finally landing a coaching job with the San Diego Chargers in the newly formed American Football League in 1960. Three years later, he was named head coach of the league's Minneapolis franchise when it moved to Oakland. In his rookie year, the Raiders went 10-4 and Davis — just 33 years old — was Coach of the Year. In 1966, Davis was named AFL Commissioner, and became the guiding force behind the merger with the NFL.

The Raiders lost to the Packers in Super Bowl II in 1968, and they didn't return to the Big Dance until 1976, when they beat the Minnesota Vikings, 32-14, in Super Bowl XI. Behind "the Snake," QB Ken Stabler, and coach John Madden, they won their second and third NFL titles in 1980 and 1983.

Since then, it's been only one trip to the AFC championship game, a 51-3 trouncing in Buffalo in 1990. In between, Davis has been vilified and criticized for moving his team from Oakland to Los Angeles and back to Oakland, and for defying his NFL brethren in the courts. But in a league where loyalty and camaraderie have been sacrificed in the name of free agency and the salary cap, Davis's focus on tending his silver-and-black flock has never wavered. The Oakland Raiders give meaning to the idea of a football "club," an organization one belongs to instead of a company that hires players.

> **did you know?**
> The face with the eye-patch in the Raider logo was modeled after actor Randolph Scott.

> "Some people walk into a room and dominate it. I'm like that."
> **— Al Davis**

Indeed, no man has been asked to present more inductees into the Pro Football Hall of Fame in Canton, Ohio. Davis, who was enshrined himself in 1992, has made eight presentations. Though he would like to improve his team's place in the standings, Davis's place in pro football history is quite secure.

—*Sal Paolantonio*

Oakland Coliseum

There's no football stadium like it in America, more because of its characters than its configuration. The Coliseum looks like a grunge concert at every Raider game. Costumed fans with painted faces are dressed in black and silver, stomping their feet, pounding on the fences behind both end zones, and screaming X-rated language at the opposition. You know you're in an unusual setting when the fans seated next to you introduce themselves as "Violator" and "Skullman."

The fans have become more demonstrative since the Raiders came back. As one visiting writer said of the Coliseum crowd: "This place looks like the end of the earth." Imagine what it would look like if the Raiders started winning again, and the place was filled — rather than half-filled — with blood-thirsty fans.

> **did you know?**
> The 1998 season marks the first time since Monday Night Football began in 1970 that the Raiders do not appear on Monday night. No other team can claim such a streak.

> "The bottom line is that I like to kick butt."
> —Defensive end Lyle Alzado, looking back on his career.

Fans are advised not to wear visiting team jerseys — especially Kansas City Chiefs— because Raiders fans are easily annoyed, and tend to say things that will stand your hair on end and make you

The "I Was There" Game

December 21, 1974: Two-time defending Super Bowl champion Miami scored first in this AFC Divisional Playoff when Nat Moore took the opening kickoff the distance. A seesaw affair had the Dolphins ahead, 26-21, with 2:08 to play, but Raiders QB Ken Stabler led his team downfield, throwing an 8-yard TD pass (just before being tackled) to Clarence Davis, who caught the ball in the middle of a crowd to put the Raiders over the top with :26 to play. Raiders 28, Dolphins 26.

The Paper Bag Game

December 23, 1972: One team's "I was there" is another team's "Paper Bag." The NFL's all-time crazy finish. Franco Harris's "Immaculate Reception" in this AFC playoff in Pittsburgh sent Oakland packing. How Immaculate? The Raiders wonder to this day if Steelers owner Art Rooney, and not George Burns, was the cigar-smoking God. Steelers 13, Raiders 7.

Great Names

Chetti Carr (WR, 1987)
Derrick Crudup (DB, 1989, 1991)
Marty Feldman (C, 1961-62)
I.M. Hipp (RB, 1980)
David Humm (QB, 1975-79, 1983-84)
Proverb Jacobs (T, 1963-64)
Howie Long (DE/DT, 1981-93)
Herb McMath (DT, 1976)
Bill Pickel (DT/DE, 1983-90)

Our Top Story

"Commitment to Davis"
January 15, 1963
Former Chargers assistant coach Al Davis was named general manager and head coach in Oakland. The Raiders would never be the same.

"Boom! I'm Head Coach!"
February 4, 1969
Thirty-two-year-old assistant coach John Madden was named head coach of the Raiders. That season, he took the Raiders to the AFL Championship Game; only twice in his ten seasons with the team did they miss the playoffs.

"Davis Takes His Ball and Goes Home"
May 11, 1981-June 30, 1985
Al Davis relocated his Raiders to Los Angeles for the 1982 season, then survived court fights with the NFL and the city of Oakland, plus an eminent domain case — all of which took more than four years — to keep his team in L.A.

"Second Thoughts"
June 23, 1995
The Raiders become the first major-league sports franchise to leave and then return to their original home. There were many reasons, but "L.A. Raiders" never sounded right, anyway.

did you know?

When QB Jeff George took the field for the Raiders in 1997, he became the seventh overall number-one pick (since the common draft began in '67) to play for the Silver and Black.

want to quicken your pace. And — jersey or no jersey — be careful not to root too loudly for the visitors. This can lead to fisticuffs.

Tailgating is a unique experience at Oakland Coliseum. Raider skull-and-crossbones flags hang from antennas across the parking lots. There is incredible camaraderie among Raider fans, even though they look like a carnival sideshow. Some of the best barbecue anywhere is prepared in those lots prior to kickoff. In the old days, Raiders players would tailgate with fans after games. But, like a lot of things in the Raiders organization, the post-game tailgate isn't what it used to be.

The Bottom Line on Oakland Coliseum

Address: 7000 Coliseum Way, Oakland, CA 94621. (510) 864-5000.

Tickets: Ticket prices are among the NFL's highest — $51 per seat on the average — and personal seat licenses climb upwards to $4,000. It's like joining an expensive country club to pay monthly dues. That explains why plenty of Raider tickets are available at the moment. Better buy them now, if you can afford them. Call the Oakland Football Marketing Association to order at 1-800-949-2626.

1998: $61/$51/$41

1994: $42/$38/$35/$25/$15 (L.A. Memorial Coliseum)

Public Transportation: Bay Area Rapid Transit has a rail stop at the Coliseum. Call BART for route information. (510) 465-2278.

Best of the Raiders

Best Team

1976 (16-1): John Madden's warriors dropped just one game during the team's first Super Bowl championship season, a 48-17 loss at Foxboro in the fourth week which the Raiders avenged in the divisional playoffs at Oakland. After being sent home by the Steelers the previous two years in the AFC title game, the third time turned out to be the charm, and the Raiders simply manhandled the Vikings in Super Bowl XI.

Greatest Players by Position

Pos:	Player
QB:	Ken Stabler
RB:	Marcus Allen
WR:	Fred Biletnikoff
TE:	Dave Casper
OL:	Art Shell
DL:	Howie Long
LB:	Ted Hendricks
DB:	Willie Brown
P/K:	Ray Guy
ST:	Tim Brown

> "I guess that's football, but I can't accept it." — Defensive back Jack Tatum, off whom the Steelers' "Immaculate Reception" rebounded in the famous 1972 AFC Playoff game.

And Don't Forget...

C: Jim Otto. These days, he's more known for having rebuilt knees. Not long ago, he defined the center position.
WR: Cliff Branch. There will always be that image of the sign at the Oakland Coliseum which read "Speed Kills." A true game-breaker.

LB: Rod Martin. The unsung hero of Super Bowl XV, his three interceptions kept the Eagles in check all afternoon.
RB: Bo Jackson. A two-sport star who flashed greatness on the football field. We just didn't get to see enough of him.
DB: Jack Tatum. A true intimidator, and arguably the most physical defensive back to ever play the game.

> "I'm glad when he plays football it's on our side." — Art Shell, about running back Bo Jackson.

Best Argument

Offensive Line: Art Shell or Gene Upshaw? You can't go wrong with arguably the best left side of an offensive line in NFL history. Shell just went about his business and was so good you may have never noticed—holding celebrated Vikings' DE Jim Marshall to zero tackles in Super Bowl XI. Upshaw was an intense competitor who missed just one league game during his 16-year career.

Best Coach

John Madden (1969-78): Before he was busy selling beer and hardware and long before there was a "Cruiser," Madden was a helluva football coach, and probably would have won more championships had he not been in a conference that boasted some of the best teams (i.e., the Dolphins and Steelers) in NFL annals. One of these days, you'll find Madden's likeness in Canton, Ohio.

Pressbox

Who to Read...

The Bay Area has many newspapers, but the consensus is that no daily covers the Raiders better than the *Oakland Tribune* and the five other Alameda Newspaper Group papers: *Hayward Review, Alameda Times-Star, Fremont Argus, Tri-Valley Herald* and *San Mateo County Times*. If you want up-to-date news on the Raiders, the ANG papers are a must read. Bill Soliday and Jerry McDonald offer daily reports, while Monte Poole, Carl Steward, Art Spander (also of ESPN.com) and Leonard Koppett write insightful columns. Jeffrey Chadiha of the *San Francisco Examiner* and Sam Farmer of the *San Jose Mercury-News* also have a strong handle on the Raiders, but the 49ers definitely get more inches in the *Examiner*.

Who to Watch...

Gary Radnich serves as KRON-TV's evening sports anchor, and hosts the highly rated "Sports Final" late Sunday nights. Raiders players frequently appear on the Sunday night wrap-up shows on KRON and KPIX.

> **"There's nothing wrong with reading the game plan by the light of the jukebox." — QB Ken Stabler on lifestyle.**

Who to Listen To...

Tim Brown and Jeff George host radio shows on the Raiders flagship station KTCT (1050 AM), which is also known as "The Ticket." Of course, they don't have too hard a time booking teammates as guests. The most popular radio personality in Oakland is Gary Radnich, who has a noon-3 p.m. talk show on KTCT's sister station KNBR (680 AM), which is also simulcast on Bay TV Cable. Both stations offer sports talk day and night, the latter station appealing to a younger demographic.

Parking: About 10,000 spaces on stadium property, plus another overflow lot a good 10-minute walk away. Spaces cost $10 for cars. Get there early because even though this isn't LA, the folks here still like to drive.

Capacity: 63,026.

Restrooms: 25 men's, 25 women's.

Where to Go . . . in Oakland

Best Bars

Best fantasy bar. An early-form of Rotisserie-style football leagues actually started in Oakland in the early 1960s. **The Kings X**, a friendly neighborhood pub, is the capital of fantasy-league activity. *4401 Piedmont Ave. (510) 653-4200. Seven days 10am-2am.*

Best place to watch "Nick at Nite." Raiders fans congregate at the number-one sports bar in the East Bay, **Ricky's Sports Lounge**, where there are TVs galore. The owner's name is Ricky Ricardo — honest. *15028 Hesperian Blvd., San Leandro. (510) 352-0200. Su-Th 10am-12pm, F-Sa 10am-2am, flexible hours for sporting events.*

Best call of the wild. Opened in 1883, **Heinold's First and Last Chance Saloon** is a spot where author Jack London drank when he was a mere lad. It's unique — saloon and a log cabin combined. *56 Jack London Sq. (510) 839-6761. Su 11am-10pm, M 4pm-12pm, T-Sa 12pm-1am.*

Best post-game destination. The **Pacific Coast Brewing Company**, a downtown microbrewery, is a great place to stop in for some home brew and food after a Raider game. *906 Washington St. (510) 836-2739. M-Sa 11:30-midnight, Su 11:30-10pm.*

Best Restaurants

Best place to be seen. One of the hottest new restaurants in Oakland, **Garibaldi's** is Mediterranean with an Asian touch. *5356 College Ave. (510) 595-4000. Su 5:30pm-10pm, M-Th Lunch: 11:30-2:30, dinner: 5:30pm-10pm, F Lunch: 11:30pm-2:30pm, dinner: 5:30pm-10:30pm, Sa 5:30-10:30pm. All major credit cards. $$*

Swami Sez:

The Raiders have all the Heisman Trophy winners and number 1 draft picks. Too bad they haven't had a winning season since they returned to Oakland.

Best place 'round midnight. Yoshi's is a popular Japanese restaurant and jazz club—the perfect place to find sushi and some Thelonius Monk, too. *510 Embarcadero West. (510) 238-9200. Su-Th 5:30-10pm (sushi bar till 10:30pm), F-Sa*

Ready For Primetime (Monday Night)

September 22, 1975: It was the first game of the season and a rematch of the stirring playoff battle with the Dolphins from the previous year, so revenge was certainly on the minds of the determined Dolphins. But it would be all Raiders this evening as Oakland jumped out to a quick 17-0 lead and never looked back. The win snapped Miami's record 31-game winning streak (including playoffs) at the Orange Bowl.
Raiders 31, Dolphins 21.

The Raiders' Monday record was a glittering 29-6-1 through 1990, but is only 4-10 since—which helps explain why Al Davis has hired four head coaches in five years since 1994.

Overall Monday night: 33-16-1
Overall Thursday night: 3-1
Overall Sunday night: 8-11

Think About the Weather

January 4, 1981: Down by two and with second down on the Oakland 9-yard line with under a minute to play in this divisional playoff, Browns' coach Sam Rutigliano had already seen place-kicker Don Cockroft miss a pair of field goals due to the elements (1 degree at Cleveland Stadium). Brian Sipe threw for the end zone, the pass was picked off by Raiders safety Mike Davis and the Raiders survived.
Raiders 14, Browns 12.

Worst Team

1997 (4-12): For the most part, "Pride and Poise" has not been a part of the Raiders' vocabulary in the 1990s as the Silver and Black have looked like a contender on paper but have failed to live up to expectations. The '97 Raiders boasted an incredible 18 former first-round draft choices and fielded a formidable offense, but their defense turned too many opponents into AFC Offensive Players of the Week.

> "Los Angeles welcomed the Raiders with closed arms."
> — San Francisco Chronicle columnist Scott Ostler.

Hall of Fame

Jim Otto	(C, 1980)
George Blanda	(QB/K, 1981)
Willie Brown	(CB, 1984)
Gene Upshaw	(G, 1987)
Fred Biletnikoff	(WR, 1988)
Art Shell	(T, 1989)
Ted Hendricks	(LB, 1990)
Al Davis	(Owner/Coach, 1992)
Mike Haynes	(CB, 1997)

5:30-11pm (sushi bar till 11pm). All credit cards. $$

Did somebody say Barney's? Barney's Gourmet Hamburger serves thirty different kinds of burgers and better french fries than McDonald's. There are three other locations in the East Bay, too. *5819 College Ave. (510) 601-0444. M-Th 11am-9:30pm, F-Sa 11am-10pm, Su 11am-9pm. Cash only. $*

Best out-of-the-way spot. A hidden treasure in Oakland's Chinatown, **Vi's Restaurant** is where the area's top chefs dine. The Vietnamese food is beautifully prepared, plentiful, and 1960s cheap. *724 Webster St. (510) 835-8375. 9am-9pm, Th closed. Cash only. $*

Best Accommodations

Travelodge. There aren't a whole lot of safe, inexpensive hotels in the city of Oakland; this one, downtown near Jack London Square, is an exception. Plus, it's only a 10-minute drive from the Coliseum. *423 Seventh St. (510) 451-6316, (800) 578-7878. $*

Lake Merritt Hotel. There's a stylish hotel within these recently renovated Art Deco walls. *1800 Madison St. (510) 832-2300, (800) 933-4683. $$$-$$$$*

Claremont Resort, Spa and Tennis Club. Pull out all the stops at this luxury establishment, 20 minutes from the Coliseum. The Terrace Bar has the best bay views in town, and no two of their

While You Were Eating Turkey

November 26, 1970: Apparently, the Raiders aren't pilgrims, to the NFL's way of thinking: They've played only once on Thanksgiving Day. On Turkey Day, 1970, in Detroit, Fred Biletnikoff burned Lem Barney twice early for touchdowns and Oakland led, 14-0. But then the Lions made a wish and scored 28 unanswered points to devour the Raiders. Lions 28, Raiders 14.
Overall, 0-1

Fans' notes

On Screen

He played just two seasons with the Raiders (1970-71), then three in the CFL before completing his degree in Theatre Arts at San Francisco State. By 1976, Carl Weathers was a world champion boxer by the name of Apollo Creed — in **Rocky**. Weathers went on to score roles in such films as **Semi-Tough**, **Close Encounters of the Third Kind** and, of course, a couple more Rocky flicks. The late John Matuszak had a memorable line in **North Dallas Forty**: "Every time I say it's a game, you say it's a business. Every time I say it's a business, you say it's a game." He also appeared in a pair of non-Oscar-contenders during the early '80s: **Caveman** and **The Ice Pirates**. Playing characters with names like Brawn, Bulk and Iron Butt, Lyle Alzado appeared in films ranging from **The Double McGuffin** to **Ernest Goes to Camp**. Bo Jackson had a cameo in 1997's **Fakin' Da Funk**. After forging a career as a studio analyst, Howie Long turned action hero. He first appeared in **Broken Arrow** then starred in **Firestorm**, in which he fought a raging forest fire while also foiling a jailbreak. Raiders fans can take a 35-minute tour of the team's history with **Los Angeles Raiders: The Team for All Decades**, from NFL Films Video.

Bookshelf

From Oakland to Los Angeles. Joesph Hession and Steve Cassady (Foghorn Press 1987).
Cruisin' With The Tooz. John Matuszak and Steve Delsohn (Franklin Watts 1987).
Snake: The Candid Autobiography of Football's Most Outrageous Renegade. Ken Stabler and Berry Stainback (Doubleday 1986).
"You're Okay, It's Just a Bruise," A Doctor's Sideline Secrets About Pro Football's Most Outrageous Team. Rob Huizenga (St. Martins Press 1995).
Black Knight: Al Davis and His Raiders. Ira Simmons (Prima Publications 1990).
Just Win, Baby: Al Davis and His Raiders. Glenn Dickey (Harcourt Brace 1991).
Slick: The Silver and Black Life of Al Davis. Mark Ribowsky (Macmillan 1991).
One Knee Equals Two Feet and Everything Else You Need To Know About Pro Football. John Madden and Dave Anderson (1987).
Final Confessions of NFL Assassin Jack Tatum. Jack Tatum and Bill Kushner, (Quality Sports Publications 1996). Contains the entire book *They Call Me Assassin*.
Fire in the Iceman: Autobiography of Tom Flores. Tom Flores and Frank Cooney (Bonus Books 1992).

You Gotta See...

▶The **Oakland A's** also play in the Coliseum, and the **Golden State Warriors** play their home games next door at The New Arena, jazzed up by a recent renovation.
▶Take the kids to **Children's Fairyland**, where a variety of rides and entertainment are available.
▶The collection at the **Oakland Museum** of California ranges from natural history to fine art — they've even put on the occasional sports-related show.

Team Leaders

Rushing Yards
8,545   Marcus Allen, 1982-92
Passing Yards
19,078   Ken Stabler, 1970-79
Passing Touchdowns
150   Ken Stabler, 1970-79
Receptions
589   Fred Biletnikoff, 1965-78
Interceptions
39   Willie Brown, 1967-78
    Lester Hayes, 1977-86
Touchdowns
98   Marcus Allen, 1982-92
Points
863   George Blanda, 1967-75

rooms are alike. *41 Tunnel Rd. (510) 843-3000. $$$$-$$$$$*

"There are some individuals in Silver and Blackdom who would rather run through a gauntlet of pit bulls wearing pork chop underwear than see me break the record for interceptions by a Raider." — Lester Hayes

Against the Odds

Winning the Heisman Trophy does not guarantee success: Just ask **Jim Plunkett** (1979-1986). He entered the NFL as the first pick overall in 1971 (New England) and the free-fall began. Two teams and eight seasons later, Plunkett was Dan Pastorini's backup in Oakland. Replacing the injured Pastorini early in the 1980 season, Plunkett led the Raiders to a 27-10 win in Super Bowl XV, making them the first wild-card team to capture the Lombardi Trophy. Plunkett had his finest season in five years, throwing for 2,299 yards with a touchdown-to-interception differential of 18-to-16.

Philadelphia Eagles

Understanding the Eagles means understanding Philadelphia sports fans, an unforgiving breed whose particularly bad behavior during the 1997 season forced the city to permanently assign a Common Pleas Court judge to Veterans Stadium to fine and jail hooligans. Of course, rowdiness and football in Philly have a long history. At Franklin Field, where the Eagles won their last NFL Championship in 1960, the fans once booed Santa Claus.

Nearly thirty years after the Eagles won that championship, Jimmy Johnson, then coach of the hated Dallas Cowboys, was pelted with snowballs. One of those throwing snowballs that day in 1989 at the Vet was a prominent Philadelphia lawyer, who was embarrassed when the incident and his name appeared in the Philadelphia *Inquirer*. The lawyer was named Ed Rendell. Two years later, he was elected mayor of Philadelphia.

Distemper among the fans has been so accepted perhaps because the Eagles have been so disappointing. Founded in 1933 by entrepreneur Bert Bell, who later started the college draft, Philadelphia's pro football franchise did not win its first NFL championship until 1948. Halfback Steve Van Buren, the Eagles' first-round pick in 1944, scored the only touchdown in a blinding snowstorm to beat the Chicago Cardinals, 7-0, at Philadelphia's old Shibe Park. The following year, Van Buren, perhaps the franchise's greatest player, fought through driving rain, wind and mud at the Los Angeles Coliseum to lead the Eagles over the Rams for their second consecutive NFL title.

Franchise History

Philadelphia Eagles
(1933–1942,
1944–present)
Phil-Pitt Steagles
(1943)

By the Numbers

(Since 1970)
Regular Season: 204-213-7
Postseason: 5-10
Division Titles: 2
Vs. Division: 100-118-4 (Playoffs: 1-4)
Playoff Appearances: 10
Home: 117-93-3
Away: 87-120-4

(Overall)
Regular Season: 382-451-24
Postseason: 9-11
Playoff Appearances: 14
Home: 220-201-12
Away: 162-250-12

Most Revered Football Figures

Chuck Bednarik. The game's last full-time two-way player; knocked Giants running back Frank Gifford unconscious in a game during the Eagles' 1960 NFL championship season.

Dick Vermeil. Built a title contender before burning out following the '82 season. Vermeil was so popular that he was still appearing on billboards in Philly 15 years later.

Bill Bergey. A fiery competitor at game time and immensely popular off the field, the defensive leader of Dick Vermeil's Birds set the tone with every tackle.

Rivalries

Separated by just 80-odd miles of the New Jersey Turnpike, the Eagles and New York **Giants** (58-67-2) have developed the deep contempt that comes only with intimate familiarity. In the 22 seasons from 1976 to 1997, the Eagles swept the Giants eleven seasons, the Giants swept the Eagles seven times. Philadelphia fans also hate the Dallas **Cowboys** (30-47) with a passion that can be disturbing at times: after John F. Kennedy was assassinated in Dallas, some Philadelphia fans began to call the Cowboys the "JFK Killers." During the late '80s, head coach Buddy Ryan was rumored to have offered "bounties" for injuries to certain Cowboys.

did you know?

Including playoffs, the Eagles are 0-14 vs. the Bears in the Windy City. In fact, Philadelphia's 1949 NFL champs lost only once, a 38-21 setback to George Halas's club in Chicago.

But while the NFL grew in stature and popularity through the 1950s, Eagles fans suffered through a decade of ineptness before the team finally reached a breakthrough in 1960. Led by Chuck Bednarik—known as "Concrete Charlie" for his vicious hits and unprecedented endurance as a two-way player—the Eagles beat the Vince Lombardi-led Green Bay Packers in 1960 to win their third and last NFL championship.

The team was sold in 1963 and then again in 1969, finally landing in the hands of trucking magnate Leonard Tose, who moved the Eagles into Veterans Stadium in 1971 and hired UCLA head coach Dick Vermeil. In 1980, Vermeil led the Eagles to their only Super Bowl appearance. But quarterback Ron Jaworski, the NFL player of the year, and the Eagles lost to the Raiders, 27-10, in Super Bowl XV in New Orleans. The loss was devastating. Vermeil, complaining of burnout, left the game during a tearful press conference in 1983. Tose threatened to move the Eagles to Arizona, then sold the team to Miami businessman Norman Braman in 1985.

Under Braman, the Eagles enjoyed a brief but troubled renaissance. Buddy Ryan, the defensive coordinator of the Super Bowl XX champion Bears, arrived as head coach in 1986. He made the flamboyant Randall Cunningham the starting quarterback and fashioned a defense much like Philadelphia itself—mean, relentless and unapologetic. But, after three uneventful trips to the playoffs in 1988, 1989 and 1990, the gruff Ryan, who often feuded with the haughty Braman, was fired. Four years later, Braman exited too, selling the team to a would-be Hollywood producer named Jeffrey Lurie, heir to the Harcourt Publishing and General Cinema fortune.

Hailed by Eagles fans as "Saint Jeffrey," Lurie set out once again to rebuild the franchise, hiring Ray Rhodes, the defensive coordinator of the San Francisco 49ers, as his new head coach. But in the era of free agency, it remains to be seen whether Lurie has the personality and purse strings to become successful in a city where the fans are desperate to back a winner.

—*Sal Paolantonio*

Veterans Stadium

In terms of physical charms, "the Vet" is lacking. One of the lamentable, multipurpose, "cookie cutter" stadiums built in the late 1960s and early 1970s, its outmoded facilities have prompted both the Eagles and their co-tenants, the baseball Phillies, to push for new homes. In 1996, the stadium replaced the uncomfortable orange, yellow and red seats from the '70s with cozier, all-blue seating from the sidelines to the 700 level. Sitting in the 700's may give you a view of everything halfway to New York, but you'll be far from the action. Sightlines are actually better for football than for baseball, although gusting winds in this perfectly circular bowl can make things uncomfortable for players and fans alike. An Astroturf-8 playing surface was installed in 1995, replacing what was considered the worst turf in the league. Unfortunately, the field is still reviled as quite dangerous; more than one career has

The "I Was There" Game

January 11, 1981: In sub-zero weather, the Eagles vanquish the Cowboys, their most hated rivals at the time, in the NFC Championship Game. Wilbert Montgomery opens the scoring with a 42-yard touchdown run and totals 194 yards on 26 carries. The defense holds the Cowboys to 202 total yards. (Eagles 20, Cowboys 7).

The Paper Bag Game

December 1, 1985: At 6-6 and battling for the playoffs, the Eagles dominate the Minnesota Vikings for 52 minutes, taking a 23-0 lead. Then comes the collapse, as shocked fans watch the team surrender 28 points in the final eight minutes. Two weeks and two losses later, coach Marion Campbell is fired (Vikings 28, Eagles 23).

"For who? For what?" — RB Ricky Watters, to a reporter asking why he had short-armed a fourth-quarter pass from Randall Cunningham rather than take a jarring hit.

Great Names

Greasy Neale (Coach, 1941-50)
Joe Panos (Zois Panagiotopoulos) (G, 1994-97)
Mike Quick (WR, 1982-90)
Vai Sikahema (KR/PR, 1992-93)
Taivale "Junior" Tautalatasi (RB, 1986-88)

Our Top Story

"Buddy Ball"
January 29, 1986
After three disappointing seasons under Marion Campbell, the Eagles hire David "Buddy" Ryan as the 17th coach in team history. Ryan, fresh off a victorious trip to the Super Bowl as the Chicago Bears' defensive coordinator, quickly guarantees that his team will win the NFC East in 1986. His prediction is belied by a 5-10-1 record, but within three seasons he built one of the league's most talented teams.

"Jerome Brown Killed"
June 25, 1992
All-Pro defensive tackle Jerome Brown, a standout on the field and a boisterous presence in the lockerroom, is killed in an automobile accident in his hometown of Brooksville, FL. The team keeps Brown's locker intact throughout the 1992 season, which is played in his memory.

"Eagles Sold"
April 6, 1994
Norman Braman, the team's owner since 1985 who had presided over the tumultuous Buddy Ryan era and alienated most of the team's best players with his predilection for profits over victories, reaches an agreement to sell the team to Boston native and Hollywood film producer Jeffrey Lurie.

did you know?

The adversarial relations between players and ownership during the Norman Braman-Buddy Ryan period in the late 1980s is perhaps the single biggest cause of the current free-agency situation in the NFL. Annual salary squabbles between the penurious Braman—referred to by Ryan as "the guy in France," because of his frequent overseas travels—and players such as Reggie White, Mike Quick, Keith Jackson and Seth Joyner led to radical changes in the relationship between players and owners.

ended with a knee or shoulder slamming into the stadium's unforgiving concrete and plastic floor.

And as if the notoriously critical Philadelphia fans needed more bad press, Veterans Stadium got a rap in 1997 as a dangerous place to visit. Eagles fans that year, frustrated by the team's lackluster play, committed various and sundry acts of mayhem in the stands, most notably in a nationally televised Monday Night loss to the 49ers. Subsequently, the team attempted to crack down on in-house lawlessness with the much-publicized "Eagles Court," in which local judge Seamus McCaffery dispensed "justice while you wait" in the bowels of the stadium. Within minutes of their offending actions, wrongdoers were brought before the judge and quickly sentenced to small fines or other minor punishment, with several fans losing their season tickets. Despite their hard-bitten reputation, Philadelphia fans are among the NFL's most knowledgeable and supportive; the team's impressive 34-14 home mark since 1992 gives some evidence of that. Eagles games rarely fail to sell out, with the team selling over 55,000 season tickets each season. During games, Big Bird, the somewhat constipated-looking team mascot, darts around the stadium goading partisans into the traditional chant "E-A-G-L-E-S EAGLES!!!" Some people even respond.

In addition to the standard overpriced stadium fare of hot dogs, nachos, fries and

Best of the Eagles

Best Team

1949 (12-1): In 1948, the Eagles' defense pitched five shutouts on the way to an NFL title. A year later, a more complete team sought to defend its championship. The lone blemish on Philly's resume would be a 38-21 loss to the Bears in Chicago. Quarterback Tommy Thompson took a back seat to RB Steve Van Buren, who led the league in rushing. The 14-0 win over the Rams was the Eagles' second straight shutout in the title game.

Greatest Players by Position

Pos:	Player
QB:	Ron Jaworski
RB:	Wilbert Montgomery
WR:	Harold Carmichael
TE:	Pete Retzlaff
OL:	Chuck Bednarik
DL:	Reggie White
LB:	Seth Joyner
DB:	Bill Bradley
P/K:	Paul McFadden
ST:	Steve Van Buren

And Don't Forget...

E: Pete Pihos. A Hall of Famer, Pihos caught 373 passes and led the NFL in receptions three times during his nine-year career in Philadelphia.
DT: Jerome Brown. His life cut short by an auto accident, Brown was the anchor of the 1991 defensive unit, one of the best in recent memory.
DE: Clyde Simmons. A former ninth-round draft choice, Simmons terrorized quarterbacks and turned their mistakes into scores.
WR: Tommy McDonald. Another Hall of Fame enshrinee, this big-play, productive pass-catcher enjoyed his

best seasons with the Birds.
Coach: Greasy Neale. Eagles coach from 1941 to 1950, he led the team to a pair of NFL titles. Neale also played pro baseball for the Philadelphia Phillies and Cincinnati Reds between 1918-22.

Best Argument

Quarterback: Ron Jaworski or Randall Cunningham? A one-time Ram, "Jaws" was the offensive leader of Dick Vermeil's teams. Just like a Timex, Jaworski took a licking and kept on ticking, perfectly suiting Vermeil's ball-control attack. Cunningham is one of the great athletes to play the position, and his elusiveness has resulted in some of the most memorable plays in NFL annals.

Swami Sez:

Even with an offense in transition, Ray understands the Rhodes to success.

Best Coach

Dick Vermeil (1976-82): Yes, it was Earle "Greasy" Neale who led the Birds to consecutive NFL titles in 1948-49, but it was Vermeil who revived a dead program, bringing out the best of a group not blessed with an overflow of talent. He may be best remembered for an early recognition of job "burnout" when he used the phrase to explain his resignation following the '82 season. His passion for his players is what made him so successful.

Pressbox

Who to Read...

The general consensus is that out of Philadelphia's two major daily newspapers, the *Daily News* provides slightly superior Eagles coverage during the week, while the *Inquirer* (which, unlike the *News*, publishes on Sundays) offers fine game-day coverage. Check out Rich Hoffman's twice-weekly Eagles columns in the *News* during the season. Veteran editor Bill Lyon's one-sentence paragraphs often convey a sense of impending doom in his Inquirer articles.

Who to Watch...

Among local TV media types, WCAU-NBC employs Vai Sikahema, a former return specialist during the early 1990s, to cover the Eagles. KYW-CBS uses Howard Eskin, a longtime Philly sports reporter who isn't shy about expressing his opinions.

Who to Listen To...

Eagles play-by-play man Merrill Reese is a Philadelphia institution, bringing fans the action since 1977. Games are broadcast on WYSP (94 FM). It's not uncommon to see fans at the game huddled over transistor radios to hear Reese's emotive delivery. For the last 14 years, his unapologetic boosterism has been balanced nicely by Stan Walters, a former All-Pro offensive tackle for the team and a very underrated analyst. Walters stepped down after the 1997 season and the team has not yet announced a replacement. Philadelphia's all-sports radio station WIP (610 AM), offers virtual 24-hour-per-day Eagles conversation from August to January.

fried chicken, Veterans Stadium offers two food courts behind the 50-yard line, on the 200 and 500 levels. These sell Pizza Hut pizza, hoagies and a variety of grilled sandwiches, including the city's trademark cheese steaks, though you'd have to be nuts to take one of these over Pat's or Geno's. Early in the season, you'll find tailgaters in the main parking lot, but like the rest of the show, it's a no-nonsense deal. Don't come expecting fine local cuisine.

The Bottom Line on Veterans Stadium

Address: 3501 South Broad St., Philadelphia, PA, 19148-5201, (215) 685-1517.

Tickets: Seat prices aren't very differentiated; $45 for all lower-level seats, $40 for everything in the upper level. For information, call (215) 463-5500.

1998: $45, $40

1994:   All seats $40

Public Transportation: The Broad Street stop of the subway's Orange Line is across the street from the stadium. Call SEPTA at (215) 580-7800 for schedule and route information.

Parking: There are about 10,000 spaces in the combined Vet/CoreStates complex, but tailgaters snap these up quickly, so come early. Nearby lots ranging in price from $5 to $15 hold around half that much again, and there is limited street parking within walking distance. Best bets are often found in the lot just off

Packer Avenue, within sight of the Walt Whitman Bridge.

Capacity: 65,352.

Restrooms: 26 men's, 30 women's

Where to Go . . . in Philadelphia

Best Bars

Best place to watch *Jaws*. A popular watering hole for fans after early Sunday games. Part-owned by former Eagles quarterback Ron Jaworski, **Legends** is no more than a five-minute walk across the parking lot from the stadium, and hosts lively discussion after wins and losses alike. *The Stadium Holiday Inn. 10th & Packer Ave., (215) 755-9500. M-Th 2pm-12am, F-Sa 11am-2am , Su 11am-12am.* All major credit cards.

Best pizza and beer joint. For true South Philly flavor, this musty but charming bar/restaurant can't be beat. Step through the door of the **Triangle Tavern** and you'll feel like you've landed in the first hour of "Rocky." Try the pizza. If possible, come in on a Saturday night before the game, when you might catch the drummer from the house band putting on one of his trademark skits. *10 Reed St, (215) 467-8683. Su-Th 3pm-11pm, F-Sa 3pm-1am. V, MC only.*

> "To take us to the next plateau."
> — Norman Braman, explaining why he had replaced Buddy Ryan with offensive coordinator Rich Kotite in January 1991.

Best native beer. Somewhat upscale by sports-bar standards, but **Dock Street**

Ready For Primetime (Monday Night)

November 12, 1979: Dick Vermeil later called it the biggest win in his coaching career. Off a surprise playoff appearance in 1978, the Eagles were an up-and-comer. Still, they had dropped nine straight to the Cowboys and hadn't won in Dallas since 1965. The biggest play of the game came from barefooted PK Tony Franklin, whose 59-yard field goal changed the momentum of the entire contest. (Eagles 31, Cowboys 21). The team has not won a Monday Night game in Ray Rhodes's tenure, going 0-5 since 1995.

Overall Monday Night: 21-18

Overall Sunday nights: 6-3

Overall Thursday nights: 1-1

did you know?
The Eagles' last NFL Championship came way back in 1960, a 17-13 victory over Green Bay. The victory was nearly forty years ago but it was the only postseason loss for legendary Packers' coach Vince Lombardi (9-1)

Think About the Weather

December 18, 1983: It was a very snowy day at Busch Stadium, and it was the sky that fell in on Eagles' QB Ron Jaworski. The Philadelphia signal-caller dropped back to pass 56 times against the Cardinals, completing 21 of his 45 throws for one score while tossing four interceptions and being dropped 11 times by St. Louis defenders. Meanwhile, St. Louis had few problems moving the ball. (Cardinals 31, Eagles 7). Also see Chicago Bears chapter for information on the "Fog Bowl."

Worst Team

1972 (2-11-1): The Eagles were in the midst of a stretch (1967-77) of 11 straight seasons without a winning record. Ed Khayat had replaced Jerry Williams as head coach after three games in '71 and led the Birds to six wins in their last 11 games. Unfortunately, there was no carry-over to next season as Philadelphia's only two wins came by a single point. The Eagles were held to a touchdown or less in half of their games.

did you know?

Early owner Bert Bell came up with the idea of the college draft in 1935, after being continually beaten to the punch on college talent by richer teams. The Eagles "won" the first first-round pick, with which they selected Jay Berwanger. He was also the first first-round bust—Berwanger never played a down of NFL ball.

Team Leaders

Rushing Yards
6,538 Wilbert Montgomery, 1977-84
Passing Yards
26,963 Ron Jaworski, 1977-86
Passing Touchdowns
175 Ron Jaworski, 1977-86
Receptions
589 Harold Carmichael, 1971-83
Interceptions
34 Bill Bradley, 1969-76
Eric Allen, 1988-94
Touchdowns
79 Harold Carmichael, 1971-83
Points
881 Bobby Watson, 1951-62

Brewing Company is responsible for some of the very best beer ever to come out of Philadelphia, and they make a killer roast beef sandwich to boot. *Two Logan Sq, (215) 496-0413. M-Th 11:30am-12am, F 11:30am-2am; Sa 12pm-2am, Su 12pm-11pm. All major credit cards.*

Best Restaurants

Best breakfast. As the slogan says, "Everybody who knows goes to Melrose." Located on the way to the stadium for those fans coming from Center City or the north and northeast suburbs, **The Melrose Diner** is the perfect place for a cup of coffee and incomparable French toast before taking in a game at the Vet. Pick up a tin of butter cookies on the way out to nosh during the third quarter. *1501 Snyder Ave., (215) 467-6644. Open 24 hours. Cash only. $$*

Best cheese steak. Before or after the game, **Pat's** and **Geno's**—two side-by-side cheese steak palaces—cater to South Philly's most dedicated fans, serving the city's best-known contribution to American cuisine. Pat's offers neophytes a clever "How to Order" primer, but if you want to sound like a native, tell 'em to "scoop the roll"—take some bread out of the middle to make a pocket for the meat, cheese and onions. Out-of-towners are recommended to try one steak from each, taste-test, then visit a cardiologist. *Pat's, 9th St. and Wharton, (215) 468-1546, open 24 hours, cash only. Geno's, 9th St. and Passyunk, no phone, open 24 hours, cash only. $*

Best real steak. Top-notch American meat and potatoes for the upscale fan, **The Palm** is a favorite of athletes playing for all four of the area's sports teams—as seen in the painted murals of Philly

Fans' notes

On Screen

The most recent and most Eagles-y Eagles movie is Tony Danza's made-for-TV **The Garbage Picking Field Goal Kicking Philadelphia Phenomenon**, about a Philadelphia sanitation worker whose vocation endows him with exceptional leg muscles. The pickings get pretty slim after that. There's **Triple Threat**. Well, it doesn't have anything to do with the Eagles, per se, but Hall of Famer Steve Van Buren appears in it. Same with **The Long Gray Line**, another cameo to remember, as Norm Van Brocklin shows up in this tale of sports at West Point. And finally, in **Black Sunday** Tom Brookshier plays himself in his former role as Pat Summerall's color man, but his number 40 was retired by the Eagles. Last, and probably least, Keith Byars and the Eagles are the team playing the Dolphins in **Ace Ventura: Pet Detective**.

Fight Songs, etc.

Not to be forgotten are the brief rap careers of Ricky Watters and Keith Jackson, who worked under the name K-Jack.

Bookshelf

I'm Still Scrambling. Randall Cunningham and Steve Wartenberg (Doubleday 1993).
Reggie White: Minister of Defense. Reggie White and Terry Hill (Wolgemuth and Hyatt 1991).
Bringing the Heat. Mark Bowden (Knopf 1993) A chronicle of the 1992 season, after Jerome Brown had been killed and Buddy Ryan replaced by Rich Kotite.

Broken Wing, Broken Promise: A Season Inside the Philadelphia Eagles. Phil Anastasia (Camino Press 1992)
The Eagle Five-Linebacker Defense. Fritz Shurmur (Harding Press 1993).
Philadelphia Eagles: The 65th Anniversary Authorized Pictorial History. David Spadaro (Summitt Publishing Group 1998).
And Every Day You Take Another Bite. Larry Merchant (1971).

You Gotta See...

▶Even if you don't appreciate the treasures inside one of America's best art museums, you can get a vicarious thrill running up **the steps of the Philadelphia Museum of Art**, the same steps Rocky Balboa climbed in the 1976 mega-hit that forever linked Sylvester Stallone with the City of Brotherly Love. Interestingly, the "Rocky" statue that now adorns the Spectrum in South Philadelphia once stood on the Art Museum patio, but highbrow patrons and museum directors quickly arranged for it to be moved to a more plebian locale.
▶The home of the Eagles from 1958 to 1970, **Franklin Field**, a West Philadelphia landmark, still hosts University of Pennsylvania football.
▶In the heart of Philadelphia's Olde City, across the street from the Liberty Bell, is the birthplace of the United States—**Independence Hall**. Stand where Jefferson stood, flirt with the gals like Ben Franklin did. C'mon, it's the most historically rich city in the United States and all you want to do is swill beer and compare Buddy Ryan to Ray Rhodes?

Hall of Fame

Bert Bell	(Owner 1963)
Steve Van Buren	(HB 1965)
Chuck Bednarik	(C/LB 1967)
Alex Wojciehowicz	(C 1968)
Earl "Greasy" Neale	(Coach 1969)
Pete Pihos	(E 1970)
Bill Hewitt	(E 1971)
Norm Van Brocklin	(QB 1971)
Ollie Matson	(HB 1972)
Jim Ringo	(C 1981)
Sonny Jurgensen	(QB 1983)
Mike Ditka	(TE 1988)
Tommy McDonald	(WR 1998)

Against the Odds

Jerome Brown (1987-91) was large in life; he was large in death as well. The Eagles defensive tackle was one of Buddy Ryan's boys and the heart and soul of a vaunted defense which also featured Reggie White, Clyde Simmons and Seth Joyner. Brown's talent, drive and outrageous ways were difficult to match, and the tragic car accident that killed him in the summer of 1992 sent shockwaves through the organization and around the league. The Eagles dedicated their 1992 campaign to their fallen comrade and spent the year on a mission to honor him.

sports stars from Harold Carmichael to Lenny Dykstra. *Broad & Walnut Sts., (215) 546-7256. M-F 11:30am-11pm, Sa 5pm-11pm, Su 4:30-9pm. V, AX, MC only. $$$$*

> **"Buddy doesn't have many rules, but one of them is don't lose to the Cowboys." — DT Mike Golic on the Eagles-Cowboys rivalry under Buddy Ryan.**

Best Accommodations

Park Hyatt Philadelphia at the Bellevue Situated along the same subway line that takes you to the Vet, this hotel makes sure you don't go hungry with three restaurants and 24-hour room service — you can work it off at their health club. *1415 Chancellor St., Philadelphia 19102-0380. (215) 893-1776. $175 per weekend night (subject to availability).*

Doubletree Hotel Philadelphia Conveniently located for those who want to give their regards to Broad Street, the Doubletree offers a health club, pool, and sauna. *237 South Broad St. (at Locust), Philadelphia 19100-0322. (215) 893-1600. $129 per weekend night including breakfast.*

Airport Tower/Stadium A budget option ideal for layovers or home games — just five minutes from the stadium. *2015 Penrose Ave., Philadelphia 19145-5623. (215) 755-6500. $60 per weekend night.*

While You Were Eating Turkey....

November 23, 1989. The word "bountiful" is often associated with Thanksgiving. But this clash between the Birds and Cowboys was allegedly "bounty filled," that is if you ask Dallas head coach Jimmy Johnson, who was suffering through a learning experience in his first NFL season. On the other side of the field was Philadelphia's Buddy Ryan, who seemed to take joy in beating and beating up the Pokes. The Eagles were having their way, but the focus after the game was on the coaches, Johnson accusing Ryan of putting bounties on Cowboys' players, in particular PK Luis Zendejas--who had been cut by Ryan just two weeks earlier. Eagles 27, Cowboys 0.
Overall, 4-0

Pittsburgh Steelers

The steel mills and coal mines of western Pennsylvania have bred a toughness into the city of Pittsburgh, a resolve in the face of hard work and hard times to hunker down and see it through. The Pittsburgh Steelers have one of the most loyal followings in football because the team has historically shared the same toughness and persistence as its fans, and when the Steelers finally rose to the top of the NFL in the '70s after decades at the bottom, Pittsburghers saw themselves up there with Bradshaw, Greene, and Harris. The bond between fans and team here is unique.

Founded by Arthur Rooney as the Pittsburgh Pirates in 1933, the Steelers are the fifth-oldest franchise in the National Football League. Later in its life the team called Forbes Field and then Three Rivers Stadium home, but in the early days the Pirates often barnstormed to compete with baseball and college football. Rooney and his Pirates became noticed in 1938 when they made Colorado All-American Byron "Whizzer" White one of the NFL's first high-paid stars. With his $15,800 in the bank, White led the league in rushing that season, and his bust is now in the Pro Football Hall of Fame. White's influence went far beyond football, though: In 1993, he retired from the Supreme Court after 31 years there. In 1940, as the war loomed, Rooney changed the name of his team to the "Steelers" to reflect the heritage of the city. Another brief name change came in 1943. With so many players and fans serving in the military, Rooney was forced to merge his team first with the

Franchise History

Pittsburgh Pirates
(1933–39)
Pittsburgh Steelers
(1940–42, 1945-present)
Phil-Pitt Steagles
(1943)
Card-Pitt
(1944)

By the Numbers

(Since 1970)
Regular Season: 256-167-1
Postseason: 21-14
Division Titles: 14
Vs. Division: 104-68 (Playoffs: 4-0)
Playoff Appearances: 18
Home: 158-54
Away: 98-113-1

(Overall)
Regular Season: 413-420-19
Postseason: 21-15
Playoffs Appearances: 19
Home: 248-166-8
Away: 165-254-11

Most Revered Football Figures

Art Rooney. The Chief, the cigar-chomping, beloved founder of the franchise. Steeler fans still go to him for comfort by sitting on his lap, courtesy of the big, bronze statue outside Three Rivers Stadium.

Joe Greene. He helped turn around a chronically losing franchise, no "Mean" trick.

Jack Lambert. Better known as Splat. With his front teeth missing, he still gnawed on opponents at middle linebacker.

Rivalries

When the Cleveland **Browns** return in 1999, they will rekindle the rivalry with the Steelers, which Cleveland leads 52-41. Pittsburgh and Cleveland are two hours apart, gritty industrialized towns with similar types of fans. Fans can easily travel to the other city, which often makes the battles in the stands more interesting than what occurs on the field. Whether they play in Houston, Memphis or Nashville, the **Oilers** and Steelers rivalry is also hot. The Steelers beat Houston in consecutive AFC Championship games in Pittsburgh in 1978 and 1979, fanning the flames. In the mid-1980s, Chuck Noll grabbed Houston coach Jerry Glanville's hand after a game, wagged a finger in his face and accused his team of spearing the Steelers. Pittsburgh upset Houston in overtime in the playoffs in 1989, and a benches-clearing-brawl erupted between the teams in Pittsburgh in 1996. Fun! The Steelers own the series, 38-20.

Eagles (Phil-Pitt Steagles) and then with the Chicago Cardinals (Card-Pitt) in 1944 — proof positive that misery loves company.

The next two decades were mostly long and cold for Steelers fans. It was the hiring of a young coach by the name of Chuck Noll which brought the team back into prominence. His first draft choice was DT Joe Greene but the results were a 1-13 finish in 1969. The following year Noll won a coin toss with the Bears and selected Terry Bradshaw with the first pick. Mel Blount was their third selection that same year, followed by Jack Ham in 1971 and Franco Harris in 1972. Those five players, all Hall of Famers, provided the foundation for what became a dynasty.

> "Running against the Steelers is like running downhill."
> — Cleveland Brown Marion Motley, who rushed for 188 yards on 11 carries against Pittsburgh on Oct. 29, 1950.

did you know?

The Steelers logo, which pays tribute to the steel industry, appears only on the right side of their helmet. They first used it in 1962 and wanted to test the reaction, so they put it only on the right side. It turned into a tradition.

From 1974 though 1979, just as the steel industry was melting and the city lay in economic shambles, the Steelers won an unprecedented four World Championships. From its humble beginnings, Pittsburgh became the first NFL franchise to display four Vince Lombardi Trophies in its office lobby. The residents of Pittsburgh found a sense of pride and hope in the Steelers, too; after all, local Pittsburgher Rooney had founded the team and endured the fire of forty years of losing before becoming the envy of the sporting world. Adversity had hardened Rooney's resolve, and his success gave fellow Pittsburghers something to believe in. The team truly became Pittsburgh's during those years. The Steel Curtain defense led by Mean Joe Greene and Jack Lambert became more than just a great unit; it exemplified the resilience of the entire beleagured city.

Rooney's death in 1988 coincided with the team's decline through the eighties. Noll retired in December 1991 after twenty-three years as head coach of the team. After a nationwide search for a new head coach, Dan Rooney chose 34-year-old Bill Cowher to succeed Noll. At the time, Cowher was the youngest head coach in the NFL. A native of Pittsburgh, Cowher brought a youthful enthusiasm back to the Steel City. The former linebacker and defensive coordinator built his team around a ferocious defense — exactly the style of football demanded by the residents of this Rust Belt city. In his first six seasons as head coach, Cowher led the Steelers to three AFC Championship games and one Super Bowl appearance. Of all NFL coaches, only Cowher and the great Paul Brown took their teams to the playoffs in each of their first six seasons.

As the league rushes forward, the complex economics of football threaten the very strength of this throwback franchise. But as you enter Three Rivers Stadium on a fall Sunday, polka music blaring in the background, it's impossible to miss the connection of the Pittsburgh people and their Steelers. Silently, a statue of Arthur Rooney sits outside, cigar in hand, a reminder of the legacy born out of fire and rust which surges through every Pittsburgh Steeler fan.

—Mark Malone

The "I Was There" Game

December 23, 1972: Not only was this the "Immaculate Reception" game, it was the first playoff victory in franchise history, which began in 1933. Franco Harris won it when he caught a disputed, deflected pass knocked backwards by Jack Tatum and "Frenchy" Fuqua, and ran into the end zone for the winning score as time expired. Steelers 13, Raiders 7.

The Paper Bag Game

September 10, 1989: Under intense pressure following a 5-11 season, Chuck Noll's Steelers opened 1989 at home by losing to the hated Cleveland Browns, 51-0, the worst loss in franchise history. There were calls for Noll's resignation. The Steelers rebounded to make the playoffs.

> "Now he's gonna have to run uphill." — Art Rooney, when Motley joined the Steelers in 1955.

Great Names

Buzz Nutter (C 1961-64)
Hugh Lickiss (LB 1974)
Bill Shakespeare (RB 1936)
John "Frenchy" Fuqua (RB 1970-76)
Bubby Brister (QB 1986-92)
Tunch Ilkin (OL 1980-92)

Our Top Story

"I Changed My Mind"
1941
After selling the Pirates, Art Rooney changed his mind and orchestrated a franchise swap between the new owner and Bert Bell, then-owner of the Eagles. Bell and Rooney co-owned the new team, the "Steelers."

"One More Time"
December 10, 1983
Terry Bradshaw's shredded right elbow kept him off the field the entire 1983 season, except for one game. The Steelers were unraveling behind QB Cliff Stoudt and needed a win to make the playoffs. Bradshaw started against the Jets in the final NFL game at Shea Stadium. He threw two TD passes, then left the field forever, clutching his ailing right arm. The Steelers won, 34-7.

"Franco Who?"
August 17, 1984
Not long after Chuck Noll referred to him as "Franco Who?," the Steelers, unable to reach a contract agreement with their holdout running back, cut him near the end of training camp in 1984. It set off a firestorm of controversy in Pittsburgh. Harris hooked on with Seattle for a few games but was cut by the Seahawks and never played again.

"Noll Steps Down"
January 21, 1992
Bill Cowher, who grew up in Pittsburgh, takes over the team after Chuck Noll resigns, marking the end of one of the greatest coaching careers in NFL history.

Three Rivers Stadium

The smell from the smoked kielbasa wafts around this stadium that, despite being one of the dreaded cookie-cutter monstrosities of the '70's, still provides one of the best football atmospheres in the NFL. The fans are the reason. Steelers games have been sold out since 1972

did you know?
Talk about consistency: In the 28-year history of Three Rivers Stadium (1970-97), the Steelers have never suffered through a losing season at home.

(scalpers abound, though, meaning that a seat can be had for the right price). Inside, the place rocks to thousands of Terrible Towel-twirling fans. This is the place where Franco's "Immaculate Reception" happened, where the Steelers won four AFC Championships, and where they lost three others in the closing minute.

This is a football stadium.

There are no club seats so the best seats are on the 400 level. These seats are protected from the elements and high enough to see all the action, even from the end zone. Low field boxes are the worst seats unless you just want to see the names and numbers of the guys on the bench.

Tailgating starts early and heats up quickly in the parking lots surrounding the stadium. Some fans pay for extra space to park their RVs or to set up tents. Many fans come without tickets and remain in the lot to watch the game on TV.

There are no 1990s versions of Gerela's Gorillas, Lambert's Lunatics or Franco's Italian Army. The crowd has grown older because many fans have kept their season tickets for the past 25 years. For annoyances, there are the typical show-offs with

Best of the Steelers

Best Team

1976 (11-5): The "Team of the '70s" won four Super Bowls in six years, but the group that lost to the Raiders in the '76 AFC title game was scary. Following a 1-4 start, the Steelers won their final nine regular-season games by giving up two touchdowns, 28 points and pitching five shutouts. But injuries to 1,000-yard RBs Franco Harris and Rocky Bleier in a 40-14 playoff win at Baltimore proved costly.

Greatest Players by Position

Pos:	Player
QB:	Terry Bradshaw
RB:	Franco Harris
WR:	John Stallworth
TE:	Randy Grossman
OL:	Mike Webster
DL:	Joe Greene
LB:	Jack Lambert
DB:	Jack Butler
P/K:	Gary Anderson
ST:	Bill Dudley

And Don't Forget...

DB: Rod Woodson. The best cornerback of his generation, he was named to the NFL's 75th Anniversary team.
DB: Mel Blount. Yet another outstanding Pittsburgh cornerback, his physical playing style and durability earned him a place in the Hall of Fame.
DT: Ernie Stautner. He was easily the Steelers' best player on a lot of their bad teams, and was mean long before Joe came to town.
C: Dermontti Dawson. Not many could fill the shoes of a Mike Webster, but this Kentucky strongman has earned his accolades.

LB: Jack Ham. Alongside Lambert and Andy Russell in one of the best linebacking units of all time, his superb anticipation helped earn him eight straight trips to the Pro Bowl.
DE: L.C. Greenwood. You couldn't miss this ferocious defender, thanks to his golden, hi-top shoes, as well as his many collisions with quarterbacks.

Best Argument

Wide Receiver: John Stallworth or Lynn Swann? This debate has persisted to the point where it seems to harm both players' chances of making the Hall of Fame. Stallworth, who scored the winning touchdown in Super Bowl XIV on a 73-yard pass play, rewrote the Steelers' record book in his 14 seasons with the team. Swann was one of the most graceful receivers ever to take the field.

Swami Sez:

The only head coach other than Bill Cowher to lead his team to the playoffs his first six years: Paul Brown.

Best Coach

Chuck Noll (1969-91): He is the only coach in NFL history to win four Super Bowls and was the guiding force of the Steelers dynasty of the '70s. But some of Noll's best coaching came when he wasn't expected to win. In 1989, Pittsburgh dropped its first two games by a combined score of 92-10, but Noll rallied his undermanned team to a 9-7 mark and qualified for the playoffs.

Pressbox

Who to Read...

The city is down to one metro paper, the *Pittsburgh Post-Gazette*. The Steelers coverage is led by Ed Bouchette who has been on the Steelers beat since 1985. Many suburban papers also aggressively cover the team. The Steelers also have their own weekly newspaper, *Steelers Digest*, run by veteran editor and columnist Bob Labriola.

> "I'd like to put my hands under Webby's butt one more time."
> —Terry Bradshaw at the 1997 Hall of Fame induction ceremony for his former center, Mike Webster.

Who to Watch...

Sam Nover of WPXI has covered the Steelers since before they ever played in a Super Bowl and handles their post-game, live locker room interviews. The team of John Steigerwald and Bob Pompeani at KDKA will become more involved with the Steelers now that their CBS-affiliated station will carry most of the games.

Veteran Pittsburgh radio broadcaster Bill Hillgrove, Andrew Stockey and Pat Parris provide the coverage for viewers at WTAE. The station also presents weekly "Steelers Insiders" reports by Hillgrove and Bouchette and produces 60-minute pregame shows when they play in prime time. Hillgrove also hosts Bill Cowher's show on WTAE.

Who to Listen To...

What Harry Caray was to the Chicago Cubs, Myron Cope is to the Steelers. Even though he no longer hosts a regular talk show, he has been the color analyst on the Steelers broadcasts since 1970, and he owns the town. He hosts a post-game call-in show on the Steelers radio network from a tent outside the stadium dubbed "Cope's Cabana." Bill Hillgrove provides the play-by-play. WTAE (1250 AM) provides a two-hour pregame show, a postgame wrapup, and a Monday call-in from coach Cowher. The best and most popular Monday through Friday sports talk show hosts are Thor Toll on KDKA (1020 AM) and Bruce Keidan on Sports Radio 1360 (1360 AM).

the painted faces, the drunks, the boisterous and the shirtless. Few run onto the field anymore. At Steelers games, it's mostly about the football.

The Bottom Line on Three Rivers Stadium

Address: 300 Stadium Circle, Pittsburgh, PA 15212. (412) 321-0650.

Tickets: The games have been sold out since 1972, but some individual tickets are held back for sale to the general public each year through a mail-in lottery. Also, check on Wednesday or Thursday before each game for tickets that may have been returned by the visiting team. Write to the Steelers for details, or call them at (412) 323-0300.

1998: $42/$37/$35

1994: $30

Public Transportation: Special Steelers buses, including two shuttle services from downtown, ferry people to the stadium throughout Allegheny County starting 1 ½ hours before kickoff. Call (412) 442-2000 for information.

Parking: Arrive early. The parking lots at Three Rivers Stadium open five hours before kickoff and fill up about an hour later. There are 4,000 spaces on stadium property, but 1,500 are sold on a yearly basis. Another 5,000 spaces are within walking distance. In addition, downtown Pittsburgh has parking and is only a brisk walk across the bridge on the Allegheny River or a quick shuttle ride by bus.

Capacity: 59,505.

Restrooms: 85

Where to Go . . . in Pittsburgh

Best Bars

Best bang for your buck. Home of the stiffest mixed drinks in town, **Froggy's** in downtown Pittsburgh has sports photos, old and new, covering the walls. *100 Market St., (412) 471-FROG. M-Sa, 11am-1am; Su (home game days only) opens 3 hours before kickoff.*

Best historical scenery. Worth the 15-minute drive from downtown, **Chiodo's** is a museum in itself, a place where memorabilia hangs from the ceiling: Pirates uniforms, footballs, bats, and hundreds of photos. Run for over 50 years by longtime Steelers fanatic, Joe Chiodo. *107 W. 8th Ave., Homestead, (412) 461-9307. M-Sa 9am-2am, Su 1am-9am.*

Best place to drink your way to a first down. Famous for its giant yard of beer,

Ready For Primetime (Monday Night)

September 13, 1982: Tom Landry's Dallas Cowboys, losers of two Super Bowls to Pittsburgh, had revenge on their minds when they hosted Chuck Noll's rebuilt squad in the first Monday night game that year. The 'Boys had won an NFL-record 17 straight season-openers, as well as 18 straight regular-season home games. But Steelers QB Terry Bradshaw and WR John Stallworth had big nights and beat the Cowboys 36-28. Under current coach Bill Cowher, the Steelers are 10-3 on MNF.

Overall Monday Nights: 25-17

Overall Thursday Nights: 1-3

Sunday Nights: 6-7

did you know?

Since regular-season overtime was instituted in 1974, the Steelers' 14-5-1 overtime record, including a 3-0 record in 1997, is the NFL's best.

Team Leaders

Rushing Yards
11,950 Franco Harris, 1972-83

Passing Yards
27,989 Terry Bradshaw, 1970-83

Passing Touchdowns
212 Terry Bradshaw, 1970-83

Receptions
537 John Stallworth, 1974-87

Interceptions
57 Mel Blount, 1970-83

Touchdowns
100 Franco Harris, 1972-83

Points
1,343 Gary Anderson, 1982-94

Think About the Weather

January 4, 1976: The night before this AFC Championship Game with the Oakland Raiders, a tarp covering the field at frozen Three Rivers Stadium tore and ice formed along the sidelines when the temperature dipped into the single digits. It prevented the Raiders from using the sidelines effectively with Cliff Branch and Fred Biletnikoff. The Steelers won 16-10. The Raiders' Al Davis cried "conspiracy."

did you know?

Tackle Ray Kemp, who joined the franchise in its first season (1933), was the Steelers first African-American player.

"I think of all the people who were involved in the Steelers organization during our Super Bowl years, Chuck Noll is by far the most deserving to be inducted into the Hall of Fame." — Hall of Fame linebacker Jack Ham.

Worst Team

1969 (1-13): Following a 2-11-1 showing the previous year, the Steelers turned to Don Shula's staff in Baltimore and hired Chuck Noll as their new coach. He rewarded the Rooney family with a 16-13 win over the Lions in his debut, but proceeded to lose his final 13 games—thanks to a lifeless offense that struggled to put points on the board and a defense (led by rookie DT Joe Greene) that simply wore down.

the largest drink in the city. A casual spot on the city's teeming Southside, **Mario's Southside Saloon** is a good start for a pub crawl to many taverns within walking distance. *1514 E. Carson St. (412) 381-5610. M-Sa11am-1:30am, Su 12pm-12am.*

Best Pittsburgh Pilsner. The oldest brewpub in town, maker of the award-winning Penn Pilsner. Plenty of other beers on tap at the **Penn Brewery**; the atmosphere is German, with a wood-paneled rathskeller and an outdoor *biergarten* during the warm months. Penn Brewery, across from the H.J. Heinz plant on the North Side. *800 Vinial St. (412) 237-9402. M-Sa, 11am-12am, Su closed.*

Best Restaurants

Most original local cuisine. Primanti's is home of the tasty, unusual sandwiches with the french fries and the coleslaw stuffed inside. *46 18th St. (412) 263-2142. Open 24 hours a day, 7 days a week. Cash only. $*

Best brunch. Renowned for elegant dining and its Sunday brunch, **Grand Concourse** is a hit with the pregame crowd. Located in the renovated and historic Pittsburgh and Lake Erie Railroad Station on the Southside, it features seafood, homemade pastas, and steaks. *1 Station Square. (412) 261-1717. M-F Lunch: 11:30am-2:30pm, M-Su Dinner: 4:30pm-10pm, Su Brunch: 10am-2:30pm. All major credit cards. $$$*

A room with a view. In the tallest building between New York and Chicago, the view here at the **Top of the Triangle** is breathtaking. Make sure to ask for a window seat. *USX Tower. 600 Grant St. (412)*

Fans' notes

On Screen

Fighting Back, based on Rocky Bleier's autobiography, is the only serious movie about the Steelers, but the Mean Joe Greene Coke commercial where he gives the kid his jersey did spawn a full-length movie, **The Steeler and the Pittsburgh Kid.** Terry Bradshaw started a silver-screen career with movies like **The Cannonball Run** and **Smokey and the Bandit II**, where he was joined by Mean Joe Greene. Bradshaw later opted for the small screen, co-hosting a short-lived morning program, **The Home Show**, at the same time he was in the studio as a football analyst. The on-the-field exploits of Bradshaw and Franco Harris find their place in the NFL Films video **Most Memorable Moments in Super Bowl History**, which has a fair larding of the Steelers', as does **Super Sunday: A History of the Super Bowl.** Franco Harris's "Immaculate Reception" is on their **NFL's Greatest Moments** tape.

Fight Songs, etc.

Yes, there's a 1981 disco anthem, "Super Steelers" by Freddie Waters, but polka is the story here. Jimmy Pol's original polka fight song is an Iron City classic. First heard in 1973, it has been revised four times since to account for changing times and faces.

Bookshelf

About Three Bricks Shy of a Load. Roy Blount (Ballantine 1986). This chronicle of a year with the Steelers is one of the best, and funniest, books on the sport.
Fighting Back. Rocky Bleier with Terry O'Neil (Warner 1976).

Looking Deep. Terry Bradshaw and Buddy Martin (Contemporary 1989).
Lost Sundays. Sam Toperoff (Random House 1989).
No Easy Game. Terry Bradshaw and Charles Paul Conn (Revell 1973).
The Game That Was. Myron Cope (Thomas Y. Crowell 1974). The voice of the Steelers presents interviews with football's early greats.
The Pittsburgh Steelers. Ed Bouchette (St. Martin's 1994).
The Pittsburgh Steelers: The Official Team History. Abby Mendelson (Taylor 1996).

Paraphernalia

The Terrible Towel. Myron Cope, the team's popular color analyst, came up with the idea in the 1970s. It's simple, inexpensive and mighty impressive when thousands are waved, not only in Three Rivers Stadium, but in enemy territory as well. In the 1970s and 1980s, Cope would call for fans to bring out the towel only for playoff games, but it has become a fixture at every game in the 1990s.

You Gotta See...

▶Step into **the Steelers lobby** in Three Rivers Stadium for a close-up view of their four Super Bowl trophies, enclosed in a glass case.
▶**Forbes Field**, where both the Pirates and Steelers played, is long-gone except for part of the left-field wall, where Bill Mazeroski socked his World Series-winning home run in 1960. It's in Oakland, on the University of Pittsburgh campus.
▶**The Allegheny Club**, the elegant restaurant in Three Rivers Stadium, has memorabilia and photos throughout.

Hall of Fame

Bert Bell	(Owner 1963)
Johnny McNally	(HB 1963)
Arthur J. Rooney	(Owner 1964)
Bill Dudley	(HB 1966)
Walt Kiesling	(G/Coach 1966)
Bobby Layne	(QB 1967)
Marion Motley	(FB 1968)
Ernie Stautner	(DT 1969)
Len Dawson	(QB 1987)
Joe Greene	(DT 1987)
John Henry Johnson	(FB 1987)
Jack Ham	(LB 1988)
Mel Blount	(DB 1989)
Terry Bradshaw	(QB 1989)
Franco Harris	(FB 1990)
Jack Lambert	(LB 1990)
Chuck Noll	(Coach 1993)
Mike Webster	(C 1997)

Against the Odds

One of the cliches to describe a Sunday in the NFL is "going to war." For **Rocky Bleier** (1968-1980), Sundays in the NFL were the furthest thing from it. Bleier, who had failed to make the roster in 1968, was severely injured in Vietnam when a grenade exploded under his right foot. Determined to return to the game, he was placed on injured reserve in 1970. By mid-1974, Bleier was teamed with Franco Harris in one of the NFL's best-ever backfields. From 1974 through 1979, Bleier and Harris rushed for a combined 10,279 yards.

471-4100. M-Th Lunch: 11:30am-3pm, dinner: 5:30pm-10pm, F-Sa Lunch: 11:30pm-3pm, dinner: 5:30pm-11pm, Sun 4pm-9pm. All major credit cards. $$$$

> "Those were the greatest teams that ever played professional football. They had the greatest players, certainly. And great coaches." — Al Davis, on the Steelers and Raiders rivalry of the 1970s.

Best place for kids. The sports theme runs throughout the family atmosphere at **Woodson's All-Star Grill**. It has televisions and game rooms everywhere and is owned by former Steeler Rod Woodson. Family atmosphere. *1 Station Square (412) 454-2600. M-Sa 11:30am-11pm, Su 11:30am-9pm. Sun. All major credit cards. $$*

Best Accommodations

Red Roof Inn. 20 minutes east of Pittsburgh. Basic, basic, basic. Plenty of shopping nearby. *2729 Mosside Blvd., Monroeville. (412) 856-4738. Triple A sales discount. $*

Shadyside Inn. Elegant suite with kitchen in the fashionable Shadyside district on the east side of town. Hollywood stars filming in Pittsburgh have stayed here, along with visiting executives. Not your typical hotel experience. *5405 Fifth Ave. (412) 441-4444. $$*

Doubletree Hotel. Next to the convention center and near the vibrant Strip District. A popular stay for visiting teams. *1000 Penn Ave. (412) 281-3700. $$-$$$.*

While You Were Eating Turkey....

Nov. 24, 1983: The Steelers were flying along under new quarterback Cliff Stoudt but were coming off a loss to Minnesota. Then they had the stuffing beat out of them on Thanksgiving Day at Detroit, 45-3. All told, Pittsburgh's 9-2 start was followed by five losses in their last six games, including a 38-10 setback to the Raiders in the playoffs. Overall, 0-2.

St. Louis Rams

"The Rams have raised the level of what class is all about in the NFL." Dick Vermeil

One of the most storied and traveled of all NFL franchises, the Rams originated as an American Football League team in 1936 before the NFL granted an expansion franchise to Cleveland in 1937. The team struggled for a decade as the Cleveland Rams before winning its final game in that city, beating Washington, 15-14, and claiming the franchise's first world championship. Owner Dan Reeves moved the team to Los Angeles in 1946, and five years later the Rams won their second title, beating Cleveland, 24-17, when future Hall of Famers Norm Van Brocklin and Tom Fears connected on a 73-yard pass late in the fourth quarter.

Though he is known for moving the team to the West Coast, it's a lesser-known fact that in 1946 Reeves also signed Woody Strode and Kenny Washington, two African-Americans, a year before Jackie Robinson broke the color barrier with the Brooklyn Dodgers. Over the next four and half decades, although the Rams were never able to repeat as world champions, they nonetheless produced Hall of Famers, including Deacon Jones, Merlin Olsen, Ollie Matson, Bob Waterfield and Elroy "Crazylegs" Hirsch. The late, great Pete Rozelle was general manager of the Rams from 1957-59 before being appointed NFL commissioner in 1960.

Dan Reeves lost a battle with cancer in 1971, and his death set the stage for one of the most historic ownership moves in the NFL: In 1972 Baltimore Colts owner Carroll Rosenbloom convinced Robert Irsay, who acquired the Rams franchise in an estate settlement, to trade the

Franchise History

Cleveland Rams (AFL)
(1936)
Cleveland Rams (NFL)
(1937–45)
Los Angeles Rams
(1946–94)
St. Louis Rams
(1995–present)

By the Numbers

(Since 1970)
Regular Season: 225-195-4
Postseason: 10-14
Division Titles: 8
Vs. Division: 92-78-2 (Playoffs: 0-1)
Playoff Appearances: 14
Home: 122-88-2
Away: 103-107-2

(Overall)
Regular Season: 416-379-20
Postseason: 13-20
Playoff Appearances: 22
Home: 229-163-10
Away: 187-216-10

Most Revered Football Figures

Elroy "Crazylegs" Hirsch. One of the game's first deep threats. Even starred in his own movie.

Merlin Olsen. The anchor of the Fearsome Foursome, long before he started peddling flowers.

Deacon Jones. Another Fearsome Foursome mainstay, the Deacon was one of the greatest pass rushers in NFL history.

Rivalries

The West Coast's first professional sports rivalry was more than just a clash of two teams. The Rams vs. the **49ers** was a clash of geography, of lifestyle, of laid-back Los Angeles vs. free-thinking San Francisco. It was the Beach Boys vs. the Grateful Dead; wine country vs. wine coolers. On the field, it was Elroy "Crazylegs" Hirsch vs. Hugh McElhenny; the Fearsome Foursome vs. the Gold Rush; John Brodie vs. Roman Gabriel. Even with the franchise moving halfway across the country to St. Louis, this is still *the* rivalry as far as the Rams are concerned. It has been lopsided in the '90s, with San Francisco winning 15 in a row, but the Rams still hold a slim 48-47-2 lead. While the rivalry with the 49ers has survived a move, the friction with the **Cardinals** was caused by a move. Most St. Louis sports fans will never forgive Bill Bidwill for moving his Cardinals to Arizona in 1988. The town stayed in a football funk for weeks after the Cardinals defeated the Rams, 31-28, in overtime in 1996, the first meeting between the city's present and past football franchises.

entire Los Angeles team for his Baltimore franchise. When Rosenbloom died in 1979, majority ownership of the Rams passed to his widow Georgia Frontiere, who made a deal to move the team out of the L. A. Coliseum to Anaheim. This was one of the more successful periods in franchise history. After losing Super Bowl XIV to Pittsburgh, the Rams made the playoffs seven out of 10 years during the '80s under head coach John Robinson.

> **did you know?**
> The Rams won an NFL-record seven straight NFC West titles from 1973-79.

In 1995, seeking a better stadium deal, the team exercised its right to terminate its lease and left Southern California after 49 years. Having lost the Cardinals in a stadium dispute just eight years earlier, St. Louis lured the Rams with a handsome financial package that included the newly-built Trans World Dome. The Gateway to the West was back in the football business. For several years, bad personnel moves and a lack of direction kept the Rams near the bottom of the NFL heap, but in 1997 the franchise hired Dick Vermeil as head coach and president of football operations. Having been out of coaching for 15 years, Vermeil now found himself at the reins of the team that gave him his first full-time job in the NFL, as a special teams coach under then-head Coach George Allen.

> **"I don't believe in riling the grain. I like a nice, hard game where everybody keeps his blood cool."**
> — Gene "Big Daddy" Lipscomb.

Vermeil, the Rams organization and the fans of St. Louis can only hope that the man once noted for leading the long-suffering Philadelphia Eagles to prominence in the

1980s can bring one of the NFL's most historic franchises back to glory in the Heartland.

—*Mark Malone*

Trans World Dome

The $300 million Trans World Dome opened midway through the 1995 season. As domes go, it's the league's second-best, but a distant second, to the Georgia Dome in Atlanta. The sight lines are good, better than in St. Louis's former football home, Busch Stadium.

> **did you know?**
>
> The Rams were the first NFL team to have insignias on their helmets. RB Fred Gehrke, a graphic artist by trade, designed the ram's-horn helmet in 1947, and the Rams began wearing them in 1948.

In November and December, when the St. Louis weather can get rough, it's a relatively cozy place to watch a game. But in September and October, when the weather can be gorgeous, you wish you could blow off the roof and let the sunshine in. Alas, the roof was nonnegotiable, a key element in securing taxpayer funding for a new stadium attached to the downtown convention center. Like most domes, the Trans World Dome can be deafening when the home team is doing something exciting — which unfortunately hasn't happened too often in St. Louis. More often, with the struggling Rams, the stadium has been like a morgue because of grand lulls in the action.

Public address announcer Jim Holder doesn't really need amplification; he must have the strongest pipes in the business. The overall P.A. system has been upgraded, but it still could be better. The rock and pop music played during breaks in the game seems deafening in certain parts of the stadium and barely audible in others.

The PSL Club offers a decent pregame

The "I Was There" Game

December 23, 1951: Coach Joe Stydahar had benched Norm Van Brocklin for arguing over play calls in the season finale, so Bob Waterfield played the first 50 minutes of this NFL Championship Game. With the score tied at 17 against Cleveland in the title game, Stydahar sent in Van Brocklin, who tossed a 73-yard TD pass to Tom Fears midway through the fourth quarter, giving the Rams a 24-17 victory over the Cleveland Browns. It was the Rams' only NFL title while in Los Angeles; it was also the first NFL game to be televised nationwide.

The Paper Bag Game

October 22, 1995: With the Rams off to a 5-1 start in their first season in St. Louis, and with Elvis Grbac making his first NFL start in place of the injured Steve Young, a changing of the guard appeared imminent in the NFC West. But it was not to be. Grbac and the 49ers jumped out to a 14-0 lead after just one offensive play and romped to a 44-10 victory at Busch Stadium.

Great Names

Jack Bighead (E, 1955)
Alex Bravo (DB, 1957-58)
Ed Champagne (T, 1947-50)
Tom Fears (E, 1948-56)
Jesse James (OT, 1995-96)
Duval Love (G, 1985-91)
Jim Mello (RB, 1948)
Lance Rentzel (WR, 1971-72, 1974)
Jack "Hacksaw" Reynolds (LB, 1970-80)
Charley Toogood (DT/OT, 1951-56)
Billy Waddy (WR, 1977-81)

Our Top Story

"Wholesale Trading"
July 14, 1972
We've all heard of "I'll give you my Mickey Mantle for your Willie Mays," but this? Baltimore Colts owner Carroll Rosenbloom traded the entire Colts franchise to Robert Irsay for the Rams. Or look at it this way: The Colts and Rams traded owners.

"One for the Books"
December 16, 1984
Wrapping up his second pro season, Eric Dickerson rewrites the regular-season record book. His 2,105 yards rushing breaks O.J. Simpson's record (2,003, set in a 14-game season), and his twelve 100-yard games set a record (broken in 1997 by Barry Sanders).

"Hasta Los Angeles"
January 17, 1995
After 49 seasons in Southern California, owner Georgia Frontiere announces that the Rams are moving from Los Angeles to St. Louis.

"Slater Christens Dome"
November 12, 1995.
Basically playing with one arm because of an elbow injury, the Eternal Ram, Jackie Slater, makes his one and only start as a St. Louis Ram in his 20th NFL season. The Rams defeat Carolina in the inaugural game at the Trans World Dome before 65,598, the largest crowd ever to see a football game in St. Louis.

did you know?

Rams players hold NFL records for most passing yards in one game (Norm Van Brocklin, 554 in 1951), most receiving yards in a game (Flipper Anderson, 336 in 1989), and most receptions in a game (Tom Fears, 18 in 1950).

buffet in the stadium, and is open to any ticket holder. Concession stands are very mainstream: hot dogs, bratwurst, beer, nachos and pretzels are the big sellers. The brats are especially good. Complaints about quality of the pizza have led to an "upgraded" brand this year.

Like many of the newest stadiums, there are advertisements splashed all over the Trans World Dome, and the scoreboards show more commercials than highlights or stats during timeouts. There aren't enough replays, especially when the opposing team does something good or when the Rams do something bad. The place is almost always full, but the Dome definitely ranks in the bottom half of the NFL in terms of atmosphere. A few more victories from the NFL's losingest franchise in the '90s would help. Right now, the fans arrive at game time and leave early. Can you blame them?

The Bottom Line on Trans World Dome

Address: 701 Convention Plaza, St. Louis, MO 63101. (314) 423-9550

Tickets: Stadium box office is open 9 a.m. to 5 p.m. Monday through Friday, and three hours prior to kickoff on game days. Each year in July, the club makes 4,000 single-game seats available per game, at $25 a ticket, on a first-come, first-served basis. There are also some club level seats available each year. Most of the seats are good. Just avoid the upper end zones. Season tickets are available with a PSL. For more information, call (314) 425-8830 or 1-800-2GO-RAMS.

1998: $45/$40/$35/$30/$25

Best of the Rams

Best Team

1967 (11-2-2): Perhaps one of the best teams not to make it to a championship game, George Allen's Rams were led by QB Roman Gabriel and a fierce defense that gave up the fewest points in the league. Still, their first playoff stop was a trip to Milwaukee to face the defending world champion Packers, who limited the top offense in the league to just 217 total yards and a single, first-quarter touchdown, winning 28-7.

> "The only man in pro football who really scares me is Merlin Olsen." — Browns guard Gene Hickerson. (1970)

Greatest Players by Position

Pos:	Player
QB:	Roman Gabriel
RB:	Eric Dickerson
WR:	Henry Ellard
TE:	Billy Truax
OL:	Jackie Slater
DL:	Merlin Olsen
LB:	Jack Reynolds
DB:	Nolan Cromwell
P/K:	Mike Lansford
ST:	Ron Brown

And Don't Forget...

LB: Isiah Robertson. Best known for getting run over by Oilers' RB Earl Campbell, but one of the premier linebackers in the '70s.

G: Tom Mack. The Rams have traditionally been known for great line play, epitomized by this 11-time Pro Bowler.

DE: Jack Youngblood. Unselfish and relentless defender who played in Super Bowl XIV despite a broken leg.

QB: Norm Van Brocklin. Fiery six-time all-star who knew how to win. Still owns NFL record for most passing yards in a game (554).

DB: Dick "Night Train" Lane. Played just two seasons with the Rams (1952-53) but as a rookie, totaled a record 14 interceptions.

Best Argument

Defensive Line: Merlin Olsen or Deacon Jones? There was a time that opposing quarterbacks had to face this pair, along with the rest of the Fearsome Foursome. Olsen was an immovable force in the middle, and was named to the Pro Bowl an NFL-record 14 times. Jones not only made the "quarterback sack" his specialty, he coined the phrase that is now an official statistic.

> "A press conference was called yesterday to announce the new head coach of the Rams. A limo pulled up, the passenger door was opened, and nobody got out." — Columnist Jim Murray of the Los Angeles Times, on the Rams' hiring of the then-unknown Chuck Knox. (1973)

Best Coach

George Allen (1966-70): The late and great Allen is probably best remembered by most for leading Washington's "Over The Hill Gang" in the 1970s. But he led some of this franchise's best teams in the late '60s, although he failed to win a playoff game in two tries. When Allen took over the Redskins in 1971, he brought more than one of his talented Rams to the nation's capital.

Pressbox

Who to Read...

Basically a one newspaper town, St. Louis has beat writer Jim Thomas and columnist Bernie Miklasz of the *Post-Dispatch* as the sources for daily information. The *Post-Dispatch* offers heavier coverage over game weekends, including weekly postgame report cards, and it has particularly good coverage during the off-season. The Belleville (Ill.) *News-Democrat* is a smaller daily which covers the team home and away during the season. Steve Korte and Dave Wilhelm are the beat writers.

Swami Sez:

Fans in this great river city are hoping the Rams will soon swim upstream in the NFC West. They haven't had a winning record since 1989.

Who to Watch...

Television stations have more of a clue as to what's going on with the team than in most markets, and all the local stations do a decent job with game coverage. KSDK, with anchor Mike Bush, has an excellent sports show on Sundays, from 10:30-11:30pm. KMOV also has an extended Sunday night highlight show. KMOV sports anchor Steve Savard was once a participant in the Dallas Cowboys training camp; even though his NFL career never materialized, he can provide some special insight into the game.

Who to Listen To...

The market is very radio-intensive, with traditional giant KMOX (1120 AM), the first all-talk radio station, and upstart KTRS (550 AM) offering significant amounts of air time to sports talk and programming. Kevin Slaten, generally on from 6:30-8pm weeknights on KTRS, is the most outspoken. Miklasz, the newspaper columunist, has a 9-11am weekday show on KFNS (590 AM) that is football intensive during the season. Randy Karraker, evenings on KMOX, avoids the outlandish, remaining thoughtful and informed. Rams games are broadcast simultaneously on the all-sports station, KFNS (590 AM), and on KSD (93.7 FM). Dick Vermeil also has a Monday night radio show which airs on these stations.

1994: $35/$30/$23 (Anaheim Stadium)

Public Transportation: Rams express buses bring fans in from Missouri and Illinois. For schedule information on bus transportation and the MetroLink light rail, call the Bi-State Development Agency, (314) 231-2345, or the agency's special events and sports hotline at (314) 982-1521.

Parking: There is no stadium garage per se, so don't bother thinking about tailgating, but there is plenty of surface and garage parking available in the immediate downtown area and the adjacent Laclede's Landing restaurant and nightclub area. Traffic seems to get in smoothly before and after the games.

Capacity: 66,053

Restrooms: 20 for women, 20 for men, and nine family restrooms.

Best Bars

Best sports bar. It's 25 minutes from downtown and the Dome, but the best sports bar in town is **Ozzie's Restaurant & Sports Bar**, owned by former Cardinal shortstop Ozzie Smith. *645 Westport Plaza, (314) 434-1000. M-Th 11am-11pm, F-Sa 11am-midnight, Su 11am-10pm.*

Best live music. For years, **Lucius Boomer's** has been one of the most popular nightspots on Laclede's Landing. Live music after the game, and you just might see some of the Rams or St. Louis Blues. *707 Clamorgan Alley. (314) 621-8155. Lunch: Seven days 11:30am-4pm, dinner: Su-Th 4-10pm, F-Sa 4-11pm.*

Best sports bar near the Dome. Popular with the 25-to-40 set, **Trainwreck on the Landing** has ten TVs, including a big screen, live music on Friday and Saturday, and a dance floor. There's also a full dinner menu, including great burgers, and it's just a few blocks from the Dome. *720 N. First St. (314) 436-1006. Sa 11am-3am; football Sundays 10am-12am. Kitchen: Seven days 11am-10pm, bar: M-Th 11am-10pm, F-Sa 11am-3am, Su 11am-11pm.*

> "I like men with bald heads. I want to win today. I don't want to wait for tomorrow. The future is now."
> — George Allen, Rams head coach from 1966-70, on his preference for veteran players.

Best brew pub. The ambience at the **Morgan Street Brewery** changes from restaurant to nightclub after dark. The microbrewery offers five or six varieties of lager daily, although Budweiser and Bud

Ready For Primetime (Monday Night)

December 9, 1985: John Robinson's club opened the season with seven straight wins, but four losses in their next six games (including an earlier setback to San Francisco) had raised doubts, and surely the Niners would bring the Rams back to earth and reclaim their hold on the NFC West. But Robinson's defense and special teams came up big, and the 27-20 win paved the way for a division title.

Overall Monday Night: 17-20

Overall Sunday Night: 3-10

Overall on Thursday Night: 2-3

Think About the Weather

December 16, 1945: Between playing in Southern California and the Trans World Dome, weather has never been much of a factor for the Rams. But while in Cleveland, the Rams defeated visiting Washington, 15-14, in this NFL Championship Game for the franchise's first NFL title. An icy field at Cleveland Stadium made for an interesting day, but didn't seem to faze Rams rookie QB Bob Waterfield, who threw two touchdown passes. The difference in the game came courtesy of Redskins' QB Sammy Baugh, whose first-quarter pass from the end zone hit the crossbar and bounced back for a safety (a rule which later changed). The team left for California the next season.

Worst Team

1991 (3-13): It's hard to choose when you think about the Rams in the 1990s, a franchise which lost 10 or more games in seven of the decade's first eight years. The 1991 season would prove to be the last for head coach John Robinson, who two years earlier had led the wild card Rams to within a game of Super Bowl XXIV. Following a 3-3 start, the team closed the season with 10 consecutive (and mostly ugly) losses.

> "My name is Deacon Jones ... and I've come to preach the gospel of winning football to the good people of Los Angeles." — Rookie Deacon Jones at his first Rams press conference. (1961)

Team Leaders

Rushing Yards
7,245   Eric Dickerson, 1983-87
Passing Yards
23,758   Jim Everett, 1986-93
Passing Touchdowns
154   Roman Gabriel, 1962-72
Receptions
593   Henry Ellard, 1983-93
Interceptions
46   Ed Meador, 1959-70
Touchdowns
58   Eric Dickerson, 1983-87
Points
789   Mike Lansford, 1982-90

Light (produced by that slightly larger brewery down the street) are available too. The restaurant offers pizza, pasta, sandwiches and Black Angus steaks. *712 N. Second St. (314) 231-9970. Seven days 11am-3am. Football Sundays 9am-3am (12:00 kickoffs), 11am-3am (3:00 kickoffs).*

Best Restaurants

Best Italian. High rollers looking for a great meal on Saturday night can't do better than **Tony's**, which serves Continental cuisine with an Italian flair. *About ⅓ mile from the Trans World Dome. 410 Market. (314) 231-7007. Reservations taken only for 5pm-11:30pm, Saturday nights. M-Th 5-11pm, F-Sa 5-11:30pm. All major credit cards. $$$$*

Best Cajun. The **Broadway Oyster Bar** specializes in Cajun/Creole food — try the barbecue shrimp. You can also get a good steak or burger, and of course, oysters. *736 S. Broadway, about ½ mile south of the Trans World Dome (just south of Busch Stadium). (314) 621-8811. M-Th 11am-1am, F-Sa 11:30am-1:30am, Su 11:30am-12am, food served till 11 p.m. MC, V. $$*

> "If I'd had the regular wrap-around hip pads, I'd have been down to my jock strap." — Elroy "Crazylegs" Hirsch after a swarm of youths accosted the retiring star and took much of his gear as souvenirs. (1954)

Best Sunday brunch. **Chestnut's** at the Adams Mark Hotel offers the best Sunday buffet in town — everything from omelettes to boiled shrimp, Asian and Greek dishes and duck l'orange. There's a full desert table, a fresh pasta station, and the $21.95 per person price includes champagne. *4th and*

Fans' notes

On Screen

Playing for the "Hollywood Rams" led a number of players right into show business. Merlin Olsen appeared in **The Undefeated, One More Train to Rob** and **Mitchell**, but he is best remembered for his TV work — **Little House on the Prairie** and **Father Murphy,** for example. And how many other defensive linemen have become spokesmen for flower delivery companies? In contrast, Olsen's neighbor on the D-line, Fred Dryer, eventually starred as a detective on TV's **Hunter**. Mike Henry, a Rams linebacker from 1962 to 1964, went on to star as Tarzan in a number of late-'60s movies. Henry also appeared in **Soylent Green** with Charlton Heston, **The Longest Yard** with Burt Reynolds and all three **Smokey and the Bandit** movies. Kenny Washington, running back for L.A. from 1946 to 1948, also has a number of film credits, ranging from **The Jackie Robinson Story** to **Tarzan's Deadly Silence**. In the 1953 autobiographical film **Crazylegs, All American,** a 30-year-old Crazylegs Hirsch played himself as a teenager — the age difference was somewhat awkward. A number of other Rams also appeared in the film, including Bob Waterfield (who married movie starlet Jane Russell). The Rams also earned a team film credit for their appearance in 1949's **Easy Living,** starring Victor Mature and Lucille Ball. Wide receiver Bernie Casey came to L.A. to play the last two years of his career, and he liked Tinseltown so much he stayed on in the local industry. Casey's acting credits include **Sons of the Magnificent Seven** and the Bond film **Never Say Never Again**. Finally, Warren Beatty is quarterback of the Rams in **Heaven Can Wait**.

Bookshelf

Great Teams' Great Years: Los Angeles Rams. Steve Bisheff (Macmillan 1973).
Rams: Five Decades of Football. Joseph Hession (Foghorn Press 1987).
Headslap: The Life and Times of Deacon Jones. John Klawitter and Deacon Jones (Prometheus 1996). An honest and revealing look at football from the leader of the Fearsome Foursome.
Pat Haden: My Rookie Season with the Los Angeles Rams. Pat Haden. (William Morrow 1977).
On the Run. Eric Dickerson and Steve Delsohn (Contemporary 1986).
Hard Knox: The Life of an NFL Coach. Chuck Knox and Bill Plaschke (Harcourt Brace 1988).

You Gotta See...

▸Head to the top of the **Gateway Arch** — elevators carry you skyward along an arc to the observation deck, where you can look out over the entire city.

▸If the Rams don't provide you with enough of a rollercoaster ride for your liking, there's still **Six Flags Over Mid-America**, about 30 miles out of town on I-44.

▸Daytime or nighttime, you can tool along the **Mississippi River** on a 19th-century replica riverboat. Tours begin at the St. Louis Levee, near the Arch.

▸And there's the **St. Louis Zoo**. Big, beautiful, well-kept—and free.

Against the Odds

Every NFL player is forced to grin and bear the pain at some time over his career — if not *all* the time. But **Jack Youngblood** (1971-84), took it a step further. Despite his somewhat small, 6'4", 245-pound frame, the Rams' tenacious defensive end never missed a game, playing in 202 straight en route to seven Pro Bowl selections. Youngblood's toughness and dedication were never more evident than in the 1979 postseason, when he shrugged off a broken fibula in his left leg to anchor the Rams defense in the NFC Championship Game and the Super Bowl.

Hall of Fame

Earl Clark	(C, 1963)
Bob Waterfield	(QB, 1965)
Dan Reeves	(Owner, 1967)
Elroy "Crazylegs" Hirsch	(WR/RB, 1968)
Tom Fears	(WR, 1970)
Andy Robustelli	(DE, 1971)
Norm Van Brocklin	(QB, 1971)
Ollie Matson	(HB, 1972)
Bill George	(LB, 1974)
Dick Lane	(DE, 1974)
Deacon Jones	(DE, 1980)
Merlin Olsen	(DT, 1982)
Sid Gillman	(C, 1983)
Joe Namath	(QB, 1985)
Pete Rozelle	(GM, 1985)
Tex Schramm	(GM, 1991)
Tommy McDonald	(WR 1998)

Chestnut Sts. (314) 241-7400. Su (Brunch) 10am-2pm. Su-Th 6am-11pm, F-Sa 6am-midnight. All major credit cards. Reservations suggested. $$$

did you know?

On January 28, 1971, the Rams sent linebacking greats Jack Pardee and Maxie Baughn and four other players and a draft choice to the Redskins for Marlin McKeever and seven draft picks.

Best Accommodations

Adams Mark Hotel. This upscale choice sits in the shadow of the Gateway Arch. *4th and Chestnut Sts. (314)241-7400. $$$$*

Marriott Pavilion. Next to Busch Stadium, but within walking distance of the Dome (1/3 mile) in all but foul weather. *1 Broadway, (314) 421-1776. $$$*

Drury Inn. Right across the street from the Dome. Convention Plaza and Broadway, *711 N. Broadway (314) 231-8100. $$*

While You Were Eating Turkey

November 23, 1967: The Rams don't have an extensive Thanksgiving history but they are undefeated against the one team in the league that is steeped in Turkey Day lore. The Rams went on the road to Detroit in 1945, 1967 and 1975 and won all three games, the last one a 20-0 shutout in which James Harris threw for three TDs. The 1967 win, keyed by the defense, was particularly impressive, though. Interceptions by Jack Pardee and Eddie Meador and a fumble recovery by Lamar Lundy on a deflected pitchout helped the Rams put a stack of points on the board, and Detroit just couldn't catch up. Rams 31, Lions 7. Overall, 3-0.

San Diego Chargers

The lightning bolt on the side of the helmet is more than just a symbol. The San Diego Chargers have been known for quick offensive firepower since their early American Football League days. In the '60s, it was John Hadl throwing to Lance Alworth, accompanied by the running of Paul Lowe and Keith Lincoln. In the late '70s and '80s, Air Coryell electrified the Pacific skies with Dan Fouts's passes. Though Stan Humphries may not have had the swagger of a Hadl or a Fouts, his ability to rifle long passes advanced the Chargers to Super Bowl XXIX, the ultimate highlight of the franchise.

So it was only fitting that General Manager Bobby Beathard would unload most of his top 1998 and 1999 draft choices to move into the position to take Washington State's Ryan Leaf. Quarterbacks are the lifeblood of this franchise, and their stadium, once named for sportswriter Jack Murphy and now for computer powerhouse Qualcomm, has been one of football's most fertile grounds for offensive innovation. Sid Gillman, the Chargers' first head coach (1960-69), was the architect of many of the passing schemes we watch today. Gillman assembled an all-star coaching staff that included Chuck Noll, John Madden and Al Davis. Under him, the Chargers were in four AFL title games in the league's first five years and blew out the Boston Patriots, 51-10, for the 1963 title.

Don Coryell was a natural hire for the Chargers in 1978 following eight seasons without a winning record. A local hero for his passing offense at San Diego

Franchise History

Los Angeles Chargers (AFL)
(1960)
San Diego Chargers (AFL)
(1961–69)
San Diego Chargers (NFL)
(1970–present)

By the Numbers

(Since 1970)

Regular Season: 191-228-5
Postseason: 6-7
Division Titles: 5
Vs. Division: 85-118-3 (Playoffs: 1-1)
Playoffs Appearances: 7
Home: 108-101-2
Away: 83-127-3

(Overall)

Regular Season: 277-276-11
Postseason: 7-11
Playoffs Appearances: 12
Home: 155-122-5
Away: 122-154-6

Most Revered Football Figures

Junior Seau: Seau's face provides the best close-up TV shot since Mike Singletary. The heart and soul of the current team.

Don Coryell: Air Coryell rekindled memories of Sid Gillman's high-flying AFL glory days for San Diego while redefining the passing game in the NFL.

Dan Fouts: He made it look so easy that it seemed as though any quarterback could have found success in the Chargers passing attack. Today, quarterbacks are lucky to make it through 16 games, much less 15 seasons with one team.

Sid Gillman: Sportswriter Jerry McGee, who covered the team for 25 years, called Gillman the single most important figure in Chargers history. His football knowledge and ruthlessness as a coach forced other teams in the AFL to raise their competitive levels in order to compete, in turn raising the level of play throughout the game.

State, he was brought in by the Chargers to run his fabled one-back offense. Under Coryell, the Chargers assembled one of the most talented offensive teams in league history. For receivers, Fouts had Charlie Joiner, Wes Chandler and Kellen Winslow, with Chuck Muncie as the powerful running back. It was a cast of Hall of Fame players performing in their prime.

The mid-1980s were impatient times for this franchise. Stockton real estate developer Alex Spanos, who bought the team in 1984, demanded titles. Coryell was gone after the 1986 season, and Spanos went through two coaches—Al Saunders and Dan Henning—and several general mangers before handing the football operations over to Beathard. As he did with the Redskins, Beathard used aggressive scouting, small-college draftees and smart trades to build the Chargers back to contender status. His best move was hiring Bobby Ross, who did for the Chargers what Joe Gibbs did for the Redskins. Ross willed his squad to win, capped by the 1994 trip to the Super Bowl.

Unfortunately, Ross was too good. Expectations ran high, and the Super Bowl loss to San Francisco led to deterioration within the organization. Ross lost some confidence in his players. The once close relationship between Ross and Beathard deteriorated to the point that Ross left for Detroit. Fitting the history of this franchise, Beathard hired an

> **did you know?**
> The Bolts have never won a regular-season game in Pittsburgh (0-11). Their two wins at Three Rivers Stadium came in the playoffs, including a 17-13 upset victory in the '94 title game.

> "The country is full of good coaches. What it takes to win is a bunch of interested players." — Head Coach Don Coryell

offensive coach as a replacement. Coach Kevin Gilbride struggled in his inaugural season, losing 12 of 16 games. In year two, he and Beathard rebuilt the offense, completely retooling the offensive line and bringing back popular running back Natrone Means.

But the future is at quarterback and the expected arrival of Leaf. He's the perfect re-charge for this franchise.

—John Clayton

Qualcomm Stadium

Opened in 1967 to replace Balboa Stadium, San Diego Stadium was initially renamed Jack Murphy Stadium in 1980, in honor of the late *San Diego Union* sports editor who did so much to attract major league franchises to the city. "The Murph" was officially dubbed Qualcomm Stadium in 1997, with the playing surface now called Jack Murphy Field.

Construction in preparation for Super Bowl XXXII made things a bit of a mess for two seasons, temporarily reducing seating and parking for Chargers and Padres games. Tailgating is huge at The Murph, with just about every local radio and television station hosting some sort of activity in the lot. Inside the stadium, Rubio's Fish Tacos (fish, cabbage, salsa, and lime) are the signature food of choice.

Since this is southern California, bikini tops and bare chests are the preferred attire for those not among the thousands painted in blue and gold. With Southern California's penchant for fitness, such sights distract only in a positive sense from the game. The Cheerleaders are once again an active part of the sideline show, and

did you know?

The '92 Chargers opened 0-4 under new head coach Bobby Ross, but rebounded to win 11-of-12 and the AFC West — the only team ever to overcome such a start and make the playoffs.

Rivalries

The Oakland **Raiders**, since their first Oakland incarnation, have been the team Chargers fans most love to hate, fueled by the many classic clashes including the 1980 AFC Championship game won by the Raiders 34-27. The defining meeting in this series was the "Holy Roller Game" on September 10, 1978. With the Raiders rallying to take the lead, defender Woody Lowe had wrapped up quarterback Ken Stabler, who fumbled the ball towards running back Pete Banaszak, who then knocked it forward towards the end zone, where tight end Dave Casper fell on it for the deciding score. After the 21-20 Raiders win, Stabler admitted the play was intentional, and in the ensuing off-season, the NFL altered the rules regarding advancing a fumble. The Raiders lead the series 46-29-2. And while Chargers fans hold a certain cold spot in their hearts for the Raiders, San Diego's management clearly finds the Kansas City **Chiefs** a more worthwhile target for their aggression in recent years, built upon a perceived arrogance in Kansas City's camp. The Chiefs lead the series 39-36-1.

The "I Was There" Game

January 5, 1964: While there were other, more exciting games in Chargers history, none compares in meaning to this AFL Championship victory. Running back Keith Lincoln provided 349 yards total offense in San Diego's 51-10 win over the Boston Patriots, the Chargers' lone win in five trips to the AFL title game.

The Paper Bag Game

December 29, 1979: No team in Chargers history could hold a candle to the 1979 incarnation of Air Coryell. Playing at home in the playoffs after a first round bye, they figured to crush a Houston team playing without Earl Campbell, Dan Pastorini, and Ken Burrough. Houston 17, San Diego 14. Go figure.

Swami Sez:

Perhaps Ryan Leaf is a member of the same family tree as Dan Fouts and Air Coryell, not to mention John Hadl and Sid Gillman. If so, buckle your seat belts for the lightning bolts.

Great Names

Lance "Bambi" Alworth (WR, 1962-70)
Coy Bacon (DE, 1973-75)
Hubert Bobo (LB, 1960)
Marion Butts (RB, 1989-93)
Larry Little (G, 1967-68)
Natrone Means (RB, 1993-95, 1998-)
Alfred Pupunu (TE, 1992-97)

did you know?

Don Coryell's high-powered offense led the NFL in first downs for four consecutive seasons from 1980 through 1983, a feat never duplicated by any other club.

crowds are generally loud and faithful. In the "Air Coryell" era, gold T-shirts were the garb of choice, and gold remains popular. Styrofoam lightning bolts adorn the heads of fans, who refer to their team as "The Bolts." There is an unofficial "Bolt Man" who wears complete superhero garb, including cape and colors. The only obstructed-view seats are between the 30-yard lines, close down to the field.

There is one strong caveat regarding Chargers games: Beware "The Cannon." No matter how many times you have been to a Chargers game, the deafening bang that comes after a San Diego score is still a wake-up call. A staple of Chargers games since the 1961 season, opposing players hate this sound more than any single aspect of visiting San Diego. More than a few unsuspecting sideliners have had their hats blown off by the force of the post-touchdown explosion. Frankly, there's not a whole lot else about the city, or visiting a Chargers game, to dislike. Depending on your attitude, that could, in fact, be a problem.

"A player comes along once in a lifetime who alone is worth the price of admission. Lance Alworth was that player." — Houston Oilers receiver Charley Hennigan

The Bottom Line on Qualcomm Stadium

Address: 9449 Friars Road, San Diego CA, 92108, (619) 874-4500

Tickets: There are season and individual tickets available, with a 10-ticket limit

Best of the Chargers

Best Team

1963 (12-3): Following a disastrous 4-10 showing in '62, Sid Gillman's club opened with three straight wins the following year before being upset in Denver. But the Raiders would be the only club to beat the Chargers (twice) the rest of the way, and the San Diego offense — led by QB Tobin Rote, WR Lance Alworth, and FB Keith Lincoln — kicked into gear late, stomping the Patriots 51-10 in the AFL title game.

Greatest Players by Position

Pos:	Player
QB:	Dan Fouts
RB:	Paul Lowe
WR:	Lance Alworth
TE:	Kellen Winslow
OL:	Ron Mix
DL:	Leslie O'Neal
LB:	Junior Seau
DB:	Gill Byrd
P/K:	Rolf Benirschke
ST:	Leslie Duncan

And Don't Forget...

WR: Wes Chandler. A speedster with 373 catches in seven seasons, Chandler gained an astounding 1,032 yards in the nine games of the strike-shortened 1982 season.

FB: Keith Lincoln. Along with Paul Lowe, he made "Lincoln and Lowe" the franchise's most effective backfield combo ever.

QB: John Hadl. 201 TD passes in 11 seasons makes Hadl one of the most productive passers absent from the Hall of Fame.

WR: John Jefferson: Though he played just three seasons for the Chargers, he had 36 TD catches over that span.

G: Walt Sweeney. A longtime fixture on the Chargers offensive fronts of the 1960s and early '70s, Sweeney was All-Pro nine times.

T: Russ Washington. Despite five Pro Bowls and being the team leader in games played and consecutive starts, Washington was the classic anonymous offensive lineman.

> "You know, the reason Pope John XXIII is so famous is because he recognized the other league." — Head coach Sid Gillman to NFL Commissioner Pete Rozelle in 1963, suggesting an interleague championship game against the NFL champion Bears.

Best Argument

Wide Receiver: Lance Alworth or Charlie Joiner? The first AFL player to be inducted into the Pro Football Hall of Fame, "Bambi" was an amazing combination of speed and sure hands, and was nearly unstoppable. Joiner was with the Oilers and Bengals before settling in with the Chargers, where he enjoyed his best seasons thanks to Dan Fouts and "Air Coryell."

Best Coach

Sid Gillman (1960-69, '71): A Hall of Famer and the father of the modern passing game, Gillman epitomized the AFL's wide-open approach. His Chargers put points on the board, one way or another. During their days in the AFL, Gillman's clubs endured just one losing season. In '71, he stepped down at midseason after a disappointing 4-6 start.

Pressbox

Who to Read...

San Diego Union-Tribune veteran Jerry Magee, currently the newspaper's NFL at-large writer, has covered the Chargers beat for 30 years and remains the most turned-to NFL source in the market. The younger fan, however, is more likely to consider the words of his replacement on the Chargers beat, Jim Trotter, or columnist Nick Canepa, a lifetime resident of San Diego who still has the ticket stub from the first Chargers game played at Balboa Park. Canepa has excellent knowledge of team history, and his current status down in the trenches with the Bolts before, during and after their Super XXIX defeat, makes him the consensus choice for the city's pre-eminent opinion-maker regarding the franchise.

Who to Watch...

For ages, a coaches/Chargers weekly television show has been aired after Monday Night Football games on KGTV–ABC, but the change in networks threw those arrangements into negotiation. When the smoke cleared, KFMB––CBS had landed the program.

Who to Listen To...

Chargers fans are active and opinion-ated, and are West Coast leaders in calling sports-talk radio; just about every San Diego radio station has some type of Chargers radio show. XTRA (690 AM) offered almost wall-to-wall Chargers coverage on game day. However, the station lost its 11-year hold on broadcast rights to the team to KFMB STAR (100.7 FM and 760 AM) starting with the 1998 season. Some wonder if the change has something to do with the outspoken criticism handed down by radio talk hosts Lee "Hacksaw" Hamilton, radio voice of the Chargers, and his station-mates, including the afternoon drive "Loose Cannons." Of course, XTRA got on the map because of the hypercritical and now-nationally syndicated Jim Rome.

> "If I went out there and missed on my first six or seven passes, he'd say, 'Screw it, you've got forty more to go.'" — Dan Fouts on playing for head coach Don Coryell.

per customer for single-game purchases. Tickets may be purchased through Ticketmaster and at the stadium box office.

1998: $99/$55/$39/$34/$25/$20

1994: $22-$35

Public Transportation: San Diego Transit offers Chargers Express bus service from various parts of the county, with single game and season ticket plans available. Call (619) 685-4900 for information.

Parking: The Qualcomm parking lot, touted as the second largest in the NFL, holds 19,000. Spring for the $10.00 reserved parking at the main gate area and around the inner ring of the stadium parking lot. Come early and expect to get out late—there aren't a lot of entrances.

Capacity: 71,000.

Restrooms: 44 men's, 50 women's.

Where to Go . . . in San Diego

Best Bars

Best owner/bouncer. Yes, you may run into the famous part-owner. Yes, **Seau's**, the restaurant, is a typical sports bar. Yes, it's a perfect post-game party spot. *1640 Camino del Rio North, San Diego. (619) 291-7328. Su-Th 11am-10pm, F 11am-12pm, Sa 9:30am-12pm.*

Best blues and suds. Television crews, league-office types, and the occasional visiting player visit **Jimmy Love's** in the Gaslamp Quarter on game weekends. Live bands, a pretty good menu, and a late-night crowd make it a good place for postgame revelry. *672 Fifth Ave. (619) 595-0123. Seven days 5pm-2am.*

Best real bar. If you're tired of all the southern California sunshine, drop in at **Dobson's**, one of the few old-time, woody bars you'll find in this part of the world. *956 Broadway Circle. (619) 231-6771. Seven days 11:30am-"whenever."*

Best place to relax. Hang Ten Brew Pub, formerly Hop's City Brew Pub, offers a casual microbrewery visit for the before- or after-game dinner when visiting the Gaslamp Quarter. Barbecue pizza is a specialty at this favorite hangout of the college crowd. *Seven days 11am daily till close. 310 Fifth Ave. (619) 232-6336.*

Best Restaurants

Best team connection. Long-time NFL executive Rick Smith prefers **Pernicano's** because of its family traditions. George Pernicano has been a minority owner of the team from its

Our Top Story

"Unitas to Lead Chargers"
January 22, 1973
General Manager Harland Svare signed 17-year Colts veteran Johnny Unitas to quarterback for San Diego. Unitas' best days were behind him, however, and injuries forced him to the bench while a third-round draft choice named Dan Fouts took over the offense.

"And In Other News..."
September 25, 1978
Chargers coach Tommy Prothro resigns the same day as a Pacific Southwest Airlines plane crash in San Diego kills more than 100 people, the worst air disaster in U.S. history at the time. Prothro was replaced by Don Coryell. The big news the previous day was the franchise's decision to can their cheerleading squad.

"No Deal."
September 10, 1984
Running back Chuck Muncie is sent back to San Diego by Miami after he fails a drug test. Muncie is suspended by the league for one year.

"We're In!!"
January 15, 1995
Called by one long-time resident the biggest news day in San Diego history, Chargers or otherwise, this is the day the Chargers went to Pittsburgh and beat the Steelers in the AFC Championship, earning a berth in Super Bowl XXIX. More than 70,000 fans packed Jack Murphy Stadium for the welcome home celebration that night.

Ready For Primetime (Monday Night)

December 20, 1982: It was "Air Coryell" at its best as the Chargers, fresh off a stirring 41-37 victory over the defending Super Bowl champion 49ers, hosted the defending AFC champion Bengals, who had stomped them in the cold at Cincinnati in the '81 AFC title game. The San Diego offense rolled up a team-record 661 yards, and Dan Fouts and company completed an impressive sweep. Chargers 50, Bengals 34.

Overall Monday Night: 14-16
Overall Sunday Night: 6-10
Overall Thursday Nights: 1-4

Think About the Weather

September 27, 1970: San Diego has maybe the best climate in mainland America, but it was the site of the only football game nearly called on account of a forest fire. Chargers fans left home this day to see the Raiders despite a wildfire raging across 280,000 acres of dry land in the back country of San Diego County. Individuals were paged over the public address system to leave the stadium to protect their homes, but how could you leave a Raiders game? As the fire came closer, the Chargers caught fire. Down two touchdowns with five minutes left, John Hadl found Jeff Queen and Lance Alworth to tie the score at 27. Daryle Lamonica got the Raiders within field goal range, but George Blanda, under a smoke-covered sky, missed the chip shot and the Chargers pulled out a moral victory with a scoreless overtime. Chargers 27, Raiders 27.

inception. *Several locations including Scripps Ranch, 9988 Scripps Ranch Blvd., San Diego, CA 92131. (619) 271-5250. Su-Th 11am-3pm, 4pm-8pm, F- Sa 11am-3pm, 4pm-9pm. MC,V. $$$*

Best seascapes. While the Continental cuisine at **Mister A's** can be expensive, the views of San Diego Bay make it a good call for out-of-towners looking for that memorable dining experience in downtown San Diego. *2550 Fifth Ave. (619) 234-7951. Lunch, M-F 11am-2:30pm, dinner 5pm-10:30pm, Sa-Su 5:30pm-10:30pm. AE, DIS, MC, V. $$$$$*

Best Mexican. You're close to the border, but if you don't want to make the crossing try a burrito at **El Indio**. Nothing fancy here—eat outside at a picnic table. *3695 India St. (619) 299-0333. Seven days 7am-9pm.*

Best chance of dining with Oprah. George's at the Cove offers another classic choice for your big meal in San Diego. A wide-ranging menu with flash-grilled ahi among the most popular items, George's was voted by the Zagat Survey as most popular restaurant in San Diego. Some fans (you know who you are) may care that George's recipe for chicken, broccoli and black bean soup is in "Oprah's Cooking with Rosie" book. For a more casual meal, there is an upstairs menu which is more modestly priced. *1250 Prospect St., La Jolla. (619) 454-4244. Fine dining (downstairs): M-Th 11:30am-2:30pm, 5:30pm-10pm, F-Sa 11:30am-2:30pm, 5-*

> **did you know?**
> In their 49-26 loss to San Francisco in Super Bowl XXIX, the Chargers might have liked to be on the receiving end of fewer kickoffs. Still, they set a Super Bowl record with 244 yards in kickoff returns.

Fans' notes

On Screen

Despite being a drive from the movie and television capital of the world, the Chargers have never really made a mark on screen aside from the annual NFL Films team video.

Bookshelf

First Down and a Billion: The Funny Business of Pro Football. Gene Klein and David Fisher (St. Martin's Press 1987).

You Gotta See...

▶What could be more appropriate for fans of America's favorite sport than a visit to another country? Though the city of San Diego might not recommend it, a trip across the border into **Tijuana** will ground you. It is advised not to over-imbibe, and do not bring the kids with you. Leave plenty of time for your return across the border, especially if you go Saturday night and try to return to the U.S.A. in time for the game Sunday. Adios, amigos!

▶Safer for the kids than Tijuana, the **Gaslamp Quarter** is San Diego's downtown outdoor restaurant and shopping district, easily accessible by car or public transit, or by foot if you are staying in the relatively small downtown area. **Sea World** and the **San Diego Zoo** are also good for young fans.

▶Or there's **the beach**. Get in your car and head west. Though this is the home of Surfin' USA, don't bother with a board: You'll be shamed off the waves by people who do nothing but surf and have an attitude about it. Stick with beach football.

11pm, Su 5-10pm, $$$$. Ocean Terrace (upstairs): Su-Th 11am-10pm, F-Sa 11am-11pm. AE, DIS, MC, V, $$.

Best Accommodations

Mission Valley Marriott. The closest major hotel to the stadium, this is where 80 percent of the visiting teams headquarter during the season. Shuttles are available, and the hotel is a one-mile walk to the game. *8757 Rio San Diego Dr. (619) 692-3800. $$-$$$*

Holiday Inn Mission Valley Stadium. Also offering shuttles to the stadium and airport, one mile north of the Murph, this Holiday Inn is as close as the MV Marriott but often has more rooms available on game weekends. Full service hotel with restaurant, bar, jacuzzi, etc. Kids stay free and eat free when accompanied by parents in hotel restaurant. *3805 Murphy Canyon Rd. (619) 278-9300, reservations only (800)-666-6996. $$; ask for the special Chargers rate.*

Wyndham Emerald Plaza. The self-proclaimed "Jewel of Downtown San Diego," the Wyndham's green glass structure stands out along the city's riverfront and offers deluxe accommodations with a view within easy access to the Gaslamp Quarter and Horton Plaza shopping mall. *402 W. Broadway. (619) 239-4500, $$$$-$$$$$; call for special package information.*

Worst Team

1975 (2-12): After winning four of their final seven games in 1974, Tommy Prothro's team looked like they had something to build on. But the San Diego offense began '75 in absentia as the Chargers were blanked in three of their first six contests. The season-opening losing streak would reach 11 games before consecutive wins over the Chiefs and Jets, followed by a humbling 47-17 setback to the Bengals.

Team Leaders

Rushing Yards
4,963   Paul Lowe, 1960-67

Passing Yards
43,040   Dan Fouts, 1973-87

Passing Touchdowns
254   Dan Fouts, 1973-87

Receptions
586   Charlie Joiner, 1976-86

Interceptions
42   Gill Byrd, 1983-92

Touchdowns
83   Lance Alworth, 1962-70

Points
766   Rolf Benirschke, 1977-86

Hall of Fame

Lance Alworth   (WR 1978)
Ron Mix   (T 1979)
Johnny Unitas   (QB 1979)
Deacon Jones   (DE 1980)
Sid Gillman   (Coach 1983)
John Mackey   (TE 1992)
Dan Fouts   (QB 1993)
Larry Little   (G 1993)
Kellen Winslow   (TE 1995)
Charlie Joiner   (WR 1996)

Against the Odds

Not many placekickers would be considered "tough guys," but **Rolf Benirschke** (1977-1986) certainly would. Playing through pain for part of 1978 and the early portion of the '79 season, Benirschke was diagnosed with Crohn's Disease (later determined to be ulcerative colitis), a serious gastrointestinal disorder. After converting four of four attempts, he was placed on injured reserve in late September. Two surgeries later, Benirschke returned in 1980 to score 118 points. The model of consistency, he led the Chargers in scoring for five consecutive seasons (1980-84).

While You Were Eating Turkey....

November 26, 1964. The Chargers and Buffalo Bills would get to know each other quite well from 1964-65, playing each other six times--including a pair of meetings in the American Football League title game (both won convincingly by the Bills), as well as consecutive Turkey Day confrontations in 1964 and '65. Earlier this season, the Bolts had been handled at Buffalo, 30-3, but were primed for a rematch. This Thanksgiving Day affair would attract a Balboa Stadium record 34,865 fans, who would unfortunately go home disappointed as the soon-to-be AFL champions edged Sid Gillman's talented club. Bills 27, Chargers 24.
Overall, 2-1-1

San Francisco 49ers

"Maybe they'll name a state after me." — Joe Montana in 1982, after being named MVP of Super Bowl XVI.

The 1981 NFC Championship Game. Just over four minutes left. Dallas 27, San Francisco 21.

When Joe Montana ducked behind center on his own 11-yard line, the 49er faithful prepared for the worst. And why not? Since joining the NFL from the old All America Football Conference in 1950 up through 1980, San Francisco had made the postseason only four times.

In 1957, Joe "The Jet" Perry, "Hurryin'" Hugh McElhenny, Y.A. Tittle, Bob St. Clair, et al, blew a 27-7 lead to the Detroit Lions in a special Western Conference Playoff, losing, 31-27. The next week, the Lions won the NFL title over Cleveland, 59-14.

It took 13 years for the Niners to recover, and when they did in the early '70's, the Dallas Cowboys broke their hearts. In 1970, Dick Nolan's team, quarterbacked by John Brodie, made it to the NFC Championship game, extending their stay at venerable Kezar Stadium for one more afternoon, only to lose to Dallas, 17-10. In 1971, they fell again to the Cowboys just one step away from the Super Bowl, 14-3.

Nineteen seventy-two brought 1957 back with a thud. In their new home, Candlestick Park, the 49ers led Dallas 28-13, in the divisional round, heading into the fourth quarter, only to see Roger Staubach lead an epic comeback to beat them, 30-28.

Their next foray into the playoffs didn't occur until 1981, which leads us back to Joe Montana at his own 11-yard line. What happened in the final four minutes of that NFC title game shook Candlestick

Franchise History

San Francisco Forty-Niners (AAFC) (1946–49)
San Francisco 49ers (NFL) (1950–present)

By the Numbers

(Since 1970)
Regular Season: 261-160-3
Postseason: 23-13
Division Titles: 16
Vs. Division: 107-63-3 (Playoffs: 1-0)
Playoff Appearances: 18
Home: 134-76-2
Away: 127-84-1

(Overall)
Regular Season: 381-288-13
Postseason: 23-14
Playoff Appearances: 19
Home: 203-131-7
Away: 178-157-6

Most Revered Football Figures

Ronnie Lott. The NFL's most dominant defensive back in the 1980s, Lott was the closest thing the 49ers defense had to Joe Montana.

Joe Montana. A third-round draft pick out of Notre Dame, Montana played in four Super Bowls and never lost one, winning Super Bowl MVP an unprecedented three times.

Jerry Rice. When Rice is done playing the game, he will have put the finishing touches on a career that should go down as the best in NFL history, certainly for a wide receiver, and perhaps for any athlete on either side of the ball.

Bill Walsh. The team he built in the 1980's was one of the most complete teams in NFL history.

Team Leaders

Rushing Yards
7,344   Joe Perry, 1950-60, 1963
Passing Yards
35,124   Joe Montana, 1979-92
Passing Touchdowns
244   Joe Montana, 1979-92
Receptions
1,057   Jerry Rice, 1985-present
Interceptions
51   Ronnie Lott, 1981-90
Touchdowns
166   Jerry Rice, 1985-present
Points
1,000   Jerry Rice, 1985-present

> **did you know?**
> For all of their Super Bowl success (5-0), the Niners are the only team to have twice been eliminated in the playoffs by the same team three straight years: the Cowboys (1970-72) and the Packers (1995-97).

a full eight years before the infamous earthquake, and rewrote football history as well.

Officially, it reads "Clark, 6 yard pass from Montana," but it will forever be known as "The Catch." San Francisco's 28-27 triumph excorcised the Dallas demons from a decade before, and erased three decades of franchise futility.

The victory opened the door for one of the most prolific two-decade runs in all of sports, let alone pro football. Oh, by the way, it also began the legend of Joe Montana.

The 49ers completed their Cinderella 1981 season by beating Cincinnati, 26-21, in Super Bowl XVI, a far cry from new owner Eddie Debartolo, Jr.'s second season in 1978, when they went 2-14, and a far cry from Bill Walsh's first season in 1979, when the Niners also went 2-14.

The rest, as they say, is history. Five Super Bowls in a 14-year span from 1981 to 1994. In 1984, the 49ers went 15-1, then cruised through the postseason, including a resounding 38-16 win over Dan Marino, Don Shula and the 14-2 Miami Dolphins in Super Bowl XIX.

In 1988, Walsh's coaching career ended with a drum roll, and Montana's legend grew geometrically when he hit John Taylor in the final minute from 10 yards out to beat Cincinnati in Super Bowl XXIII, 20-16.

> "Steve, a pleasure meeting you, and oh, by the way, nice shoes you're wearing."
> — Joe Montana upon meeting Steve Young, who had borrowed a pair of Montana's shoes for a workout.

In case Jerry Rice's 22 touchdown receptions in 1987 weren't convincing enough, his 11 catches for 215 yards and MVP performance in Super Bowl XXXII put him into the wide receiving stratosphere.

In 1989, with George Seifert at the helm, the 49ers didn't miss a beat, finishing a 14-2 season and skating through the playoffs with a 55-10 lambasting of the Denver Broncos in Super Bowl XXIV behind five Montana TD passes, three to Rice.

In 1994, it was Steve Young shedding Montana's lurking shadow in a huge way as the 49ers blasted San Diego, 49-26. Young threw six TD passes, three to Rice.

Starting in 1983, the 49ers have won 10 or more games 15 straight seasons. Montana is regarded by many as the greatest quarterback to ever play in the NFL, and while that might be debatable, four for four in Super Bowls is not.

Walsh already is in the Pro Football Hall of Fame, as 20 years after he began, his "West Coast Offense" with its newer wrinkles is still the most vaunted attack in the game.

Ronnie Lott will join Walsh in Canton as one of the best to ever play cornerback or safety.

When Roger Craig retired at running back, he was in the all-time top 20 for both rushing and receiving.

Young owns the highest ranking for a passer in NFL history, and has won six individual passing titles. As for Jerry Rice, suffice it to say he is the NFL's greatest receiver of all-time, despite missing almost the entire 1997 season with knee and leg injuries. His 1057 catches are over 100 more than anyone else, his 16,445 yards are over 2000 yards more than anyone else, and his 166 total touchdowns are 21 more than anyone else.

Nineteen ninety eight will be the second

Rivalries

Even though the 49ers lead the overall series (14-12-1), no team in the NFL has caused them more angst than the Dallas **Cowboys**. Dallas has beaten San Francisco five times in the teams' seven playoff encounters, including six NFC Championship games over three decades. The Niners have taken 10 of the 14 meetings since 1981, but two of those losses were in the conference title tilt. The Los Angeles (now St. Louis) **Rams** (47-48-2) provided the 49ers closest rivalry for many years. After 97 games the series remains nearly dead even, despite 15 consecutive victories for the 49ers dating to 1990. The Rams held the upper hand over the years at the L.A. Coliseum, with a 21-9-1 record in 31 meetings there. One would expect a decent rivalry between the **Raiders** (3-5) and 49ers, but because of rare head-to-head meetings and a markedly different fan base, no real sense of competition between the two teams has emerged during the Raiders' two tenures in the Bay area. Also cooling the rivalry is the fact the Raiders' success came in the 1960's and 70's, while the 49ers' glory years began in 1981 and continue to the present day.

did you know?

In five Super Bowls, no 49ers quarterback (including reserves) has ever thrown an interception, while starters Joe Montana and Steve Young have combined for 17 TD passes.

The "I Was There" Game

January 10, 1982: The greatest moment in 49ers history didn't come in a Super Bowl, but this victory certainly announced the arrival of the "Team of the '80s." Despite six turnovers, the Niners found themselves down by just six with 4:54 to play and 89 yards in front of them. "The Catch" in the back of the end zone of a Joe Montana throw-away pass by a reaching Dwight Clark gave the 49ers the dramatic come-from-behind, 28-27, win over the Dallas Cowboys in the NFC Championship game, erased a history of shortcomings for the franchise, and propelled the 49ers into the Super Bowl.

The Paper Bag Game

December 22, 1957: Though there may have been darker games involving more talented teams, the early 49ers consistently demonstrated a failure to "get over the hump" as a competitive franchise. In 1957, a 49ers team with a penchant for the dramatic, led by Y.A. Tittle's "alley-oop" passing to rookie halfback R.C. Owens, made the playoffs for the first time as a member of the NFL. They led the Detroit Lions, 27-7, in the third quarter, but eventually lost, 31-27, at Kezar Stadium.

Great Names

Forrest Blue (C, 1968-74)
Bob Hoskins (T-G, 1969-75)
Israeli Ifeanyi (LB, 1996)
Woody Peoples (G, 1968-77)
Iheanyi Uwaezuoke (WR, 1996-present)

year under head coach Steve Mariucci and once again, San Francisco will be among the top Super Bowl contenders. To have stayed at or near the top for this long in this day and age of the NFL with rule changes making it harder to do so every year, is testimony to a unique organization that can focus on both the daily and annual nuts and bolts while exhibiting X-ray vision into the future. Nobody would have believed this was possible after looking at the 49ers during their first 30 years.

—Chris Berman

Candlestick Park/ 3Com Park

Though original ground breaking took place in 1958, Candlestick Park was not expanded to house the NFL's 49ers until 1969. The facility finally entertained its first NFL regular season game in 1971. Expanded twice more to the current capacity of 70,207, the renamed 3Com Park is one of the most cramped facilities in all of pro football. While sight lines vary inside the stadium, the show has been good enough for the last two decades to offset the lack of creature comforts throughout the park.

This might explain why you could walk up and buy a ticket on just about any game day until about 1981. Today, the 49ers are riding a string of 152 consecutive sellouts which began on October 11, 1981 (pre-, regular and post-season) and have a season ticket waiting list estimated between 15,000 and 20,000 names long. Why? The team is great, the weather, despite outside perception, is often mild and comfortable on Sunday afternoons, and as for the stadium — well, the wine and cheese crowd the 49ers are famous for attracting can live with it.

Though the 49ers and the DeBartolo fam-

Best of the 49ers

Best Team

1989 (17-2): After their Super Bowl XXIII victory and the subsequent retirement of Bill Walsh, some 49ers felt "The Genius" got too much credit for the team's success. Led by new coach George Seifert, the Niners proved that it wasn't all Walsh's doing by dominating the league in 1989. They lost just two games by a total of five points, while demolishing the Vikings, Rams and Broncos in the postseason by a combined 100 points.

Greatest Players by Position

Pos:	Player
QB:	Joe Montana
RB:	Roger Craig
WR:	Jerry Rice
TE:	Ted Kwalick
OL:	Leo Nomellini
DL:	Cedrick Hardman
LB:	Charles Haley
DB:	Ronnie Lott
P/K:	Ray Wersching
ST:	John Taylor

And Don't Forget...

T: Bob St. Clair. Five-time all-star who also played on goal line defense and special teams, blocking 10 field goals during his career.

QB: Steve Young. Six NFL passing titles in seven years (1991-97) and one of the most gifted athletes to ever play the position.

WR: Dwight Clark. Clutch receiver who made the most of his abilities. Not bad for a 10th-round pick from Clemson.

CB: Jimmy Johnson. Excelled in man-to-man coverage with 47 interceptions. He also saw some action as a wide receiver early in his career.

RB: Hugh McElhenny. Big-play threat from anywhere on the field, still ranks amongst the club's all-time leaders in total yards.

QB: John Brodie. Often lost in the shadow of his successors, he led the 49ers during the early stages of their rivalry with Dallas in the '60s and '70s.

Best Argument

Running Back: Roger Craig or Joe Perry? A big part of three of the 49ers' Super Bowl title teams, Craig, the former fullback, became "Mr. Versatility" and remains the only player in league history to total both 1,000 yards rushing and 1,000 yards receiving in the same season (1985). Perry was a big-play back dating back to the Niners' days in the AAFC, and was the first NFL player to run for 1,000 yards in consecutive seasons.

Swami Sez:

It's been almost 20 years since the 49ers weren't a legitimate Super Bowl contender. Nobody else could even dream of making that claim.

Best Coach

Bill Walsh (1979-88): This celebrated offensive mind inherited a team that finished 2-14 in 1978 and wound up equaling that mark in Walsh's first year. The 49ers tripled their win total in 1980 — including a 38-35 OT win over the Saints which featured what was then the greatest comeback (28 points) in regular-season annals. The seeds were planted, and Walsh won three Super Bowls in the next eight years.

Pressbox

Who to Read...

The area papers treat the 49ers with front page respect. Art Spander, long-time Bay area resident and columnist, recently jumped ship from the *San Fransisco Chronicle* to the *Oakland Tribune*. For every other imaginable speck of 49ers news, consult the *Chronicle* and the *Examiner*, which go very heavy on the Niners. Beat writers Ira Miller of the *Chronicle* and John Crumpacker of the *San Francisco Examiner* are thorough and witty, as are the myriad of other columnists available.

> "Good liquor and a big sweat relax me. I'm a guy under a good deal of tension." — Tackle Bob St. Clair, nicknamed "The Geek".

Who to Watch...

Television station KPIX–CBS broadcasts pre-season, non-network games. KRON–NBC offers the popular "Sports Final" on Sunday nights hosted by Gary Radnich, and KTVU–FOX has a weekly pre-game show with Mark Ibanez and a preview show with former Niner Harris Barton on Sunday nights. Ken Norton Jr. has a show on KNTV–ABC out of San Jose on Monday nights.

Who to Listen To...

KGO-AM (810 AM) is the flagship station for a 33-station radio network that reaches south to Los Angeles; east to Boise, Idaho; north to Fairbanks, Alaska and west to Hilo, Hawaii. Joe Starkey is the play-by-play voice for the 49ers on radio, with Gary Plummer doing color. Coach Steve Mariucci will have his own show Wednesday nights on KGO. Several of the San Francisco stations have featured 49ers shows hosted by players; the list is always changing. Listeners on both sides of the Bay tune into Gary Radnich on KNBR (680AM) from noon to 3, which is also simulcast on Bay TV Cable, and for quarterback Steve Young's show.

---

ily trumpeted the approval of a new stadium at Candlestick Point to be built by the year 2000, politics have put the project on frequent hold, and no ground has been broken. Despite being one of the most isolated facilities in all of the NFL, Candlestick/3Com draws on fans from all directions geographically. Tailgating is common and encouraged, although you have to get a parking space first to enjoy it.

While You Were Eating Turkey....

The John Brodie-led 49ers headed into Dallas looking to avenge a 14-3 loss in the 1971 NFC Championship game. And avenge they did, walloping the Cowboys, 31-10, and handing them their first home loss of the season. The Niners went on to win their division and host the Cowboys in the first round of the playoffs, where a quarterback named Staubach came off the bench to help eliminate San Francisco, 30-28.
Overall, 3-0

The Bottom Line on 3Com Park

Address: San Francisco, CA 94124.

Tickets: With games perpetually sold out, tickets are hard to come by. For information, call (415) 468-2249.

1998: $50

1994: $39.75

Public Transportation: Bay Area Rapid Transit (BART) provides shuttles to the stadium from various rail stops in the region. For more information, call (415) 992-2278.

Parking: There is very little parking at 3Com park, with room for only 7,000 cars and 300 buses. It costs $20 a game, but don't worry; it's all taken. The Park is surrounded with other lots, though, so if you must drive, you should be able to find a spot.

Capacity: 70,207.

Restrooms: 70.

Where To Go . . . in San Francisco

Best Bars

Best Irish bar in the financial district. One of the best-known pubs in the city, **Harrington's**, is a weathered old saloon and an island of tradition in a more yup-scale neighborhood. *245 Front St. (415) 392-7595. M-Tu 9am-10:30pm, W-Th 9am-11pm, F 9am-midnight, Sa 11am-10pm.*

Best neighborhood dive. Gino and Carlo, a very local kind of place in San Francisco's North Beach, provides ample opportunity to embroil yourself in a sports-related argument with other patrons. *548 Green St. (415) 421-0896. 7 days 6am-2am.*

Our Top Story

"World Champs"

January 24, 1982

The 49ers made up for a troubled team history by beating Cincinnati in Super Bowl XVI. Ray Wersching kicked four field goals, and San Francisco jumped out to a 20-0 halftime lead as the Niners held off Ken Anderson and the Bengals, 26-21. It was the first of four 49er Super Bowl victories in the decade.

> **did you know?**
> In 1953, fullback Joe Perry rushed for 1,018 yards. For his trouble, he was awarded a bonus of $5,090, or $5 per yard.

"Joe Hangs 'Em Up"

April 18, 1995

Joe Montana's retirement from the Kansas City Chiefs was an unofficial holiday for the City of San Francisco. Thousands packed a downtown plaza to honor the return of their hero. It was a day that rivaled the Super Bowl parades in that it gave the 49ers faithful the chance to honor Montana in a way they could not after the trade to Kansas City.

"DeBartolo Steps Down"

December 2, 1997

Indicted in an investigation into the business dealings surrounding the state of Louisiana's last available gaming license, Eddie DeBartolo, the 49ers' well-known and popular owner, gave up his role in the organization.

Ready For Primetime (Monday Night)

December 11, 1989: John Robinson's club had already defeated the 49ers in San Francisco and owned a 27-10 lead in the fourth quarter in this rematch at Anaheim. Joe Montana led his team to 20 points in the final 10 minutes, but the star of the evening was WR John Taylor, who by night's end had turned a pair of short receptions into touchdowns of 92 and 95 yards — an unprecedented feat (49ers 30, Rams 27). In 1997, the 49ers beat the eventual Super Bowl Champion Broncos at 3Com Park, 34-17, in a game which included the retirement of Joe Montana's jersey and the return of Jerry Rice from knee surgery. Rice caught a TD pass, reaching the 1,000 point plateau, and subsequently broke his kneecap and was lost for the balance of the season.

Overall Monday night: 30-18
Overall Thursday night: 2-0
Overall Sunday night: 8-3

Hall of Fame

Leo Nomellini	(DT 1969)
Joe Perry	(FB 1969)
Hugh McElhenny	(HB 1970)
Y.A. Tittle	(QB 1971)
O.J. Simpson	(RB 1985)
John Henry Johnson	(FB 1987)
Bob St. Clair	(T 1990)
Bill Walsh	(Coach 1993)
Jimmy Johnson	(DB 1994)

did you know?

During the 1990s, the Niners' ground game has struggled, but back in 1948, it was unstoppable. Behind the running of Johnny Strzykalski and Joe Perry, San Francisco rushed for 3,663 yards that year, an average of 262 per game, and scored 35 touchdowns on the ground.

Best blues with brews. Dating back to the early part of the century, **The San Francisco Brewing Company** abounds in old-time ambience. Live jazz and blues performances complement the house brews. *155 Columbus Ave. (415) 434-3344. S-Th 11:30am-1:30am, F-Sa noon-1:30am.*

Best Restaurants

Best steaks. This ain't no Philly cheese steak at **Harris'**. Dry-aged on the premises, the steaks at this luxurious Van Ness Avenue restaurant are the city's best. The martinis aren't bad, either. *2100 Van Ness Ave. (415) 673-1888. M-F 5:30-close, S-Su 5-close. All major credit cards. Reservations recommended. $$$.*

Best all-night eats. Open all day and all night, this Castro-Upper Market diner serves up a big menu which includes good burgers and breakfasts. **Sparky's Diner.** *242 Church St. (415) 621-6001. 24 hours. AE, D, MC, V. $.*

Best Haight fest. So you came to San Francisco to get a glimpse of the '60s Haight-Ashbury scene? You're about 30 years too late. The **Sacred Grounds Cafe**, which keeps the faith with poetry readings and the work of local artists, will have to do for now. *2095 Hayes St. (415) 387-3859. 7am-10pm. No credit cards. $.*

Best burger. In fact, the burgers are so good here they named the place **Hamburger Mary's**. Goofy flea market decor, big juicy burgers, live music. *1582 Folsom St. (415) 626-5767. DC not accepted. $.*

Fans' notes

On Screen

The 4,008 yards and 27 touchdown receptions recorded by 49er Bernie Casey may not rival Jerry Rice's numbers, but does Rice have a filmography to compare? **Cleopatra Jones, Never Say Never Again, Revenge of the Nerds** and **I'm Gonna Get You Sucka** (also starring the great Jim Brown) are among Casey's acting credits. Southpaw quarterback Frankie Albert, who joined the 49ers when they were still part of the All America Football Conference (AAFC), didn't stretch his acting skills as much when he played himself in the 1942 film **Spirit of Stanford**. More recent San Francisco quarterbacks have earned their fair share of TV ad time: Concussion-prone Steve Young hawks pain relievers, and Joe Montana left his number 16 on the hanger for a series of underwear ads. To see what happened when Montana put that jersey on, check out **The Joe Montana Story** from NFL Films video. And for the truly devoted, the appeal of NFL Films releases like team history **Pure Gold: San Francisco's Fabulous 49ers** and **San Francisco 49ers: Super Bowl XXIX Champions** is self-evident.

Bookshelf

America Has A Better Team: The Story of Bill Walsh and San Francisco's World Champion 49ers. Glenn Dickey (PGW 1982).
Forty-Niners: 49th Anniversary Collector's Edition. Joseph Hession, (Foghorn Press 1995).
Rice. Jerry Rice and Michael Silver (St. Martin's Press 1996). A photo-laden autobiography of the best wide receiver in NFL history.
The San Francisco 49ers, The First Fifty Years. Glenn Dickey (Andrews and McMeel 1995).
Total Impact: Straight Talk From Football's Hardest Hitter. Ronnie Lott and Jill Lieber (Doubleday 1991).
All the Rage: The Life of an NFL Renegade. Charles Haley and Joe Layden (Andrews and McMeel 1997). The often controversial former Cowboy and Niner tells his side of the story.
Audibles, My Life In Football. Joe Montana and Bob Raismann (William Morrow 1986).
Building a Champion, On Football and the Making of the 49ers. Bill Walsh and Glenn Dickey (St. Martin's Press 1992). Football philosophy and insider stuff from Walsh.

You Gotta See...

▶Easily accessible by trolley and cab is the city itself; gaze across the **Golden Gate Bridge**, reminisce at **Haight-Ashbury**, play tourist at **Alcatraz**, stroll **Chinatown** and wind down **Lombard Street**, the world's "crookedest" street.
▶Located not far from the Wharves, **The San Francisco Museum of Contemporary Art** is first class and features an outstanding casual restaurant. And bring money: Even tough guys like to dance in San Francisco's **downtown shopping district.**
▶Once out of the city you'll find some of the United States' most beautiful driving country as you visit **wine country, Muir Redwood Forest, Carmel, Monterey, Sausalito, Tiburon** and more.

Think About the Weather

Jan. 8, 1989: Earlier in the season on a Monday night at Soldier Field, the Chicago defense came up big in a 10-9 triumph over the Niners. This title game rematch featured a minus-26 wind chill factor and a game time temperature of 17 degrees. You would think the denizens of the West Coast would have had their problems, but it was the Bears offense that never came in from the cold (49ers 28, Bears 3). Back at home, 3Com can be a veritable quagmire for months at a time, due to the fog and rain of the Bay area in the late fall and the fact that the stadium's high rims do not allow for the top layers of dirt to dry out. In 1982, "The Catch" game was played on an atrocious surface, which obviously did not hamper the 49ers. Soggy sod will remain the late season norm as long as the 49ers play at 3Com Park, and will remain an advantage for the team used to playing on it.

Worst Team

1978 (2-12): In 1976, the 49ers looked like a team on the rise, finishing a respectable 8-6 but losing tough games to some good teams. Two years later, the franchise fell upon hard times as head coaches Pete McCulley (1-8) — fired after nine games — and Fred O'Connor (1-6) struggled through a forgettable season which saw the club set a dubious NFL record by turning over the football 63 times.

Best Accommodations

Days Inn. Basic accommodations in downtown San Francisco; indoor parking and a continental breakfast. *895 Geary St. (415) 441-8220. $$*

The Phoenix. An outrageously popular, offbeat hotel known for the entertainment industry guests oft seen poolside. A surprisingly good deal, all things considered. *601 Eddy St. (415) 776-1380, 800-248-9466. $$*

Sheraton Fisherman's Wharf. A simple, pet-friendly hotel with a heated outdoor pool, strategically situated by San Francisco's Fisherman's Wharf tourist mecca. Convenient location, if not the biggest bang for your buck. *2500 Mason St. (415) 362-5500, (800) 325-3535. $$$-$$$$*

Mark Hopkins Intercontinental. Views, views, views from this luxury hotel with a fashionable Nob Hill address. Featuring the "Top of the Mark" restaurant and cocktail lounge, offering a full view of the evening skyline. *1 Nob Hill. (415) 392-3434, (800) 327-0200. $$$$$*

Against the Odds

The team's drafting of **Dwight Clark** (1979-87) in 1979 drew far more yawns than cheers. Tenth-round picks usually elicit such a response. But it didn't take long for Clark to move from unknown to well known. He retired in 1987 as the 49ers' all-time leading receiver (later passed by Jerry Rice) with 506 catches for 6,750 yards and 48 touchdowns. His most memorable grab — "The Catch" — will be forever linked with the greatest moment in team history, as it sent the '81 Niners to their first Super Bowl. Clark continues to contibute to the 49ers' glory as the team's vice president/director of football operations.

Seattle
Seahawks

"...I know that I am responsible for some of the woes that they have felt there in Seattle."— Brian Bosworth

The Seattle Seahawks have been a tale of three ownerships. In 1974, the Nordstrom family of department store fame stepped forward to provide the final financial clout necessary for the $16 million franchise fee and the team's 1976 debut. It took seven years for the Nordstroms to find the right management team, but the Seahawks didn't lack for excitement while they waited. Quarterback Jim Zorn fired pass after pass to sure-handed Hall-of-Famer Steve Largent, and head coach Jack Patera filled his game plans with trick plays and some of the most aggressive special teams calls of the past three decades. On defense, tackle Manu Tuiasosopo and veterans Mike Curtis and Carl Eller held the line. By their third and fourth seasons, the Seahawks were 9-7 overachievers who thrilled the nation as the ultimate underdog.

Franchise History

Seattle Seahawks
(1976–present)

Three consecutive losing seasons to start the 1980s cost Patera his job but allowed the Nordstroms to find the perfect front office combo. Mike McCormack, the Hall of Fame offensive lineman for the Cleveland Browns, filled in as interim coach in 1982 and became team president the next season. McCormack hired Chuck Knox, a master of franchise turnarounds. The Seahawks were no longer an expansion team—they were contenders. With the Nordstroms pouring profits back into the team for personnel, McCormack and Knox had the Seahawks in the 1983 AFC title game, where they were defeated by the Los Angeles Raiders, 30-14. Running back Curt Warner, quarterbacks Zorn and Dave Krieg, and Steve Largent formed an explosive offensive unit and

By the Numbers

(Overall)

Regular Season: 156-184-0
Postseason: 3-4
Division Titles: 1
Vs. Division: 66-96 (Playoffs: 2-1)
Playoff Appearances: 4
Home: 91-80
Away: 65-104

despite the disappointing performance of highly touted linebacker Brian Bosworth, the Seahawks kept winning. But times started changing in 1988 when the Nordstroms, concentrating on the nationwide expansion of their stores, sold the team to California real-estate developer Ken Behring.

Behring turned a success story into a

Most Revered Football Figures

Steve Largent. Largent was never the most athletically gifted player, but he never failed to get the most out of what he had. He was voted NFL Man of the Year in 1988 and is a member of the Seahawks "Ring of Honor."

Chuck Knox. Head coach from 1983 until 1991. The team realized its best and most consistent success with Knox, compiling an 80-63 record, three wild card spots, one division title and an appearance in the 1983 AFC championship game.

Jim Zorn. The Seahawks picked him off the NFL's scrap heap, and the lefty quarterback helped lift his team over .500 in just their third season. In 1978, Zorn led the league in passing yardage, attempts and completions.

Joe Nash. He made just one Pro Bowl (1984 season), but his 15 years of service at defensive tackle made him the eternal Seahawk.

Rivalries

People in Seattle love to hate John Elway and the Denver **Broncos**. Seattlelites have had John Elway as a thorn in their side since he tortured the beloved University of Washington during his college years. The Seahawks hold a mark of just 16-26 against the Broncos, although they did beat Denver in the 1983 playoffs. There is animosity among the Seahawk faithful for the **Raiders**, against whom Seattle is 20-22. Raider fans always turn out in force. Though the teams are bitter AFC West rivals, this rivalry is definitely even more rabid between the fans.

disaster. In 1989, he fired McCormack, replacing him with first-time general manager Tom Flores. Because Flores detested free agency, the Seahawks watched their talent base dwindle. Starved for talent, Knox couldn't maintain his winning touch. Fans became frustrated. A franchise which had kept a 62,000 season ticket base and a waiting list of 30,000 more under the Nordstroms couldn't fill the Kingdome anymore, even with players such as Cortez Kennedy, Derrick Fenner and Brian Blades. Flores replaced Knox as head coach in 1992, but that only made things worse. The Seahawks didn't have a winning season during the eight Behring years,

did you know?

The first jersey ever retired by the Seahawks was #12 In honor of "The Fans." It happened on December 15, 1984 and the jersey was presented to Mr. & Mrs. Randy Ford of Tukwila, Washington, who originated the idea. To date, the only other retired number is Steve Largent's number 80.

and the half-filled Kingdome encouraged him to decide to move the franchise to Anaheim in the winter of 1996.

That's when Paul Allen came to the rescue. Co-founder of Seattle area-based Microsoft, Allen saved the day in 1996 when he exercised an option to buy the Seahawks for the then-staggering price of $200 million. Under Allen, money isn't a problem. On the first day of free agency in 1997, Allen wrote a $7 million check to lure Pittsburgh Steelers linebacker Chad Brown to town. Former University of Washington quarterback Warren Moon arrived in 1997, throwing for a club-record 3,678 yards and 25 touchdowns in the exciting passing offense of head coach Dennis Erickson. On the horizon is a new state-of-the-art stadium at the site of the Kingdome, to be built by the year 2002. The fans are starting to come back in out of the Seattle rain, eager to get charged up by something other than coffee.

—John Clayton

Seattle Kingdome

The beginning of the end for the Kingdome came in 1994. While the Mariners and Seahawks pressed for a new or refurbished stadium, a new problem arose, or, rather, fell into sight. On July 19 ceiling tiles in the Kingdome came crashing down into several empty seating sections hours before a Mariners baseball game. The damage was judged to be severe enough that the remainder of the Mariners' home games were relocated and the Seahawks moved their preseason games to University of Washington's Husky Stadium. Roof repairs that were initially estimated at $4 million eventually cost over $50 million. There is only one more season of football left for the Kingdome — starting in 1999, the Seahawks are scheduled to play in Husky Stadium until their new open-air facility is built on the site of the Kingdome. The Kingdome is scheduled to be demolished once the new Mariners ballpark opens in summer of 1999. As for the football experience at the Kingdome, it won't be missed.

> **did you know?**
>
> The Seahawks' first game was a 30-24 loss to the Cardinals in 1976. Excluding recent additions (Panthers, Jaguars and Ravens), the Cards are the only team in the NFL they've failed to beat through 1997 (0-5).

> "As a rookie in the NFL, it's like you play the game with blinders on ... It's the same way in Congress." Steve Largent, who joined the House of Representatives in 1994.

The "I Was There" Game

December 31, 1983: Chuck Knox's surprising 'Hawks had just pasted the Broncos, 31-7, in the Wild Card Game at the Kingdome, but facing red-hot rookie QB Dan Marino and the Dolphins in the AFC Divisional Playoffs at the Orange Bowl figured to be a different story. But Seattle rallied for 10 points in the final two minutes as Seahawks' rookie Curt Warner stole the headlines, rushing for 113 yards and two scores. Seahawks 27, Dolphins 20.

The Paper Bag Game

August 31, 1997: The New York Jets matched their 1996 victory total with a stunning 41-3 road victory in their first game of 1997. Paul Allen had just purchased the team, gone out and brought in a lot of top-line free agents on defense and expectations were high. Neil O'Donnell hit 18 of 25 passes for 270 yards and threw a career-high five touchdown passes, while running back Adrian Murrell ran for 131 yards. Seahawk fans were stunned. Jets 41, Seahawks 3.

Great Names

Sam Adams (DT, 1994-present)
Lou Brock (CB, 1988)
Nesby Glasgow (S, 1988-92)
Andy Heck (T/G, 1989-93)
Ron Howard (TE, 1976-78)
Ed Marinaro (FB, 1977)
Vic Minor (S, 1980-81)
Mack Strong (FB, 1994-)

Our Top Story

"The Blessed Event"
August 23, 1975
Professional football had finally come to Seattle. Fans immediately embraced the club—after only three weeks, the team suspended sales of season tickets when order totals reached 59,000.

"'Hawks Flying South?"
February 2, 1996
Seahawks owner Ken Behring announces his intention to move the team to Southern California.

"Kingdoom"
June 30, 1997
With the vote to demolish the Kingdome and build a new open-air football stadium having passed, Paul Allen exercises his option to buy the Seattle Seahawks and keep professional football in Seattle.

"The Darkest Day"
January 9, 1998
Seattle Seahawks running back Lamar Smith pleaded guilty to vehicular assault, saying he made "a terrible decision" by drinking and driving before a 1994 car crash that left teammate Mike Frier paralyzed. Smith later signed with the New Orleans Saints.

did you know?
Never has a team had a worse day offensively than did the Seahawks on November 4, 1979. The fourth-year franchise set an NFL-record with minus 7 total yards in a 24-0 loss to the Rams.

The food service in the Kingdome is poor. There is nothing beyond the standard hot dog, pretzel, nachos and popcorn. You are allowed to bring food in from the outside, so plan accordingly. Tailgating is not allowed on the streets and in the parking lots. But the team puts on a tailgater in the convention center south of the Kingdome with various sponsors starting three hours before kickoff each game day. You get it all — grub, dancing girls, live bands, celebrities, etc.

Swami Sez:
Watters in the rain...if it doesn't work, Seattle will be all wet.

Even if the Kingdome is no Lambeau Field, you do get some local flavor out in the stands. There's a peanut vendor whose behind-the-back tosses traverse seating sections with deadly accuracy, a chubby guy in overalls who goes from section to section starting cheers and The Wave, and a guy with his face painted blue and green with a flapping bird on his head — he makes the stadium video screen every game. If the score is close people stay. If you get to the fourth quarter and there's a 10-point spread either way, prepare for a mass exodus. These days, you can't imagine how important it is to be a Seahawk fan AND beat game traffic.

The Bottom Line on Seattle Kingdome
Address: 201 South King St., Seattle, WA 98104.

Best of the Seahawks

Best Team

1984 (13-5): While the 'Hawks' lone division title came in 1988, Chuck Knox had fielded a more imposing team four years earlier. Despite losing RB Curt Warner to a season-ending knee injury in Week 1, QB Dave Krieg and WRs Steve Largent and Daryl Turner took up the slack, and they were aided by an opportunistic defense. Still, the Seahawks lost the AFC West title by falling at home to the Broncos in the season finale.

Greatest Players by Position

Pos:	Player
QB:	Dave Krieg
RB:	Curt Warner
WR:	Steve Largent
TE:	Mike Tice
OL:	Bryan Millard
DL:	Cortez Kennedy
LB:	Fredd Young
DB:	Kenny Easley
P/K:	Norm Johnson
ST:	Rufus Porter

And Don't Forget...

DE: Jacob Green. One of the more underrated pass-rushers of the '80s, he remains the team's all-time sack leader.
RB: Chris Warren. A kick returner early in his career, the former fourth-round pick from Ferrum has exceeded expectations.
FB: John L. Williams. One of the league's best blocking backs during his career and deadly as a receiver, especially on screens.
DB: Dave Brown. An original Seahawk, thanks to the '76 expansion draft and the team's all-time interception leader (50).

DB: Eugene Robinson. One of the most opportunistic defenders in team history (56 takeaways in 11 seasons).

Best Argument

Quarterback: Dave Krieg or Jim Zorn? A free agent from Milton College, Krieg is now one of the NFL's noted journeyman quarterbacks, but Seattle saw him lead the 'Hawks to their only four playoff appearances. Southpaw Zorn brought excitement to the expansion Seahawks, and led the club to back-to-back 9-7 finishes in their third and fourth campaigns, respectively.

> "It rips away at the very being of yourself. I don't know how to put it. I wish I was a poet."
> — Christian Fauria, on the losing habits of a talent-laden Seahawks team in 1997.

Best Coach

Chuck Knox (1983-91): After successful stints with the Rams and Bills, Knox took his celebrated act to the great Northwest and led the 'Hawks to the AFC title game in his first season, the team's only division title in '88 and all four of the team's playoff berths. In '90, the team opened 0-3 but rallied for a 9-7 finish. Expectations were high in '91, and a 7-9 mark ended the Knox Era in Seattle.

Pressbox

Who to Read...

The Seattle Times and Seattle Post-Intelligencer both offer in-depth coverage of the Seahawks. Look for Steve Kelley and Glenn Nelson in the Times and Art Thiel and Laura Vescey in the PI. Clare Farnsworth's "Seahawks Notebook" column in the PI is a must. On Sundays the Times and the PI combine to put out one paper. All columnists and writers for both newspapers are included in the Sunday (and gameday) editions of the Sports page.

Who to Watch...

On television, tune in to KIRO–CBS, a popular favorite of the older and established crowd, where Tony Ventrella is the sports anchor. KIRO is usually the best source for breaking Seahawk news because KIRO radio is the Seahawks' flagship station. Sports anchor Paul Silvi on KING–NBC is a favorite among younger adults. Northwest Cable News is a 24-hour regional news channel with sports updates every hour. This station hosts a live broadcast with head coach Dennis Erickson every Tuesday evening throughout the sea-

son. KOMO–ABC and KCPQ–FOX also cover the local sports scene.

Who to Listen To...

KJR (950 AM) in Seattle has some of the best sports radio programming and personalities you'll find anywhere, and Seattle sports fans are always tuned in. You've got Mitch Levy (Mitch In The Morning) and Jeff Aaron (Mr. Trivia) in the AM, New York Vinnie during lunchtime, Dave Grosby (The Groz) in the afternoon, Mike Gastineau (The Gas-man) in the late afternoon and Dave Mahler (Softy) in the evening. The station has developed a rabid, educated sports community in Seattle. KIRO (710 AM) is the flagship station of the Seahawks and Mariners. Steve Thomas handles play-by-play and Steve Raible does color. Ron Callan and Dori Monson do the Seahawk pre- and post-game coverage on game day, and Callan also does the sports segments on the daily morning radio show. Weeknights from 7 to 9, KIRO airs "Rudman and Thiel on Sports," a sports talk show featuring Art Thiel and Steve Rudman.

Tickets: Seahawks tickets are easily purchased by calling the (888) NFL-HAWK number. There is no waiting period, and the process is simple. The Seahawks will now have slightly over 10,000 seats at the lowest price, but the problem is that they're on the third level in the end zone.

1998: $38/$22/$10

1994: $38/$32/$28/$19

Public transportation: The Kingdome is a focal point of downtown Seattle, so there are many ways of getting there without a car. During the season, a shuttle makes stops along Fourth and Second streets every 10 minutes to and from the Kingdome, and so do approximately 50 bus lines that pass within a few blocks. Call (206) 553-3000 for more information. Of course if you must, you can take a cab.

Parking: Parking close to the stadium has always been limited and very expensive, and it's gotten worse now that construction on the Mariners' new baseball stadium has knocked out some garages. The best bet if you are driving is to leave early—really early—and park in the street spots and parking garages in the area of downtown 5-6 blocks north of the Kingdome, but don't get your hopes up for a free spot because they get snagged first. Traffic is not that bad on game day.

Extras: Public tours of the Kingdome are available from mid-April through September, and group tours can be arranged year-round. A one-hour excursion visits the playing field, press box, a locker room and a private lounge. You'll see how they turn the Kingdome from a football stadium to a baseball park in less than 24 hours. The Kingdome Sports Museum features the Royal Brougham collection, sports memorabilia dating back to the 19th century and hailing from around the world. (206) 296-3128.

Capacity: 66,400

Restrooms: 34

Where to Go . . . in Seattle

Best Bars

Best slice of history. The J&M Cafe is one of Seattle's oldest watering holes. Depending on the day and the hour, you can experience almost every variety of clientele. *201 First Ave. S. (206) 292-0663. Seven days 11am-2am (opens 10:00am on Seahawk game days).*

Ready For Primetime (Monday Night)

November 30, 1992: Seattle would win just two games all year, but had enough to outlast a Broncos team playing without QB John Elway. In one of the more amusing contests in prime time history, Seattle tied the score on the final play of regulation via Stan Gelbaugh's 3-yard TD pass to WR Brian Blades, and PK John Kasay ended it in overtime with a 32-yard field goal. Seahawks 16, Broncos 13.

Overall Monday night: 11-5
Overall Thursday night: 0-1
Overall Sunday night: 8-5

> **did you know?**
> The Seahawks have the world's largest NFL pennant. Measuring 12 feet by 30 feet, it sits atop the Kingdome and was manufactured by Swirling Silks in Skippack, PA.

Think About the Weather

December 4, 1988: When you play the majority of your games indoors, it's pretty difficult to come up big in bad weather. Six days after a rousing Monday night win over the Raiders which saw the Seattle offense roll up 35 points and 459 yards, the chilled Seahawks managed 65 total yards in frigid Foxboro where the 30-plus mile-per-hour winds dropped the temperatures below freezing. Patriots 13, Seahawks 7.

Worst Team

1992 (2-14): The firing of Chuck Knox put former Raiders coach Tom Flores on the Seattle sidelines, and it's too bad he couldn't have suited up. Despite an unsung defense that featured Player of the Year Cortez Kennedy, the 'Hawks missed QB Dave Krieg. The team set a record for fewest points scored in a 16-game season (140), never topping the 17-point mark in any contest that year.

> "To add insult to injury, not only are we getting hurt, but we're losing to crappy teams." Christian Fauria, after the Seahawks had lost four of five in 1997.

Hall of Fame

Franco Harris	(FB 1990)
Steve Largent	(WR 1995)

Team Leaders

Rushing Yards
6,705   Curt Warner, 1983-89
Passing Yards
26,132   Dave Krieg, 1980-91
Passing Touchdowns
195   Dave Krieg, 1980-91
Receptions
819   Steve Largent, 1976-89
Interceptions
50   Dave Brown, 1976-86
Touchdowns
101   Steve Largent, 1980-91
Points
810   Norm Johnson, 1982-90

did you know?

The Seahawks won the highest-scoring game since the 1970 merger — a 51-48 overtime squeaker against the Kansas City Chiefs in 1983.

Best micro-brew. The Pyramid Ale House is a popular spot for the younger, middle-class crowd. Beer is brewed on the premises and good, though typical pub fare is on the menu. *1201 First Ave. S. (206) 682-3377. Su-Th 11am-10pm, F-Sa 11am-11pm (opens early on Seahawk game days).*

Best location. The closest bar/restaurant to the Kingdome is **Chippers.** *539 Occidental Ave. S. (206) 654-8070. Open Su-Th 11:30am-11pm, F-Sa 11:30am-1:00pm (opens 10:00 AM on Seahawk game days).*

Best Restaurants

Best place to see Frasier and Niles. The most popular place with the affluent Seahawk fans, **FX McRory's** has a great menu, including killer steaks and an impressive bar offering any drink you are looking for. *419 Occidental Ave. S. (206) 623-4800. Seven days 11:30am-12am (opens at 9:30am on game days). All major credit cards. $$$$*

Best barbecue. Mac's Smokehouse opened the day before the roof tiles fell in the Kingdome. It was a struggle, but it survived and is now the destination of choice for the beer-drinking, no-nonsense Seahawk fan. Mac's serves some of the best BBQ in the Northwest, and it's a great place to catch the early Sunday games and stuff yourself prior to kickoff. *1006 First Ave. S. (206) 628-0880. Seven days 11am-8pm (opens at 10am on Seahawk game days). All major credit cards. $*

> "I'm not saying I'm a great football player. I've also been very lucky." Steve Largent.

Fans' notes

On Screen

The only Seahawk to "go Hollywood" was former LB Brian Bosworth. In fact, one might argue that "the Boz" went Hollywood before he went pro. He has appeared in several cheesy action movies, including **Stone Cold**, **One Tough Bastard** and **Midnight Heat**. If you thought Bosworth's pro football career was a disappointment, wait till you check out these flicks.

Bookshelf

Fighting Chance: An NFL Season with the Seahawks. Fred Moody (Sasquatch Books 1989).
The Boz: Confessions of a Modern Anti-Hero. Brian Bosworth and Rick Reilly (Doubleday 1988).

Paraphernalia

After the tiles on the Kingdome roof fell, merchandisers started selling silver hard-hats with Seahawk colors and logos on them. They also came out with a slew of T-Shirts calling the line the "Seattle Seahawk Hard-Hat Crew." But there's yet a better story behind another piece of paraphernalia. Back when Brian Bosworth played for the Seahawks, a popular item in Denver was an orange T-shirt with the slogan "No Boz" surrounded by a red circle with slash through it. Bronco fans bought them by the thousands, especially because Bosworth had declared Denver QB John Elway a "marked man." The real kicker is that Bosworth himself produced and sold the T-shirts, and the Bronco fans had no idea.

You Gotta See...

▶Located in the heart of the city, **Seattle Center** is a 74-acre civic complex which serves as the region's center for cultural, educational and recreational entertainment. Situated on a landscaped campus, Seattle Center houses museums, theaters, arts centers and galleries, tourist attractions, an amphitheater, as well as an amusement park and the 605-foot Space Needle.
▶**Pike Place**, an old-time fish market on Seattle's waterfront, is one of the city's largest tourist attractions. There's still fish to be had, but there are also a variety of non-fish eateries and craft shops about.
▶Make a pilgrimage to the **grave of Jimi Hendrix** in Greenwood Cemetery, located on NE 3rd Street in Renton (take Route 405 South from Seattle to the Sunset Boulevard exit). The guitar legend's grave is in the back on the left, located near a sundial and a couple of marble benches.

While You Were Eating Turkey

November 27, 1980: The powerhouse Dallas Cowboys invited the Seahawks over for Seattle's first Thanksgiving on the gridiron. Unfortunately, turkey wasn't the fowl being served at Texas Stadium that day—Dallas simply obliterated the Seahawks, handing them the worst loss in franchise history. Cowboys 51, Seahawks 7. The Seahawks have seen Thanksgiving action just once since, but they took the opportunity to throw a 31-14 decision back in the Cowboys' faces.
Overall, 1-1

Against the Odds

After a sensational rookie season in which he established a new NFL rookie record for yards (1,449) and a team rookie record in receptions (42), **Curt Warner's** (1983-1989) career was thrown for a loss. Warner, the first-round pick out of Penn State, suffered a season-ending knee injury in the first game of 1984. But he returned the following year, eclipsing the 1,000-yard plateau (1,094) and catching 47 passes for 307 yards. Over the next three seasons, Warner averaged 213 rushes for 1,163 yards.

---

did you know?

Paul Allen is the first NFL owner to also own an NBA franchise, the Portland Trailblazers. The NFL granted him an exemption from the league rule banning ownership of multiple sports franchises.

Best upscale seafood. An old world, meat-eating feeling, from the waiters in black tie to the woody bar, make **McCormick & Schmick's** a heartier version of your usual seafood place. Try the salmon; this is Seattle, you know? *1203 1st Ave. (206) 623-5500. M-F 11am-11pm, Sa 5-11pm, Su 5-10pm. All major credit cards. $$$*

Best big fat steak. **Metropolitan Grill** is where big-money Seattle gets its steak fix satisfied. The nearby financial district, as well as tourists from both sides of the Pacific Rim, keep this handsome restaurant filled. *820 2nd Ave. (206) 624-3287. M-F 11am-3:30pm lunch, 5-11pm diiner, Sa 4-11pm, Su 4:30-10pm. All major credit cards.$$$$*

Best burgers. Dutch Neds is a very popular full-service bar close to the dome, but more importantly, it serves up the best burgers anywhere. *206 First Ave S. (206) 340-8859. Tu-Su 11am- 2am (closed Mondays, opens at 10am on Seahawk game days). All major credit cards. $$*

Best Accommodations

Westin. The best and most centrally located of the high-end downtown Seattle hotels. *2001 6th Ave. (206) 443-5000. $$$$.*

Ramada. Located just north of central downtown, it has the best combination of location and price. *2200 5th Ave. (206) 441-9785. $$*

West Coast Vance Hotel. Cool atmosphere and local know-how make this a great downtown choice. *620 Stewart St. (206) 441-4200. $$*

Tampa Bay
Buccaneers

"We'll be back ... maybe not in this century, though."— Head coach
John McKay in 1977, after an 0-14 inaugural season in 1976.

I f history were the only lesson, Chris Berman would be the professor, the man who helped color the Tampa Bay Buccaneers as — well, let's face it — the "Yuccaneers" who played in the "Big Sombrero." The Tampa Bay organization built a reputation for being out of step almost from the start, when it was awarded the NFL's 27th franchise on April 24, 1974. A Philadelphia construction executive named Tom McCloskey was selected to be the team's owner, but he withdrew his name. That left it in the hands of Hugh Culverhouse, an attorney and real estate investor from Jacksonville, Florida.

Franchise History

Tampa Bay Buccaneers
(1976–present)

If there is a tie that binds the Buccaneers, it is held by a father and son — John and Rich McKay. John McKay was the first coach of the Buccaneers, the man who held the reins on a team which began its venture into the NFL with an 0-26 record. McKay, one of the game's sharp-tongued leaders, composed a book of humor based solely on his team's ineptitude. When asked about his off-season plans after the Bucs' 0-16 1976 campaign, McKay said "I'll probably take a little time off and go hide someplace."

Lo and behold, by 1979, it was the Buccaneers who executed opponents regularly, winning their first NFC Central title as running back Ricky Bell became the franchise's first 1,000-yard rusher. The next year, the Bucs stunned the league by reaching the NFC championship game, only to lose 9-0 to the Los Angeles Rams. Led by quarterback Doug Williams and defensive end Lee Roy Selmon, the Bucs won another NFC Central title in 1981 and made the playoffs again in '82. But the Bucs stopped there. They would not see another winning season again until Rich McKay, who was just 17 years old when his father became the Bucs coach, was named general manager.

The younger McKay oversaw the retooling of a sorry team, the sale of the club to Malcolm Glazer and the notable

By the Numbers

(Overall)
Regular Season: 110-229-1
Postseason: 2-4
Division Titles: 2
Vs. Division: 54-107-1 (Playoffs: 1-1)
Playoff Appearances: 4
Home: 70-99-1
Away: 40-130

Most Revered Football Figures

Lee Roy Selmon. The Bucs' only Hall of Fame player and one of the league's dominating defensive ends during the late 1970s and early 1980s.

John McKay. The original coach of the Bucs, who quipped his way through an 0-26 start to lead the team to three playoff berths before retiring in 1984.

Doug Williams. The quarterback of those playoff teams, who jumped to the USFL in a contract dispute and then returned to the NFL to lead the Redskins to a Super Bowl victory.

> "I'm all for it." — Bucs head coach John McKay in 1976, when asked about his team's execution.

Rivalries

Thanks to the late sportswriter Pete Axthelm, Tampa Bay-Green Bay **Packer** games earned the moniker of "The Bay of Pigs" when both teams were struggling throughout the 1980s. In 1997, this rivalry turned the corner as the Packers and Bucs finished in first and second place, respectively, in the NFC Central and eventually battled in the playoffs for the first time ever. The Packers lead the series overall, 25-13-1. Largely because of their great Chicago teams of the 1980s, the **Bears** hold the largest series advantage of any of the Bucs' division opponents, 30-10. Even during their 1997 struggles, the winless Bears rose up to smite the playoff-bound Buccaneers, 13-7.

hiring of Tony Dungy as head coach in January 1996. Almost instantly, a series of shrewd draft-day moves brought in exciting young players like Warrick Dunn, Mike Alstott and Warren Sapp, and Dungy had the Bucs in the playoffs in 1997. Tampa fans started coming back to games. Gone are the orange jerseys. Gone are the Yuccaneers. And, gone too is the "Big Sombrero," as the Bucs move into a new stadium with new prospects for a bright future.

—Chris Mortensen

Tampa Stadium

The "Big Sombrero" is history, but that may not be such a bad thing for the Bucs. When you suffer 14 consecutive losing seasons, how many memorable games could you have at home? Besides, the new Tampa Stadium will wipe away any nostalgic feelings for the old place. When it makes its debut the third week of September, the new 65,000-seat, state-of-the-art stadium will feature full-color video replay scoreboards at both ends of the field, luxury suites, and club seats with private lounges as well as 19-inch wide seats with chairbacks, armrests and extra legroom for the basic fan.

The Glazers promise there won't be a bad seat in the house. The best seats no doubt will be the club seats, which will include preferred parking areas, a private entrance and access to an air-conditioned atrium with an 84-foot ceiling and imported marble floor. Escalators will carry club-seat ticket holders to the main club level with an additional 120,000 square feet of air-conditioned comfort. The club seats them-

did you know?
Although Tampa Bay has enjoyed just four winning seasons in 22 years of existence (1976-97), those are also the only four times the Buccaneers have made the playoffs.

selves are extra wide and padded. Also, club seat owners will be able to enjoy a Sunday brunch, four sports bars and other food choices not available to those in the cheap seats. They also can order from an extensive in-seat menu and have a waiter deliver food and beverages right to their seat. Club-seat prices are $2,450, $1,750 and $950 annually and must be reserved for five, seven or ten years. However, those prices are guaranteed for only the 1998 and 1999 seasons.

> "I'd like to think we could beat them if we gave them the play-book."
> — Steelers defensive end Dwight White about the 1976 Buccaneers. Pittsburgh beat Tampa Bay, 42-0, that year.

The Bottom Line on Tampa Stadium

Address: Dale Mabry Highway, Tampa, FL 33607. (813) 879-2827.

Tickets: Season ticket packages cost $480, $360, $260 and $190, plus a deposit equal to the price of the ticket that will be held for 10 seasons and refunded in five percent increments after each season, with the full balance refunded at the end of the 10th season. To order tickets, write to: Tampa Bay Buccaneers, 1998 New Stadium Season Ticket Application, P.O. Box 20608, Tampa, FL, 33622. For ticket information, call (800) 282-0683.

1998: Single game prices not set.

1994: $40/$20 (old Tampa Stadium).

Public Transportation: Hillsborough Area Regional Transit will provide bus service with two stops at the new stadium. Call (813) 254–4278 for information.

Parking: Just like the former stadium, there will be plenty of parking on site as well

The "I Was There" Game

December 29, 1979: Tampa Bay's first playoff game was a stunning upset of a Philadelphia team that would make it to the Super Bowl the following season. The Bucs took the opening kick-off and drove to a touchdown before the Eagles knew what hit them and, as they say, the final score wasn't indicative of Tampa Bay's domination. (Buccaneers 24, Eagles 17).

The Paper Bag Game

November 27, 1983: You've heard of the Super Bowl. Well, the Bucs and Houston Oilers met at Tampa Stadium in what *The Tampa Tribune* dubbed the "Repus Bowl," or Super Bowl spelled backward. That's because, unlike the Super Bowl that pits the top teams from the NFC and AFC, the Bucs-Oilers game matched the two worst teams in the league. By the way, the Bucs won, 33-24.

did you know?
The Bucs are 0-17 when the game-time temperature is 40 degrees or lower.

Great Names

Hasson Arbubakrr (DE, 1983)
Donald Igwebuike (PK, 1985-89)
Gary Puetz (G/T, 1978)
Mark Studaway (DE, 1985)
Mark Vlasic (QB, 1993)

Hall of Fame

Lee Roy Selmon   (DE 1995)

Our Top Story

"From Worst to First"
December 12, 1979
The 1979 season saw the Bucs, who lost their first 26 games and finished last in the NFC Central a year earlier, post a 10-6 record on their way to the division title, a first-round playoff upset of Philadelphia and an NFC Championship Game loss to the Los Angeles Rams.

"Glazers Buy Bucs"
January 17, 1995
The franchise was in turmoil when Palm Beach investor Malcolm Glazer bought the Bucs for a then-professional sports record $192 million. Glazer, who put his sons Bryan and Joel in charge of the team, promised to turn Tampa Bay into the San Francisco 49ers of the East Coast.

"Bucs Make Playoffs"
December 21, 1997
After a 14 straight years without playoffs, the 1997 Buccaneers earned a wild-card playoff berth with a 10-6 record. They went on to defeat the Lions in the wild card round before losing in Green Bay.

Worst Team

1986 (2-14): It would be easy to point the finger at the Buccaneers' first two years in the league, but a stronger case can be made for this squad, which won its only two games by a total of 10 points. Steve Young saw the majority of action at quarterback but received little or no help, especially from a porous defense. Ten of the team's 14 losses were by double-digits.

as nearby. As always, fans will have a choice of paying at nearby Al Lopez Park, Hillsborough Community College, and Jesuit High School, or they can park for free at Tampa Bay Center mall. Two negatives for parking at the mall: a longer walk and awful traffic jams after games.
Capacity: 65,000
Restrooms: 16 men's, 20 women's.

> **did you know?**
> The Bucs have never returned a kickoff for a touchdown in their history.

Where To Go . . . in Tampa

Best Bars

Best place to catch a late meal. One of Tampa's oldest sports bars — **Press Box Sports Emporium** — is located about 10 minutes away from the stadium and serves food until the wee hours of the morning. You can catch the action on several large-screen TVs as well as smaller ones spread around, or shoot pool/throw darts in the back room. *222 Dale Mabry Highway South. (813) 876-3528. Seven days 11am-3am.*

Best place to catch a great tale. The **Chatterbox**, another Tampa legend that's wall-to-wall with the college crowd on weekends. Outstanding juke box and pool tables overshadow the sports usually playing on several small-screen TVs, but if you're lucky, the man behind the bar will be Dan Lea, who actually knew John Matuszak and has the stories to prove it. *709 S. Howard Ave. (813) 251-3628. Seven days 11am-3am.*

Best place to spot a celebrity. Located off the lobby of the Westshore Marriott Hotel, **Champions Sports Bar** offers the

Best of the Buccaneers

Best Team

1997 (11-7): Tony Dungy's young club actually began its ascent late in '96. The offense was anchored by the Pro Bowl backfield of QB Trent Dilfer, RB Warrick Dunn and FB Mike Alstott, while DT Warren Sapp was the heart and soul of an emerging defense that set a team record for sacks. The Bucs made the playoffs for the first time in 15 years, and won a postseason game for the first time since 1979.

Greatest Players by Position

Pos:	Player
QB:	Doug Williams
RB:	James Wilder
WR:	Mark Carrier
TE:	Jimmie Giles
OL:	Paul Gruber
DL:	Lee Roy Selmon
LB:	Hardy Nickerson
DB:	Ricky Reynolds
P/K:	Donald Igwebuike
ST:	Karl Williams

And Don't Forget...

DB: Cedric Brown. Reliable defender with a nose for the football, and a key veteran on the Bucs' first three playoff teams.

WR: Kevin House. Back when Doug Williams was playing bombs away, House was the strong-armed passer's favorite target.

C: Tony Mayberry. In '97, the veteran pivot became the first Buccaneers' offensive lineman to be voted to the Pro Bowl.

FB: Mike Alstott. The former Purdue standout epitomizes the modern Bucs with his pounding runs and solid blocking.

DT: Warren Sapp. From controversial first-round pick to all-star, Sapp may be the Bucs' best defensive lineman since Lee Roy Selmon.

Best Argument

Running Back: James Wilder or Ricky Bell? Wilder, a former Missouri standout, was not only a reliable ball-carrier but a sure-handed pass catcher, and is still the franchise's top rusher and receiver. Bell was the league's top pick in 1977. Two years later he ran for 1,263 yards and seven TDs and was the workhorse in the 24-17 playoff upset of Dick Vermeil's Eagles.

> "If I hadn't done that I would have been lynched. I'm not too popular around here anyway."
> — John McKay in 1984, after his last game as Bucs coach. His defense allowed the Jets to score a meaningless touchdown so that James Wilder had a chance to break Eric Dickerson's all-purpose yardage record.

Best Coach

Tony Dungy (1996-current): Yes, he has only been on the job two years, but you have to be impressed at what he's done. Dungy's coaching career began at 1-8 but then his team rallied for five wins in their last seven games in '96, and carried that momentum into the next season, rewarding Tampa fans with a winner for the first time since 1982. The best is yet to come.

Pressbox

Who to Read...

The *Tampa Tribune* features columnists Tom McEwen, Martin Fennelly and David Whitley. McEwen, a Red Smith award winner, is the all-world veteran who has been chronicling Tampa Bay sports since the 1950s. Fennelly and Whitley are equally capable of making readers laugh or stirring up controversy. The *St. Petersburg Times* has columnists Hubert Mizell and Gary Shelton. Mizell has been writing about Tampa Bay sports for three decades and also hosts a morning radio show. Shelton isn't afraid to tackle a tough issue.

Who to Watch...

On television, WFLA's Chris Thomas is easily the most outspoken critic of the Bucs among the TV set and one of the funnier guys in TV sports, earning him a popular following. Dick Crippen has been covering Tampa Bay area sports for four decades. The poor guy. Bay News 9 features ex-Buc defensive tackle David Logan hosting a nightly half-hour call-in show that features players and sports media types discussing the issues of the day.

Who to Listen To...

On the radio, WZTM (820 AM) starts off the day with "The Team," a lineup which consists of Mizell and T.J. Rives. They truly relish getting into it with each other. They're followed by Tom Korun, who loves to stir it up in the midday, and ex-Buc linebacker Scot Brantley and Rob Weingarten — a real Odd Couple — in the late afternoon. Bucs coach Tony Dungy has a Monday afternoon show during the season. On WDAE (1250 AM), you can hear "The Sports Animal," irreverent sports chatter from Rock Riley, Chris Thomas and Steve Duemig.

---

usual big-screen TVs and pool tables as well as a slightly better atmosphere than your basic sports bar. *1001 Westshore Blvd. North. (813) 286-2201. Seven days 11:30am-2am.*

Best Restaurants

Best Cuban. There are dozens of top-notch Cuban restaurants in Tampa, but you can't beat **La Teresita** for good food, huge portions and low prices. Plus, it's within walking distance of the stadium. *3248 W. Columbus Dr. (813) 879-4909. Hours: Breakfast, lunch and dinner. S-Th 8am-10pm, F-Sa 8am-11pm. All major credit cards. $*

Best celebrity Italian. What can you say about a place that counts Jimmy Johnson, John McKay, and Wayne Fontes among its favorite customers? Good Italian food and atmosphere and solid service has made **Malio's** a long-time favorite. *301 Dale Mabry Highway South. (813) 879-3233. M-Th 5-11pm, F-Sa 5-11:30pm. All major credit cards. $$*

Best primadonna. The owner of **Primadonna Trattoria**, Cesar Tini, is a huge Bucs fan who will gladly talk football with anyone interested. Northern Italian food; don't miss the Rollatini Frank Sinatra, veal stuffed with shrimp and scallops and created specially for Ol' Blue Eyes. *915 S. Howard Ave. (813) 258-3358. Hours: Lunch M-F 11:30am-2pm, dinner 7 days 5:30-10pm. All major credit cards. $$$*

Best stop for carnivores. If you want a perfect steak, a wine list longer than 100 yards and outstanding service, **Bern's Steak House** is the place to go. But don't miss the upstairs dessert room, an experience unto itself. *1208 S. Howard Ave. (813) 251-2421. Seven days 5-11pm. All major credit cards. $$$*

"If I believed in a turning point, I'd say that was probably it." — Head Coach Ray Perkins, after the Bucs lost a 28-3 fourth quarter lead over the Cardinals in the eighth game of the strike-shortened 1987 season. Tampa Bay didn't win another game all season, turning a 4-3 start into a 4-11 finish.

Best Accommodations

Holiday Inn Express. Located a short walk from the stadium, you can't get any closer than this to the action. *4732 Dale Mabry Highway North. (813) 877-6061. $*

Radisson Bay Harbor Inn. Owned by George Steinbrenner — yes, that George Steinbrenner — this hotel is located on Tampa Bay and is about 15 minutes from the stadium. *7700 Courtney Campbell Cswy. (813) 281-8900. $$*

Hyatt Regency Westshore. Located off Tampa Bay (the actual bay, that is) and about 15 minutes from the stadium, this hotel also features a roof-top four-star restaurant, Armani's, and lounge with a great view of the bay and nearby airport. *6200 Courtney Campbell Cswy. (813) 874-1234. $$-$$$*

Ready For Primetime (Monday Night)

Nov. 29, 1982: The Bucs made just three Monday night appearances in their first 22 seasons. In this affair, the team was 0-3 and hosted the eventual AFC champion Dolphins in both clubs' second game following the two-month strike. Tampa scratched out a victory, 23-17, then rallied to make the playoffs.

Overall Monday Night: 1-2
Overall Thursday Night: 1-0
Overall Sunday Night: 4-4

Think About the Weather

December 16, 1979: John McKay's club appeared to be a playoff cinch with a 9-3 mark and four games to go. But a three-game slide followed, and they found themselves facing the Chiefs at Tampa Stadium in a rainstorm that would have made Noah flinch. Neil O'Donoghue's 19-yard field goal was the only score as the Bucs wrapped up the NFC Central, 3-0.

Team Leaders

Rushing Yards
5,957   James Wilder, 1981-89
Passing Yards
14,820 Vinny Testaverde, 1987-92
Passing Touchdowns
77   Vinny Testaverde, 1987-92
Receptions
430   James Wilder, 1981-89
Interceptions
29   Cedric Brown, 1977-84
Touchdowns
46   James Wilder, 1981-89
Points
416   Donald Igwebuike, 1985-89

Fans' notes

On Screen

Even though success has embraced the Bucs recently, the franchise's history is not necessarily the happiest of stories. One particularly somber chapter is commemorated in the 1991 TV movie **A Triumph of the Heart: The Ricky Bell Story.** Tragically, during the middle of his career, Tampa Bay running back Bell was killed by a rare muscle disease. Based on actual events, the plot focuses on the friendship between Bell (Mario Van Peebles) and a fatherless handicapped child. Susan Ruttan, Lynn Whitfield, and even Marcus Allen play supporting roles.

Bookshelf

Quarterblack: Shattering the NFL Myth. Doug Williams (Bonus Books 1990). Although better known for being the first black quarterback to lead a Super Bowl team, the Redskins, Williams was an early draft choice for Tampa Bay and led the club to its first playoff appearance.

You Gotta See...

▶It may be second fiddle to Disneyworld among Florida theme parks, but **Busch Gardens** is the Tampa area's single biggest tourist attraction. You'll find the largest roller-coaster in the southeastern U.S. here, as well as a zoo complete with a simulated veldt.

Swami Sez:

How far have the Bucs come?? In 1998, the Bay of Pigs, Green Bay at Tampa Bay, will be on Monday Night Football.

▶This is prime Gulf Coast beach territory. Hit the sand at one of the many barrier-island beaches off the **St. Petersburg peninsula**, or drive a bit further south to find more beachfront property.

▶Is it spring yet? We're talking baseball. The Tampa-St. Petersburg region is one of the main spring training zones in the baseball world, and a number of minor league clubs inhabit the area as well. Plus the brand-spanking new **Tampa Bay Devil Rays** first hit the majors in 1998.

> "They were absolutely horrible, and that's the nicest thing I can say about them." — John McKay, after Tampa Bay's 28-19 loss to the Chiefs in 1976.

Against all Odds

Ricky Bell (1977-81) was never one to give up — not in his football career, and certainly not in life. But he was robbed of both on November 28, 1984, when he died after an arduous fight with two degenerative diseases, dermatomyositis and cardiomyopathy. The first overall pick in the 1977 draft, Bell never wanted or asked for sympathy, and he took great pains to hide an illness which forced him out of football in 1982, curtailing what had appeared to be a promising career. On the field, Bell carried the Bucs to the 1979 NFC Championship Game with huge performances during the regular season (1,263 yards) and the playoffs.

Tennessee Oilers

The oil business is a lot trickier than being a cowboy. It's a boom or bust game, and when a well runs dry you just gotta move along. The Houston Oilers know that well. Businessman K.S. "Bud" Adams Jr. struck football first in Texas when he founded the Oilers, the first professional football franchise in this football-crazy state. The cycle of ups and downs was established right away in the '60s, as names such as George Blanda, Elvin Bethea and Ken Houston wowed the fans of Houston. The Oilers also showed signs of a flashiness and speed that would be associated with their great years, a style that was more Brothers Ewing than Hoss and Little Joe Cartwright. It was not a player who epitomized the team in those early days of the space race and Mission Control as much as it was their ultra-modern stadium, the Houston Astrodome. The stadium and the Oilers AFL championships in 1960 and 1961 added to the city's image. The team didn't keep up through the balance of the '60s, though. Men landed on the moon, but the well went dry in Houston and the Oilers went down.

Franchise History

Houston Oilers (AFL)
(1960–69)
Houston Oilers (NFL)
(1970–96)
Tennessee Oilers
(1997–present)

By the Numbers

(Since 1970)
Regular Season: 189-233-2
Postseason: 7-10
Division Titles: 2
Vs. Division: 73-99 (Playoffs: 1-4)
Playoff Appearances: 10
Home: 112-99-1
Away: 77-134-1

(Overall)
Regular Season: 259-299-6
Postseason: 9-13
Playoff Appearances: 15
Home: 155-125-2
Away: 104-174-4

It took Earl Campbell, Robert Brazile, Dan Pastorini and coach Bum Phillips in the '70s to bring back a winning attitude. Pastorini's free-wheeling style at quarterback, Ken Burrough's speed at wide receiver and the powerful running of Earl Campbell made the "Luv Ya Blue" Oilers one of the best shows in the league. The 1979 AFC Championship Game between the Oilers and the Steelers helped introduce another kind of show — instant replay. A disputed catch in the end zone led to a long confab between the officials that left the Oilers without a crucial

Most Revered Football Figures

O. A. "Bum" Phillips. In his six years with the team, Phillips took Houston to within a game of the Super Bowl twice with an equal mixture of humility, Texas twang and a Yogi-esque philosophy.

Earl Campbell. An overall number one draft pick who became a Hall of Famer, Campbell gave his all for the team and the fans loved him for it.

Dan Pastorini. Pastorini quarterbacked the "Luv Ya Blue" Oilers with reckless abandon and lived it up off the field as well. The fans loved him for both efforts.

Bruce Matthews. A multiple Pro-Bowler on the offensive line, Matthews, an NFL and Oiler veteran of 16 years, has been a study in class throughout his career.

Rivalries

There's still a lot of animosity in the air, but the rivalry peaked when the Cincinnati **Bengals** and Oilers were coached by Sam Wyche and Jerry Glanville, respectively. Annually, the Bengals would go to Houston and get crushed, and Cincinnati would return the favor when the Oilers came to town. The series is knotted at 29-29-1. During the Oilers' "Luv Ya Blue" days, their toughest opponent was the Pittsburgh **Steelers** (20-38), who sent them home from the AFC Championship Game in 1978 after a 34-5 rout and beat them again in 1979, 27-13. The Dallas **Cowboys** (4-5) used to provide the Oilers with an intrastate rivalry which was focused less on the field than in the hearts and minds of Texans.

touchdown and a lot of people with the feeling that there were better ways to solve these things (a feeling many still have).

The '80s brought six straight losing seasons (1981-1986), but the likes of perennial Pro Bowlers Warren Moon, Ray Childress, Mike Munchak and Bruce Matthews changed the franchise's fortunes. By the end of the decade and continuing into the early '90s, winning had found its way back to the Astrodome — then nicknamed "The House of Pain" — with the team posting seven consecutive winning records and earning seven playoff appearances.

> **did you know?**
> Before eventually moving the Oilers to Tennessee, Bud Adams had shopped his team to three other cities: Atlanta (1965), Seattle (1967), and Jacksonville (1987)

A new era for the Oilers began in 1994. With the hiring of coach Jeff Fisher and the departure of quarterback Warren Moon, many changes were in store for the franchise. After spending some prosperous years in the city of Houston, the Oilers found their fan base dwindling. They averaged just 31,000 fans per game their last year in Houston. The well was dry for good, and suddenly geography was the big story for the Oilers, not football. In 1996 Bud Adams struck a deal with the city of Nashville to bring his team to the state of Tennessee. There was only one hitch in the plan: With the stadium and training facility no more than blueprints, they had no place to move into. As a result, the Oilers found themselves setting up shop in Memphis for the 1997 season. There wasn't much in Memphis worth drilling for, though. Attendance for the Oilers' Memphis home games in 1997 averaged approximately 3,000 less than their final days in Houston. The Oilers finally took the dive and moved to Nashville in the summer of 1998, albeit in temporary digs at Vanderbilt Stadium.

On the field, though, Jeff Fisher has tried to keep it business-as-usual for the players.

Since he took over in November 1994 (the team limped to a 2-14 finish) he steadily brought the Oilers to a respectable .500 in 1997. Veterans such as strong safety Blaine Bishop and center Mark Stepnoski, along with budding stars such as running back Eddie George and quarterback Steve McNair, seem to solidify the franchise's future on the field. Meanwhile, the job of solidifying the Oilers' future off the field must be left to Bud Adams and the fans of Tennessee.

—Mike Golic

Vanderbilt Stadium

Vanderbilt Stadium will play host to two preseason and eight regular season home games for the Tennessee Oilers, who negotiated to play there for a season while awaiting the completion of their new stadium in 1999. When the Oilers finally get into their permanent home, it will be their fourth home stadium in as many seasons: They played in Houston's Astrodome in 1996 and the Memphis Liberty Bowl in 1997. The major downside to the Oilers tempo-

> "I feel like someone who inherited a million dollars in tarnished silverware. All I did was polish it." — Head coach Wally Lemm on the success of his teams in the early '60s.

The "I Was There" Game

December 29, 1979: AFC Divisional Playoff; Oilers 17, Chargers 14: Playing without RB Earl Campbell, QB Dan Pastorini and WR Ken Burrough, the undermanned Oilers faced a San Diego squad that appeared Super Bowl-bound. But S Vernon Perry was superb, picking off four Dan Fouts passes, while backup QB Gifford Nielsen connected with WR Mike Renfro on a 47-yard touchdown play which proved to be the difference.

The Paper Bag Game

Jan. 3, 1993: AFC Wild Card Playoffs: Bills 41, Oilers 38 (OT). The Bills pulled off the greatest comeback in NFL history by rallying from a 35-3 deficit early in the third quarter to defeat the bumbling Oilers in overtime. This historic loss is more embarassing than any other in team history. And the Oilers have a lot of embarassing losses.

Great Names

Billy Cannon (RB, 1960-63)
B.W. Cheeks (RB, 1965)
Jimmy Dean (DE, 1978)
Elbert Drungo (OT, 1969-77)
Henry Ford (DE, 1994-present)
Ron Lou (C, 1972-73, 1976)
Calvin Loveall (CB, 1988)
Oliver Luck (QB, 1982-86)
Kent Nix (QB, 1972)
Johnny Peacock (S, 1969-70)
Dick Swatland (G, 1968)
Mike Teeter (DE, 1993-94)

Our Top Story

"AFL Strikes Oil in Texas"
October 31, 1959
Owner Bud Adams Jr. announced that he'll be naming his franchise, one of the original six members of the AFL, the Oilers — "for sentimental and social reasons."

"Take It Inside"
February 10, 1968
Three years after turning down a lease on what would be dubbed the Astrodome, owner Bud Adams Jr. announces that the Oilers would move from Rice Stadium to Harris County domed Stadium for the 1968 season.

"Drafting Genius"
April 24, 1978
The Oilers trade TE Jimmie Giles and three draft picks to the Tampa Bay Buccaneers in exchange for the first pick in the 1978 draft. They use that pick to select that year's Heisman Trophy winner, running back Earl Campbell.

"Houston, We Have a Problem"
June, 1997
Undoubtedly the biggest day in Oilers history came in June 1997 when the Oilers finally packed up their powder blue uniforms and *adiosed* for Tennessee after owner Bud Adams' cries of poverty went unheard. The Tennessee years started out badly: Oddly, the team was not renamed, and the team's lame-duck presence in Memphis before the final move to Nashville had an ill effect on attendance.

did you know?

The Bills of the '90s get a lot of flack for losing four Super Bowls. But consider that the Oilers went to the playoffs seven straight years from 1987-93 and never made it to the AFC title game.

rary home is the artificial turf field. The players loved playing on grass in Memphis, and look forward to the natural field at their new stadium. For one season, though, they're willing to give up grass in a trade that gives them home games in their home city after a miserable year of commuting 200 miles to Memphis. Vanderbilt Stadium is in the heart of the Vanderbilt campus, nestled between two main drags, West End Avenue and 21st Street. Although the Oilers played two preseason games at Vanderbilt in 1997, it will be different playing there in the fall when school is in session. Many neighborhood residents voiced loud concerns about what the team's presence will mean on Sunday afternoons. But the team, the school and the community ironed it all out, and extra clean-up crews and security will be on hand. Vanderbilt University wanted to be a good citizen, and the Oilers hope their fans won't abuse the hospitality. No beer will be sold.

The Bottom Line on Vanderbilt Stadium

Address: Jess Neely Boulevard, Vanderbilt University, Nashville, TN 37212. (615) 322-4636.

Tickets: For the 1998 season, fans who have bought PSLs for the new stadium starting in 1999 have first shot at tickets. Since the Oilers have sold over 46,000 PSLs and since Vandy holds just over 41,000 fans, it is likely that few if any tickets will be available to the general public. How available seats will be through scalpers remains to be seen.

Best of the Oilers

Best Team

1961 (11-3-1): The Oilers won the first two American Football League championships, and their second title team could win any number of ways. Amazingly, the club got off to a 1-3-1 start but won its final nine games. By year-end, the Oilers had scored 513 points in 14 games, thanks to QB George Blanda, WR Charley Hennigan and a strong cast. But it was the defense that shackled San Diego (10-3) in the AFL title tilt.

Greatest Players by Position

Pos:	Player
QB:	Warren Moon
RB:	Earl Campbell
WR:	Charley Hennigan
TE:	Mike Barber
OL:	Bruce Matthews
DL:	Elvin Bethea
LB:	Robert Brazile
DB:	Ken Houston
P/K:	Al Del Greco
ST:	Billy "White Shoes" Johnson

"As the judge said, I was naive. I didn't know what the Rams were doing to me." — RB Billy Cannon, who signed contracts with both the Rams and Oilers in 1959 before a court ruled that the "naive country boy" could play for Houston in his rookie season.

And Don't Forget...

WR: Drew Hill. Acquired in a trade with the Rams in 1985, he proved to be a steal for the Oilers, totaling 480 catches in just seven seasons.

G: Mike Munchak. The former Nittany Lion was named to nine Pro Bowls during his standout 12-year career.

WR: Ernest Givins. A combination of sure hands and deceptive speed, Givins was one of the toughest receivers to ever play the game.

DT: Curley Culp. The one-time Kansas City Chief had his best years in Houston and was a force on the Oilers' defensive front.

LB: Al Smith. Unsung for most of his career, this tackling machine earned a pair of Pro Bowl appearances.

Best Argument

Defensive Line: Elvin Bethea or Ray Childress? A force on some very good and some very bad Oilers squads, Bethea played 16 seasons for the club and was named to the Pro Bowl in half of those years. Childress was a standout from Texas A&M who began his career at defensive end and was then asked to move inside. He grudgingly accepted and enjoyed his most productive years.

Best Coach

Bum Phillips (1975-80): One of the most popular head coaches ever, Phillips inherited a team that two years earlier had managed back-to-back 1-13 seasons (1972-73). The Oilers finished 10-4 in his debut season and just missed the playoffs. In 1978 and '79, they made consecutive appearances in the AFC title game, but just couldn't "kick in the door" in two losses at Pittsburgh.

Pressbox

Who to Read...

Nashville is a one-newspaper town, and *The Tennessean* is the city's primary source of Oiler news. Paul Kuharsky covers the beat on a daily basis, and Jeff Legwold helps out on the Oilers while also covering the NFL and writing columns. Each has covered other AFC teams in the past; Kuharsky the Oakland Raiders and Legwold the Pittsburgh Steelers. The paper's primary sports columnist, David Climer, frequently writes about the team as well. The weekly *Nashville Scene* also chimes in on the team periodically.

Who to Watch...

WKRN–ABC's John Dwyer is the leader of the pack among the local sportscasters. Dwyer brings a professional attitude to what is still primarily a college market, as he worked in Jacksonville when the Jaguars started up. He hosts "Monday Night Live with Jeff Fisher" during the season, broadcast from Planet Hollywood downtown. Fans are invited to watch the show live and mingle with Fisher and player guests.

Who to Listen To...

As the Oilers and NHL Predators get started in Nashville, the radio banter is growing. Still, the University of Tennessee is typically the hottest topic, no matter the season. WLAC (1510 AM) broadcasts a nightly sports talk show hosted by Bob Bell and Bill King. While the pair haven't spent much time around the team yet, they often have Oilers on the air, and Kuharsky is a regular guest during the season. Another member of *The Tennessean*'s staff, popular columnist Joe Biddle, co-hosts "Sports Night" on WWTN (99.7 FM) with voice of Vanderbilt George Plaster and former Commodore hoopster Willie Daunic. Weak-signaled WHBQ (560 AM) is all-sports all the time.

Swami Sez:

By 1999, the Oilers will have had four home fields in four years. Jeff Fisher's keeping this team's head above water rates with one of the best unsung coaching jobs in recent years.

1998: $48/$36

1994: $38/$36/$31/$27/$20

Public Transportation: The Oilers and Vanderbilt University will run shuttles from parking lots scattered around town to the stadium on game days to alleviate traffic in the university neighborhood. There will be a small, still-to-be-determined charge.

Parking: Fans will be urged to buy parking with their tickets for this season, and they will be pre-assigned to lots. Only the very fortunate will draw spots within walking distance. The rest will be asked to hop on the shuttle.

Capacity: 41,448.

Restrooms: 5 men's, 5 women's.

Where to Go . . . in Nashville

Best Bars

Best Oilers atmosphere. To be determined. As has been well-documented, while the Oilers commuted to Memphis last season, Nashvillians were largely non-responsive to the team. All signs indicate that things are looking up, but where the fanatics will hang out isn't clear yet.

Best sports bar. The best sports bar in town is **Jonathan's Village Cafe** in Hillsboro Village, on the fringes of Vanderbilt. The beer is cold, and for bar food, it's top-notch. Try the chicken-herb pizza. *1803 21st Ave. (615) 385-9301. M 4pm-12:30am, T 11am-12:30am, W-Sa 11am-2am, Su 2pm-12:30am.*

Best sports bar II. Another favorite is the **Second and Goal Sports Bar** in Graham Central Station. Good bar food, lots of beers on tap and a back room that opens up to overlook the Cumberland River and stadium. *128 Second Ave. North. (615) 244-5340. M-F 11am-midnight, Sa-Su 11am-1am.*

Best place to play pool. Buffalo Billiards is *the* place to shoot a few games and get a great glimpse of Nashville's prettiest people. Upstairs is Havana Lounge, a cigar bar that's reportedly popular among the Oilers, including Steve McNair. *154 2nd. Ave. North (615) 313-7665. M-Th 4pm-2am, F 4pm-3am, Sa 1pm-3am, Su 1pm-2am (Havana Lounge closed Su).*

---

did you know?

In 1980, the Oilers dealt QB Dan Pastorini to Oakland for QB Ken Stabler. Pastorini broke his leg and was replaced by Jim Plunkett, who beat Stabler and company in the play-offs that year, 27-7.

Ready For Primetime (Sunday Night)

January 2, 1994: The franchise's most infamous moment came during a Sunday night (24-0) win over the New York Jets in the 1993 season finale. The victory, a dominating performance to cap the season and send the Oilers to the playoffs, was marred when irascible defensive coordinator Buddy Ryan threw a Gerry Cooney-esque jab at offensive coordinator Kevin Gilbride, citing unhappiness with Gilbride's play-calling as the rationale for his flying fist. An 11-game winning streak was abruptly halted two weeks after "The Punch," when Joe Montana and the Chiefs rallied for 21 points in the fourth quarter to squash the Oilers' season with a 28-20 playoff loss.

Overall Monday night: 11-11

Overall Thursday night: 2-2

Overall Sunday night: 8-5

Think About the Weather

December 31, 1978: Oilers 31, Patriots 14. Chilly Foxboro was the setting for one of the team's most impressive postseason victories in this AFC Divisional Playoff game. Bum Phillips's club jumped out early as QB Dan Pastorini threw three second-quarter touchdown passes and the 31-14 rout was on. This game was exceptional, as the Oilers usually performed poorly outside of the temperature-constant Astrodome.

Worst Team

1973 (1-13): Dan Pastorini was in his third season and still learning. And the Oilers were taught a lesson which lasted all season as their lone victory came in a close 31-27 contest at Baltimore. That victory was preceded by seven losses and followed by six more setbacks, most of those of the lopsided variety. It was a rough two months for Sid Gillman, who replaced Bill Peterson (1-18 as Oilers' head coach from 1972-73) after five games.

Hall of Fame

George Blanda	(QB/PK 1981)
Sid Gillman	(Coach 1983)
Ken Houston	(DB 1986)
John Henry Johnson	(FB 1987)
Earl Campbell	(HB 1991)
Charlie Joiner	(WR 1996)

Best place to nurse a beer and catch the breeze. The Bound'ry has a very cool balcony and a great happy hour. It's a better place to enjoy Nashville's own Market Street Vanilla Beer than Market Street Brewery itself, and the food is terrific. *911 20th Ave. South. (615) 321-3043. Seven days 4pm-2am.*

Best place for country. Try **Tootsie's Orchid Lounge**, but be forewarned — it's tailor-made for tourists. Still, all the bartenders are country music wannabes who often hop up on stage and join the band for a song or two. Country music plays all day long. *422 Broadway. (615) 726-0463. Seven days 9:30 am-3am.*

Best Restaurants

Best burger. Boscos Nashville Brewing Co., a brew pub restaurant next door to Jonathan's Village Cafe has top-rate burgers and plenty of other good stuff on the menu. Only one TV though, so if you're looking for a game, head next door. *1805 21st Ave. (615) 385-0050. M-Th 11am-1:30am, F-Sat 11am-2:30 pm, Sun 11am-12:30am. AX, MC, V. $$*

Best place to run into Oilers unwinding on a Friday night. Try **The Trace** in Hillsboro Village. It replaced the once famous Faison's. A great place for a nice dinner, but later in the night it turns

While You Were Eating Turkey

November 27, 1997: It doesn't matter that this was little more than kicking a team when it was down. The Oilers went into Texas Stadium last Thanksgiving and put a butterball-sized spanking on the Cowboys in front of God, Texas, and a national television audience. The Oilers' 27-14 win in their first Thanksgiving Day appearance was possibly the low point of Dallas' season. It drove another nail into the hated Cowboys' playoff coffin and moved head coach Barry Switzer one step closer to the exit door.
Overall: 4-0.

Best of Oilers

On Screen

Defensive tackle John Matuszak, the Oilers' and the NFL's first overall pick in the 1973 draft, stayed with the team for just one year before an attempted defection to the WFL, a court battle and a trade ended his Oilers career. Unfortunate, then, that Matuszak is the team's most illustrious Hollywood alum, with credits including **North Dallas Forty** (1979), **Caveman** (1981) and **The Ice Pirates** (1984).

Fight Song, Etc.

The Oilers' fight song "Luv Ya Blue" — infectious as hell, and not wholly devoid of simple charm — contains the rhyme "We give the other team no hope/You know we're gonna hold the rope." Exactly what that line means is not clear.

> "Don't ever quote me again unless I speak to you or I'll sue your ass." — QB Dan Pastorini to Houston Post writer Dale Robertson in 1980.

Bookshelf

Loser Takes All: Bud Adams, Bad Football, & Big Business. Ed Fowler. (Longstreet 1997).

The Year of Pain: The 1989 Houston Oilers Season. Kenny Hand (Eakins 1980). Title is actually applicable to a number of other Oiler seasons.

Elvis Don't Like Football: The Life and Raucous Times of The NFL's Most Outspoken Coach. Jerry Glanville and J. David Miller. (Macmillan 1990). The book itself is only a tad more annoying and self-serving than its title.

Oilers Anonymous: A Twelve Step Program for Houston Oiler Fanatics. Mike Vance (Gulf Publications 1995).

You Gotta See...

▶Country music stars of the past and present frequently pop in to join the nightly performances at the **Grand Ole Opry at Opryland**, which is being converted from an amusement park to an enormous retail mall. Weekends at the Opry you can be in the audience for the longest-running radio show around. Big fans might also want to check out the Country Music Hall of Fame & Museum in the heart of Nashville's Music Row.

▶**Ryman Auditorium** at Fourth and Commerce, home of the original Opry, still hosts concerts.

▶Take a walking tour of downtown and poke into shops, restaurants and bars with music along **Broadway and 2nd Avenue** in the heart of downtown. Find **Printer's Alley**, too, an historic street that's been an entertainment area since the Civil War. It's not what it once was, but it's still fun.

▶The **Parthenon** and **Centennial Park** are just across West End Avenue from Vanderbilt University and an easy walk from Vanderbilt Stadium. The Parthenon was built for the Tennessee Centennial Exposition in 1897 and redone in 1931. The Athena in the Parthenon is the largest indoor sculpture in America. There are also plaster castings of the famous Elgin marbles.

Team Leaders

Rushing Yards
8,574   Earl Campbell (1978-84)
Passing Yards
33,685   Warren Moon (1984-93)
Passing Touchdowns
196   Warren Moon (1984-93)
Receptions
542   Ernest Givins (1986-94)
Interceptions
45   Jim Norton (1960-68)
Touchdowns
73   Earl Campbell (1978-84)
Points
596   George Blanda (1960-66)

did you know?

Despite playing "home" games in Memphis in '97, the Oilers trained and practiced in Nashville, flew to Memphis on Saturdays then flew back after the game was over. Adams paid a Liberty Bowl rent of only $1 per-ticket-sold, and the Memphis Stadium Authority chipped in $300,000 to the Oilers for their weekly trips.

Against the Odds

He was an electrifying presence, with the ability to change the direction of a game any time he touched the ball. **Billy "White Shoes" Johnson** is credited with reinventing the position of kick returner, turning it into an offensive weapon. Johnson was never more dangerous than in 1975, when he returned four kicks (three punts, one kickoff) for touchdowns. A respectable receiver (37-393-1), he averaged 15.3 yards per punt return and 24.2 yards per kick return that year.

into a high-class bar, free of Vandy students because it's more expensive and a little dressier. *2000 Belcourt Ave. (615) 385-2200. Seven days 5pm-3am. All major credit cards. $$*

Best places for dinner. Green Hills Grille is always full. Grab a pager at the front desk and chat with the cool bartenders while you have a drink at the bar and wait. *2122 Hillsboro Dr. (615) 383-6444. Su-W 11am-10pm, Th 11am-11pm, F-Sa 11am-12am. All major credit cards. $$.*

Best downhome food. It's a bit of a drive out to Nashville, but the **Loveless Cafe** has some of the best southern food you'll ever have. *8400 Tenn. Hwy. 100 (615) 646-9700. M-F Lunch: 8am-2pm, dinner: 5-9pm, Sa-Su 8am-9pm. $*

Best Accommodations

Days Inn-Vanderbilt/Music Row. The place to stay if you spent too much on tickets. Well located, particularly if you want to experience the country music scene. For a little extra you can get a room with a hot tub and a steam bath. *1800 West End Ave. (615) 327-0922 $*

Union Station Hotel. Close to everything downtown, this hotel is housed in the Union Station railway site and is rated Nashville's most elegant place to stay. The stained glass vaulted ceiling in the lobby, which was the station's main hall, is something to behold. *1001 Broadway. (615) 726-1001. $$*

Loews Vanderbilt Plaza Hotel. Right in the heart of the Vanderbilt neighborhood, this hotel hosts a load of conventions and conferences but still comes across as quiet and high-class. *2100 West End Ave., (615) 320-1700. $$$$*

Washington Redskins

When you talk about the Washington Redskins, start at the beginning with George Preston Marshall and the team's original name, the Boston Braves. Marshall changed it to the Redskins a year later, but changing the name didn't help. The organization struggled for five years, and Marshall's disappointment with the lack of support in Boston grew. He finally moved the franchise out of Fenway Park to Griffith Stadium in Washington, D.C., on February 13, 1937. The early Redskins teams featured such Hall of Famers as Sammy Baugh, Cliff Battles, Turk Edwards, and Wayne Millner, who quickly created support for the new franchise. In 1940, the Redskins won their second Eastern Championship, but were humiliated in a record-breaking 73-0 demolition by the Chicago Bears in the championship game. Just three weeks earlier, the Redskins had beaten the same Chicago team 7-3 in a defensive battle. Under Sammy Baugh, the Redskins continued their winning ways, but the era ended when Baugh decided to retire in 1952.

Franchise History

Boston Braves
(1932)
Boston Redskins
(1933–1936)
Washington Redskins
(1937–Present)

By the Numbers

(Since 1970)

Regular Season: 251-171-2
Postseason: 18-10
Division Titles: 5
Vs. Division: 125-96-2 (Playoffs: 3-1)
Playoffs Appearances: 13
Home: 142-67-2
Away: 109-104

(Overall)

Regular Season: 456-399-27
Postseason: 21-14
Playoffs Appearances: 19
Home: 263-176-11
Away: 193-223-16

The '50s marked the start of another Redskins legend when Eddie LeBaron began throwing touchdowns for the burgundy and gold. More Hall of Fame names were added to the Redskins roster, such as Bobby Mitchell, Charley Taylor and Sonny Jurgensen. Moving into the late sixties, the Redskins continued to be an offensive power, and in 1967, even though they were only 5-6-3, they scored 347 points. Unfortunately the defense gave up 353.

Another legendary name took over the helm in 1969 when Vince Lombardi left Green Bay and brought his magic to D.C.

Most Revered Football Figures

Sonny Jurgensen. He could close a bar at dawn and throw six touchdown passes that afternoon. When the Eagles traded Jurgy to Washington in 1964, all the bartenders in Philadelphia wore black armbands.

George Allen. The legendary coach filled the sizable shoes of Vince Lombardi, led the team to a pair of Super Bowls, and built the Redskins-Cowboys rivalry into the stuff of legend.

John Riggins. As much a throwback-style player as Jurgensen, the wild and crazy Riggins was nearly unstoppable behind those 'Hogs. His performance in Super Bowl XVII was the highlight of a great career.

Rivalries

In 1975, the Redskins used a ninth-round draft choice on California DE Dallas Hickman, who was reportedly asked by George Allen to change his first name because the coach "didn't like Dallas." It's that kind of story, along with some great games and players, that makes it the incredibly fun feud it is. Is it any wonder we've seen **Cowboys**-Redskins an NFL-best 10 times on Monday Night Football? The Cowboys lead this series 41-33-2, but the Skins have come out on top in both of their playoff meetings. The New York **Giants** are an older and only somewhat less hated foe. New York leads this series, 74-54-4, with the teams splitting their two postseason appearances. In 1966, the Redskins beat the Giants, 72-41, in the highest-scoring NFL game of all time.

Having battled baseball's now-defunct Senators for the fans' affections, the Redskins now became the city's favorite team. After Lombardi's death two years later, George Allen was hired and another era of Redskins football was born. Allen created an atmosphere of fun and excitement for both the fans and his team. He brought in the "Over the Hill Gang" — players that teams thought were too old—to lead his Redskins, and in 1972, only his second year, the team went to the Super Bowl. Allen was a defensive genius, the originator of the emphasis on special teams as well as the term "nickel defense." Among Allen's most noted accomplishments is the creation of the Cowboys-Redskins rivalry. He often said, "I hate the Cowboys so much, I wish I could just fight Tom Landry on the fifty-yard line one-on-one." Eccentric, yes. A winner, without question.

Moving from a defensive philosophy to an offensive one, the Redskins hired Joe Gibbs in 1981 and became the best team of the '80s. Joe Gibbs' Redskins won three World Championships with John Riggins running the football, Art Monk catching touchdowns, Dave Butz stopping the run, Darrell Green defending the pass and a little quarterback by the name of Joe Theismann.

After Gibbs' retirement in 1993, Norv Turner, another offensive-minded coach, was brought in. The names have changed:

> **did you know?**
> Politics and football may be two very different things, but this is Washington, and the Redskins haven't made the playoffs during a Democratic presidency since 1945.

> "Loosen up, Sandy, baby."
> — John Riggins, dinner banquet chit-chat to Supreme Court Justice Sandra Day O'Connor.

Gus Frerotte is the quarterback, Terry Allen is the running back, and people like Dana Stubblefield and Dan Wilkinson anchor the defense, but one thing that hasn't changed for the team in their new home, Jack Kent Cooke Stadium, is the love affair that the city of Washington has with its Redskins.

—Joe Theismann

Jack Kent Cooke Stadium

For 36 years, the Redskins enjoyed perhaps the greatest homefield advantage in the NFL at RFK Stadium. For big games like Dallas, the place would literally shake. But with 55,000 seats, RFK was the smallest stadium in the NFL. In the late '80's, owner Jack Kent Cooke announced he would build a new stadium for what he called "The best bloody fans on the face of the earth." Easier said than done.

After years of roadblocks in the District of Columbia and Virginia, Cooke finally broke ground in October 1995 on a site in Landover, MD just inside the Beltway. As Cooke predicted, the new stadium opened in time for the 1997 season, but Cooke didn't live to see it. Only five months before the opening game, he died at the age of 84. As a tribute, son John Kent Cooke announced at the funeral that the stadium would be named Jack Kent Cooke Stadium.

With 80,116 seats and a grass field, what fans now call "The Big Jack" is one of the largest stadiums in the NFL. The average ticket price, $52.92, is the highest in the NFL. But luxury boxes are the name of the game, running just under $160,000 for the season. There is also a ring of yellow

did you know?

Only once has a team been ousted at home by the same opponent two straight years in the postseason. The Redskins did it to the Bears at Chicago in the 1986 and '87 Divisional Playoffs.

The "I Was There" Game

December 31, 1972: Dallas was the defending Super Bowl champion fresh off yet another miracle playoff win against the 49ers, but there was no magic in this NFC Championship Game. The Redskins were dominant. The sight of Charley Taylor hauling in a Billy Kilmer spiral (A Billy Kilmer spiral!) for a touchdown to make it 17-3 will forever be etched in the minds of the burgundy and gold faithful. (Redskins 26, Cowboys 3).

The Paper Bag Game I

December 8, 1940: Bears 73, Redskins 0. Of course, anyone old enough to have seen this NFL Championship Game is probably too old to remember it. Let's just say the game was as close as the 73-0 score indicated.

The Paper Bag Game II

January 22, 1984: Super Bowl XVIII should have been the crowning achievement of one of the great seasons in NFL history: a record 541 points and only two losses by a total of two points. They opened the playoffs with a 51-7 win over the Rams, then beat a 49ers team that would rule the league for the rest of the decade. But it all fell apart on Super Bowl Sunday. Jack Squirek's interception of Joe Theismann's "Rocket Screen" for a touchdown was the killing blow. (Raiders 38, Redskins 9).

Our Top Story

"Dallas Foils Nixon's
Debut"
November 16, 1969
Nine months after coach Lombardi encouraged him to come to the stadium in order to show his true fanhood, Richard Nixon became the first sitting U.S. president to attend a regular-season NFL game. With the chief executive watching, Washington fell to the Cowboys, 41-28. Later in his term, Nixon telephoned head coach George Allen with play-calling advice.

"Skins Sign Allen"
January 7, 1971
Seven days after the 9-4-1 Los Angeles Rams released head coach George Allen, the Redskins outjock-eyed several other teams to sign him.

"LT Ends Theismann's
Career"
November 18, 1985
Before a Monday Night Football audience, quarterback Joe Theismann suffered a gruesome compound fracture of his right leg when hit by Lawrence Taylor and Harry Carson of the Giants on a flea-flicker play. It was a premature end to a 12-year career which saw Theismann pass his way to over 25,000 yards and a Super Bowl title.

Great names

Ken Barefoot (E, 1968)
Danny Buggs (WR, 1976-79)
Cris Crissy (WR, 1981)
Don Doll (DE, 1953)
Art Gob (E, 1959-60)

did you know?
The franchise's second head coach, hired in 1933, was full-blooded Native American William Lone Star Dietz. That same year, the team name was changed from Braves to Redskins.

club seats which are available, but at a premium and only on a season-ticket basis. The seats sold to the general public are also locked up by season-ticket holders. The waiting list to buy these seats numbers more than 50,000.

RFK didn't provide enough room for quality tailgating. However, with the traffic mess around The Big Jack, fans who want to beat the jams get there early, say 10 am for 1 pm kickoffs. You haven't lived until you've eaten a burger with the works on a bagel. Once inside, things get fancier. And pricier. Nothing like a cappucino and a crab cake sandwich at a football game, eh? You can have that here if you like, but traditionalists can get that hot dog and beer with a $10 bill.

Despite the newness and beauty of the new place, a few grumbles have been heard. Access roads are choked with traffic, the subway doesn't run directly to it, those upper deck seats are a long way from the field, and it tends to be awfully quiet. And even 80,000 fans haven't been able to shake it.

The Bottom Line on Jack Kent Cooke Stadium

Address: Raljon, MD 20785
Tickets: Essentially unavailable — Senators could easily filibuster by reading aloud the Redskins' season ticket waiting list. If you want to find out for yourself, you can call (301) 276-6060 (club and executive seats) or (301) 276-6050 (regular seats).
1998: $60/$55/$40
1994: $45/$40/$35/$30 (RFK Stadium)

Best of the Redskins

Best Team

1991 (17-2): The 'Skins have captured five NFL championships, but none more impressive than their Super Bowl XXVI title squad, which rolled over and through nearly every opponent on its way to dominating the Bills in Minneapolis. An explosive, balanced attack was orchestrated by QB Mark Rypien, who enjoyed a career campaign, while LB Wilber Marshall spearheaded an unsung defense.

Greatest Players by Position

Pos:	Player
QB:	Sammy Baugh
RB:	John Riggins
WR:	Art Monk
TE:	Jerry Smith
OL:	Len Hauss
DL:	Dave Butz
LB:	Chris Hanburger
DB:	Ken Houston
P/K:	Mark Moseley
ST:	Brian Mitchell

"He's something else. He calls all the time. He even called the coach on election night to talk about the game."
— Quarterback Billy Kilmer, on President Richard Nixon.

And Don't Forget...

RB: Larry Brown. Ran with great authority and determination, and only John Riggins gained more yards rushing for the 'Skins.

WR: Gary Clark. A vital component in Washington's passing attack and a charter member of the Redkins' fabled "Posse."

RB/WR: Bobby Mitchell. The Redskins' first African-American star and a Hall of Famer, he retired with over 14,000 yards rushing, receiving and returning.

OL: Joe Jacoby. The "Hogs" may be the game's most famous set of blockers, and this four-time Pro Bowler was a rock for 13 seasons.

CB: Darrell Green. Drafted by the 'Skins in 1983, he remained fast and consistent as he concluded his 15th season in '97.

QB: Sonny Jurgensen. Known more sometimes for that paunch, but one of the most incredible arms in the game's history.

Best Argument

Wide Receiver: Art Monk or Charley Taylor? If you are looking for one player who epitomized the word consistency, look no further than Monk, a great possession-receiver and blocker who could also make the big play. Taylor was an electifying talent who began his career as a running back, then was named to eight Pro Bowls and was the NFL's all-time leader in receptions when he retired.

Best Coach

Joe Gibbs (1981-92): A hard-working strategist with a brilliant offensive mind, Gibbs' first club in 1981 started 0-5 but rallied for an 8-8 finish. That season was followed by a pair of Super Bowl appearances. Despite a humbling loss in Super Bowl XVIII, his '83 Redskins scored an NFL-record 541 points. And Gibbs remains the only coach to win Super Bowls with three different quarterbacks.

Pressbox

Who to Read...

Washington, D.C. could be the worst sports town in America. There's been no baseball since 1971, when the Senators left to become the Texas Rangers. The Wizards and Capitals have a new building and a few flashy young stars, but make no mistake about it: This is a Redskin town. Only in Washington could a local columnist gain fame for jumping on the bandwagon. During the 1991 season Tony Kornheiser of *The Washington Post* climbed aboard and rode it all the way to the Super Bowl. As the Redskins cruised to victory after victory and a Super Bowl blowout of Buffalo, the sarcastic Kornheiser cranked out weekly columns about the greatness of "Coach Joe" and his wonderful players that managed to reflect the rah-rah mood of the town and still be tongue-in-cheek. Richard Justice and Michael Wilbon of *The Washington Post* cover the Redskin beat better than anyone ever has, and the *Post*'s Sunday football section is a massive, beautiful thing to football fans. *The Washington Times* is by far the secondary paper in town, but they devote a serious effort to the Redskins.

Who to Watch...

On television, George Michael of WRC-TV–NBC has the horses and resources to kick the competition's behind. Michael uses Sonny Jurgensen for Monday and Friday analysis on his sportscasts. And must-see TV for 'Skins fans is Michael's Saturday evening show "The Redskin Report," on the same station. Michael, Jurgensen, John Riggins and local columnist Michael Wilbon give you solid discussion and criticism of the team. Games are broadcast on the local Fox affiliate, WTTG, with "Redskins Playbook" afterwards. Coach Norv Turner has a show on WJLA–ABC, and former Redskin Charles Mann is a reporter on WUSA–CBS.

Swami Sez:

Washington brought in everyone to play defensive line except Norman Schwartzkopf. If it works, they'll be back in the playoffs.

Who to Listen To...

Radio broadcasts are heard on WJFK (106.7 FM). Jurgensen, Sam Huff and play-by-play man Frank Herzog have been together for nearly 20 years. Weeknights at 7pm, "The Sports Junkies" draw many listeners. WTEM (980 AM), Washington's all-sports radio station, does its postgame show from Pitchers Sports Pub in the Greenbelt Marriott. Former Redskin greats Joe Jacoby and Monte Coleman join sports director Andy Pollin to talk about the game. Weekdays, listen for Ken Beatrice.

Parking: If you're thinking about leaving for the stadium about an hour or so before kickoff, prepare to miss the first half. There are 23,000 parking spaces around the stadium, but getting into one is another story. Traffic starts backing up a couple of hours before gametime. Your best bet may be parking at the old U.S. Airways Arena and walking about a mile.

Public Transportation: The Washington Metro Area Transit Authority (WMATA) runs shuttle buses from the Addison Road, Cheverly and Landover Metro stations. (202) 331-1671. There are also buses from various restaurants in the area.

Capacity: 78,600.

Restrooms: 74.

Where to Go . . . in Washington, D.C.

Best Bars

Best beer selection. If you've drunk it, you can probably find it in **The Brickskeller**, a basement bar near D.C.'s Dupont Circle. They claim to have the world's largest selection of beer here; even if that's not true, you won't be hurting for options with a menu that includes nearly 1,000 brews (but no drafts). *1523 22nd St. NW. (202) 293-1885. M-Th 11:30am-2am, F 11:30am-3am, Sa 6pm-3am, Su 6pm-2am.*

Best football bar. The classic sports bar right in the heart of Georgetown, **Champions: The American Sports Bar and Restaurant**, is where you want to be the night before the game. Also not a bad spot to be after the game. Don't be surprised to see a player or two drop by. *1206 Wisconsin Ave., NW. (202) 965-4005. M-F 6pm-2am, Sa-Su 11:30am-3am.*

> "Ron [Reagan] may be president, but tonight I'm king."
> — John Riggins, after being named MVP of Super Bowl XVII.

Ready For Primetime (Monday Night)

October 8, 1973: Twenty-four seconds left in the game. The Redskins lead 14-7. Dallas had fourth and goal at the Washington four. Craig Morton took the snap, rolled right and threw to Walt Garrison, whose offseason activities included bullriding. Garrison caught the ball at the goal line, where Kenny Houston rammed his shoulder into Garrison's back, wrapped his arms around the fullback and dragged him to the ground before he could get into the end zone. This time, Garrison was the bull. Against their greatest rival and with the entire nation watching, Ken Houston made the greatest tackle in Redskins history. (Redskins 14, Cowboys 7)

Overall Monday Night: 23-21

Overall Sunday Night: 6-6-1

Overall Thursday Night: 1-0

> **did you know?**
> The night before earning MVP honors in Super Bowl XXII, Quarterback Doug Williams underwent emergency root canal surgery. The media was not notified.

Think About the Weather

October 25, 1976: Even the United States Post Office would have refused to deliver on this Monday evening in Washington. A continuous downpour turned RFK Stadium into an audition for a mud wrestling tournament. Despite more than doubling the 'Skins in total yardage, St. Louis turned over the football an incredible 10 times, losing an NFL-record eight fumbles in the process (a mark since tied). (Redskins 20, Cardinals 10).

Worst Team

1961 (1-12-1): Bill McPeak inherited a Redskins squad that had lost its final eight games in 1960. His club picked up where the other left off, dropping its first nine contests before forging a 28-28 tie with the second-year Cowboys. The winless streak ended in the season's final game with a 34-24 triumph over Dallas. Still, these 'Skins scored an NFL-low 174 points, and only the expansion Vikings gave up more.

did you know?

Washington gave up an NFL-record 73 points in the infamous shutout loss to the Bears in the 1940 title game. The 'Skins scored a team-record 72 points in a 1966 victory over the Giants.

Team Leaders

Rushing Yards
7,472   John Riggins, 1976-79, 1981-85

Passing Yards
25,206   Joe Theismann, 1974-85

Passing Touchdowns
187   Sammy Baugh, 1937-52

Receptions
888   Art Monk, 1980-93

Interceptions
41   Darrell Green, 1983

Touchdowns
90   Charley Taylor, 1964-77

Points
1,206   Mark Moseley, 1974-86

Best local TV hangout. You can get good tips about the game from members of the local media, as well as a pretty good meal, at **Chadwicks Friendship Heights**, a classy joint situated about 15 minutes from downtown and a half-hour from the stadium. *5247 Wisconsin Ave. NW. (202) 362-8040. M-Th 11:30-2am, F-Sa 11:30am-3am, Su 10am-2am.*

Best Restaurants

Best spot for player sightings. The Alpine is not far from Redskin Park, the 'Skins training site. You might come across a Redskin eating the Alpine's good Italian fare (probably for free). *4770 Lee Highway, Arlington, VA. (703) 528-7600. M-Sa 11:30am-11pm, Su 12pm-10pm. All major credit cards. $$$*

Best power meal. The elite come to meet, greet, and eat at the **Palm Restaurant**. Senators and congressmen are regulars, and so is Larry King ("Buffalo, Hello what's your question?"). Redskin coach Norv Turner even showed up to celebrate a big win in 1997. *1225 19th St., NW, near Dupont Circle. (202) 293-9091. M-F 3pm-10pm, Sa 6pm-10:30pm, Su 5pm-9:30pm. All major credit cards. $$$$*

Best historical ambience. There's another **Morton's of Chicago** in Georgetown, but

While You Were Eating Turkey....

November 28, 1974: The Redskins needed a win over the Cowboys to clinch a wild card spot, and the Cowboys were down to Clint Longley at QB. After Roger Staubach was knocked out with the Skins up 16-3, Longley, who'd never taken a snap in an NFL game, came in and led the Cowboys to two touchdowns. The Redskins took the lead back in the fourth quarter, and with 35 seconds to go and Dallas on the 50 yard line, Skins fans prepared to get up from the couch and head to the table. But Longley sidestepped the blitz and connected with Drew Pearson. An Efren Herrera extra point sealed it. (Dallas 24, Washington 23).
Overall, 1-5

Fans' notes

On Screen

You've seen Joe Theismann's face somewhere; not just inside his single-bar helmet, not just as a TV analyst — that's right, you remember him from the silver screen, from the 1984 crash-and-burn release **Cannonball Run II**. Joe also ducked out of the huddle to appear in 1980's **Sam Marlowe, Private Eye** before hitting prime time full-time.

Fight Songs, etc.

No team anthem in football is loathed so much by opponents as **Hail to the Redskins**. The song, with music by band leader Barnee Breeskin and lyrics by Corinne Griffith, wife of team founder George Preston Marshall, made its debut on August 17, 1938. Marshall, no multiculturalist by today's standards, dressed up a band in imitation Indian garb to perform the first recorded half-time shows, which featured the team's fight song. In later years, the Hogs and their fellow fans have bellowed "Fight on, fight on/Till you have won/Sons of Wash-ing-ton!" to create an intimidating din in RFK Stadium.

Bookshelf

Washington Redskins: An Authorized History. Thomas Loverro (Taylor 1997). A must for every Redskin fan of any age.
Day by Day in Washington Redskins History Ken Denlinger (Macmillan 1983). Anything not in Loverro's book is in here.
Coach: A Season With Lombardi Tom Dowling (Norton 1970). The legend's time in Washington at the end of his career is nicely documented here.
Joe Gibbs: Fourth and One Joe Gibbs

and Jerry Jenkins, (Thomas Nelson 1991).
Theismann Joe Theismann and Dave Kindred (Contemporary 1987). The straight-talking ESPN broadcaster that we all know and love doesn't pull any punches here either.
Sam Baugh: Best There Ever Was. Whit Canning and Dan Jenkins (Masters Press 1997). Any football fan will benefit from learning about Slingin' Sammy and from merely reading Dan Jenkins.
My Life with the Redskins. Corinne Griffith (1947). The colorful memories of Mrs. George Preston Marshall.
All These Mornings. Shirley Povich (Prentice Hall 1969). These collected pieces by the famed *Post* writer include much on the Redskins.

You Gotta See...

▶You might still be able to find a few polystyrene Hog noses strewn about the floor of **RFK Stadium**, the Redskins' old home. The strains of "Hail To the Redskins" are no longer audible here, now that the D.C. United soccer club is the primary tenant, but it's a piece of team history that will bring back Super Bowl memories for diehards.
▶The new **MCI Arena** is now the home of the Wizards, the Capitals and the Georgetown Hoyas. It was built in central Washington because everyone complained about having to haul out to Landover. Do the Redskins know something we don't?
▶Everything else. If you're only going to do one non-football thing, take a walk along the **Mall** towards the **Vietnam Memorial** and the **Lincoln Monument**, preferably at dusk.

Hall of Fame

Sammy Baugh	(QB 1963)
Earl "Curly" Lambeau	(Coach 1963)
George Preston Marshall	(Owner 1963)
Otto Graham	(QB 1965)
Bill Dudley	(HB 1966)
Cliff Battles	(HB 1968)
Wayne Millner	(E 1968)
Albert Glen "Turk" Edwards	(T 1969)
Vince Lombardi	(Coach 1971)
Ray Flaherty	(E/Coach 1976)
Deacon Jones	(DE 1980)
Sam Huff	(LB 1982)
Sonny Jurgensen	(QB 1983)
Bobby Mitchell	(WR 1983)
Charley Taylor	(WR 1984)
Ken Houston	(DB 1986)
Stan Jones	(G 1991)
John Riggins	(FB 1992)
Joe Gibbs	(Coach 1996)
Paul Krause	(DB 1998)

Against the Odds

Everything seemed to conspire against the possibility of **Pat Fischer** (1968-77) ever becoming a star. But the little guy made good. He was a 17th-round draft pick out of Nebraska whose ability to cover receivers and knock down running backs belied his size (5'9", 170 pounds). His determined play resulted in 56 interceptions over his career, including 27 after he became a key member of George Allen's "Over the Hill Gang." Fischer was a starter on the 1972 Redskins team that fell to Miami in Super Bowl VII.

did you know?
Norv Turner has been able to get his team off to some good starts, but his record over the second half of his first four seasons was just 10-21-1.

we threw in the Connecticut Avenue one because the location used to house Duke Zeibart's. Duke's was the place to be in Washington for lunch. Never mind that most of the food was terrible. Late owner Jack Kent Cooke was such a regular that he put the team's three Super Bowl trophies in Duke's lobby. Cooke died in April of 1997, and Duke died a few months later, signaling an end to one of the great eras in Washington history. *1050 Connecticut Ave., NW. (202) 955-5997. M-F Lunch: 11:30am-2:30pm, dinner: 5pm-11pm; Sa 5pm-11pm, Su 5-10pm. AE, MC, V. $$$$*

Best Accommodations

Allen Lee Hotel. Situated in the Foggy Bottom section of D.C., right on George Washington University's campus, this simple hotel has some of the lowest rates you'll find. *2224 F St. NW. (202) 331-1224. $*

Greenbelt Marriott. The Redskins stay at this hotel before home games. It's not all that close to D.C. proper, but this hotel provides shuttle bus service to Redskins games. *6400 Ivy Lane, Greenbelt, MD. (301) 441-3700. $$-$$$*

> "The nice thing about owning a pro football team is that all you have to do to move is pack your trunks."
> — **George Preston Marshall**

Sheraton Washington. A huge, convention-center-type hotel in a town which is always hosting large groups of visitors. *2660 Woodley Rd. NW (at Connecticut Ave.). (202) 328-2000. $$$-$$$$*

The Draft

A Review of the NFL Draft since 1970

by Mel Kiper, Jr.

Arizona Cardinals

1st Round

A very inconsistent record. From 1979 to 1983, they did well by bringing in Ottis Anderson, Curtis Greer, E.J. Junior, Luis Sharpe and Leonard Smith. But they also had busts like Clyde Duncan, Anthony Bell and Kelly Stouffer. They got back on track with Ken Harvey, Eric Hill, Joe Wolf and Eric Swann. But then they also picked Garrison Hearst and Ernest Dye. Jamir Miller was a nice pick in 1994, and so was Simeon Rice in 1996. But the Cardinals have missed often, and in many years they haven't even had a first round pick. Overall a **C**.

Late Round Best Steal

In 1971, the Cardinals drafted wide receiver **Mel Gray** in the sixth round out of Missouri and he was an outstanding player, emerging as one of the best deep threats of the '70s.

Best Class by Year

In **1971**, the Cardinals drafted Norm Thompson, Dan Dierdorf, Mel Gray and Ron Yankowski. Gray was just great and Dierdorf made the Hall of Fame. That's as good as it gets for a team like the Cardinals.

Best Position

In 1972 they took **defensive lineman** Dave Butz, who did nothing for the Cardinals but was a great player for the Redskins. In 1980, they took Curtis Greer in the first round and the aptly named Rush Brown in the tenth. Both played well. In 1985, they took Freddie Joe Nunn in the first round, and he worked out for them. Other good picks have been Eric Swann, Michael Bankston, and Simeon Rice. In 1997 they got Mark Smith in the seventh round but he could end up starting. And in 1998 they took Andre Wadsworth, and if he doesn't pan out it will surprise every GM in the league.

Worst Position

The Cardinals have drafted with unbelievable inconsistency so this is hard; there are booms and busts at every position. But in 1981 they had a nice second-round pick with **quarterback** Neil Lomax, and in 1997 they had what should prove to be a good pick with Jake Plummer. But they have made some big mistakes at this position, as in 1973, when they took Gary Keithley ahead of Joe Ferguson and Dan Fouts. In 1977, they took Steve Pisarkiewicz ahead of Tommy Kramer and Vince Ferragamo. They have also drafted Rusty Lisch, Rick McIvor, Kelly Stouffer (6th overall!), Tony Sacca and Stoney Case.

Atlanta Falcons

1st Round

The Falcons have been horrible over the years in the first round. Their hits have been Steve Bartkowski, Bill Fralic, Mike Kenn, Junior Miller and Gerald Riggs, none of whom were truly outstanding. Other good picks were Deion Sanders and Tony Casillas, who left and did better elsewhere. There have just been too many busts like Aundray Bruce and Bruce Pickens and other poor defensive backs like Clarence Ellis and Bobby Butler. Overall a **D**.

Late Round Best Steal

Even a bad drafting organization will eventually wake up and take a good player late in the draft, as the Falcons did in 1988 with wide receiver **Michael Haynes** in the seventh round out of Northern Arizona.

Best Class by Year

It says a lot about the Falcons that their best class, **1991**, would feature a complete flop with their first rounder and that the rest of the class would do more for other teams, though not playing much better than solid journeymen. The Falcons drafted cornerback Bruce Pickens with the third overall pick and he was a complete flop. They missed a solid corner in Todd Lyght as well as Eric Swann and Herman Moore. That flub really helped other teams. They also got Mike Pritchard in the first round and Erric Pegram in the third. Both of the those players did well on other teams. And so did their second round pick, Brett Favre. The one time they nab a great player, they trade him.

Best Position

The Falcons have drafted **quarterbacks** Steve Bartkowski, Chris Miller and Brett Favre. Alright, so they traded Favre away, but they *did* draft him. At **running back**, over the years the Falcons have found some pretty decent guys too, such as Art Malone, William Andrews, Gerald Riggs, Steve Broussard, Erric Pegram, Bob Christian, Jamal Anderson and Byron Hanspard.

Worst Position

Even though they drafted Deion Sanders, **defensive back** is still their worst position. Here's why: Clarence Ellis, Maurice Spencer, Charles Johnson, Earl Jones, Scott Werner, Vaughn Mansfield, James Britt, Rod McSwain and Reggie Pleasant (who was anything but). Ellis and Butler were first rounders and, most painfully, Pickens was a bust as the third player chosen in 1991. There's more, but you get the picture.

Baltimore Ravens

1st Round

In their first two drafts, the Ravens have done well. In 1996, they selected special teamer Jermaine Lewis, offensive tackle Jonathan Ogden and linebacker Ray Lewis. All in all a solid draft, and they topped it in 1997. The 1997 Ravens draft may eventually produce five, maybe six, starters in Peter Boulware, Jamie Sharper, Tyrus McCloud, Cornell Brown, RB Jay Graham and DB Ralph Staten. The only mistake they've made so far was trading up to get DeRon Jenkins in the second round in 1996. Jenkins doesn't ruin the class, but he has not been a player worth trading up for. Overall a **B**.

Best Late Round Steal

So far the Ravens haven't pulled off any late round surprises.

Best Class by Year

They have only had two drafts, and both were pretty good. The 1996 draft of Ogden and the two Lewises is very strong. Any draft that produces a starting left tackle AND a starting middle linebacker is one to be proud of. But in **1997**, the Ravens selected six players who may eventually start for them. That's the name of the game on draft day, so the class of '97 is the benchmark in Baltimore.

Best Position

The Ravens drafted their entire starting **linebacker** corps in the organization's first two drafts. In 1996 they took Ray Lewis, who is one of the best defensive players in the NFL, and in 1997 they grabbed Peter Boulware and Jamie Sharper. Their depth at linebacker also came in the draft, when they selected Tyrus McCloud and Cornell Brown in 1997, with Brown a nice pick in the sixth round.

Worst Position

Given that they've done fairly well in their two drafts, the Ravens get away clean in this category.

Buffalo Bills

1st Round

A mixed bag. They took Al Cowlings in 1970, and he's known for his off-field exploits and choice of friends more than anything else. Other first-round busts: J.D. Hill, Walt Patulski, Phil Dokes, Tom Cousineau, Perry Tuttle, Booker Moore and Tony Hunter. Good choices were Joe DeLamielleure, Jerry Butler, Greg Bell, Bruce Smith, Ronnie Harmon, Will Wolford, Shane Conlan, Henry Jones, John Fina and Ruben Brown. A few great picks, several good ones and a lot of busts. Overall a **C**.

Late Round Best Steal

They haven't done well at this position, but two of their best late round grabs were wide receivers. In 1971 they got **Bob Chandler** in the seventh round, and in 1985 they picked **Andre Reed** in the fourth out of Kutztown. Fourth isn't that late, but for the Bills to get anything from a wide receiver is a steal.

Best Class by Year

Buffalo is not an outstanding draft team. Their best class appears to be **1979**, even though their top pick, Tom Cousineau, was a bust. They also got Jerry Butler in the first round, as well as Fred Smerlas and Jim Haslett in the second round.

Best Position

They have used number ones and later picks at **defensive back** and done well. In the mid-'70's they drafted Mario Clark, Keith Moody and Charles Romes, all of whom contributed. In 1987, Nate Odomes was a second-round pick, and he started for some of their Super Bowl teams. Martin Mayhew played his best for the Redskins, but the Bills got him in the tenth round in 1988. Henry Jones was a first round pick in 1991, and he's been a good safety. Other good picks have been Matt Darby (5th round in 1992) Kurt Schulz (7th round in 92), Thomas Smith (1st round in 1993) and Jeff Burris (1st round in 1994).

Worst Position

An example of the tough luck that the Bills have had at **wide receiver** is the draft of 1982. They traded up for Perry Tuttle, who did nothing, and missed out on Mike Quick. From third-rounder John Kimbrough in 1977 to first-rounder Eric Moulds in 1996, the Bills just haven't been able to draft wide receivers. Jerry Butler in the first round in 1979 was good, and they hit it big with Andre Reed in 1985 in the fourth round, but after him it's Danny Fulton, Bucky Brooks and Byron Franklin.

Carolina Panthers

1st Round

Not that good. In 1995 they had three picks. Kerry Collins started out well but took a big step backward in 1997. Tyrone Poole was a good rookie, but is now on the trading block, and Blake Brockermeyer has been fine. In 1996, Tim Biakabutuka was a major bust, and Rae Carruth in 1997 has been just OK. Overall a **C-**

Late Best Round Steal

In 1995, defensive back **Chad Cota** from Oregon was a seventh round pick.

Best Class by Year

1995 stands out, and it wasn't that good. The Panthers got Kerry Collins, Shawn King, Frank Garcia and Chad Cota. For their sake, let's hope this draft doesn't last too long as their best.

Best Position

With only four drafts under their belt, the Panthers have shown a strength in drafting for the **offensive line**. Blake Brockermeyer, Frank Garcia and Norberto Garrido-Davidds make for the nucleus of a strong unit.

Worst Position

In four drafts, the Panthers have used seven picks at **defensive line** and **defensive back** and have underwhelmed. Given how high some of these picks were, Shawn King, Steve Strahan, J.C. Price, Kerry Hicks, Matt Finkes, Kinnon Tatum and Tarek Saleh are either gone or disappointments.

Chicago Bears

Overall, the Bears drafts have been pretty vanilla; nothing to sink your teeth into on the good or bad side. They have done fairly well, though, in the first round. They were shaky in the early 70's with guys like Wally Chambers and Dennis Lick. Walter Payton in 1975 was their big hit. And they did pick it up starting in 1979 with Dan Hampton and Al Harris. They continued with Otis Wilson, Keith Van Horne, Jim McMahon, Jimbo Covert, Willie Gault, Wilber Marshall, William Perry, Neal Anderson and Jim Harbaugh. In 1988, they got two OK players in Brad Muster and Wendell Davis. In 1989 they also got two decent players in Donnell Woolford and Trace Armstrong. Other nice picks have been Mark Carrier, Alonzo Spellman and Curtis Conway. Recent busts have been Stan Thomas and Rashaan Salaam. Overall a **B**.

Best Late Round Steal

In 1983, the Bears chose **Richard Dent** in the eighth round out of Tennessee State who went on to win MVP honors in Super Bowl XX. Pretty nice value for the eighth round.

Best Class by Year

In **1983**, the Bears stocked up for a great run with Jimbo Covert, Willie Gault, Mike Richardson, Dave Duerson, Tom Thayer, Mark Bortz and Richard Dent.

Best Position

Defensive tackle, but only because I had to pick one. In 1975, they got Mike Hartenstine, who was pretty good. In 1978, they took Brad Shearer in the third round, who was OK. In 1979 they made a great pick in the first round with Dan Hampton. In 1985, they took The Refrigerator, William Perry, in the first round. In 1991, they took Chris Zorich in the second, and in 1994 they got Jim Flanigan in the fourth round. That's as good as it gets for the Bears.

Worst Position

A lot of busts at **wide receiver**. The Bear have drafted players such as Wayne Wheeler, Ricky Watts, James Maness, David Williams, Ron Morris, Tony Moss, Jack Jackson and Marcus Robinson. All of these guys were unspectacular.

Cincinnati Bengals

1st Round

From 1984-97, the Bengals had 18 first-round picks and with the exception of WR Eddie Brown (1985) and Tim McGee (1986), they've not lived up to billing, at least as Bengals. In 1984, they chose Ricky Hunley. Later problems suggest that the Bengals really hadn't done their homework anyway. In 1984, they also chose Pete Koch and Brian Blados in the first round. Ugh. In 1992, QB David Klingler at number six overall was a great pick — for the team who picked seventh. In 1994 and 1995, the Bengals had the number one pick overall and essentially blew it both times. Dan Wilkinson in 1994 was a profound underacheiver who has since left the team (he's now a Redskin), and Ki-Jana Carter in 1995 was lost to injury his first year and has produced little since. Overall a **D**.

Late Round Best Steal

Boomer Esiason was a good second-round pick in 1984 but his teammate **Tim Krumrie** was a true steal. In 1983, the Bengals took Krumrie, who attended Wisconsin, in the tenth round. Krumrie played solid defensive line for the Bengals for many years and played in Super Bowl XXIII.

Best Class by Year

Gee ... let's hope 1998 is! Cincinnati got Takeo Spikes and Brian Simmons in the first round.

Best Position

Going back to 1973, when they chose Isaac Curtis in the first round, the Bengals have had a knack for finding excellent **wide receivers**. In 1976, another first-round pick was used on Billy Brooks. In 1981, they selected Cris Collinsworth. Eddie Brown arrived in 1985, another first-round selection. University of Tennessee has provided the Bengals with two solid wide receivers, Tim McGee in 1986 and Carl Pickens in 1992. More recent receiver picks that have paid off for the Bengals are Darnay Scott and David Dunn.

Worst Position

The 1997 selection of Florida State's Reinard Wilson is symbolic of the Bengals' woes in drafting good **linebackers**. Wilson was a first-round choice and he bombed out. Other busts include third-rounder Steve Shine in 1994, third-rounder Bernard Clark in 1990 and Kevin Walker, a third-rounder in 1988. James Francis was a chosen in the first round in 1990 and was nothing special after a solid rookie campaign. In 1984, the Bengals chose Ricky Hunley number seven overall but could not sign him. Naturally, he went on to a decent, if not troubled career with the Denver Broncos.

Cleveland Browns

It's important to remember that the organization that made these picks, Art Modell and company, is now in Baltimore running the Ravens. This is their legacy in Cleveland. The new Browns may have the old names, dates and records but they are starting from scratch as an organization on draft day.

Not a bad job here. They got Greg Pruitt and 1976. In 1978 they really hit it big with Ozzie Newsome and Clay Matthews. You can't draft much better than that. Other top picks have been Hanford Dixon, Chip Banks, Don Rogers, Eric Metcalf, Eric Turner, Steve Everitt, Antonio Langham and Derrick Alexander (though these last two guys are essentially Ravens). Players such as Charles White and Tommy Vardell have been OK and the busts have been Willis Adams, Michael Junkin, Clifford Charlton and Craig Powell. Overall a **B**.

Late Round Best Steal

Two stand out. In 1988, they selected safety **Thane Gash** in the seventh round out of East Tennessee State and he was a pretty good player. And in 1987, they got **Frank Winters** in the tenth out of Western Illinois and he started for the Packers when they won it all in 1996.

Best Class by Year

1978 was great with Matthews and Newsome but there was nothing after them. So you have to say **1990** based on sheer volume. They had no first rounder but they came up with Leroy Hoard, Anthony Pleasant, Harlon Barnett, Rob Burnett, Randy Hilliard and Scott Galbreath. That's three key guys in Hoard, Pleasant and Burnett and three serviceable backups and situational guys.

Best Position

In 1975, the Browns took Dick Ambrose in the twelfth round and he was an outstanding player. Other great **linebacker** picks made between 1976 and 1982 were Robert Jackson, Clay Matthews, Cliff Odom, Eddie Johnson and Chip Banks. That's six top shelf linebackers in eight years. Matthews and Banks had a lot to live up to as first round picks and they did.

Worst Position

Linebacker also comes up as the Browns worst position because they wasted some early picks on complete busts. In 1987, they took Mike Junkin in the first round and he was a washout. Same goes for their first rounder in 1988, Clifford Charlton. In 1988, they also wasted a third rounder on Van Waiters. And in 1995 they took Craig Powell in the first round and he was a complete bust.

Dallas Cowboys

1st Round

The Cowboys have been hot and cold in the first round. They had a nice run in the early 1970s with Duane Thomas, Billy Joe Du Pree, "Too Tall" Jones, Randy White, Thomas Henderson, Aaron Kyle and Tony Dorsett. Then they hit a bad streak with Larry Bethea, Robert Shaw, Howard Richards and Rod Hill. Jim Jeffcoat was a nice pickup in 1983, but then they hit the skids again with Billy Cannon Jr. in 1984 and Kevin Brooks in 1985. Things finally picked up from 1988 to 1992 with Michael Irvin, Troy Aikman, Emmitt Smith, Russell Maryland, Alvin Harper, Kevin Smith and Robert Jones. They had no first rounders in 1993, 1995 and 1996, and Shante Carver was a bust in 1994. Another bad run? Overall a **C+**.

Late Round **Best Steal**

The Cowboys have a few nice late-round picks but none better than defensive tackle **Leon Lett** of Emporia State in the seventh round of 1991. Safety Brock Marion was also a seventh-round pick in 1993.

Best Class by Year

Two stand out. Gil Brandt drafted White, Henderson, Burton Lawless, Bob Breunig, Pat Donovan, Mike Hegman and Mitch Hoopes in 1975. But Jimmy Johnson outdid him in **1991** when he got Maryland, Harper, Dixon Edwards, Erik Williams and Lett.

Best Position

The Cowboys have had two streaks of drafting high quality **defensive linemen**. From 1973 to 1975, they drafted Harvey Martin, Jones and White. In 1978, the had a first-round bust in Bethea, as well as two more with Kevin Brooks in 1985 and Danny Noonan in 1987, but they did get Jim Jeffcoat in 1983. Then starting in 1988, they went on another roll. In 1988, the Cowboys drafted Chad Hennings, Tony Tolbert in '89, Jimmie Jones in 90, and then Maryland and Lett in '91.

Worst Position

Despite the success of recent years at this position, the Cowboys have had trouble at **linebacker**. In 1980, they drafted Bill Roe and got nothing. In 1981, Scott Pelluer and Derrie Nelson. Both did nothing. In 1982, Jeff Rohrer and Jim Eliopulos. In 1983, the Cowboys took Mike Walter — he did nothing for Dallas but starred in San Francisco. Billy Cannon Jr. was a major first-round washout in 1984. And Jesse Penn was a second-round bust in 1985. In six years, they spent eight picks on linebackers and got nothing. Finally things picked up from 1988 to 1993, with Ken Norton Jr, Edwards, and Robert Jones, then Barry Minter and Darrin Smith. Then they went back to drafting the likes of DeWayne Dotson, Dana Howard and Linc Harden.

Denver Broncos

1st Round

The Broncos have been spotty in the first round, often not even having a pick. They have had two good runs in the first round. From 1972 to 1975, they got Riley Odoms, Otis Armstrong, Randy Gradishar and Louis Wright. Then from 1981 to 1989 they got Dennis Smith, Chris Hinton (read John Elway) and Steve Atwater. And in 1996, they got John Mobley, a great pick. Also sprinkled in there, however, are Tommy Maddox, Gerald Willhite, Steve Sewell, Ted Gregory and Mike Croel, none of whom performed at the level expected of a first rounder. Overall, **C+**.

Late Round Best Steal

The Broncos have had several late-round steals. In 1975, they got Steve Foley in the eighth. In 1987, they got Tyrone Braxton in the 12th round. In 1990, they got All-Pro TE Shannon Sharpe in the seventh round. And in 1994, they chose Tom Nalen in the seventh round, and he has been one of the better centers in the league. But the best late-round steal the Broncos have made was in 1983, when they took the outstanding linebacker **Karl Mecklenburg** in the 12th round out of Minnesota.

Best Class by Year

In **1983**, they selected offensive lineman Chris Hinton and traded him, with Mark Herrmann and a first round pick in 1984, for John Elway. That's a great draft.

Best Position

Denver has had a strong run in drafting players for the **defensive backfield**. In 1973 the Broncos drafted Lyle Blackwood in the ninth round. He did not play in Denver but excelled in Miami and Baltimore. In 1975 they drafted Louis Wright, a great cornerback, in the first round, and they also got Steve Foley in the eighth round. Then in 1981 they took Dennis Smith in the first round, another very good player. In 1987, they absolutely stole Tyrone Braxton in the 12th round. In 1989, they did another double dip with Steve Atwater in the first round and the solid Darren Carrington in the fifth.

Worst Position

First of all, they didn't draft John Elway or Craig Morton. When Denver has actually selected a **quarterback**, here are some of the names: Mike Franckowiak, Craig Penrose and Rick Leach. In 1981, they took Mark Herrmann, who was included in the Elway trade but never amounted to much. In 1983, they drafted Gary Kubiak, who spent his career as Elway's backup and is now the team's offensive coordinator. Other misses were Todd Ellis and Tommy Maddox, a total bust in the first round of 1992.

Detroit Lions

1st Round

For a team that really hasn't perfromed all that well over the years, the Lions have had a recent string of pretty good drafts. Since 1985, they have had nine very good picks and only three busts. The nice picks were guys like Lomas Brown, Bennie Blades, Barry Sanders, Herman Moore, Robert Porcher, Johnnie Morton, Luther Elliss and Bryant Westbrook. The stinkers have been Chuck Long, Andre Ware and Reggie Rogers. Overall a **B**.

Late Best Round Steal

In 1980, the Lions got a good kicker when they took **Eddie Murray** in the seventh round out of Tulane.

Best Class by Year

There was not a lot to choose from, but **1988** was a decent year. They got Bennie Blades, Chris Spielman, Eric Andolsek, William White and Pat Carter. Blades and Spielman were the stars but the others were steady and solid players.

Best Position

Draft day hasn't brought much to remember in Detroit. Barry Sanders alone makes **running back** their best draft position. They got a decent player in the third round in 1974 with Dexter Bussey. Billy Sims was a smart pick in 1980 and Sanders in 1989. That's it.

Worst Position

In 1971, they took Frank Harris in the sixth round. Other late picks were spent on **quarterbacks** the likes of Dennis Franklin, Steve Mathieson, Jeff Komlo, Eric Hipple, Mike Machurek, John Witkowski. They spent a first rounder on Chuck Long in 1986 and probably wished they hadn't. In 1989, they took Rodney Peete in the sixth round, and he was OK for that low a pick. They took Andre Ware in the first round in 1990, and that did not work out. Not much success but they did learn — Detroit didn't draft a quarterback from 1991 to 1997.

Green Bay Packers

1st Round

Before Ron Wolf arrived as the General Manager, the Packers were shaky on draft day. Some of their busts were guys like wide receiver Barry Smith in 1973, fullback Barty Smith in 1974 and offensive tackle Mark Koncar in 1976. They did well with James Lofton in 1978 and Sterling Sharpe in 1988, but they followed up Sharpe in 1989 with Tony Mandarich, the number two pick overall and one of the more celebrated flops in league history. But since 1993, the Packers have drafted guys who can play such as Wayne Simmons, George Teague, Aaron Taylor, Craig Newsome, John Michels and Ross Verba. Overall a **C-**.

....

Late Round Best Steal

In 1990, the Packers selected **Bryce Paup** in the sixth round out of Northern Iowa, and he has been a tremendous player in the NFL, especially after he moved on to Buffalo where he won the Defensive Player of the Year award in 1995.

....

Best Class by Year

The Packers and Ron Wolf really hit it big in **1993** with Wayne Simmons, George Teague, Earl Dotson, Mark Brunell, James Willis, Doug Evans and Bob Kuberski — a lot of talent to add in one year.

....

Best Position

The Packers were not that great for a long time, so it's hard to find much here. We'll say **wide receiver**, based on just five players, but they're good ones. In 1978, they drafted James Lofton. Ten years later they picked Sterling Sharpe. In 1992, the Packers chose Robert Brooks, and in 1995 they selected Antonio Freeman. In 1996 it was Derrick Mayes. It would be easier to find 20 positions at which they were bad, but at least Green Bay has been passable.

....

Worst Position

Remember that they did not draft Brett Favre but did choose Jerry Tagge, David Whitehurst, Dennis Sproul and Keith Myers. In 1981, they took Rich Campbell with the sixth pick overall. Other bad picks at **quarterback** were Randy Wright and Robbie Bosco. In 1987, Don Majkowski was a pretty good tenth-round pick, but he didn't last long. In 1992, Ty Detmer was a decent pick, and in 1993 they drafted Mark Brunell, but then traded him. Jay Barker was a washout in 1995. There were a few others, but the bottom line is that Favre has been their only real guy since Bart Starr retired — and they traded for him.

Indianapolis Colts

1st Round

In 1972, they had a major bust with Tom Drougas, an offensive tackle out of Oregon. They bounced back in 1973 with Bert Jones at QB and Joe Ehrmann, a great defensive tackle. 1974 was also solid with John Dutton and Roger Carr. But then in 1975 they took Ken Huff over Walter Payton. Since then they have made lousy picks and bad decisions. Ken Novak, Randy Burke and Reese McCall were all terrible. In 1982 they took Johnie Cooks over Chip Banks at linebacker and Art Schlichter over Jim McMahon at QB. In 1983, they drafted John Elway, but Robert Irsay traded him before Ernie Accorsi could sign him, which I think he would have done eventually. Then there's Jon Hand, Steve Emtman, Jeff George, Trev Alberts. A lot of busts. Overall a **C-**.

Late Round **Best Steal**

In 1972, late in the 17th and final round, the Colts selected **Stan White** out of Ohio State. He was a very good outside linebacker for many years. Not bad for the 438th player taken.

Best Class by Year

They had a great first round in **1973** with Bert Jones and Joe Ehrmann. They followed up with Mike Barnes in the second round. David Taylor was a solid fifth-round pick as a guard out of Catawba. And they finished if off with Ray Oldham in the eighth round, who was a backup in the secondary and a great special teams player.

Best Position

Not an easy call, but they had Norm Bulaich in 1970 as a first rounder at **running back**, a good pick. In 1971, the first round brought Don McCauley from North Carolina, a good third down type of back. Lydell Mitchell in the second round in 1972 was a strong pick, too. Then you have to go to 1990 for another winner, Anthony Johnson in the second round. Marshall Faulk has been OK as a first rounder in 1994. There are no Hall of Famers here, but it's their best position.

Worst Position

Their **defensive linemen** have just not done it. In 1975, they picked Dave Pear in the third round, and he was no peach. Paul Linford came in the fourth round that year, and he was no better. In 1976, they got Ken Novak in the first round. The list goes on. In 1986, their first rounder and the fourth pick overall, Jon Hand, was a major washout. Mitchell Benson, their third rounder in 1989, did nothing. In 1992, the first pick overall, Steve Emtman, was solid when healthy but couldn't stay healthy.

Jacksonville Jaguars

1st Round

The Jaguars know how to draft. In 1995, they drafted two anchors for their offensive lines in Tony Boselli and Brian DeMarco and solid running back James Stewart. In 1996, they looked at defense and came up with DE Tony Brackens, LB Kevin Hardy and CB Aaron Beasley. In 1997, DT Renaldo Wynn arrived as a first rounder for more defensive help. Overall a **B**.

Late Round Best Steal

In 1995, the Jags selected **Rob Johnson** in the fourth round. That same year, Buffalo took Todd Collins in the second round. Cut to 1998. The Bills trade their first-round pick, ninth overall, for Johnson. The Jaguars turned a fourth-round player, with little NFL experience, into a top ten pick.

Best Class by Year

Hard to say after four drafts, but **1995** looks pretty good. In addition to Boselli, DeMarco, Stewart and Johnson, they also grabbed linebacker Bryan Schwartz and S Chris Hudson.

Best Position

So far no one position has emerged as particularly strong for the Jaguars

Worst Position

On the other hand, they haven't shown any patterns on the downside, either.

Kansas City Chiefs

They've had seven booms, eight OK picks and 12 busts. Gary Green was a very good cornerback out of Baylor in 1977. They also got those great defensive players in Art Still, Bill Maas, Neil Smith and Derrick Thomas. In 1984, along with Maas, they drafted John Alt in the first round, a very good offensive tackle, and Dale Carter was a nice pick in 1992. Some of the busts were Trezelle Jenkins, Greg Hill, Paul Palmer, Willie Scott, Brian Jozwiak (seventh overall pick in 1986 and a huge bust), Todd Blackledge and Anthony Hancock. A bunch of bad picks from 1979 to 1986. Overall a **C+**.

Late Round **Best Steal**

In 1990, they got **Dave Szott** in the seventh round from Penn State. Szott has been an outstanding player at offensive guard and was named All-Pro in 1997.

Best Class by Year

It was hard to find a strong consistent draft in Kansas City, but go with **1996**. They got Jerome Woods, a defensive back in the first round. Reggie Tongue, another defensive back, came in the second round. Other picks were John Browning, Donnie Edwards and Joe Horn. All of these guys made the team. The Chiefs have not had a lot of great drafts, although things have picked up a bit since GM Carl Peterson arrived.

Best Position

In 1978, the Chiefs took an outstanding player, Art Still, in the first round. The next year they went back to the **defensive line** and picked Mike Bell, who was also good. The seventh round in 1979 provided a decent player in Ken Kramer. Other top picks on the D line have been Bill Maas in 1984 and Neil Smith in 1988. In 1989, they drafted Derrick Thomas, who has played defensive end and linebacker — wherever he plays, he's been a great pass rusher. And in 1996 in the third round they got John Browning, a player the Chiefs very much like.

Worst Position

In 1974, they picked **running back** Woody Green in the first round; he was OK but not great. In 1977, they took Tony Reed from Colorado in the second round, who ran for 1,053 yards in '78. That year they also took Mark Bailey and other washouts include Earl Grant, Ethan Horton and Paul Palmer. In 1991 they took Harvey Williams in the first round. He's had his moments but was inconsistent. And Greg Hill was a major bust in the first round in 1994.

Miami Dolphins

1st Round

Not a great track record. First the good news. In 1976 they took Larry Gordon and Kim Bokamper, and in 1977 they got A.J. Duhe — three good players. Jon Gisler in 1979 was a fine pick for the offensive line. They hit the jackpot with Dan Marino in 1983. Richmond Webb was a good pick in 1990. In 1992, they got Troy Vincent and Marco Coleman, who were decent picks. But there's also David Overstreet in 1981, Jackie Shipp in 1984, Lorenzo Hampton in 1985, John Bosa in 1987, Eric Kumerow in 1988 — each one a bust. In 1989, there was Sammie Smith and Louis Oliver. Oliver was OK but Smith did nothing. Billy Milner was a major bust in 1995. Overall a **C**.

Late Round Best Steal

Veterans will remember Vern Den Herder, a ninth rounder in 1971 who played well at defensive end for years. They have also drafted good kickers with late picks, like Joe Danelo in 1975's tenth round. Uwe Von Schamann (1979) and Fuad Reveiz (1985) were both seventh rounders. And they got Pete Stoyanovich in the eighth in 1989. Still, **Mark Clayton** in the eighth round in 1983 is about as good a late pick as you can make.

Best Class by Year

They got TE Jim Mandich in the second round in **1970**, Tim Foley at DB in the third round, and Curtis Johnson, another DB, in the fourth round. Jake Scott was a seventh rounder who made big contributions at safety (MVP in Super Bowl VII). Hubert Ginn was a decent running back in the ninth round, and they finished it off with a solid linebacker, Mike Kolen, in the twelfth round.

Best Position

The names at **wide receiver** say it all. Nat Moore was a third rounder in 1974, Freddie Solomon a second rounder in 1975. In 1978, Jimmy Cefalo was a reliable receiver. Mark Duper came in the second round in 1982, and the eighth-round pick in 1983 was Mark Clayton, a tremendous pick. In 1993 they got O.J. McDuffie in the first round.

Worst Position

The names at **linebacker** say it all here, too. In 1982, Charles Bowser was a bowser in the fourth round. In 1984, they wasted a first rounder on Jackie Shipp and got just a little from Jay Brophy. Then there's Alex Moyer, Rick Graf, Eric Kumerow (a first rounder) — all picked between the first and third rounds and all busts. In 1994, the Dolphins picked Aubrey Beavers in the second round and Ronnie Woolfork in the fourth round, both of whom did nothing.

Minnesota Vikings

1st Round

The Vikings have done pretty well in the first round. The best were Chuck Foreman, Jeff Siemon, Fred McNeill, Mark Mullaney, Chris Doleman, Randall McDaniel, Tommy Kramer, Keith Millard, Joey Browner, Todd Steussie and Robert Smith. Some of the busts were James White, Randy Holloway, Gerald Robinson and D.J. Dozier. For several years the Vikings did not have a number one pick. Overall a **B-**.

Late Round Best Steal

The Vikings have grabbed several good players in later rounds, such as ninth-rounder Scott Studwell, a linebacker from Illinois (1977), and a seventh rounder from Brown in tight end Steve Jordan (1982). Quarterback Brad Johnson was another enviable ninth-round pick in 1992. But in 1990 they got a great running back in the ninth when they took **Terry Allen** from Clemson.

Best Class by Year

The Class of **1992** stands out even without the benefit of a pick in the first round. They still ended up with Johnson, Robert Harris, Roy Barker, Brad Culpepper and Ed McDaniel on defense and fullback Charles Evans.

Best Position

In 1975, they got a good **defensive lineman** in Mark Mullaney. Doug Martin was also a solid first rounder from 1980. In 1984 and '85 they really hit with Keith Millard and Chris Doleman respectively. They have also hit with Joe Phillips, Henry Thomas, Al Noga, Robert Harris, Roy Barker and Brad Culpepper. In 1993, the Vikings drafted Gilbert Brown in the third round. Other decent players have been Mike Wells, Derrick Alexander and Duane Clemons. They did have a few busts in there but overall they have done well at this position.

Worst Position

In 1972 they drafted Jeff Siemon, a good middle **linebacker**, and in '74 they got Fred McNeill and Matt Blair, but after that, from 1978 to 1993, the Vikings did some awful things on draft day. They took guys like Whip Walton, Jerry Meter, Robin Sendlein, Jim Fahnhorst, Walker Lee Ashley, Mark Stewart, Tim Meamber, Ray Berry and David Braxton, all of whom did nothing. That was it, until Minnesota took Ed McDaniel in 1992.

New England Patriots

1st Round

Over the years, the first round has been very good to the Patriots. Jim Plunkett in 1971. In 1973, they had a tremendous first round with John Hannah, Sam Cunningham and Darryl Stingley. Russ Francis came in 1975. Nineteen seventy six was another great year with Mike Haynes, Pete Brock and Tim Fox. Nineteen seventy seven delivered Raymond Clayborn and Stanley Morgan, two of the best players in team history. Other good first-round picks include Roland James, Brian Holloway, Irving Fryar, Bruce Armstrong, John Stephens, Leonard Russell, Pat Harlow, Drew Bledsoe, Ty Law and Terry Glenn. There have been busts (Vagas Ferguson, Eugene Chung, Hart Lee Dykes, Chris Singleton, Ray Agnew and Reggie Dupard), but overall a **B+**.

Late Round Best Steal

Nineteen ninety one, fifth round, **Ben Coates**, TE, Livingstone College. Coates is a Pro Bowl player who holds the record for receptions in a season by a tight end.

Best Class by Year

Despite their great drafts from 1973 to 1977, the **1995** draft may be their best. This draft included Ty Law, Ted Johnson, Curtis Martin, Jimmy Hitchcock and Dave Wohlabaugh, all of whom played in the Super Bowl in their second year. Martin was an absolute gem but is now a Jet. Hitchcock was traded to the Vikings for a third-round pick in 1999, but the other players are big contributors.

Best Position

The Patriots have found some **quarterback** talent in the draft. In 1971, they took Jim Plunkett with the first pick overall, and he was worth it. Ask the Raiders. In 1975, they chose Steve Grogan in the fifth round. They chose Tony Eason in 1983, and he played in as many Super Bowls as Dan Marino. In 1987, they selected Rich Gannon in the fourth round, still an effective NFL backup. Round four in 1991 delivered Scott Zolak, still their number two guy, and Drew Bledsoe has more than lived up to his promise as the number one overall in 1993.

Worst Position

In 1982, they had the first pick overall and the last pick in round one and blew them both on mediocre **defensive linemen** Kenneth Sims and Lester Williams. The list goes on; Ben Thomas in 1985, Mike Ruth in '86, Chris Gannon in 1989. In 1990, they wasted the tenth pick overall on Ray Agnew. There's more: Kevin Johnson in 1993 and Ervin Collier in 1994. Busts.

New Orleans Saints

1st Round

Not a great story here. Archie Manning was a smart call in 1971. Chuck Muncie (1976) was a good running back for a few years, as was George Rogers (1981). Other fine picks have been Wes Chandler, Wayne Martin, Joe Johnson and William Roaf. That leaves a lot of room for Rick Middleton, Larry Burton, Kurt Schumacher, Joe Campbell, Russell Erxleben, Lindsay Scott, Alvin Toles, Shawn Knight and Vaughn Dunbar. You can see why they have so rarely made the playoffs. Overall a **D**.

Late Best Round Steal

In 1985, the Saints selected wide receiver **Eric Martin** in the seventh round. It may have helped that he played at LSU.

Best Class by Year

For such a weak drafting team, the Saints surprisingly put together a strong year in **1986**, when they drafted Jim Dombrowski, Dalton Hilliard, Pat Swilling, Barry Word and Rueben Mayes. They got help on both sides of the ball and even grabbed a surplus at running back with Hilliard and Mayes.

Best Position

For a team that has not drafted well overall, the Saints do have something to be proud of at **running back**, even showing a knack for getting more than one good runner in a single draft. They got Chuck Muncie and Tony Galbreath in 1976, and then in 1986, they hit three times with Dalton Hilliard, Rueben Mayes and Barry Word, though Word had his best years with the Chiefs. In 1981 New Orleans made a good choice with George Rogers. In 1988, Craig Heyward got the nod as their first-round choice. They did miss with Vaughn Dunbar in the first round of 1992 but have since bounced back with Mario Bates in 1994 and Ray Zellars in 1995.

Worst Position

For the most part, the Saints have not spent high draft picks at **defensive back** and have paid the price, even though in 1980 they scored big with Dave Waymer (second round) the team's all-time interception leader. From 1978 to 1988, New Orleans picked Eric Felton, Ricky Ray, Mike Jolly, Jitter Fields and Mike Adams, none of whom panned out. In 1989, they picked defensive backs in the second, third and fourth rounds and busted out with Robert Massey, Kim Phillips and Mike Mayes. The Saints did OK with Vince Buck as a second rounder in 1990 until he got hurt, and 1996 first rounder Alex Molden has been acceptable.

New York Giants

1st Round

Not a great story here. In the 1970's the Giants had washouts like Rocky Thompson, Troy Archer, John Hicks, Gordon King and Gary Jeter. Things pick up in 1979 with Phil Simms. In the '80s, they go on a nice roll with Mark Haynes, Lawrence Taylor, Terry Kinard, Carl Banks and William Roberts. Since then, however, they have had nine busts in 11 years, with Ingram in 1987 and Rodney Hampton in 1990 being the only bright spots from 1985 to 1996. That's a lot of mistakes. Overall a **C**.

Late Round Best Steal

The Giants have done well in later picks out of necessity. Not surprisingly, their top two late steals are defensive players. In 1975, they selected **George Martin** in the 11th round, and he became a mainstay of their defensive line for years. And in the eighth round in 1993, the Giants drafted Jesse Armstead, who has become one of the best outside linebackers in the league.

Best Class by Year

Their best year was **1983**, with Terry Kinard, Leonard Marshall, Karl Nelson, Perry Williams, Andy Headen and Ali Haji-Sheikh. But in 1984 they really hit it with Carl Banks, William Roberts, Jeff Hostetler, Gary Reasons and Lionel Manuel.

Best Position

The Giants have a solid history at two positions, a rarity in the NFL. New York won two Super Bowls with **linebackers** Harry Carson, Byron Hunt, Lawrence Taylor, Carl Banks, Gary Reasons, Pepper Johnson and Andy Headen. Later strong performers at linebacker have been Corey Miller, Corey Widmer and Jesse Armstead. But don't forget their **defensive backs**. From Mark Haynes, Terry Kinard and Mark Collins to Jason Sehorn and Phillippi Sparks, the Giants have also done very well at the last line of defense.

Worst Position

In the 1970s, they selected busts at **wide receiver** such as Rocky Thompson, Danny Buggs, Johnny Perkins and Earnest Gray. The misfires continued in the '80s with Danny Pittman, John Mistler, and Mel Hoover. They did draft some competent guys such as Stacy Robinson, Mark Ingram and Stephen Baker. In 1991, they drafted Ed McCaffrey but did nothing with him. In 1997, he won a Super Bowl with Denver, and the Giants selected Joe Jurevicius in the '98 draft, who is compared most often to . . . Ed McCaffrey. Ike Hilliard, whom they chose in 1997 but then was injured, doesn't have a lot to live up to.

New York Jets

1st Round

John Riggins was a nice pick in 1971. Jerome Barkum in 1972 was good, too, but they also took Mike Taylor at linebacker, who wasn't much. Carl Barzilauskas was mediocre in 1974. Richard Todd in 1976 wasn't bad. Marty Lyons was nice in 1979. Nineteen eighty brought Johnny "Lam" Jones, who did very little. In 1981, Freeman MacNeil was a good pick. You see the trend. Ken O'Brien (1983) was OK, but he was not Dan Marino. Al Toon (1985) was a good pick, but he was followed by guys like Mike Haight, Dave Cadigan, Roger Vick, Blair Thomas (number two overall in 1990), Johnny Mitchell and Kyle Brady. Keyshawn Johnson, number one overall in 1996, has shown only flashes of worth. Overall a **C**.

Late Best Round Steal

They've had a few, like Joe Klecko in the sixth round in 1977. But center **Joe Fields** in the 14th round from Widener College (1975) was an awfully productive player for that low a pick.

Best Class by Year

There have not been many good years here, let alone great. Because we have to pick one, it's **1976**. They got Richard Todd in the first round and Greg Buttle in the third. They took Larry Faulk (a.k.a. Abdul Salaam), a fair defensive lineman. A nice little running back, Louie Giammona, came in the eighth round, and they rounded it out with Lawrence Pillers, a defensive end in the 11th, who was not bad. That's the Jets. Their best draft class consists of two above average players and three guys who didn't stink.

Best Position

In 1976, they took **linebacker** Greg Buttle, and in 1980 they grabbed Lance Mehl. Both were third rounders and fine picks. In 1982, they got Bob Crable, a first rounder, who was just OK. In 1984, they got Kyle Clifton in the third round, who was very productive for many years. Nineteen ninety one delivered Mo Lewis in the third round, a nice pick. And in 1993, they got Marvin Jones in the first round. With four third-round picks, they did pretty well with Buttle, Mehl, Clifton and Lewis.

Worst Position

In 1983, they took **quarterback** Ken O'Brien, and Dan Marino went only three picks later. In 1991, they took Browning Nagle, a complete bust, in the second round, missing Brett Favre, who had just been picked by the Falcons. The Jets missed two Hall of Fame quarterbacks by a total of four picks. NFL history would be a lot different if the Jets had just had a little luck with these two picks.

Oakland Raiders

Since 1970, the Raiders have had many first-round booms and only a few busts. They got Ray Chester, a top tight end, in 1970. Jack Tatum came in 1971. In 1973 they drafted Ray Guy, probably the best punter of all time. Other great first rounders include Marcus Allen, Don Mosebar, Tim Brown, Chester McGlockton, Napoleon Kaufman and Rickey Dudley. Last year's number one, Darrell Russell, is already one of the best young defensive linemen in the league. There were busts like Marc Wilson, Todd Marinovich, Jessie Hester, Bob Buczkowski, John Clay and Patrick Bates, but overall a **B+**.

Late Round Best Steal

In 1977, the Raiders drafted **Lester Hayes** in the fifth round and Rod Martin in the twelfth. Hayes was a forceful, intimidating presence at corner for years, and Martin was a very good outside linebacker.

Best Class by Year

In **1974**, the Raiders drafted offensive tackle Henry Lawrence in the first round, tight end Dave Casper in the second and running back Mark van Eeghen in the third round. Plus, they got wide receiver Morris Bradshaw in the fourth, and he was OK. That's a good draft.

Best Position

In 1971, the Raiders took **defensive back** Jack Tatum in the first round. A few years later, in 1975, they drafted Neal Colzie, a good corner, in the first round and in the second they took Charles Phillips, who was an excellent safety. In 1977, they also got two defensive backs, picking Mike Davis in the second round and Lester Hayes in the fifth. There's five in a row that they hit on. Later drafts included solid players like Stacey Toran, Vann McElroy, Sam Seale and Terry McDaniel. They missed on a few, like Ted Watts in 1981, but overall that's a pretty good run. Will Charles Woodson add to their legacy?

Worst Position

In 1975, they took **quarterback** David Humm in the fifth round, who was supposed to be the next Ken Stabler. Instead, he was the first David Humm. In 1976, in the second round they took Jeb Blount. I don't know who he is, and I don't think he ever played. Later picks were equally poor. In 1980, they took Marc Wilson from BYU in the first round, and he was a bust, starting some games but never very effective. Other picks were Rusty Hilger, Steve Beuerlein, Jeff Francis, Major Harris, Todd Marinovich and Billy Joe Hobert.

Philadelphia Eagles

Dick Vermeil liked to trade picks, so there were several years that they didn't have a pick. It's just as well, because they haven't done that well when they keep a pick anyway. Over the years, the Eagles have drafted solid players like Jerry Robinson, Roynell Young and Mike Quick in the first round. From 1986 to 1990, they hit it big with four players in a row, drafting Keith Byars, Jerome Brown, Keith Jackson and Ben Smith. But more often than not, they have drafted disappointments like Michael Haddix, Kenny Jackson, Kevin Allen, Antone Davis, Lester Holmes, Bernard Williams, Mike Mamula and Jermane Mayberry. Overall a **C**.

Late Round Best Steal

In 1986, the Eagles stole two great players in late rounds. They got linebacker Seth Joyner out of UTEP in the eighth round and defensive end Clyde Simmons in the ninth from Western Carolina, two pretty big pieces of those Buddy Ryan defenses of the late 1980's.

Best Class by Year

Not easy to pick one because the Eagles just haven't drafted that well, but **1986** was pretty good. That year they came up with Keith Byars, Anthony Toney, Matt Darwin, Seth Joyner and Clyde Simmons. Byars (a Pro Bowler with the Dolphins) and Toney were nice players, but they got two Pro Bowlers in the eighth and ninth rounds with Joyner and Simmons.

Best Position

There wasn't a lot to chose from, but these five **linebackers** make up the Eagles' strongest draft area. In 1974, they took Frank LeMaster in the fourth round, and he was a good player. Jerry Robinson came in the first round in 1979, and he was very good. In 1986, Seth Joyner was an excellent eighth-round pick. The next year the Eagles took Byron Evans in the fourth round and, finally, in 1991, they got William Thomas in the fourth round.

Worst Position

This was easier because there were so many busts, including first rounders. From 1984 to 1996, the Eagles spent eight high draft choices trying to shore up the **offensive tackle** and didn't hit on one. They took guys like Rusty Russell in 1984, Kevin Allen in 1985, Matt Patchan in 1988, Rob Selby and Antone Davis in 1991, Bernard Williams in 1994, Barrett Brooks in 1995 and Jermane Mayberry in 1996, and they all were big underacheivers. Allen, Davis, Williams and Mayberry were first-round selections.

Pittsburgh Steelers

1st Round

A mixed bag. For example, in the 1980's they picked great players like Louis Lipps and Rod Woodson in the first round, but almost every other pick in that decade was, at the least, a disappointment. Does anyone remember Darryl Sims, John Rienstra, Aaron Jones or Keith Gary? In 1989, they had two first-round picks, Tim Worley and Tom Ricketts. Both bombed out as did linebacker Huey Richardson, a first-round pick in 1991. Overall a **C+**.

Late Round Best Steal

They have had two that stand out. In 1987, **Greg Lloyd** was a sixth-round pick, and in 1990 they got Justin Strzelczyk in the 11th round. He has started for them every year since.

Best Class by Year

They've had two remarkable years. In **1974**, they got Lynn Swann, Jack Lambert, John Stallworth and Mike Webster. And in 1992, they got Leon Searcy, Levon Kirkland, Joel Steed and Darren Perry. Give the nod to '74, because those guys won four Super Bowls.

Best Position

The Steelers' great **linebackers** have come almost exclusively from the draft; in fact, the turnaround of the entire franchise started when they took Jack Lambert, leader of the fabled Steel Curtain defense, in the second round in 1974. Three years earlier, Jack Ham was a second-round pick. Robin Cole and Dennis Winston were nice picks in 1977. In 1987, they got Hardy Nickerson in the fifth round and Greg Lloyd in the sixth. Jerry Olsavsky was a tenth rounder (1989) that has panned out. Levon Kirkland and Chad Brown were second rounders, in 1992 and 1993, respectively. Jason Gildon was a third rounder in 1994.

Worst Position

There were a lot of duds at **offensive line** between Mike Webster in the fifth round in 1974 and Leon Searcy in the first round in 1992. Mark Behning, a second-round pick from Nebraska in 1985, was a bust. Other high picks in the 1980s were spent on guys like John Meyer (second round in 1982), John Rienstra (first in 1986) and Tom Ricketts (first in 1989), all major busts.

St. Louis Rams

1st Round

The Rams have drafted fairly well over the years. In the 1970's they rarely missed with picks like Jack Reynolds, Isiah Robertson, Jack Youngblood, John Cappelletti, Mike Fanning, Dennis Harrah and Doug France. Other strong first rounders include Bob Brudzinski, George Andrews, Eric Dickerson, Sean Gilbert, Jerome Bettis and Kevin Carter. There have been busts, though, like Elvis Peacock, Mike Schad, and both Gaston Green and Aaron Cox in 1988, plus Bill Hawkins, Cleveland Gary and Lawrence Phillips. Overall a **B+**.

....

Best Late Round Steal

In 1979, the Rams did well in selecting wide receiver **Drew Hill** out of Georgia Tech in the 12th round.

....

Best Class by Year

In **1975**, the Rams had three first-round picks and hit it big with Mike Fanning, Dennis Harrah and Doug France. They also picked up cornerback Rod Perry in the fourth round and quarterback Pat Haden in the seventh.

....

Best Position

In 1970, the Rams got **linebackers** Jack Reynolds and Rich Saul. The next year, Isiah Robertson. After that came an outstanding run: Jim Youngblood, Carl Ekern, Bob Brudzinski, George Andrews, Mel Owens and Jim Collins. In 1985, they picked Kevin Greene. Throw in Fred Strickland and Roman Phifer, and you have a lot of nice linebackers.

....

Worst Position

Despite earlier success, since 1976 the Rams have been awful at drafting **defensive linemen**. Some of their picks have been Eary Jones, Stan Johnson (who was average) Jerry Wilkinson, Greg Meisner, Robert Cobb, Doug Barnett, Doug Reed and Hal Stephens. Donald Evans was good later, but did nothing with the Rams. The busts continue with Scott Mersereau, Mike Piel, Jeff Knapton, Bill Hawkins and Brad Ottis. Sean Gilbert was a good player but he moved on, and Kevin Carter in 1995 is also good. From 1976 to 1994, outside of Gilbert and Carter, they didn't get anything.

San Diego Chargers

The Chargers have done all right in the first round over the years, with many solid picks, several OK picks and relatively few busts. With Bobby Beathard in charge, though, they often don't have a first-round choice. They have traded away their first rounders for 1999 and 2000 and did not have one from 1994 to 1997. The jury hasn't even convened on Ryan Leaf but other first-round Chargers are John Jefferson, Kellen Winslow, James Brooks, Jim Lachey, Rod Bernstine, Leslie O'Neal, Darrien Gordon, Stanley Richard and Junior Seau. Overall a **B**.

Late Round Best Steal

In 1989, the Chargers got a great, big bruiser of a runner in **Marion Butts** from Florida State in the seventh round. And another seventh rounder was tight end Pete Holohan in 1981, who turned into a nice target over the years for Dan Fouts.

Best Class by Year

In **1975**, the Chargers drafted a slew of very solid defensive players. In the first round they got Gary "Big Hands" Johnson, a great defensive lineman, and a solid corner in Mike Williams. The second round delivered two monster defensive lineman in Louie Kelcher and Fred Dean, the great pass rusher who finished up in San Francisco. Their third rounder was defensive back Mike Fuller, and they finished off this great draft with offensive tackle Billy Shields in the sixth.

Best Position

In 1993, the Chargers selected **running back** Natrone Means in the second round. In 1991, the second-round pick was Eric Bieniemy who has been pretty decent. Marion Butts was a steal in 1989. Rod Bernstine was chosen in the first round in 1985, and the Chargers made a pretty effective running back out of this former tight end. Other top picks at running back have been Lionel James, Gary Anderson, James Brooks and Joe Washington.

Worst Position

While they have drafted John Jefferson, Yancey Thigpen, Anthony Miller and Quinn Early, the Chargers have missed on a lot of other picks at **wide receiver**. The real bad run came in the 1990s. Miller was OK but Thigpen did nothing in San Diego. The other bad picks were guys like Walter Wilson, Ray Ethridge, Andre Coleman and Jimmy Oliver. These and three other '90s busts at wide receiver forced Bobby Beathard to trade his number one pick in 2000, so he could draft Mikhael Ricks in the late second round this year. Ryan Leaf has to throw to somebody.

San Francisco 49ers

1st Round

Bill Walsh did very well with Ronnie Lott, Jerry Rice and Harris Barton. The 49ers continued to do well with picks like Ted Washington, Bryant Young and Dana Stubblefield. There were some busts like Ken MacAfee, Todd Shell, Terrence Flagler, Todd Kelly, Keith DeLong, Dexter Carter and Dana Hall. But you have to remember how bad the Niners were for how long before Bill Walsh arrived, Cedrick Hardman was the only first-round pick worth remembering pre-Walsh. Lott and Rice only bring the grade up to a **C+**.

Late Round Best Steal

Solid players like center Fred Quillan, cornerback Don Griffin and quarterback Elvis Grbac were all late picks, but the best one was offesive lineman Jesse Sapolu taken in the 11th round in 1983.

Best Class by Year

The **1986** draft was a masterful job as Bill Walsh traded down twice, once to the late first and once to the second, and still ended up with eight players of consequence. The Niners drafted Larry Roberts, Steve Wallace, Tom Rathman, Tim McKyer, John Taylor, Charles Haley, Kevin Fagan and Don Griffin.

Best Position

In the 1970s the Niners selected **defensive linemen** such as Cedrick Hardman, Cleveland Elam and Archie Reese. In the 1980's they drafted Jim Stuckey, John Harty, Michael Carter and Larry Roberts. In 1986, they picked it up a notch higher with Charles Haley and Kevin Fagan, both fourth rounders that year. In 1988 they hit it big with two second rounders in Daniel Stubbs and Pierce Holt. Dennis Brown and Martin Harrison, a serviceable situational pass rusher, came in 1990. And Ted Washington was a great first-round pick in 1991, as were Dana Stubblefield in 1993 and Bryant Young in 1994.

Worst Position

The Niners have drafted consistently over the years and have actually taken some nice **linebackers** like Keena Turner, Riki Ellison, Bill Romanowski and Lee Woodall. But there were a lot of busts at this position like Greg Collins, Craig Puki, David Hodge, Patrick Miller, Keith DeLong, Kevin Mitchell and Antonio Armstrong.

Seattle Seahawks

1st Round

The Seahawks have done well over the years. In the 1980s, they got several top players like Jacob Green, Kenny Easley, Jeff Bryant, and Curt Warner. That decade also brought some other fairly decent guys like Andy Heck, Tony Woods and John L. Williams. Cortez Kennedy was obviously a great pick. So was Pete Kendall in 1996, a solid offensive guard from Boston College. Their big busts were Steve Niehaus in 1976, Steve August in 1977 and the two quarterbacks from the '90s, Dan McGwire and Rick Mirer. Overall a **B**.

Best Late Round Steal

In 1993, they took pass rusher **Michael McCrary** in the seventh round. Michael Sinclair was taken in the sixth round in 1991 and he's been very good, but the nod goes to McCrary.

Best Class by Year

1994 was a good draft that produced defensive lineman Sam Adams, offensive lineman Kevin Mawae, running back Lamar Smith, excellent special teamer (for New England) Larry Whigham, and tight end Carlester Crumpler. But 1990 was better with Cortez Kennedy, linebacker Terry Wooden, defensive back Robert Blackmon and running back Chris Warren, a steal in the fourth round.

Best Position

Ironically, the first pick the team ever made was a bust on the **defensive line** — Steve Niehaus out of Notre Dame. They have recovered, though, to make it their best position in the draft. In 1979 they took Manu Tuiasosopo, a solid defensive tackle. In 1980, they got Jacob Green, a top pass rusher. In 1982 they took Jeff Bryant, who was very reliable for them. Cortez Kennedy in 1990 speaks for himself. Another top level player on the defensive line has been Michael Sinclair, taken in 1991. In 1993, they got Michael McCrary in the seventh round, and he later led the AFC in sacks. Sam Adams was a first rounder in 1994 and has been a good player. And Phillip Daniels has been an impressive starter since he was drafted in the fourth round in 1996.

Worst Position

They have not drafted a **quarterback** of consequence in their history. They have had to go out and get guys like Warren Moon and John Friesz. In 1976 they drafted Steve Myer, who did nothing. Later they had two high pick disasters at quarterback: Dan McGwire in 1991 and Rick Mirer, who was the second pick overall in 1993. Both were complete busts, though Mirer had a decent rookie year.

Tampa Bay Buccaneers

1st Round

They have had some real booms in Lee Roy Selmon, Doug Williams, Hugh Green, Paul Gruber, Warren Sapp and Derrick Brooks. Trent Dilfer has been just OK but is still improving. The busts have been Ray Snell, Rod Jones, Broderick Thomas, Keith McCants, Charles McRae and Eric Curry. Sean Farrell and Vinny Testaverde were just OK. Overall a **C**.

Late Round Best Steal

In 1992, the Bucs drafted another one of their solid defensive linemen when they took tackle **Santana Dotson** from Baylor in the fifth round. Chidi Ahanotu was a sixth-round steal in 1993.

Best Class by Year

The Buccaneers have set themselves up for the future in **1996** with a draft that included Regan Upshaw, Marcus Jones, Mike Alstott, Donnie Abraham and Jason Odom.

Best Position

Their first pick ever was a Hall of Famer — Lee Roy Selmon out of Oklahoma. The rest of their picks for the **defensive line** aren't on that level, but Dave Logan, Ron Holmes, Shawn Lee, Reuben Davis, Rhett Hall and Mark Wheeler have been decent players. There were some busts, such as Marcus Jones, Booker Reese and especially Eric Curry, who was a real bust as a top ten choice. Recently, they have been back on track with Ahanotu, Sapp and Regan Upshaw

Worst Position

The Buccaneers have drafted very few **wide receivers** of consequence. There's Kevin House in 1980 and Mark Carrier who has been OK at best.

Tennessee Oilers

1st Round

The solid offensive line picks demonstrate how well the Oilers have done in the first round. Other strong first-round contributors have been Lorenzo White, Lamar Lathon, Henry Ford and Kenny Holmes. Recently, the Oilers have also drafted two potential offensive cornerstones in the first round, Steve McNair and Eddie George; the latter was the NFL Rookie of the Year in 1996. Overall a **B**.

Late Best Round Steal

In 1993, the Oilers chose **Blaine Bishop** of Ball State in the eighth round. A terrific player, he regularly averages over 100 tackles a year and has been named to the Pro Bowl three times as a strong safety.

Best Class by Year

In addition to the great late round pick of Bishop, the Oilers had a great draft in **1993**. The first round delivered starting offensive tackle Brad Hopkins. Talented linebacker Micheal Barrow, now with Carolina, was chosen in the second round. In his rookie season, Barrow played regularly in passing situations and led the team in special team tackles. Rounding out this solid draft was John Henry Mills, an excellent special teamer who made the Pro Bowl in 1996 after two years as an alternate. Mills is now a linebacker with the Oakland Raiders.

Best Position

As far back as 1982, when they drafted nine-time Pro-Bowler Mike Munchak and future Hall of Famer Bruce Matthews in 1983, the Oilers have consistently selected solid **offensive linemen**. In 1989, they picked OT David Williams, a solid player who is best known for "Babygate," when the team fined him for missing a game to attend the birth of one of his children. In the third round in 1991, they picked Kevin Donnalley, a Pro Bowl-type player now with the Dolphins. In 1993, they grabbed starting left tackle Brad Hopkins in the first round, and in 1996 they drafted Jason Layman and Jon Runyan. Runyan now starts, and the talented Layman played in every game his rookie year and also contributed on special teams.

Worst Position

The Houston-Tennessee Oilers have been consistently solid drafters; no glaring positional weaknesses jump out.

Washington Redskins

1st Round

First of all, with George Allen and Bobby Beathard in charge you don't have a lot of first-round picks. From 1970 to 1979, they had NO first-round picks. Now *there's* a trend. In the early 1980s, they grabbed Art Monk, Mark May and Darrell Green, all Pro Bowlers. But they only had those three number ones in the 1980s, giving them a *total* of three first rounders from 1970 to 1990. When they started using picks in the 1990s, they had busts like Bobby Wilson, Desmond Howard, Heath Shuler, Michael Westbrook and Andre Johnson. Overall a **C-**.

Late Round Best Steal

Obviously, with no first rounders the Redskins have had to be good in the late rounds. Tight end **Clint Didier** was a 12th round pick in 1981. **Monte Coleman** was a great linebacker for many years after being taken in the 10th round in 1979. And **Gus Frerotte**, a seventh rounder in 1994, beat out the first rounder that year, Heath Shuler, for the quarterback job.

Best Class by Year

It's tough to evaluate the Redskins. Not only did they often not have a first-round pick, but for many years they had very few picks at all. In 1972, they didn't have a pick until the eighth round. And from 1972 to 1979, their earliest picks were often fourth rounders, sometimes even later. But they did come up with a nice class in **1981**, when they drafted Mark May, Russ Grimm, Dexter Manley, Charlie Brown, Darryl Grant and Didier. When they put their minds to it, they really came through.

Best Position

Not a lot to pick from, since the Redskins have always liked to trade picks, but in 1979 they got two good outside **linebackers** — Rich Milot in the seventh round and Monte Coleman in the 10th. Then in 1986 they got two more decent linebackers in Ravin Caldwell and Kurt Gouveia. After that they got Lamont Hollinquest in 1993. In 1997, they took Greg Jones and Derek Smith.

Worst Position

Again, not a lot to pick from here, but **defensive line** is probably the weakest spot. In the '80s, they drafted Mat Mendenhall, Todd Liebenstein, Steve Hamilton, Bob Slater, Markus Koch, Lybrant Robinson and Tracy Rocker. Have you heard of them? Other busts include Kent Wells, Bobby Wilson, Shane Collins and Sterling Palmer.

Postseason

by Russell S. Baxter

Top 10 AFC/AFL Postseason Games

1. 1981 Divisional Playoffs: Chargers 41, Dolphins 38 (OT)

Called by some the best game in NFL history, many forget that the Chargers actually owned a 24-0 first-quarter lead before their shaky defense let Miami get back in the game. Both Dan Fouts and Don Strock (replacing an ineffective David Woodley) threw for 400-plus yards, and Chargers' PK Rolf Benirschke's 29-yard field goal late in overtime saved it for San Diego.

2. 1974 Divisional Playoffs: Raiders 28, Dolphins 26

This battle of powers in Oakland got off to a fast start as Dolphins' WR Nat Moore returned the opening kickoff 89 yards for a score. Raiders' QB Ken Stabler answered the two-time defending Super Bowl champions at every turn in this see-saw affair, and Stabler's thread-the-needle TD pass (while falling down) to RB Clarence Davis in a crowd with 26 seconds to play capped an amazing afternoon.

3. 1971 Divisional Playoffs: Dolphins 27, Chiefs 24 (OT)

In the final game at Municipal Stadium, both teams were stretched to the limit. Despite Chiefs' RB Ed Podolak's 350 all-purpose yards and two touchdowns, Miami could not be put away. And when Chiefs' PK Jan Stenerud missed a field goal at the end of the game and had another blocked in overtime, it opened the door for the 'Fins to win the NFL's longest game ever.

4. 1977 Divisional Playoffs: Raiders 37, Colts 31 (OT)

Led by QB Ken Stabler and TE Dave Casper, the Raiders' potent offense rolled up 491 yards. The Colts' defense and special teams kept them in the game and gave them a 31-28 lead in the fourth quarter, but Stabler-to-Casper for 42 yards (a.k.a the "Ghost to the Post") set up the tying field goal, and the duo's third TD connection just 43 seconds into the second overtime gave Oakland the win.

5. 1992 Wild Card Game: Bills 41, Oilers 38 (OT)

The greatest comeback in any NFL game, Marv Levy's undermanned Bills and Jack Pardee's underachieving Oilers staged a classic in Orchard Park. Down 35-3 in the third quarter, Bills' QB Frank Reich (starting for injured Jim Kelly) threw four TD passes to give his team the lead. The Oilers sent the game into overtime, but Bills' PK Steve Christie's 32-yard boot capped a remarkable rally.

6. 1986 Championship Game: Broncos 23, Browns 20 (OT)

The game that turned Broncos' QB John Elway into a legend, and Marty Schottenheimer's best chance at that elusive Super Bowl. The host Browns had a 20-13 lead with 5:32 to play and Denver pinned on its 2-yard line, but Elway moved his team 98 yards, the last five on a TD toss to WR Mark Jackson. A 60-yard march in overtime led to Rich Karlis's winning field goal.

7. 1976 Divisional Playoffs: Raiders 24, Patriots 21

John Madden would finally get his Super Bowl ring this season, but not without a struggle from the upstart Patriots, who had handed the Raiders their only loss of the '76 regular season (48-17) in Foxboro. New England had a 21-10 lead after three quarters, but watched the eventual Super Bowl champions rally for a pair of touchdowns, including a Ken Stabler 1-yard TD run with 10 seconds to play.

8. 1995 Championship Game: Steelers 20, Colts 16

Thanks to upsets at San Diego and Kansas City, Jim Harbaugh ("Captain Comeback") and company found themselves in the Steel City. Bill Cowher's Steelers trailed, 16-13, with 3:03 left, until QB Neil O'Donnell made the big plays on a 67-yard TD drive. The Colts' final bid for victory was an unanswered Hail Mary pass off the hands and chest of WR Aaron Bailey.

9. 1968 Championship Game (AFL): Jets 27, Raiders 23

If the Jets were to shock the Colts in Super Bowl III, they'd first have to survive a shootout at frigid Shea Stadium. Neither Joe Namath nor Daryle Lamonica were accurate, but Lamonica threw for 401 yards and a score. Namath threw for three touchdowns, including a 6-yard strike to WR Don Maynard late in the fourth quarter to put his team ahead to stay.

10. 1981 Wild Card Game: Bills 31, Jets 27

Before you could say J-E-T-S, Walt Michaels's team found itself behind, 24-0, in the second quarter at Shea Stadium. New York fought back in a big way and late in the fourth quarter, had narrowed the deficit to four points. Jets' QB Richard Todd threw for 377 yards and two scores, but his errant pass was picked off by Bills' S Bill Simpson at the Buffalo 1-yard line with two seconds on the clock.

Top 10 NFC/NFL Postseason Games

1. 1981 Championship Game: 49ers 28, Cowboys 27

A back and forth affair from the start, the Niners made things tough on themselves with six turnovers. Trailing 27-21 with 4:54 to play, 49ers' QB Joe Montana needed to drive 89 yards, and coach Bill Walsh fooled the Cowboys by relying on the run. With 51 seconds left, Montana threw to the back of the end zone to WR Dwight Clark, and "The Catch" sent the Niners to their first Super Bowl.

2. 1966 Championship Game (NFL): Packers 34, Cowboys 27

The first title meeting between the Cowboys and Packers at the Cotton Bowl was a real heart-stopper from the start. After Green Bay jumped to a 14-0 lead, Dallas tied the game in the first quarter with a pair of touchdown runs by Dan Reeves and Don Perkins. Tom Landry's team trailed by seven late and had first-and-goal on the Packers' 2-yard line, but failed to crack the end zone on four tries.

3. 1958 Championship Game (NFL): Colts 23, Giants 17 (OT)

Often dubbed "The Greatest Game Ever Played," this title contest brought the NFL into prominence. Colts' QB Johnny Unitas threw for 349 yards and led a game-tying drive ending with PK Steve Myhra's 20-yard field goal with seven seconds left to send the game into overtime. After a three-and-out by New York, Baltimore's 80-yard drive ended with Alan Ameche's famed 1-yard TD plunge.

4. 1967 Championship Game (NFL): Packers 21, Cowboys 17

It was minus-13 degrees at kickoff time at Lambeau Field and the Cowboys looked frozen, as a pair of Bart Starr TD passes gave Vince Lombardi's club a 14-0 lead. Dallas rallied for a 17-14 edge, but Starr took over with 4:50 to play and drove his team downfield. On third-and-goal, from the 1-yard line, he followed G Jerry Kramer into the end zone, and the Pack survived the Ice Bowl.

5. 1972 Divisional Playoffs: Cowboys 30, 49ers 28

Tom Landry's Cowboys had defeated the 49ers in the 1970 and '71 NFC Championship games, but here was host San Francisco with a 28-13 lead late in the third quarter. Then it was Roger Staubach to the rescue, as the future Hall of Famer came off the bench to rally Dallas to 17 unanswered points, the game-winner a 10-yard TD pass to WR Ron Sellers with just 52 seconds to play.

6. 1980 Divisional Playoffs: Cowboys 30, Falcons 27

In his first season as the Cowboys' starting quarterback, Danny White proved he had a little Roger Staubach in him at Fulton County Stadium. Trailing 24-10 entering the fourth quarter, Dallas outscored the Falcons, 20-3, in the final 15 minutes. White found WR Drew Pearson twice for touchdowns in just over three minutes to erase a 27-17 Atlanta lead and send the Pokes to the NFC title game.

7. 1983 Divisional Playoffs: 49ers 24, Lions 23

Another heroic effort by 49ers' QB Joe Montana, or a blown opportunity by the Lions? Detroit trailed, 17-9, going into the fourth quarter, but would take a 23-17 lead thanks to a pair of TD runs by RB Billy Sims. Montana drove his team 70 yards to take the lead, and usually dependable Lions' PK Eddie Murray missed a 43-yard field goal with five seconds to play to save the Niners.

8. 1990 NFC Championship Game: Giants 15, 49ers 13

Earlier in the season, the 49ers had outlasted the Giants, 7-3, on a Monday night at Candlestick Park, and once again, New York failed to score a touchdown. Protecting a 13-12 lead, 49ers' RB Roger Craig fumbled with 2:36 to play, and Giants' QB Jeff Hostetler drove his club 33 yards to set up PK Matt Bahr's fifth field goal, good from 42 yards as time expired.

9. 1969 Western Conference Playoff (NFL): Vikings 23, Rams 20

Imposing Metropolitan Stadium — which became a house of horrors for the Rams — was the setting for this battle, which saw Los Angeles ahead at halftime behind QB Roman Gabriel. But the Joe Kapp Show took center stage down the stretch as the Vikings' field general took over in the second half, his 2-yard TD run in the fourth quarter putting his team ahead to stay.

10. 1957 Western Conference Playoff (NFL): Lions 31, 49ers 27

The winner would meet the Browns in the NFL title game, and San Francisco appeared on its way after celebrating a 24-7 edge after 30 minutes and increasing the lead to 20 just after the half. But Detroit's offense was unstoppable the rest of the way, and the shell-shocked Niners coughed up the ball four times in the fourth quarter to squelch their own comeback.

Top 10 Postseason Upsets

1. Super Bowl III: Jets 16, Colts 7

Considering that the AFL's first two representatives in the Super Bowl (Chiefs and Raiders) were stomped by a combined score of 68-24 by the Packers, New York figured to have little chance against a Colts, squad that had lost just once during the regular season and then pounded the Browns, 34-0, in the NFL title game. But Jets' QB Joe Namath guaranteed a win and made history at the Orange Bowl.

2. 1979 AFC Divisional Playoffs: Oilers 17, Chargers 14

Don Coryell's Chargers looked super and owned the home field edge in the conference. The Oilers had been led by RB Earl Campbell and QB Dan Pastorini, but both of them and WR Ken Burrough were out with injuries. However, QB Gifford Nielsen, RB Rob Carpenter and WR Mike Renfro made the plays, and S Vernon Perry stole four Dan Fouts, passes and blocked a field goal.

3. 1996 AFC Divisional Playoffs: Jaguars 30, Broncos 27

Undefeated at home and tied for the best record in the league, the Broncos were supposed to make quick work of the second-year Jaguars, who had just handed the Bills their first-ever playoff loss at Orchard Park a week earlier. Host Denver jumped out to a 12-0 first-quarter lead, but trailed by one at the half and never caught up, thanks to Jaguars' QB Mark Brunell.

4. 1987 NFC Divisional Playoffs: Vikings 36, 49ers 24

The Niners rolled through the strike-plagued season en route to a 13-2 finish. Visiting Minnesota had slipped into the playoffs on the final regular-season weekend, but had thrashed the upstart Saints in the wild card game. 49ers' QB Joe Montana had a rare off day, while Vikings' WR Anthony Carter frolicked at Candlestick Park, catching 10 passes for 227 yards.

5. 1994 AFC Championship Game: Chargers 17, Steelers 13

In the season finale at San Diego, the Chargers had outlasted the Steelers, 37-34, in a game in which Bill Cowher sat most of his regulars. Overconfident Pittsburgh figured a raucous Three Rivers Stadium crowd was enough to ensure victory, but Chargers' QB Stan Humphries' 43-yard TD pass to WR Tony Martin in the fourth quarter sent the Bolts to Super Bowl XXIX.

6. 1986 NFC Divisional Playoffs: Redskins 27, Bears 13

Mike Ditka's mighty Bears had cruised through the 1985 season on their way to winning Super Bowl XX, and followed that up with a 14-2 mark in '86. They figured to battle the Giants for the NFC title, but Joe Gibbs' Redskins spoiled that much-anticipated showdown, aided by QB Jay Schroeder and an opportunistic defense that put the clamps on Bears' QB Doug Flutie.

7. 1995 AFC Divisional Playoffs: Colts 10, Chiefs 7

The Colts didn't figure to be in this position, but here they were against the Chiefs, owners of the best record in football (13-3) and perfect (8-0) at home. Ted Marchibroda's upstart Colts had made a habit of knocking off the big boys in '95, and one week after dethroning defending AFC champion San Diego, held on for dear life thanks to three missed field goals by Chiefs' PK Lin Elliott.

8. 1983 AFC Divisional Playoffs: Seahawks 27, Dolphins 20

Coach Chuck Knox was in his first year in Seattle and had to lead the young franchise to its first playoff campaign. The Seahawks routed Denver, 31-7, in the wild card game, but here were the Dolphins at the Orange Bowl led by phenomenal first year QB Dan Marino. Fellow rookie Curt Warner stole the show from Marino, running for 113 yards and two scores in this upset of Don Shula's club.

9. 1984 AFC Divisional Playoffs: Steelers 24, Broncos 17

The '84 AFC title game was supposed to feature second-year QBs Dan Marino and John Elway as their teams won 14 and 13 games, respectively. Chuck Noll's club captured the weak AFC Central with a 9-7 mark and hardly looked like a match for the confident Broncos, but Steelers' QB Mark Malone and the Pittsburgh defense came up big at Mile High and spoiled Denver's plans.

10. Super Bowl IV: Chiefs 23, Vikings 7

As if the Jets' shocking victory over Baltimore the previous year wasn't proof enough that the soon-to-be-absorbed AFL could play with the established NFL, Hank Stram's Chiefs found themselves big underdogs to Bud Grant's Purple Gang. But Kansas City's massive defensive front beat up Vikings' QB Joe Kapp, and Stram's masterful play-calling (65 Toss Power Trap) proved decisive.

Top 5 Super Bowls

1. Super Bowl XIII: Steelers 35, Cowboys 31

The first rematch in Super Bowl history would mean an unprecedented three Super Bowl titles for one of these clubs. Each team's roster and coaching staff was filled with future Hall of Famers. Steelers QB Terry Bradshaw starred with WRs Lynn Swann and John Stallworth, but brash Cowboys LB Hollywood Henderson and teammate Jackie Smith's dropped TD pass are just as memorable.

2. Super Bowl XXXII: Broncos 31, Packers 24

You could easily make a case that this was the greatest. The defending champion Packers figured to make it 14 straight NFC wins over the AFC, but the stars this day in San Diego were MVP Terrell Davis (157 yards rushing, 3 touchdowns) and an offensive front that dominated the game. Packers' QB Brett Favre and WR Antonio Freeman had their moments, but it wasn't enough.

3. Super Bowl XXV: Giants 20, Bills 19

The right game at the right time. The Gulf War had cast its shadow over the country, and the talk of terrorism turned Tampa Stadium into a high security area. On the field, the underdog Giants knew they would have to play ball control to keep Buffalo's explosive attack off the field, and they executed to perfection. Bills PK Scott Norwood missed a 47-yard field goal at the gun.

4. Super Bowl XIV: Steelers 31, Rams 19

Chuck Noll's Steelers had won three Super Bowls in five seasons, but were pushed hard by a scrappy Rams' squad and raw QB Vince Ferragamo at the Rose Bowl. Los Angeles took a 19-17 lead into the fourth quarter, but Steelers QB Terry Bradshaw connected with WR John Stallworth on a 73-yard scoring pass (the sixth lead-change of the game) to put Pittsburgh ahead for good.

5. Super Bowl XVII: Redskins 27, Dolphins 17

A two-month strike had reduced the '82 season to nine games, so the 'Skins and 'Fins arrived in Pasadena the survivors of a Super Bowl tournament. Miami led most of the way, thanks to big plays from WR Jimmy Cefalo and a 98-yard kickoff return from Fulton Walker. But Don Shula's Killer B's defense couldn't stop Redskins' RB John Riggins, who rumbled for 166 yards and a score.

Top 5 Super Bores

1. Super Bowl VII: Dolphins 14, Redskins 7

The end result was a perfect 17-0 season for Don Shula's Dolphins, but this affair at the L.A. Coliseum was hardly a thriller. George Allen's "Over The Hill Gang" looked its age as their offense was stymied all day, and Miami spent the second half sitting on a 14-0 lead. If not for PK Garo Yepremian's infamous botched pass attempt off a blocked field goal, there was little worth remembering.

2. Super Bowl XX: Bears 46, Patriots 10

On the game's second play from scrimmage, Bears RB Walter Payton fumbled and the underdog Patriots had the ball on Chicago's 19-yard line. Raymond Berry's team managed only a quick field goal, and it was all downhill from there as his club managed a Super Bowl-low seven yards rushing. As for Payton, he was about the only Bear not to score this day at the Superdome.

3. Super Bowl VI: Cowboys 24, Dolphins 3

Once upon a time, the Cowboys were the team that couldn't win the big one, having lost in the playoffs four consecutive years to the Packers and Browns, respectively, then Super Bowl V to the Colts. On the other hand, Don Shula's Dolphins were making the first of three straight Super Bowl visits, but they were no match at Tulane Stadium for a determined Dallas defense that gave up just 185 total yards.

4. Super Bowl XXVI: Redskins 37, Bills 24

Joe Gibbs was in his fourth Super Bowl with his third different quarterback, while the Bills were confident that their loss a year earlier in Tampa was a learning experience. Buffalo highlights at the Metrodome included RB Thurman Thomas forgetting his helmet at the start of the game, and WR Andre Reed throwing his in disgust before halftime. A Washington rout from the start.

5. Super Bowl XXIX: 49ers 49, Chargers 26

Earlier in the season at Jack Murphy Stadium, the Niners rolled over Bobby Ross's Bolts, 38-15, and just to prove how consistently good George Seifert's club was in '94, they won this game by 23 points as well. 49ers' QB Steve Young threw a record six TD passes as his team reached the end zone on each of its first three possessions, and the Chargers' title hopes melted in Miami.

Top 10 Postseason Plays

1. 1981 AFC Divisional Playoffs: Dolphins RB Tony Nathan vs. Chargers

After narrowing the Chargers 24-0 first-quarter lead to 14 points, Miami was at the San Diego 40-yard line just seconds before halftime. Dolphins QB Don Strock threw a 15-yard pass to WR Duriel Harris, who quickly lateraled to the trailing Nathan, who went the remaining 25 yards for the score. The stunned Chargers would see Miami eventually take the lead before San Diego rallied for the 41-38 OT win, but give the nod to Don Shula for a gutsy call.

2. 1972 AFC Divisional Playoffs: Steelers RB Franco Harris vs. Raiders

Trailing 7-6, it came down to Steelers QB Terry Bradshaw, fourth-and-ten on his own 40-yard line with 22 seconds left. He evaded the Raiders defense and spotted RB "Frenchy" Fuqua downfield. The ball was deflected by Raiders S Jack Tatum (or was it Fuqua, making it an illegal play at the time?) but before it touched the ground, Harris caught the ball at his shoe-tops, never broke stride and crossed the goal line with five seconds left for the 13-7 victory.

3. Super Bowl X: Steelers WR Lynn Swann vs. Cowboys

The Pittsburgh wideout pulled down four passes for 161 yards, including the game-winning 64-yard touchdown in the fourth quarter, but his amazing 53-yard catch in the second quarter is unforgettable. Steelers QB Terry Bradshaw threw deep down the middle to Swann, who leaped over Cowboys' CB Mark Washington. Both men fell to the Orange Bowl floor, but Swann kept his concentration and pulled in the ball just before he hit the turf.

4. 1981 NFC Championship Game: 49ers WR Dwight Clark vs. Cowboys

Trailing 27-21 with 4:54 to play and pinned down on his own 11, 49ers QB Joe Montana used a dozen plays to move his team to the Cowboys' six-yard line. San Francisco faced third-and-three with 58 seconds remaining, and Montana rolled deep to his right with three Dallas defenders in his face. In what looked like an attempt by Montana to throw the ball away, the lanky Clark leaped above Cowboys CB Everson Walls and made "The Catch" in the back of the end zone.

5. Super Bowl XVIII: Raiders RB Marcus Allen vs. Redskins

The Silver and Black played a near-perfect game against a Redskins team that had set an NFL record for points scored in a season. With his Raiders ahead, 28-9, in the third quarter, Allen headed left, reversed his field, ran up the middle of the

Washington defense and veered left toward the sidelines and into the end zone. When it was all over, his scintillating run covered 74 yards, still the longest in Super Bowl history, and the score broke the spirit of Joe Gibbs's team for good.

6. 1975 NFC Divisional Playoffs: Cowboys WR Drew Pearson vs. Vikings

Underdog Dallas was the better team this day at Metropolitan Stadium, but Minnesota owned a 14-10 lead late in the game. With the ball at midfield, Cowboys QB Roger Staubach heaved a pass to Pearson down the right sideline. The ball was a bit underthrown, but the Dallas wideout made the catch (some say he pushed off Vikings' DB Nate Wright) and Tom Landry's "Hail Mary" prayer was answered in a stunning 17-14 triumph.

7. 1971 AFC Championship Game: Dolphins S Dick Anderson vs. Colts

En route to their first of three consecutive Super Bowl appearances, Miami used a stifling defense to shackle the defending world champions. Trailing 7-0 in the third quarter, Colts QB Johnny Unitas overthrew WR Eddie Hinton, and Dick Anderson picked off the ball at the Baltimore 38-yard line. Benefiting from near picture-perfect blocking, Miami's ballhawk weaved his way through the Colts offense for a 62-yard touchdown.

8. 1958 NFL Championship Game: Colts RB Alan Ameche vs. Giants

It was hardly spectacular or extraordinary, but it ended "The Greatest Game Ever Played." In the first-ever overtime affair in postseason history, the Giants won the toss but punted after three plays. Weeb Ewbank's Colts got the ball on their own 20-yard line, and QB Johnny Unitas drove his club toward the New York end zone. On third-and-one, Ameche pierced the middle of the Giants defense and scored, disappointing the Yankee Stadium crowd.

9. 1967 NFL Championship Game: Packers QB Bart Starr vs. Cowboys

Late in the fourth quarter of the fabled "Ice Bowl," Dallas owned a 17-14 edge. Starr drove his team 66 yards to the Cowboys three-yard line in just over four minutes. Two runs by RB Donny Anderson failed to dent the end zone, and Vince Lombardi's club faced third-and-goal at the one-yard line. Rather than opt for the sure field goal, Starr (thanks to a key block from G Jerry Kramer) gave his team the lead with 13 seconds to play with his one-yard sneak.

10. 1974 AFC Divisional Playoffs: Raiders QB Ken Stabler vs. Dolphins

Trailing 26-21 to the two-time defending Super Bowl champs, "The Snake" was big in the clutch. Taking over with just over two minutes to play, Stabler hit five straight passes in a drive that would reach the Miami eight-yard line. Dropping back to throw again, he barely evaded Dolphins DE Vern Den Herder and as he was falling to the ground, pushed a pass to RB Clarence Davis. The Raiders runner made the catch in a crowd, and Oakland dethroned the Fins, 28-26.

Top 10 Postseason
Performances

1. 1963 AFL Championship Game: Chargers FB Keith Lincoln vs. Patriots

Talk about having a day where everything goes right. Lincoln touched the ball just 21 times and accounted for 349 yards, rushing for 206 yards (second-most in postseason history) and a touchdown on only 13 carries, snaring seven passes for 123 yards and a score and even completing a pass for 20 yards. San Diego's offense amassed 610 yards in a 51-10 rout.

2. 1971 AFC Divisional Playoffs: Chiefs RB Ed Podolak vs. Dolphins

It was just his third year in the pros, but the versatile runner enjoyed a career in one day. Podolak rolled up 85 yards rushing and a touchdown, pulled down eight passes for 110 yards and a score, totaled 155 yards on kick returns and even attempted a pass. But it went for naught as the Dolphins eventually prevailed, 27-24, in double OT in the NFL's longest game to date.

3. 1943 NFL Championship Game: Bears QB Sid Luckman vs. Redskins

What figured to be a battle between Redskins QB Sammy Baugh and Luckman never really came to pass as Baugh left the game in the first quarter with a concussion (he would return). Still, it was Chicago's signal-caller who provided the knockout punch, throwing for 286 yards and five touchdowns and rushing for 64 yards in the Bears' 41-21 triumph.

4. Super Bowl XXI: Giants QB Phil Simms vs. Broncos

With just under two minutes remaining in the first half and his team trailing Denver, 10-9, Simms overthrew TE Mark Bavaro on third down. That toss would be his last misfire of the day, as the Giants signal-caller hit on 22-of-25 passes for 268 yards and three touchdowns in the Big Blue's 39-20 triumph. Simms' amazing accuracy rate (88 percent) remains a postseason record for one game.

5. 1987 NFC Divisional Playoffs: Vikings WR Anthony Carter vs. 49ers

In one of the biggest upsets in playoff annals, the Minnesota wideout came up aces despite not reaching the end zone. Carter pulled in 10 passes for an NFL postseason record 227 yards, ran 30 yards on a reverse in the third quarter that set up a Vikings touchdown and contributed on punt returns as the Purple Gang prevailed, 36-24, at Candlestick Park.

6. Super Bowl XXII: Redskins QB Doug Williams vs. Broncos

While he started the season backing up Jay Schroeder, the former Buccaneer got the nod for Joe Gibbs's club down the stretch. Down 10-0 in the first quarter and nursing a twisted knee that sidelined him for a play, Williams keyed an attack that piled up 35 points — including four touchdown passes — and 356 yards in the second quarter alone as the 'Skins rolled, 42-10.

7. 1981 AFC Divisional Playoffs: Chargers TE Kellen Winslow vs. Dolphins

The sight of the Hall of Famer being helped off the Orange Bowl field by teammates after the game is etched in our memories. And Winslow had good reason to be exhausted, amassing 166 yards and a score on 13 catches (an NFL postseason record since tied by several people), and blocking a field goal with four seconds left to force overtime, in which the Chargers prevailed, 41-38.

8. 1943 NFL Divisional Playoffs: Redskins QB Sammy Baugh vs. Giants

During a season in which he led the league in passing, punting and interceptions, Baugh put all of those talents on display in this 28-0 shutout of New York. The multi-talented performer threw for 199 yards and a score, averaged better than 40 yards per kick and also stole a pair of Giants passes, the second setting up his 11-yard TD pass to TE Ted Lapka.

9. 1979 AFC Divisional Playoffs: Oilers S Vernon Perry vs. Chargers

Bum Phillips's squad headed to the West Coast missing offensive standouts RB Earl Campbell, QB Dan Pastorini and WR Ken Burrough, so it was up to the defense to take matters into its own hands. Perry took this literally, stealing four Dan Fouts passes and blocking a field goal in Houston's 17-14 upset of the supposedly Super Bowl-bound Chargers.

10. 1954 NFL Championship Game: Browns QB Otto Graham vs. Lions

It was supposed to be the last game of his magnificent career (he returned in 1955), and when Graham's first pass of the game was intercepted, it didn't figure to be his day against the two-time defending NFL champions. But Cleveland's field general was just getting warm, and he wound up throwing for 163 yards and three touchdowns and running for three scores in a 56-10 rout.

5 Infamous Oops... Postseason Plays

1. Super Bowl VII: Dolphins PK Garo Yepremian vs. Redskins

With his team up 14-0 with just over two minutes to play, the Miami kicker lined up for a 42-yard field goal that would put the nail in Washington's coffin. The attempt was blocked by Redskins DT Bill Brundidge, but Yepremian made matters worse by picking up the pigskin and looking to pass. The ball slipped out of his hand, he batted it into the air and Redskins CB Mike Bass grabbed the prize and raced into the end zone for Washington's only score of the day.

2. Super Bowl XIII: Cowboys TE Jackie Smith vs. Steelers

This game saw plenty of momentum changes, but this may have been Dallas's costliest mistake of the day. Down 21-14 late in the third quarter, the Cowboys faced a third-and-three at the Steelers 10-yard line. Smith was wide open in the end zone thanks to a Pittsburgh blitz, and Cowboys QB Roger Staubach hit him right in the numbers. But the Hall of Famer inexplicably dropped the ball, and Dallas had to settle for a field goal rather than the tie in an eventual 35-31 loss.

3. Super Bowl XXVII: Cowboys QB Leon Lett vs. Bills

Call it carelessness or great hustle. Up 52-17, Dallas came up with its ninth takeaway of the day, as Cowboys DE Jim Jeffcoat forced Bills QB Frank Reich to fumble and DT Lett scooped up the ball. About five yards away from a sure touchdown, the Dallas defender held out the ball. Bills wideout Don Beebe knocked the ball out of Leon's hand, resulting in a touchback and egg on Lett's face.

4. Super Bowl III: Colts QB Earl Morrall vs. Jets

There were many factors that led to the Colts upset loss, but one play stands out. Down 7-0 but with the ball on the Jets 42-yard line and 25 seconds left before halftime, Morrall handed off to RB Tom Matte, who ran right, then threw the ball back to Morrall. Instead of throwing to wide-open WR Jimmy Orr, he opted for RB Jerry Hill down the middle, and Jets S Jim Hudson intercepted at the 12-yard line.

5. 1987 AFC Championship Game: Browns RB Earnest Byner vs. Broncos

Down 28-10 in the third quarter at Mile High Stadium, Browns QB Bernie Kosar forged a 31-all tie in the final period until Broncos QB John Elway put Denver back ahead by seven. On his way to the tying touchdown, Byner coughed up "The Fumble," Cleveland's final chance, at the Denver three-yard line, forced and recovered by Broncos DB Jeremiah Castille with 1:05 to play.

About the Authors

Joe Adams is the former sports editor of the *Detroit Sunday Journal*.

Russell S. Baxter is the chief NFL researcher for ESPN and senior reporter for *ESPN The Magazine*.

Chris Berman is one of television's most popular and entertaining sports commentators. He has been selected the National Sportscaster of the Year five times.

Ed Bouchette has covered the Pittsburgh Steelers since 1985 for the *Pittsburgh Post-Gazette*. He has written two books, contributed to several others and keeps his family in shoes with his work on radio and TV in Pittsburgh.

Jason Alan Brame, a lifelong Steelers fan, attended the University of Pittsburgh, where he received his B.A. in English Writing.

Nick Cafardo is the football beat writer for the *Boston Globe*.

John Clayton, NFL writer for *ESPN The Magazine*, contributes to SportsCenter's "Inside the Huddle" and serves as a NFL analyst on all ESPN Radio shows, including The NFL on ESPN Radio, NFL Draft programming, ESPN's Sunday pregame show, and NFL Countdown.

Gary Cohl, a former sportscaster at WSOC-TV in Charlotte, North Carolina, is now sports director at WFTV-TV in Orlando.

Jason Cole covers the Miami Dolphins for the *Fort Lauderdale Sun-Sentinel*.

Debi Faubion is news anchor and host of Panther specials at WSOC-TV in Charlotte, North Carolina

Larry Felser, former president of Pro Football Writers Association and winner of the McCann Award in 1983, is the current sports editor/columnist for the *Buffalo News*. He has covered the Bills in one form or another since the inception of the team.

David Fischer, a lifelong Eagles fan and supporter of various other lost causes, is a former writer/producer for NBC Sports on the Internet.

Greg Garber, a sportswriter for the *Hartford Courant*, provides reports for NFL Countdown and SportsCenter. He is also a regular contributor to ESPN's Outside the Lines and a columnist for ESPN SportsZone.

Peter Ginsberg is a freelance writer living in Venice, California, who yearns for the Jets' return to Shea Stadium.

Hank Goldberg, former play-by-play commentator for the Miami Dolphins, reports regularly on the NFL for SportsCenter and NFL Countdown. He is a frequent contributor on ESPN Radio, and continues to host all-sports radio WQAM's afternoon drivetime program, Hammer Time.

Mike Golic, an eight-year NFL veteran with the Houston Oilers, the Miami Dolphins, and the Philadelphia Eagles, is an NFL reporter for ESPN.

Eric Greene is an Emmy award winning television news anchor and talk show host.

John Hassan is the former editor of the *Information Please* Sports Almanac. He is now a senior editor at *ESPN The Magazine*.

Peter Hayes is the managing editor of *College and Pro Football Newsweekly*.

Tom Jackson, a former Denver Broncos linebacker, is ESPN's NFL studio analyst for NFL Countdown and NFL PrimeTime—ESPN's Sunday pre-game and wrap-up NFL shows.

Teresa Joyce is a freelance journalist living and working in Indianapolis.

Neil Justin is popular culture critic for the *Minneapolis Star Tribune*.

Mel Kiper, Jr. has served as expert analyst for ESPN's annual NFL Draft coverage since 1984. He is a frequent contributor to ESPN's SportsCenter and is responsible for all aspects of *NFL Draft Report* and *Draft Preview*.

Andrea Kremer provides reports for SportsCenter, NFL Countdown, NFL Monday Night Countdown, and NBA Today. She also contributes to ESPN Radio, ESPN SportsZone and ESPNEWS, and has covered every Super Bowl since 1985.

Bob Kurson is the entertainment editor for the *Chicago Sun-Times*.

Ellen Levy is the pro football editor of *College and Pro Football Newsweekly*.

André Maillho is an LSU graduate and the news editor for *Gambit Weekly* in New Orleans. Despite a lifetime of lessons learned the hard way, he remains a Saints season ticket holder.

Mark Malone, a 10-year NFL veteran with the Pittsburgh Steelers (eight years), San Diego Chargers and New York Jets, is host of the new daily NFL2Night program on ESPN2.

Chris Mortensen is the prinicpal NFL reporter for SportsCenter and all ESPN NFL studio programming. Formerly the NFL columnist for *The Sporting News* and a contributing writer for *Sport* magazine, he has received 18 awards in journalism, including the George Polk Award for reporting in 1987.

Jim Nagy spent the 1996 NFL season working in the public relations department of the Green Bay Packers, and assisted best-selling author and host of ESPN's The Sports Reporters, Dick Schaap, in writing *Green Bay Replay: The Packers' Return To Glory*.

David Newhouse is a sports columnist for the *Oakland Tribune*/Alameda Newspaper Group.

Sal Paolantonio, a SportsCenter correspondent, was a political reporter for the *Philadelphia Inquirer*, then covered the Eagles beat.

Andy Pollin is the sports director of WTEM-AM, Washington D.C.'s all-sports station. He's also Tony Kornheiser's sidekick on the nationally-syndicated Tony Kornheiser Show on ESPN Radio.

Pete Prisco covers the Jacksonville Jaguars for the *Florida Times-Union*. Prisco has covered the team since it was awarded to the city in 1984.

Nick Pugliese has been a sports writer for *The Tampa Tribune* for 20 years. He is currently the Pro Football Editor, overseeing coverage of the Tampa Bay Buccaneers and the NFL.

Adam Shefter covers the Denver Broncos for the *Denver Post*, and is co-author of *TD*, the autobiography of Terrell Davis.

Dana Sims is the Manager of Artist Affairs at Sub Pop Records in Seattle.

Howard Slatkin has covered the NFL, NBA, and Major League Baseball for NBC sports on the Internet.

Kent Somers has been a sportswriter at the *Arizona Republic* for 13 years. He covered the Cardinals for three seasons and his duties include writing in-depth features and project reporting.

Mickey Spagnola is a columnist for *The Insider*, a fax newsletter covering the Dallas Cowboys, and freelance writer in Dallas. He has been covering the Cowboys for the past 14 seasons, and co-authored the book, *America's Rivalry—The 20 Greatest Redskins–Cowboys Games*, published in 1997.

Vito Stellino covers pro football for the *Baltimore Sun*. The 1989 winner of the Dick McCann Memorial Award at the Pro Football Hall of Fame in Canton, Ohio for long and distinguished reporting in the field of pro football, Stellino has covered the last 26 Super Bowls.

Adam Teicher covers the Kansas City Chiefs for the Kansas City *Star*.

Joe Theismann, the former Washington Redskins quarterback, is ESPN's Sunday Night NFL color commentator. He formerly served as an in-studio analyst for the network's NFL Countdown and NFL Prime Monday.

Jim Thomas is a St. Louis native who covers the Rams and the NFL for the *St. Louis Post-Dispatch*.

Mike Tirico hosts ESPN's NFL Monday Night Countdown. He also hosts ABC's coverage of the PGA tour.

Brent Weber is main sports anchor for Orange County Newschannel in Santa Ana, California. He was formerly a sports correspondent and anchor at CNN.

Lonnie Wheeler co-authored the autobiographies of Bob Gibson and Henry Aaron and has been a regular contributor to, among others, The *New York Times*, *Sport*, and *Inside Sport*.

Acknowledgments

Football is a team game, so it's only appropriate that the ultimate book on football was created by a team. A huge team.

First, we'd like to thank all the writers, both the local contributors and the commentators from ESPN, every one of them smart, professional and passionate about the game.

Second, the reviewers at ESPN: Drew Hayes, Mike King, Patrick Caulfield, Chuck Salituro, Eric Karabell, Ed Schimmel, Barry Sacks, Seth Markman, Bob Stevens, David Lloyd, Mark Malone, Art Berko, Chris McKendry, Jeremy Schaap, Shireen Saski, Linda Willhite, Kerwin Hudson, Vince Doria, Trey Wingo, Neil Wolf, Rick Paiva, Tim Scanlan, Rick Mickler, Stu Scott, Solomon Wilcots, John McCormick, Jay Levy, Jim Allegro, Larry Beil, Charlie Moynihan, Jim Bowdon, John Hernandez, Beth Faber, Don Barone and Steve Cyphers. Your comments took the book to another level. We'd also like to thank Bob Eaton, Howie Schwab, Fred Gaudelli, and Bob Rauscher for their close attention, important contributions and, above all, patience.

At Hyperion, Jennifer Morgan held down the fort with good sense and good humor and our editor Gretchen Young always believed we could do it. Thanks, Gretchen!

At ESPN, helmets off to Shelley Youngblut and Jenny Ford, who opened the doors, and Sharyn Taymor, who led us through them with calm and confidence, both of which were greatly appreciated. This book would never have been completed without the efforts of Eric Schoenfeld, who pulled all the pieces together at the end. And finally John Walsh, whose high standards inspired us.

—Thomas Dyja

I would like to thank Tom Dyja, Howard Slatkin, Russell Baxter, Eric Schoenfeld, and Mel Kiper, each one a first-round pick with a huge upside, for their help in putting this book together. As usual, I could not have worked on this project without the help and support of my wife Karen Mynatt. Go Vols.

—John Hassan

To Mom and Dad, to my family and friends. To Janette my love, and Kil-Jae my partner in crime. Thank you... No one could have a better fan club.

—Russell S. Baxter